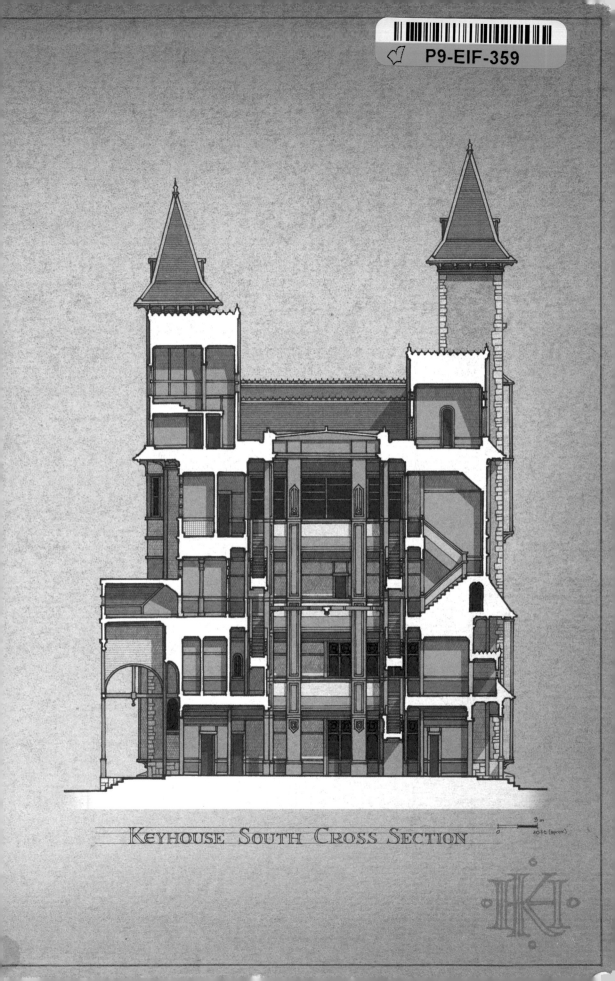

KEYHOUSE SOUTH CROSS SECTION

3 m
0
10 ft (aprox.)

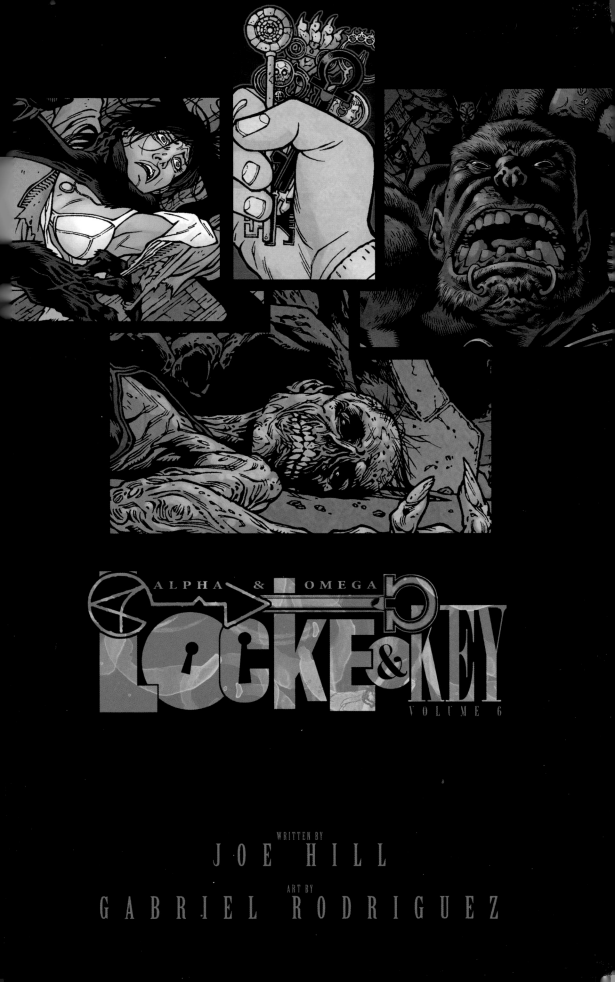

ALPHA & OMEGA

LOCKE & KEY

VOLUME 6

WRITTEN BY

JOE HILL

ART BY

GABRIEL RODRIGUEZ

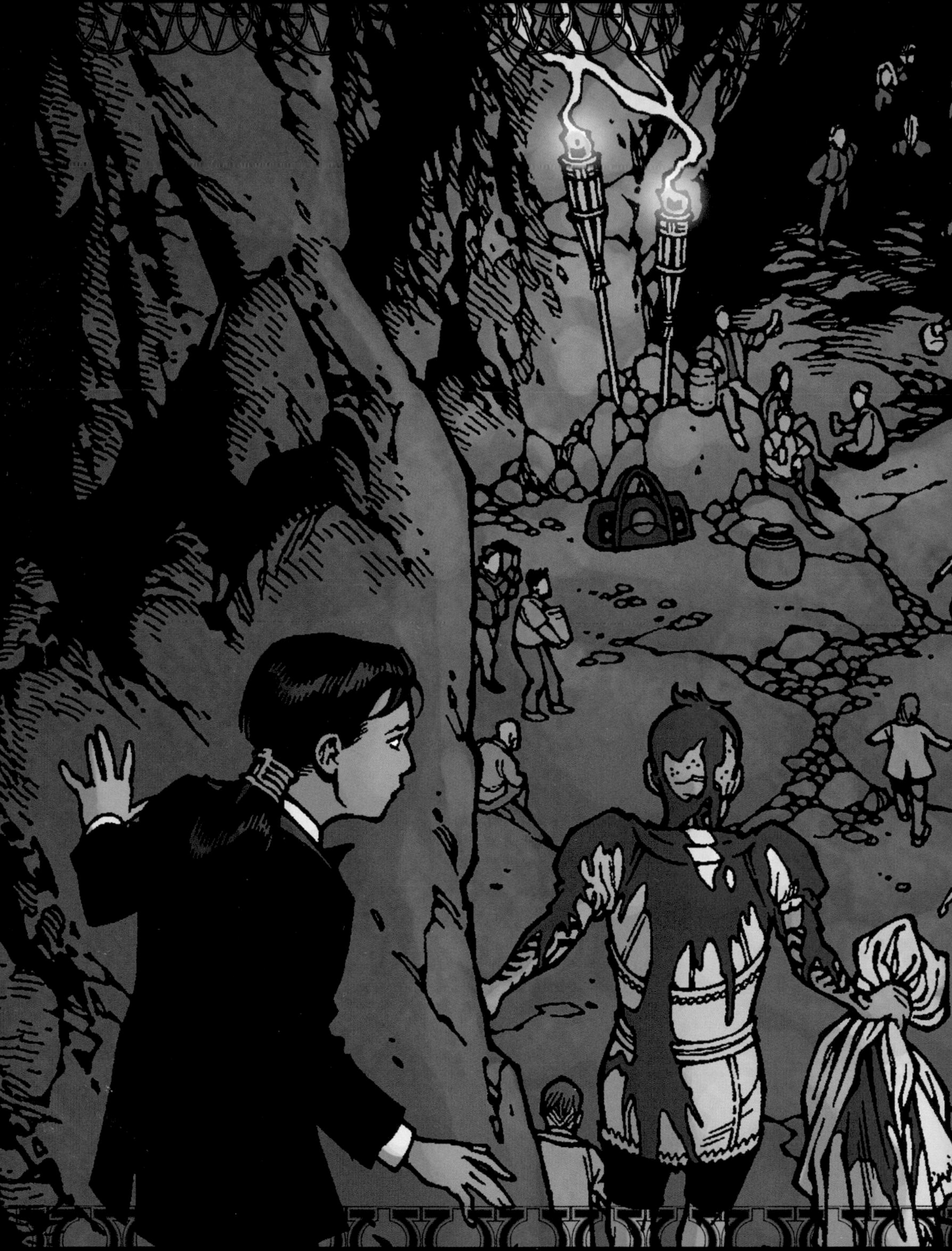

Locke & Key created by Joe Hill and Gabriel Rodriguez | Follow Joe Hill on Twitter @joe_hill • Follow Gabriel Rodriguez on Twitter @GR_comics

ISBN: 978-1-61377-853-1

17 16 15 14 1 2 3 4

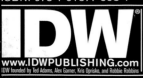

IDW®
www.IDWPUBLISHING.com
IDW founded by Ted Adams, Alex Garner, Kris Oprisko, and Robbie Robbins

Ted Adams, CEO & Publisher
Greg Goldstein, President & COO
Robbie Robbins, EVP/Sr. Graphic Artist
Chris Ryall, Chief Creative Officer/Editor-in-Chief
Matthew Ruzicka, CPA, Chief Financial Officer
Alan Payne, VP of Sales
Dirk Wood, VP of Marketing
Lorelei Bunjes, VP of Digital Services
Jeff Webber, VP of Digital Publishing & Business Development

Facebook: facebook.com/idwpublishing
Twitter: @idwpublishing
YouTube: youtube.com/idwpublishing
Instagram: instagram.com/idwpublishing
deviantART: idwpublishing.deviantart.com
Pinterest: pinterest.com/idwpublishing/idw-staff-faves

Originally published as LOCKE & KEY: OMEGA issues #1–5 and LOCKE & KEY: ALPHA issues #1- 2.

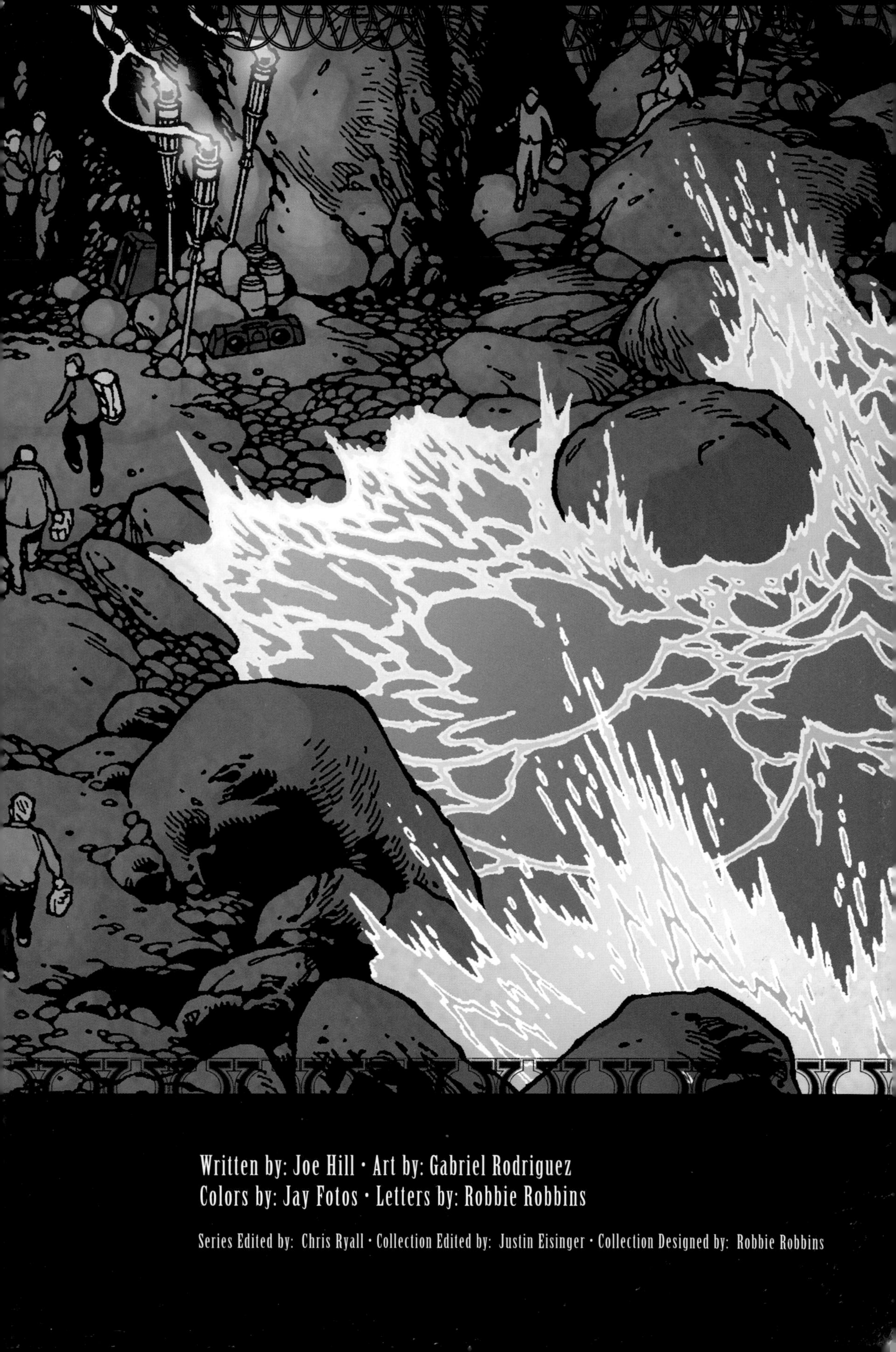

Written by: Joe Hill • Art by: Gabriel Rodriguez
Colors by: Jay Fotos • Letters by: Robbie Robbins

Series Edited by: Chris Ryall • Collection Edited by: Justin Eisinger • Collection Designed by: Robbie Robbins

JOE HILL:
To Catalina, for letting me take so much of her husband's time;
and to Matías and José, for sharing their daddy with me.

GABRIEL RODRIGUEZ:
To Joe, Chris, Jay, and Robbie, thanks for an amazing journey.
To Catalina, your love made it possible.

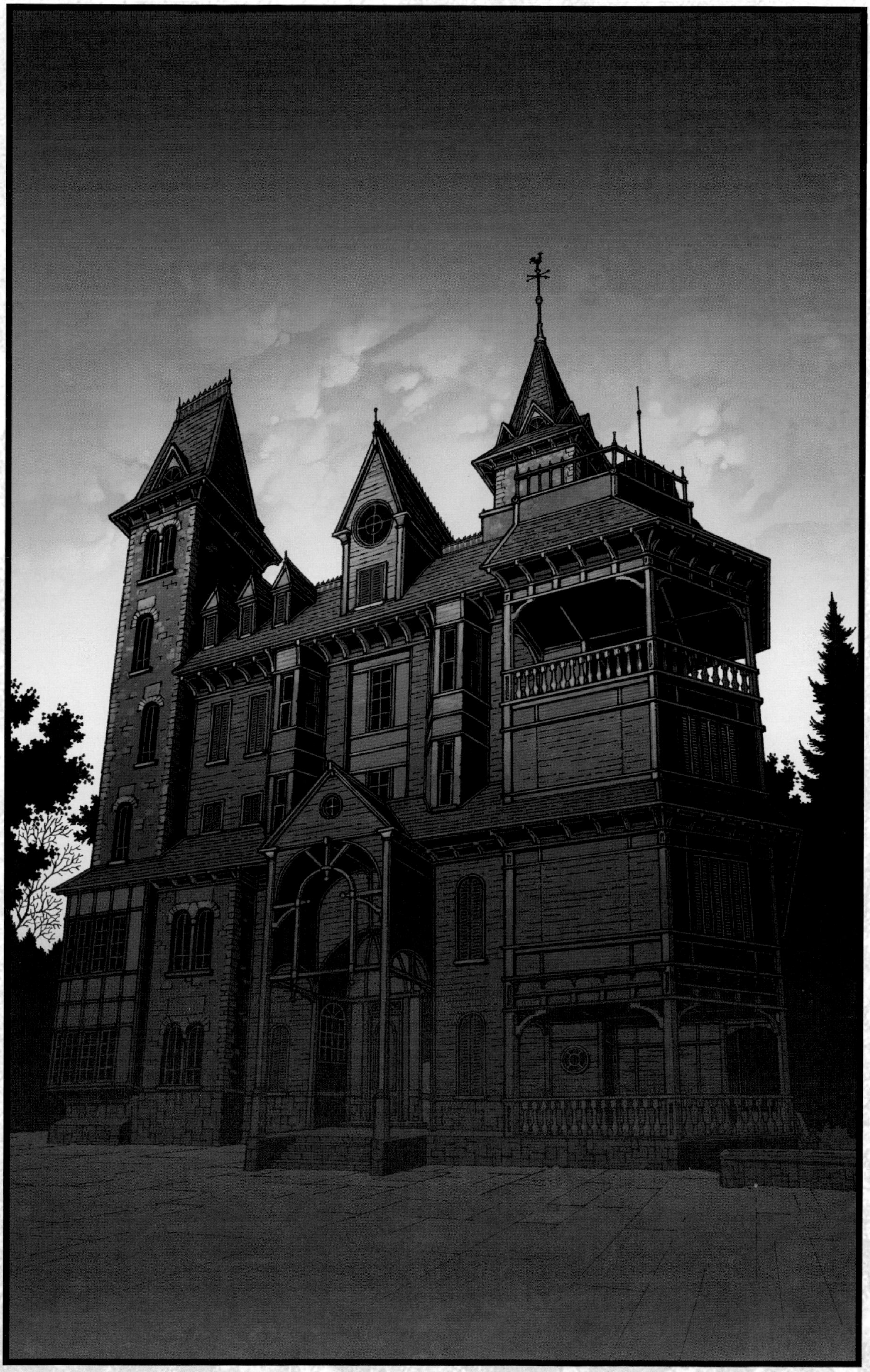

- ALPHA & OMEGA -

Chapter One

OUR REGRETS

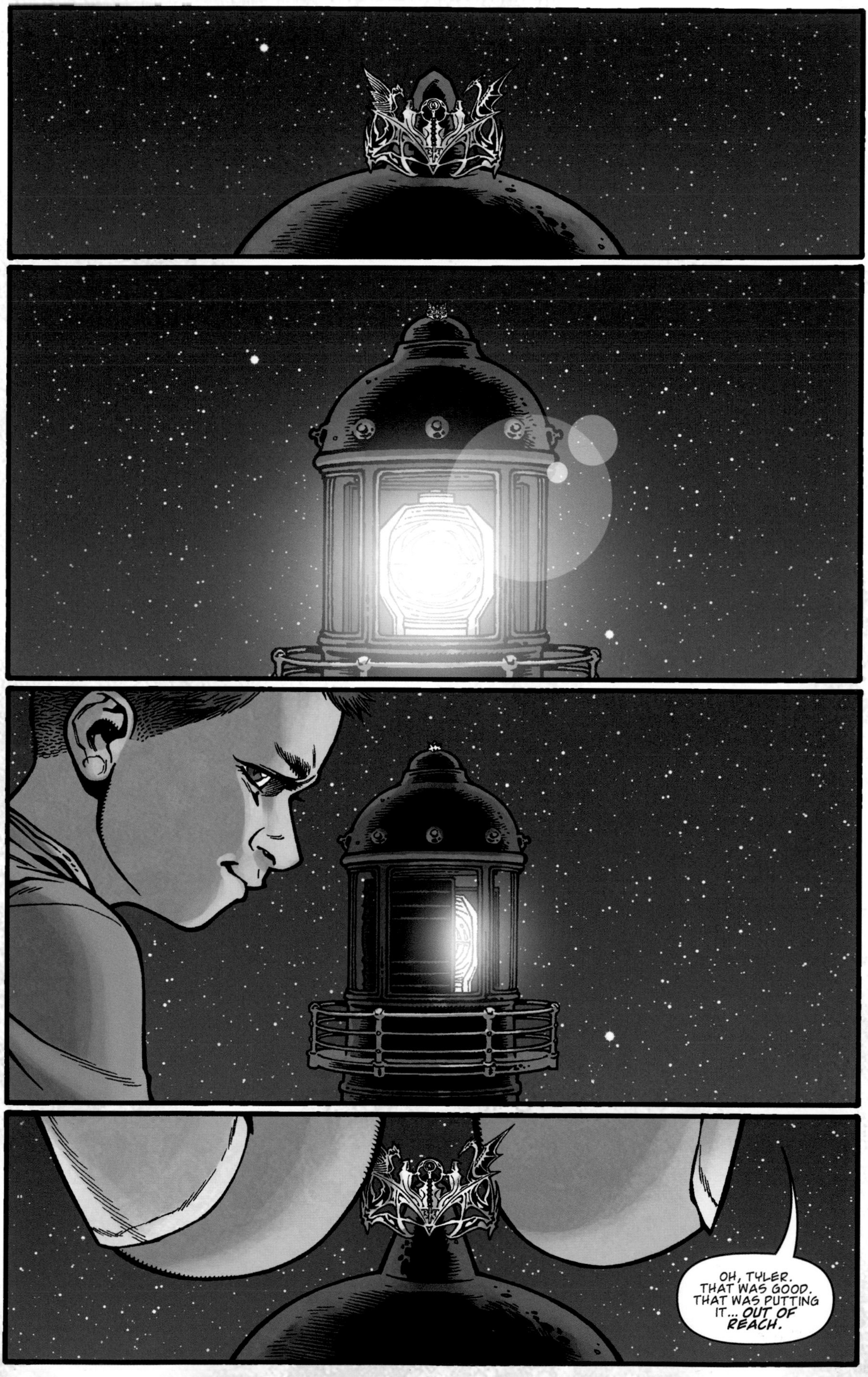
OH, TYLER. THAT WAS GOOD. THAT WAS PUTTING IT... *OUT OF REACH.*

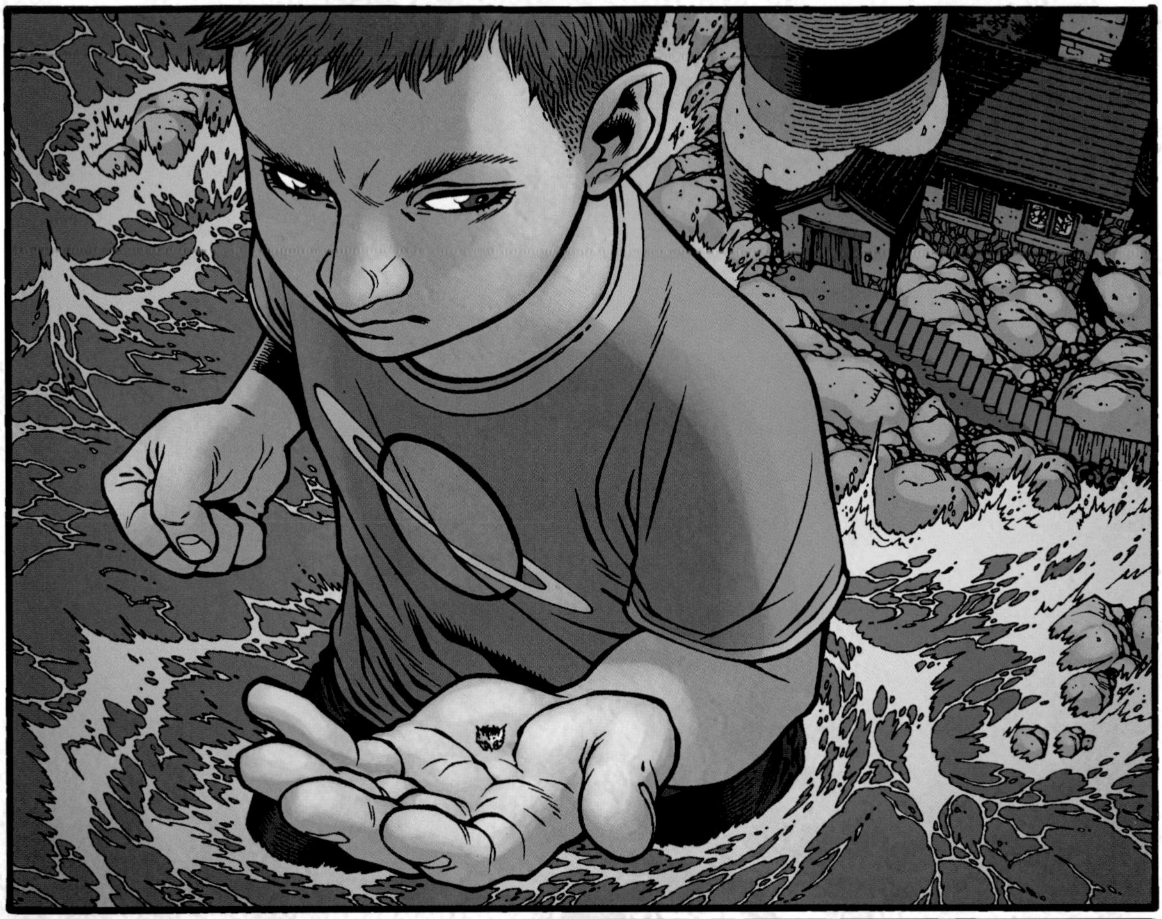

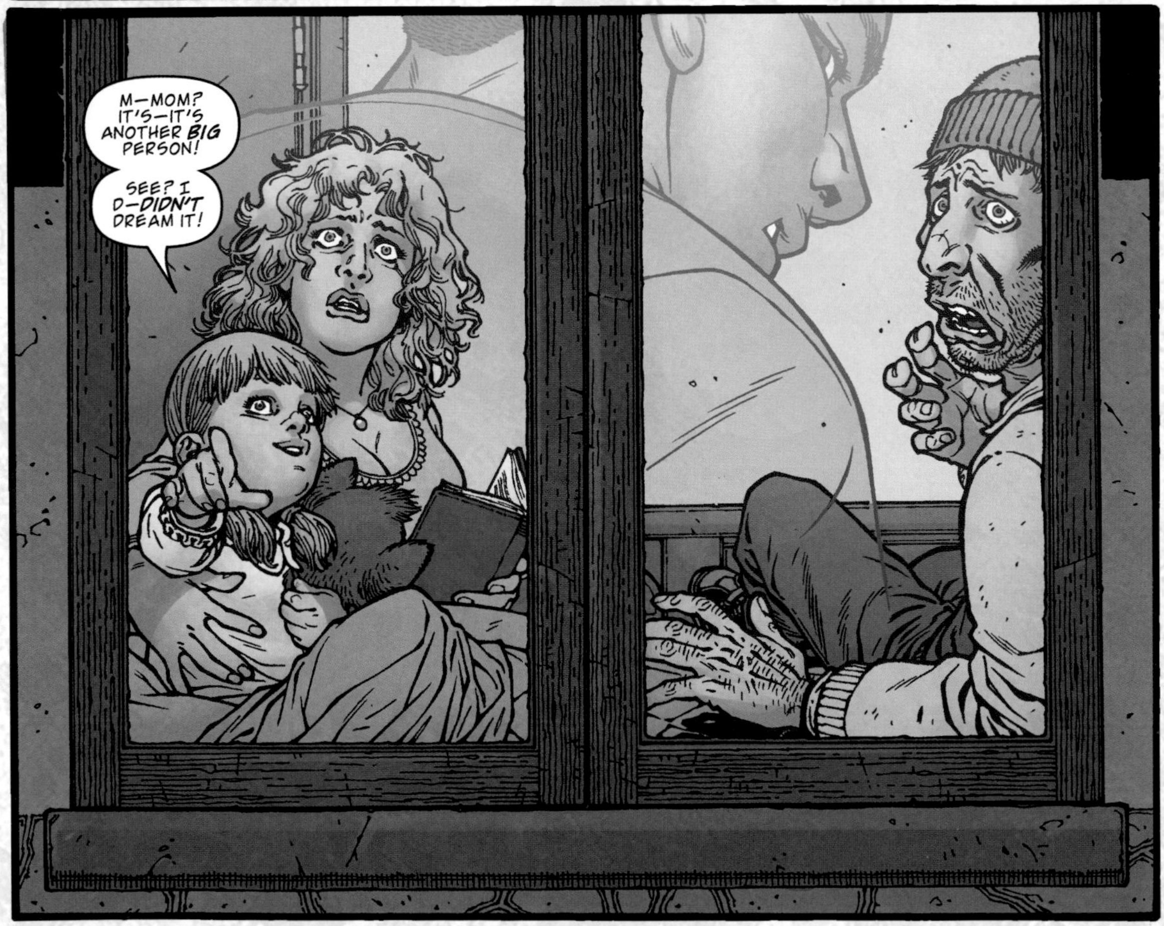
M—MOM? IT'S—IT'S ANOTHER BIG PERSON!
SEE? I D—DIDN'T DREAM IT!

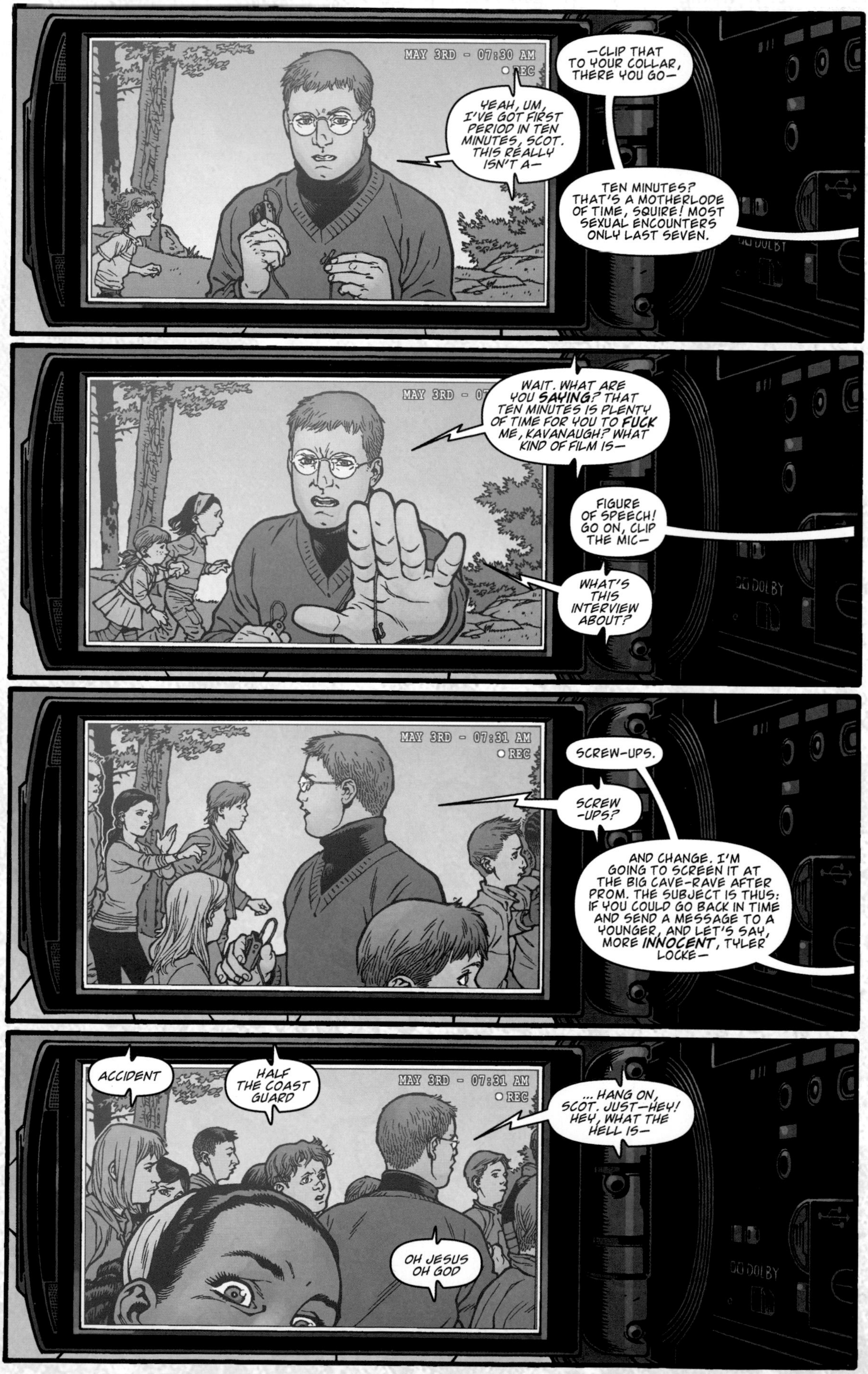
MAY 3RD - 07:30 AM
REC
—CLIP THAT TO YOUR COLLAR, THERE YOU GO—
YEAH, UM, I'VE GOT FIRST PERIOD IN TEN MINUTES, SCOT. THIS REALLY ISN'T A—
TEN MINUTES? THAT'S A MOTHERLODE OF TIME, SQUIRE! MOST SEXUAL ENCOUNTERS ONLY LAST SEVEN.
DOLBY
MAY 3RD
WAIT. WHAT ARE YOU SAYING? THAT TEN MINUTES IS PLENTY OF TIME FOR YOU TO FUCK ME, KAVANAUGH? WHAT KIND OF FILM IS—
FIGURE OF SPEECH! GO ON, CLIP THE MIC—
WHAT'S THIS INTERVIEW ABOUT?
DOLBY
MAY 3RD - 07:31 AM
REC
SCREW-UPS.
SCREW -UPS?
AND CHANGE. I'M GOING TO SCREEN IT AT THE BIG CAVE-RAVE AFTER PROM. THE SUBJECT IS THUS: IF YOU COULD GO BACK IN TIME AND SEND A MESSAGE TO A YOUNGER, AND LET'S SAY, MORE INNOCENT, TYLER LOCKE—
MAY 3RD - 07:31 AM
REC
ACCIDENT
HALF THE COAST GUARD
...HANG ON, SCOT. JUST—HEY! HEY, WHAT THE HELL IS—
OH JESUS OH GOD
DOLBY

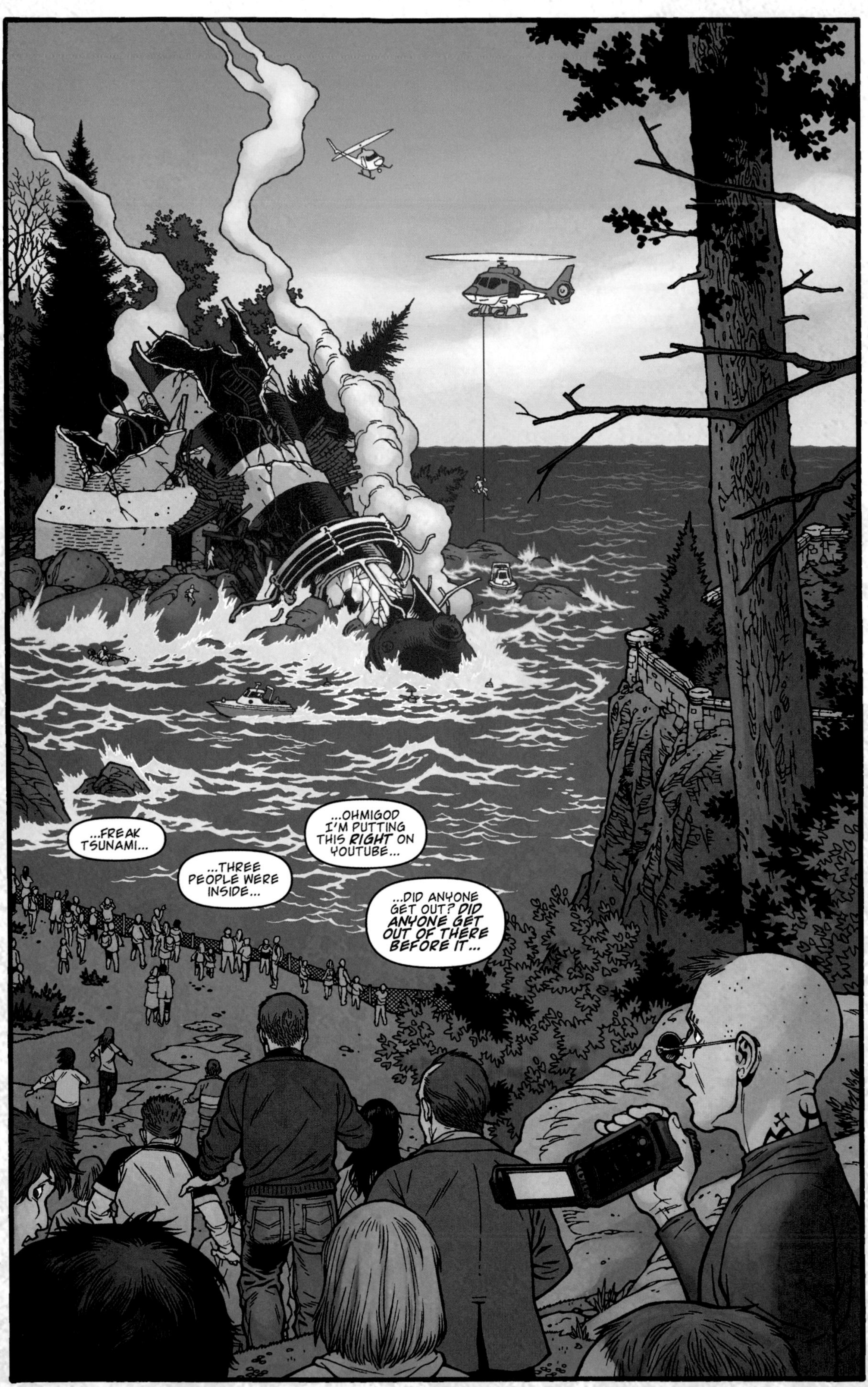
...FREAK TSUNAMI...
...THREE PEOPLE WERE INSIDE...
...OHMIGOD I'M PUTTING THIS RIGHT ON YOUTUBE...
...DID ANYONE GET OUT? DID ANYONE GET OUT OF THERE BEFORE IT...

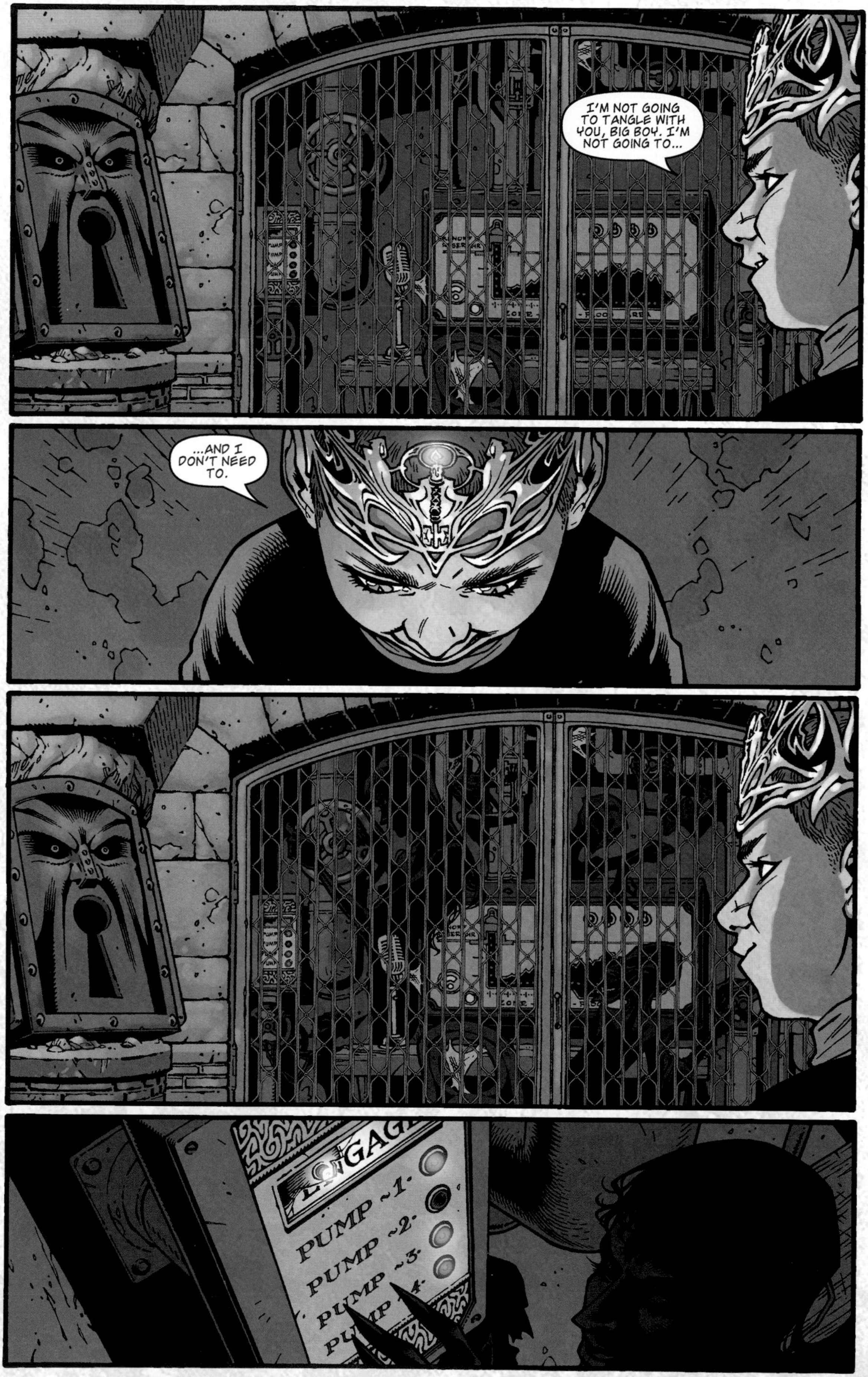
I'M NOT GOING TO TANGLE WITH YOU, BIG BOY. I'M NOT GOING TO...
...AND I DON'T NEED TO.
PUMP ~1·
PUMP ~2·
PUMP ~3·
PUMP ~4·

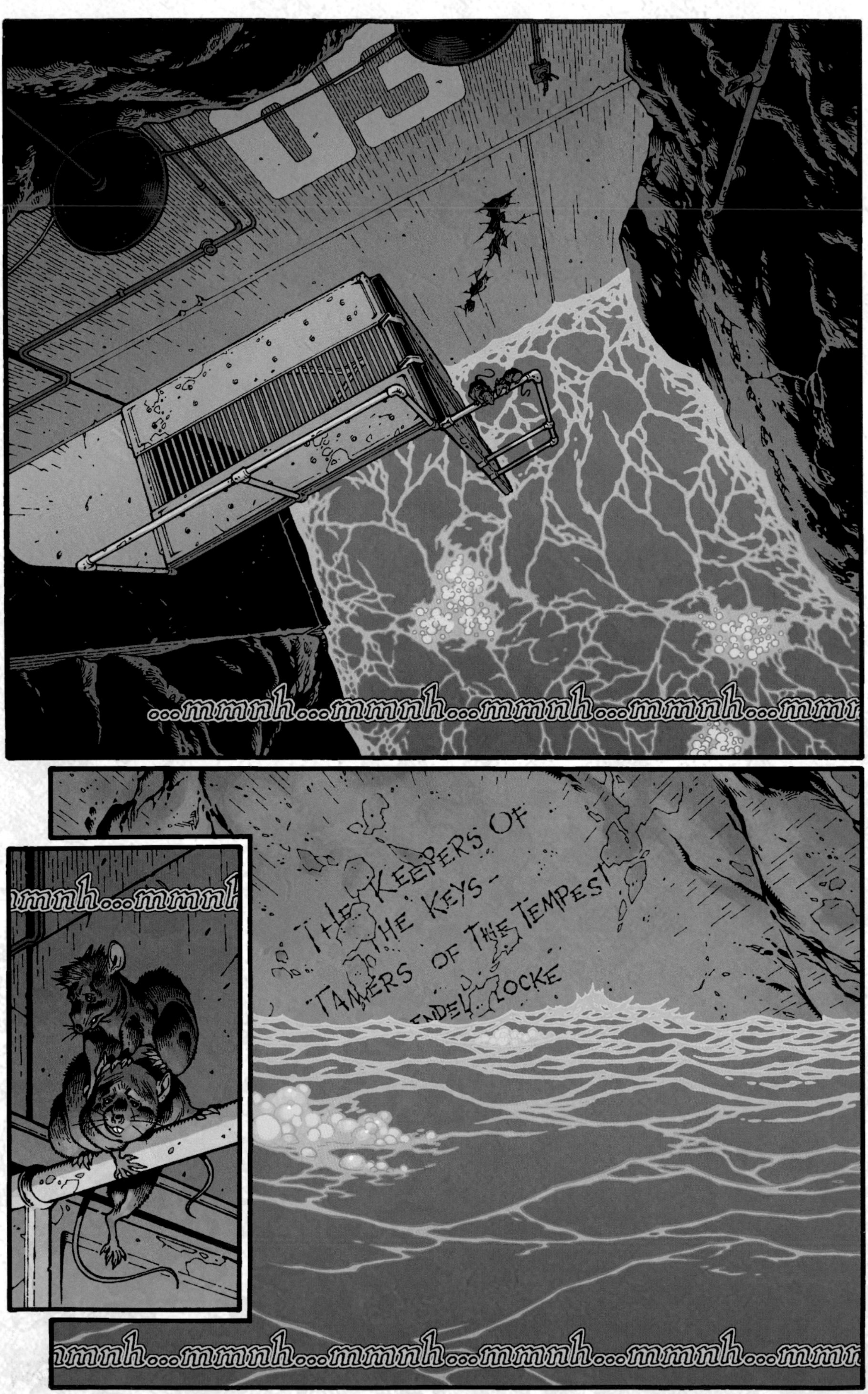
...mmnh...mmnh...mmnh...mmnh...mmn
mmnh...mmnh
The Keepers of
he Keys -
Tamers of The Tempest
endel Locke
mmnh...mmnh...mmnh...mmnh...mmnh...mmn

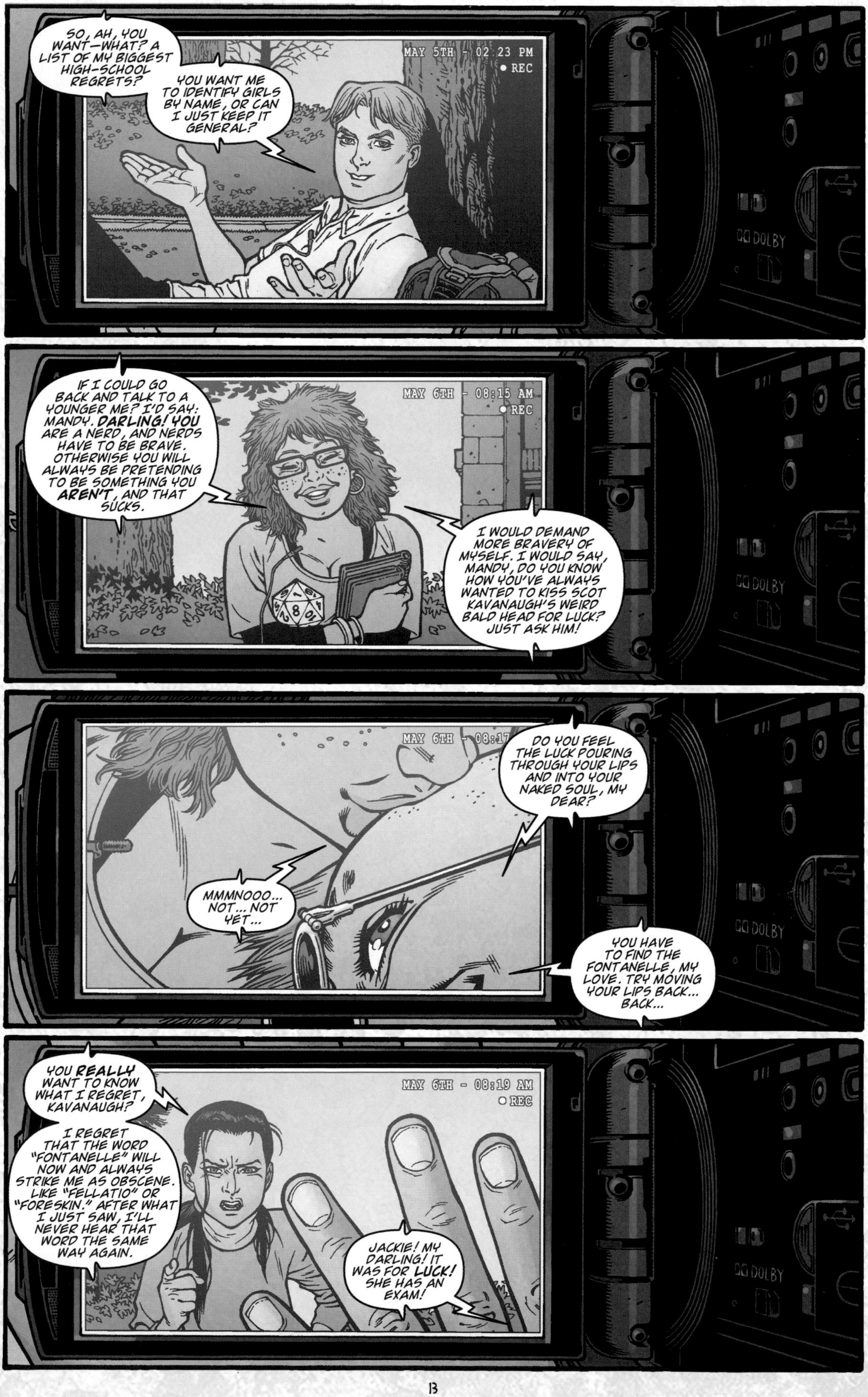
SO, AH, YOU WANT—WHAT? A LIST OF MY BIGGEST HIGH-SCHOOL REGRETS?
MAY 5TH - 02:23 PM
● REC
YOU WANT ME TO IDENTIFY GIRLS BY NAME, OR CAN I JUST KEEP IT GENERAL?
DOLBY
IF I COULD GO BACK AND TALK TO A YOUNGER ME? I'D SAY: MANDY. DARLING! YOU ARE A NERD, AND NERDS HAVE TO BE BRAVE. OTHERWISE YOU WILL ALWAYS BE PRETENDING TO BE SOMETHING YOU AREN'T, AND THAT SUCKS.
MAY 6TH - 08:15 AM
● REC
I WOULD DEMAND MORE BRAVERY OF MYSELF. I WOULD SAY, MANDY, DO YOU KNOW HOW YOU'VE ALWAYS WANTED TO KISS SCOT KAVANAUGH'S WEIRD BALD HEAD FOR LUCK? JUST ASK HIM!
DOLBY
MAY 6TH - 08:17
DO YOU FEEL THE LUCK POURING THROUGH YOUR LIPS AND INTO YOUR NAKED SOUL, MY DEAR?
MMMNOOO... NOT... NOT YET...
YOU HAVE TO FIND THE FONTANELLE, MY LOVE. TRY MOVING YOUR LIPS BACK... BACK...
DOLBY
YOU REALLY WANT TO KNOW WHAT I REGRET, KAVANAUGH?
MAY 6TH - 08:19 AM
● REC
I REGRET THAT THE WORD "FONTANELLE" WILL NOW AND ALWAYS STRIKE ME AS OBSCENE. LIKE "FELLATIO" OR "FORESKIN." AFTER WHAT I JUST SAW, I'LL NEVER HEAR THAT WORD THE SAME WAY AGAIN.
JACKIE! MY DARLING! IT WAS FOR LUCK! SHE HAS AN EXAM!
DOLBY

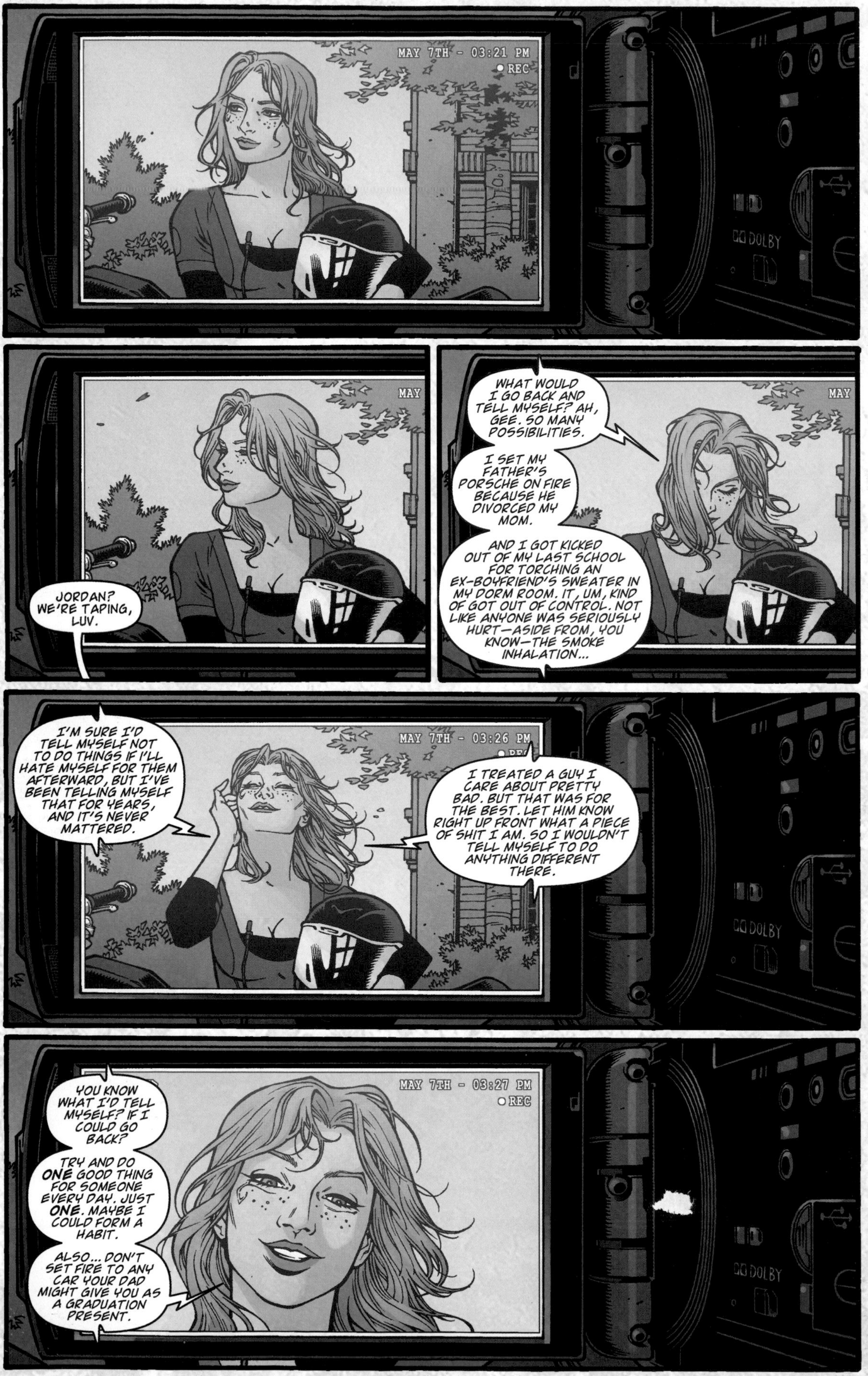
MAY 7TH - 03:21 PM
REC
MAY
JORDAN? WE'RE TAPING, LUV.
MAY
WHAT WOULD I GO BACK AND TELL MYSELF? AH, GEE. SO MANY POSSIBILITIES.
I SET MY FATHER'S PORSCHE ON FIRE BECAUSE HE DIVORCED MY MOM.
AND I GOT KICKED OUT OF MY LAST SCHOOL FOR TORCHING AN EX-BOYFRIEND'S SWEATER IN MY DORM ROOM. IT, UM, KIND OF GOT OUT OF CONTROL. NOT LIKE ANYONE WAS SERIOUSLY HURT—ASIDE FROM, YOU KNOW—THE SMOKE INHALATION...
MAY 7TH - 03:26 PM
I'M SURE I'D TELL MYSELF NOT TO DO THINGS IF I'LL HATE MYSELF FOR THEM AFTERWARD, BUT I'VE BEEN TELLING MYSELF THAT FOR YEARS, AND IT'S NEVER MATTERED.
I TREATED A GUY I CARE ABOUT PRETTY BAD. BUT THAT WAS FOR THE BEST. LET HIM KNOW RIGHT UP FRONT WHAT A PIECE OF SHIT I AM. SO I WOULDN'T TELL MYSELF TO DO ANYTHING DIFFERENT THERE.
MAY 7TH - 03:27 PM
REC
YOU KNOW WHAT I'D TELL MYSELF? IF I COULD GO BACK?
TRY AND DO ONE GOOD THING FOR SOMEONE EVERY DAY. JUST ONE. MAYBE I COULD FORM A HABIT.
ALSO... DON'T SET FIRE TO ANY CAR YOUR DAD MIGHT GIVE YOU AS A GRADUATION PRESENT.
DOLBY

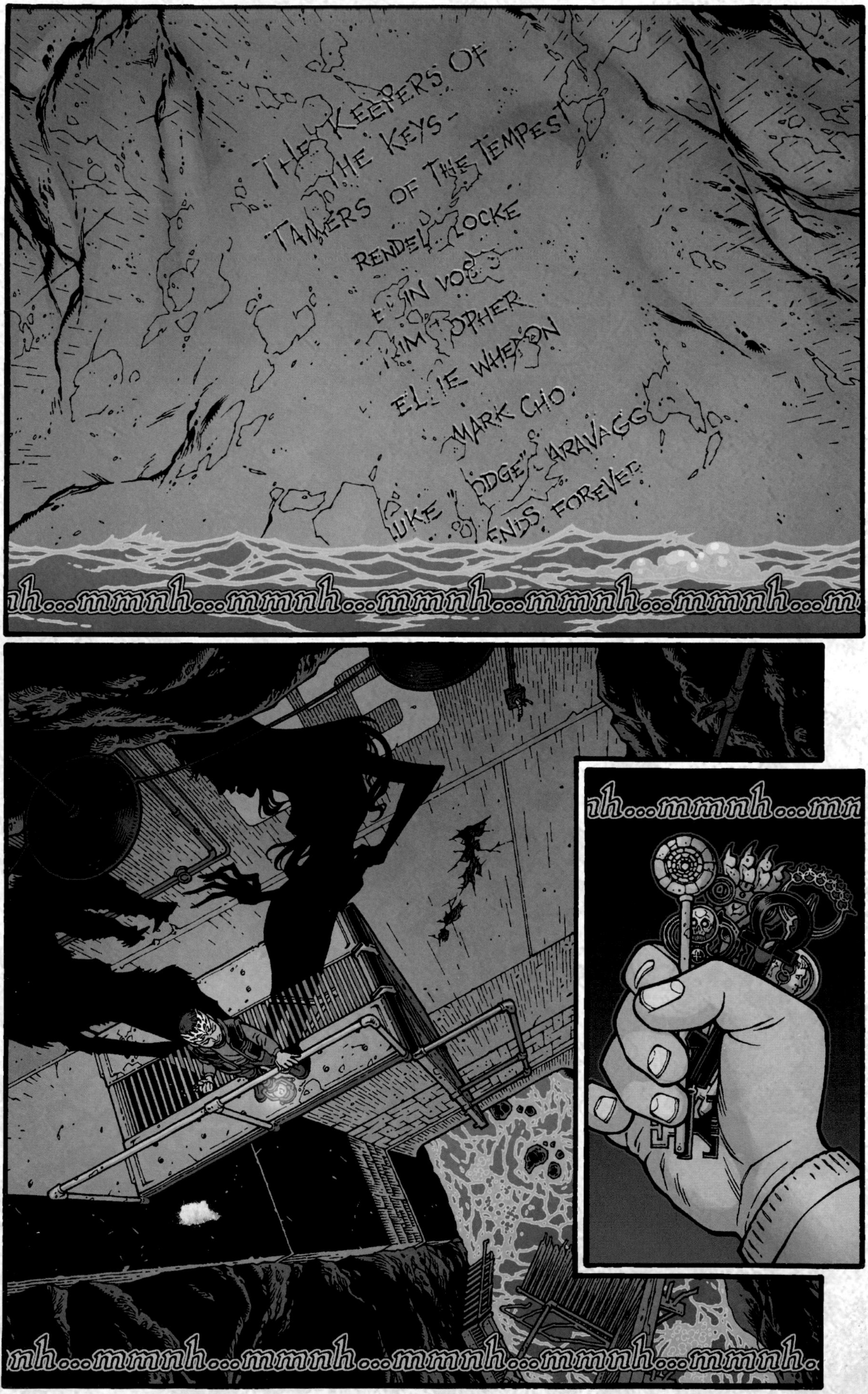
THE KEEPERS OF
THE KEYS -
TAMERS OF THE TEMPEST
MARK CHO
FOREVER
...mmnh...mmnh...mmnh...mmnh...
...mmnh...
...mmnh...mmnh...mmnh...mmnh...

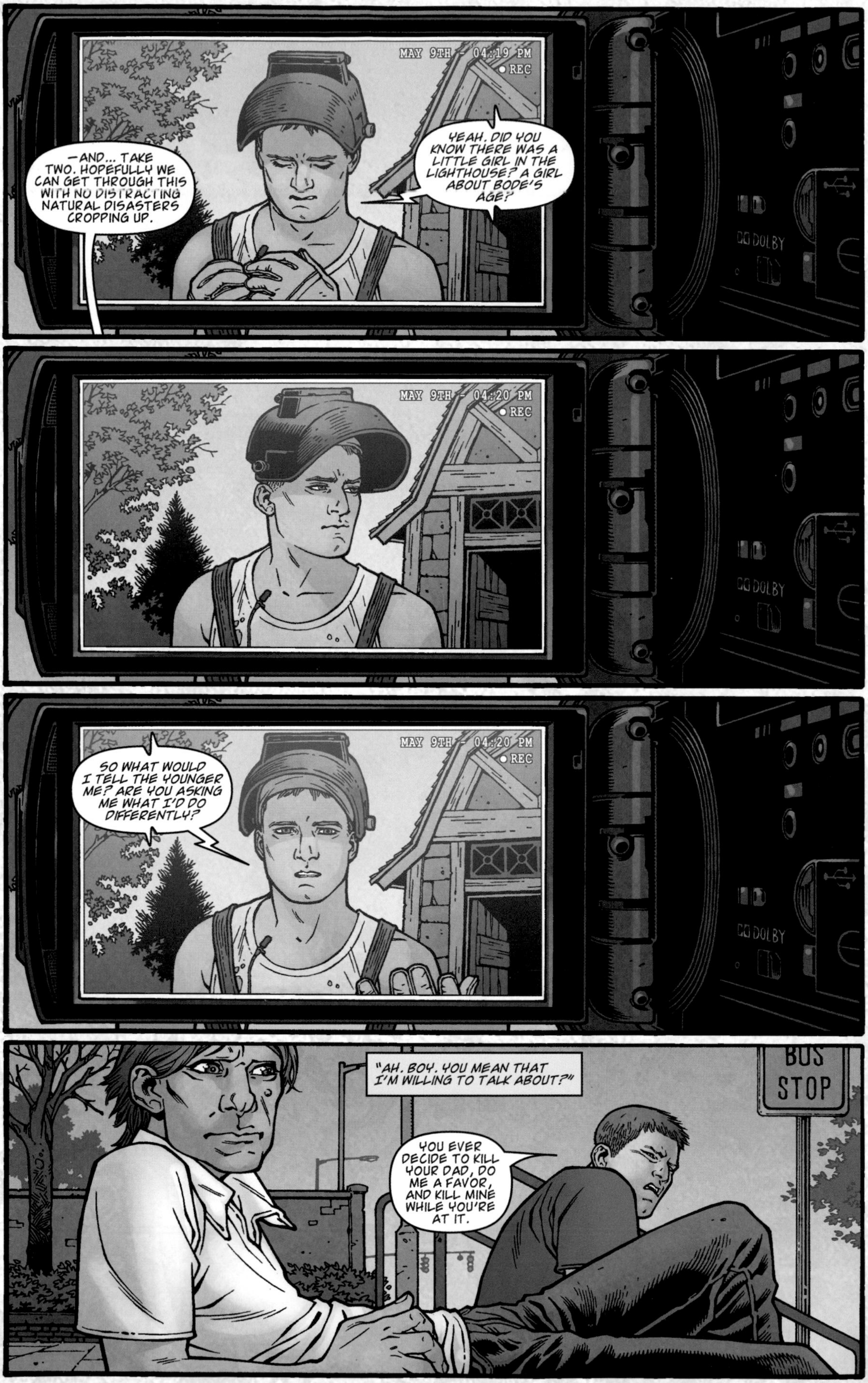
MAY 9TH - 04:19 PM
REC
—AND... TAKE TWO. HOPEFULLY WE CAN GET THROUGH THIS WITH NO DISTRACTING NATURAL DISASTERS CROPPING UP.
YEAH. DID YOU KNOW THERE WAS A LITTLE GIRL IN THE LIGHTHOUSE? A GIRL ABOUT BODE'S AGE?
DOLBY
MAY 9TH - 04:20 PM
REC
DOLBY
MAY 9TH - 04:20 PM
REC
SO WHAT WOULD I TELL THE YOUNGER ME? ARE YOU ASKING ME WHAT I'D DO DIFFERENTLY?
DOLBY
"AH. BOY. YOU MEAN THAT I'M WILLING TO TALK ABOUT?"
BUS STOP
YOU EVER DECIDE TO KILL YOUR DAD, DO ME A FAVOR, AND KILL MINE WHILE YOU'RE AT IT.

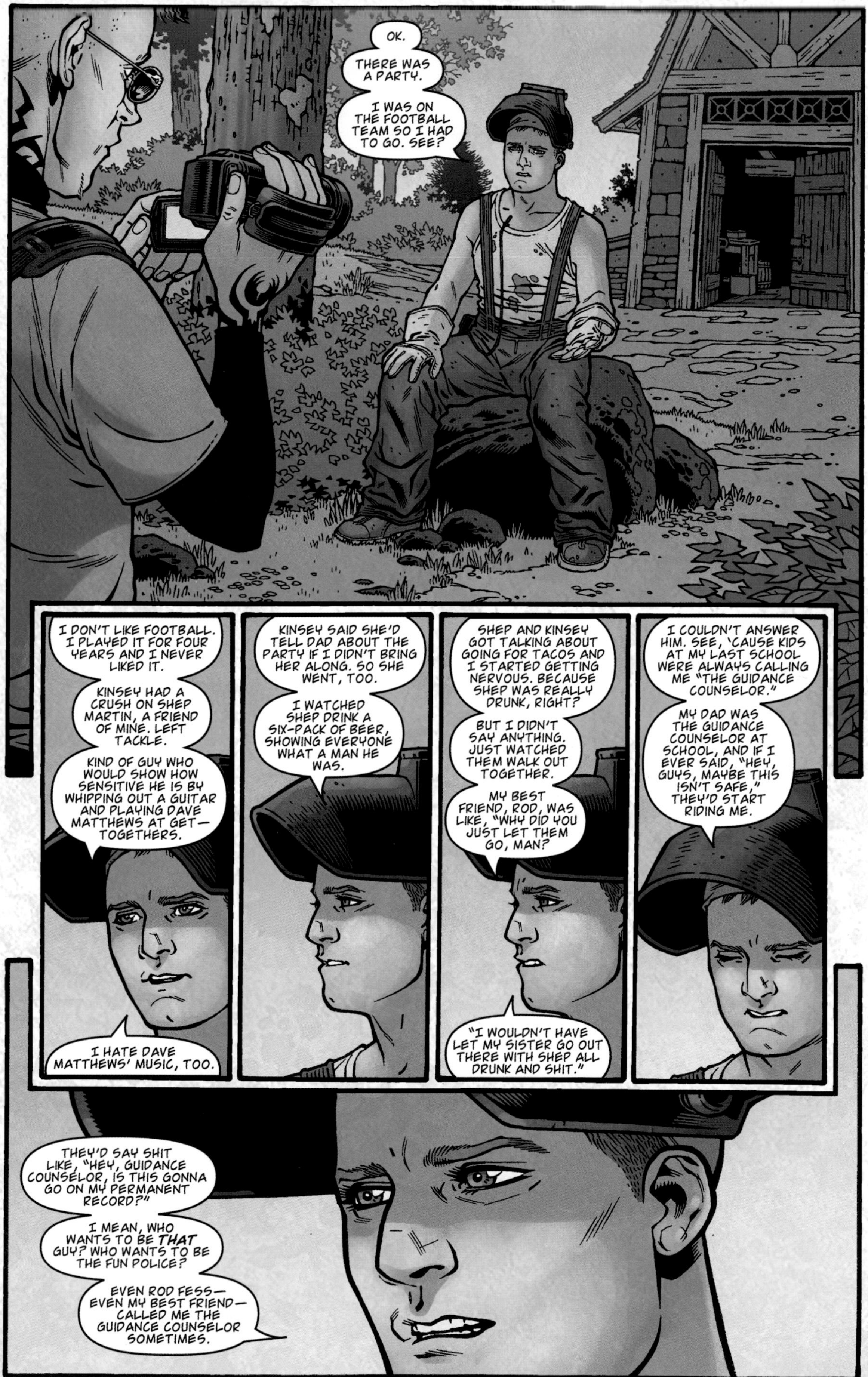
OK.
THERE WAS A PARTY.
I WAS ON THE FOOTBALL TEAM SO I HAD TO GO. SEE?
I DON'T LIKE FOOTBALL. I PLAYED IT FOR FOUR YEARS AND I NEVER LIKED IT.
KINSEY HAD A CRUSH ON SHEP MARTIN, A FRIEND OF MINE. LEFT TACKLE.
KIND OF GUY WHO WOULD SHOW HOW SENSITIVE HE IS BY WHIPPING OUT A GUITAR AND PLAYING DAVE MATTHEWS AT GET-TOGETHERS.
I HATE DAVE MATTHEWS' MUSIC, TOO.
KINSEY SAID SHE'D TELL DAD ABOUT THE PARTY IF I DIDN'T BRING HER ALONG. SO SHE WENT, TOO.
I WATCHED SHEP DRINK A SIX-PACK OF BEER, SHOWING EVERYONE WHAT A MAN HE WAS.
SHEP AND KINSEY GOT TALKING ABOUT GOING FOR TACOS AND I STARTED GETTING NERVOUS. BECAUSE SHEP WAS REALLY DRUNK, RIGHT?
BUT I DIDN'T SAY ANYTHING. JUST WATCHED THEM WALK OUT TOGETHER.
MY BEST FRIEND, ROD, WAS LIKE, "WHY DID YOU JUST LET THEM GO, MAN?
"I WOULDN'T HAVE LET MY SISTER GO OUT THERE WITH SHEP ALL DRUNK AND SHIT."
I COULDN'T ANSWER HIM. SEE, 'CAUSE KIDS AT MY LAST SCHOOL WERE ALWAYS CALLING ME "THE GUIDANCE COUNSELOR."
MY DAD WAS THE GUIDANCE COUNSELOR AT SCHOOL, AND IF I EVER SAID, "HEY, GUYS, MAYBE THIS ISN'T SAFE," THEY'D START RIDING ME.
THEY'D SAY SHIT LIKE, "HEY, GUIDANCE COUNSELOR, IS THIS GONNA GO ON MY PERMANENT RECORD?"
I MEAN, WHO WANTS TO BE *THAT* GUY? WHO WANTS TO BE THE FUN POLICE?
EVEN ROD FESS— EVEN MY BEST FRIEND— CALLED ME THE GUIDANCE COUNSELOR SOMETIMES.

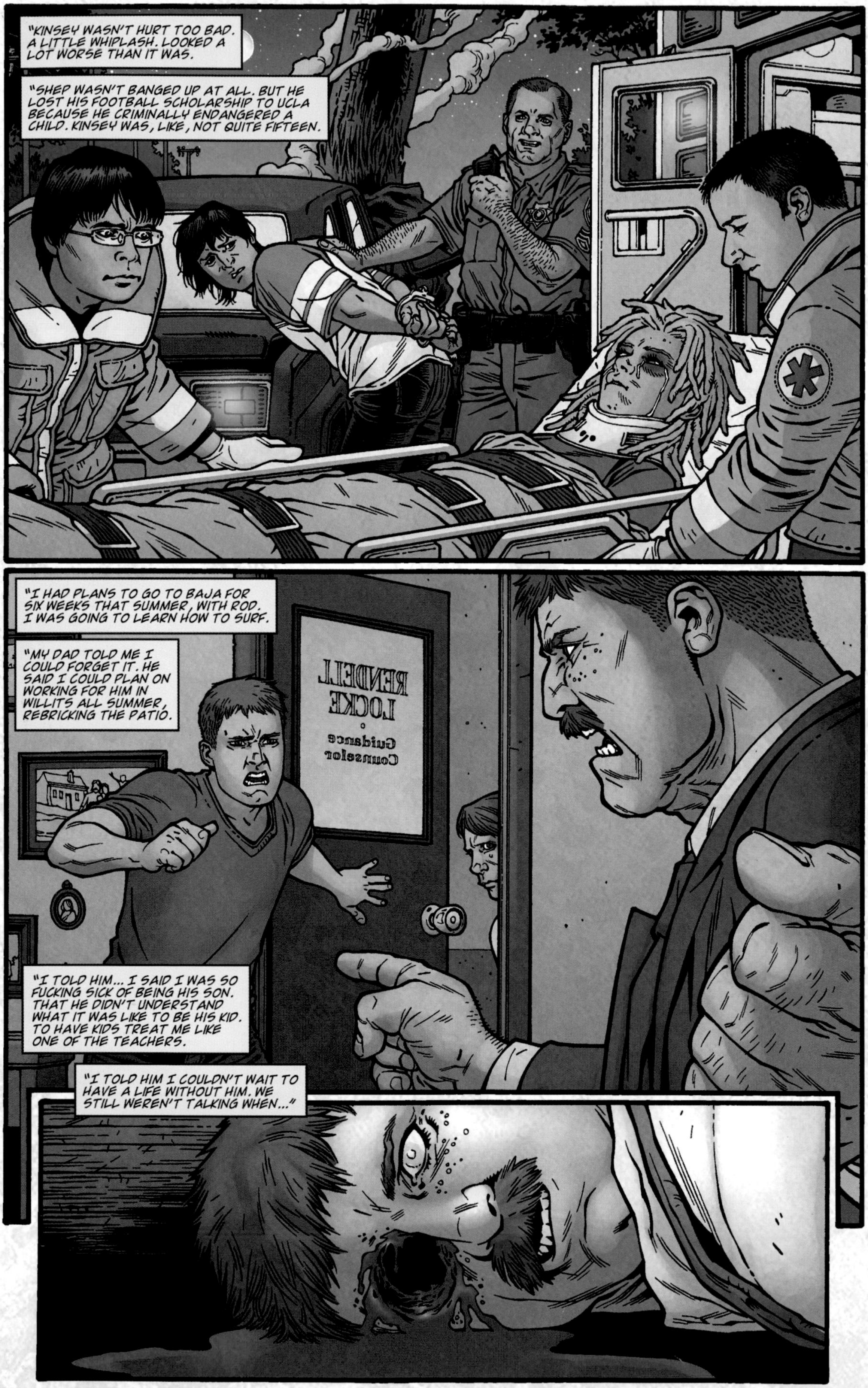
"KINSEY WASN'T HURT TOO BAD. A LITTLE WHIPLASH. LOOKED A LOT WORSE THAN IT WAS.
"SHEP WASN'T BANGED UP AT ALL. BUT HE LOST HIS FOOTBALL SCHOLARSHIP TO UCLA BECAUSE HE CRIMINALLY ENDANGERED A CHILD. KINSEY WAS, LIKE, NOT QUITE FIFTEEN.
"I HAD PLANS TO GO TO BAJA FOR SIX WEEKS THAT SUMMER, WITH ROD. I WAS GOING TO LEARN HOW TO SURF.
"MY DAD TOLD ME I COULD FORGET IT. HE SAID I COULD PLAN ON WORKING FOR HIM IN WILLITS ALL SUMMER, REBRICKING THE PATIO.
RENDELL LOCKE Guidance Counselor
"I TOLD HIM... I SAID I WAS SO FUCKING SICK OF BEING HIS SON. THAT HE DIDN'T UNDERSTAND WHAT IT WAS LIKE TO BE HIS KID. TO HAVE KIDS TREAT ME LIKE ONE OF THE TEACHERS.
"I TOLD HIM I COULDN'T WAIT TO HAVE A LIFE WITHOUT HIM. WE STILL WEREN'T TALKING WHEN..."

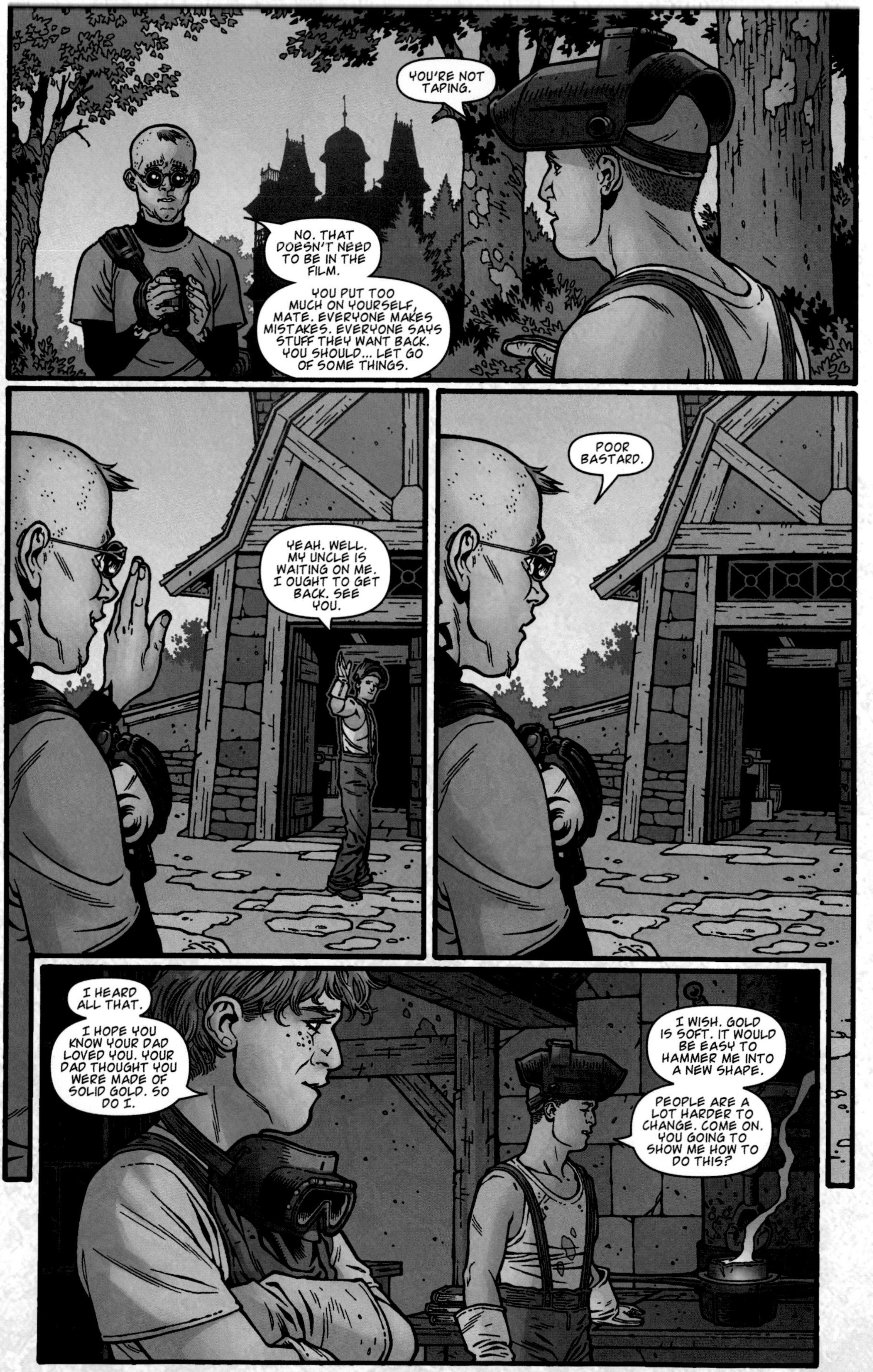
YOU'RE NOT TAPING.
NO. THAT DOESN'T NEED TO BE IN THE FILM.
YOU PUT TOO MUCH ON YOURSELF, MATE. EVERYONE MAKES MISTAKES. EVERYONE SAYS STUFF THEY WANT BACK. YOU SHOULD... LET GO OF SOME THINGS.
YEAH. WELL. MY UNCLE IS WAITING ON ME. I OUGHT TO GET BACK. SEE YOU.
POOR BASTARD.
I HEARD ALL THAT.
I HOPE YOU KNOW YOUR DAD LOVED YOU. YOUR DAD THOUGHT YOU WERE MADE OF SOLID GOLD. SO DO I.
I WISH. GOLD IS SOFT. IT WOULD BE EASY TO HAMMER ME INTO A NEW SHAPE.
PEOPLE ARE A LOT HARDER TO CHANGE. COME ON. YOU GOING TO SHOW ME HOW TO DO THIS?

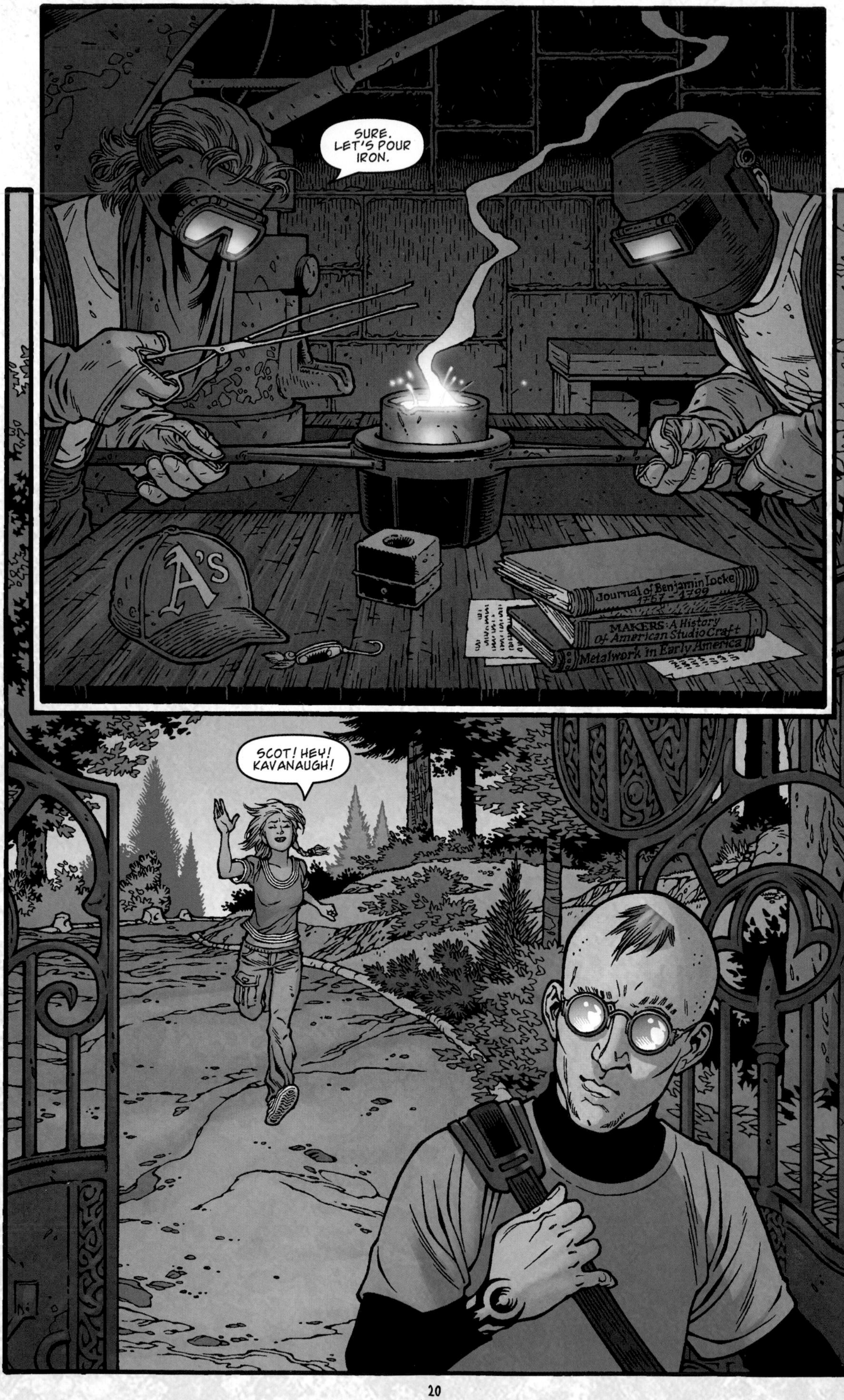
SURE. LET'S POUR IRON.
Journal of Benjamin Locke 1757 - 1799
MAKERS: A History of American Studio Craft
Metalwork in Early America
SCOT! HEY! KAVANAUGH!

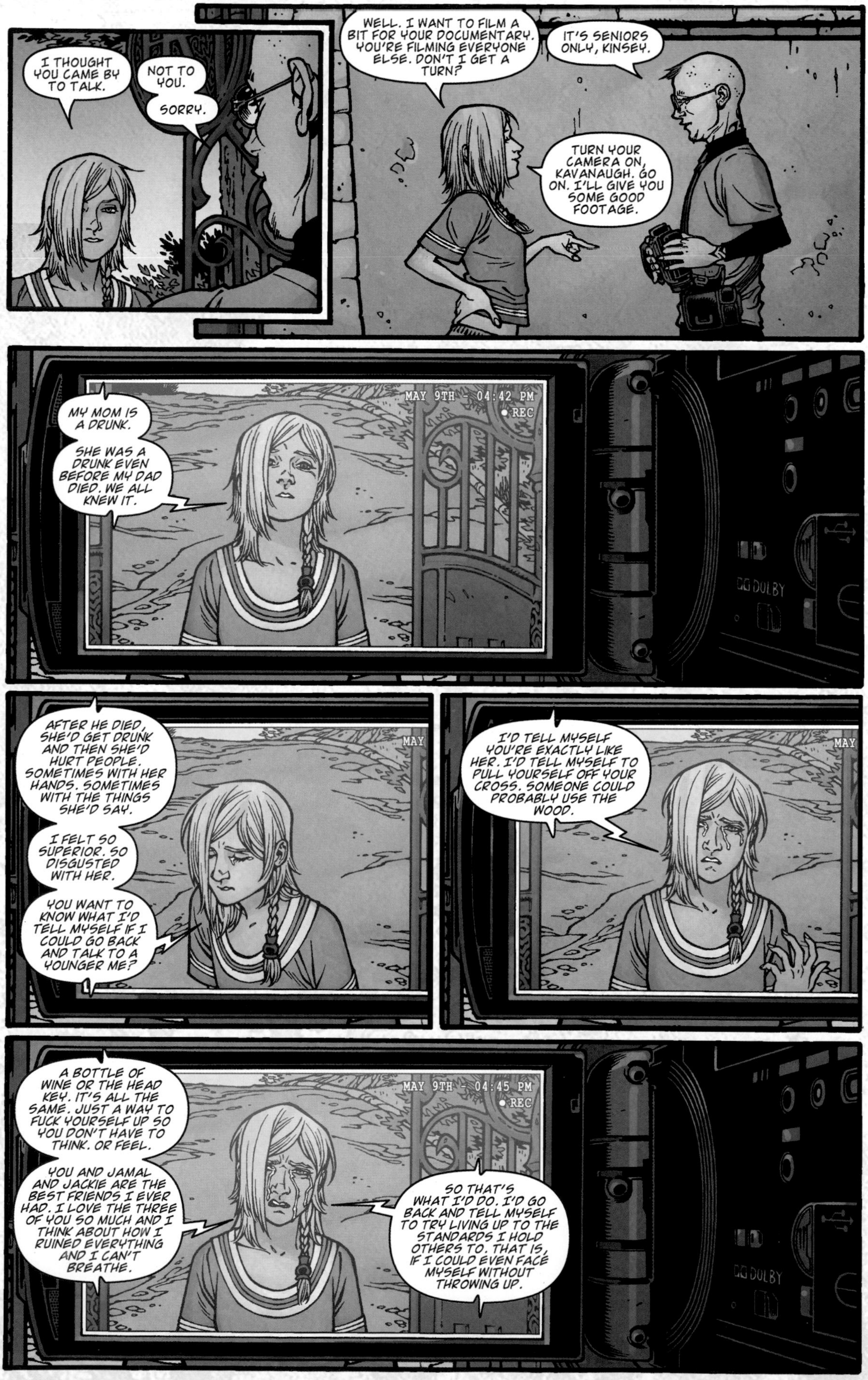
I THOUGHT YOU CAME BY TO TALK.
NOT TO YOU.
SORRY.
WELL. I WANT TO FILM A BIT FOR YOUR DOCUMENTARY. YOU'RE FILMING EVERYONE ELSE. DON'T I GET A TURN?
IT'S SENIORS ONLY, KINSEY.
TURN YOUR CAMERA ON, KAVANAUGH. GO ON. I'LL GIVE YOU SOME GOOD FOOTAGE.
MAY 9TH - 04:42 PM
● REC
MY MOM IS A DRUNK.
SHE WAS A DRUNK EVEN BEFORE MY DAD DIED. WE ALL KNEW IT.
DOLBY
MAY
AFTER HE DIED, SHE'D GET DRUNK AND THEN SHE'D HURT PEOPLE. SOMETIMES WITH HER HANDS. SOMETIMES WITH THE THINGS SHE'D SAY.
I FELT SO SUPERIOR. SO DISGUSTED WITH HER.
YOU WANT TO KNOW WHAT I'D TELL MYSELF IF I COULD GO BACK AND TALK TO A YOUNGER ME?
MAY
I'D TELL MYSELF YOU'RE EXACTLY LIKE HER. I'D TELL MYSELF TO PULL YOURSELF OFF YOUR CROSS. SOMEONE COULD PROBABLY USE THE WOOD.
MAY 9TH - 04:45 PM
● REC
A BOTTLE OF WINE OR THE HEAD KEY. IT'S ALL THE SAME. JUST A WAY TO FUCK YOURSELF UP SO YOU DON'T HAVE TO THINK. OR FEEL.
YOU AND JAMAL AND JACKIE ARE THE BEST FRIENDS I EVER HAD. I LOVE THE THREE OF YOU SO MUCH AND I THINK ABOUT HOW I RUINED EVERYTHING AND I CAN'T BREATHE.
SO THAT'S WHAT I'D DO. I'D GO BACK AND TELL MYSELF TO TRY LIVING UP TO THE STANDARDS I HOLD OTHERS TO. THAT IS, IF I COULD EVEN FACE MYSELF WITHOUT THROWING UP.
DOLBY

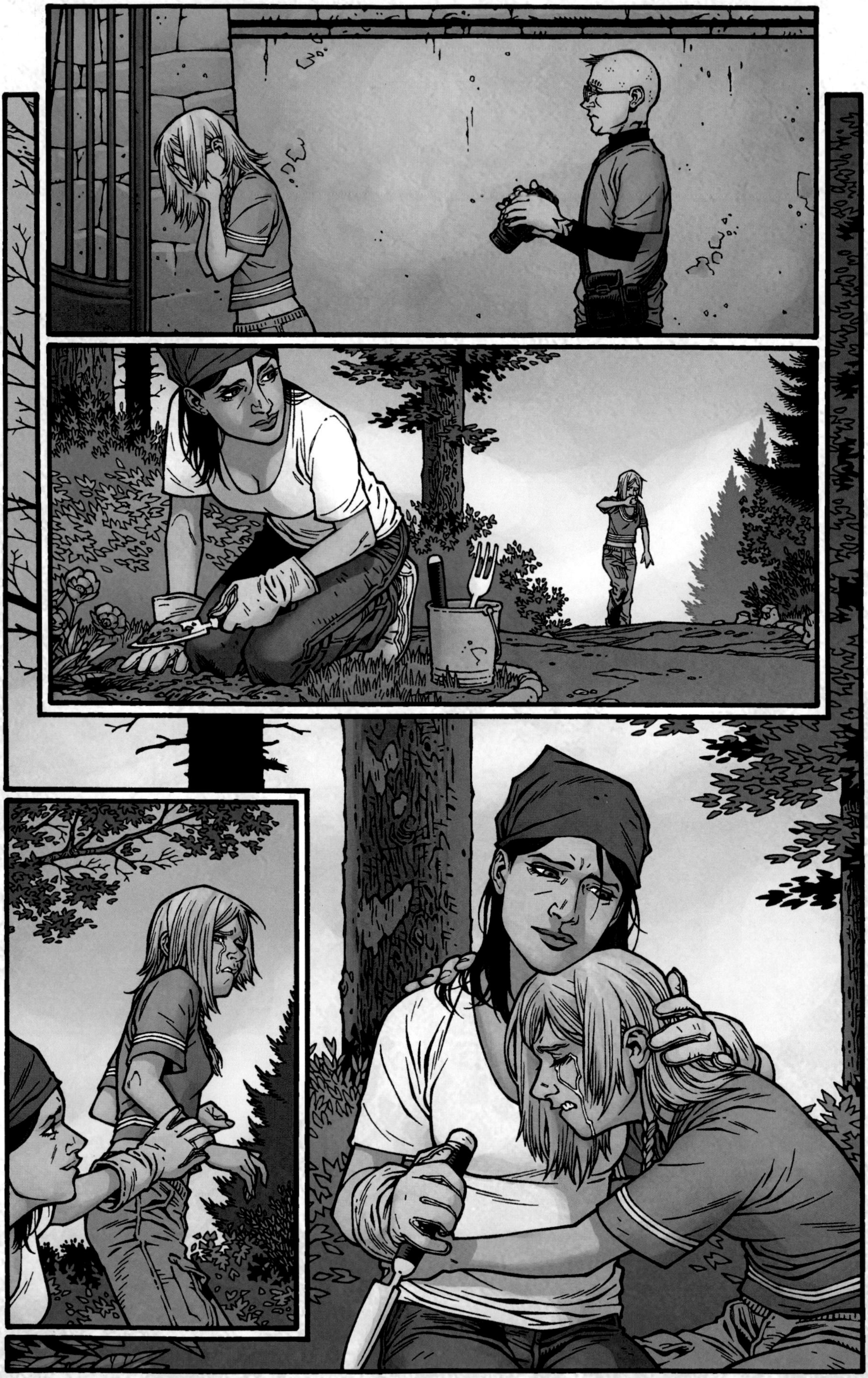

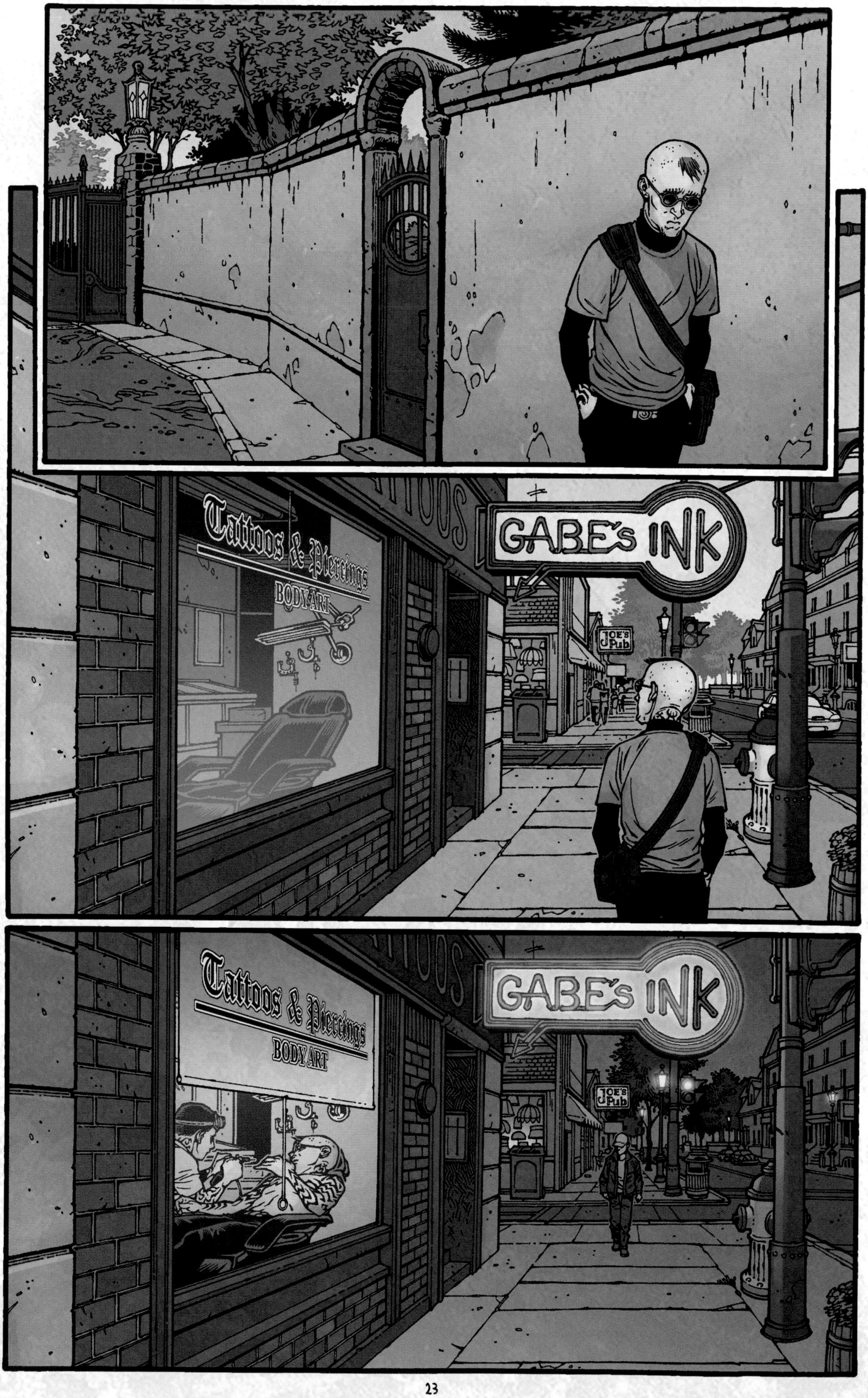
Tattoos & Piercings
BODY ART
GABE's INK
JOE'S Pub
Tattoos & Piercings
BODY ART
GABE's INK
JOE'S Pub

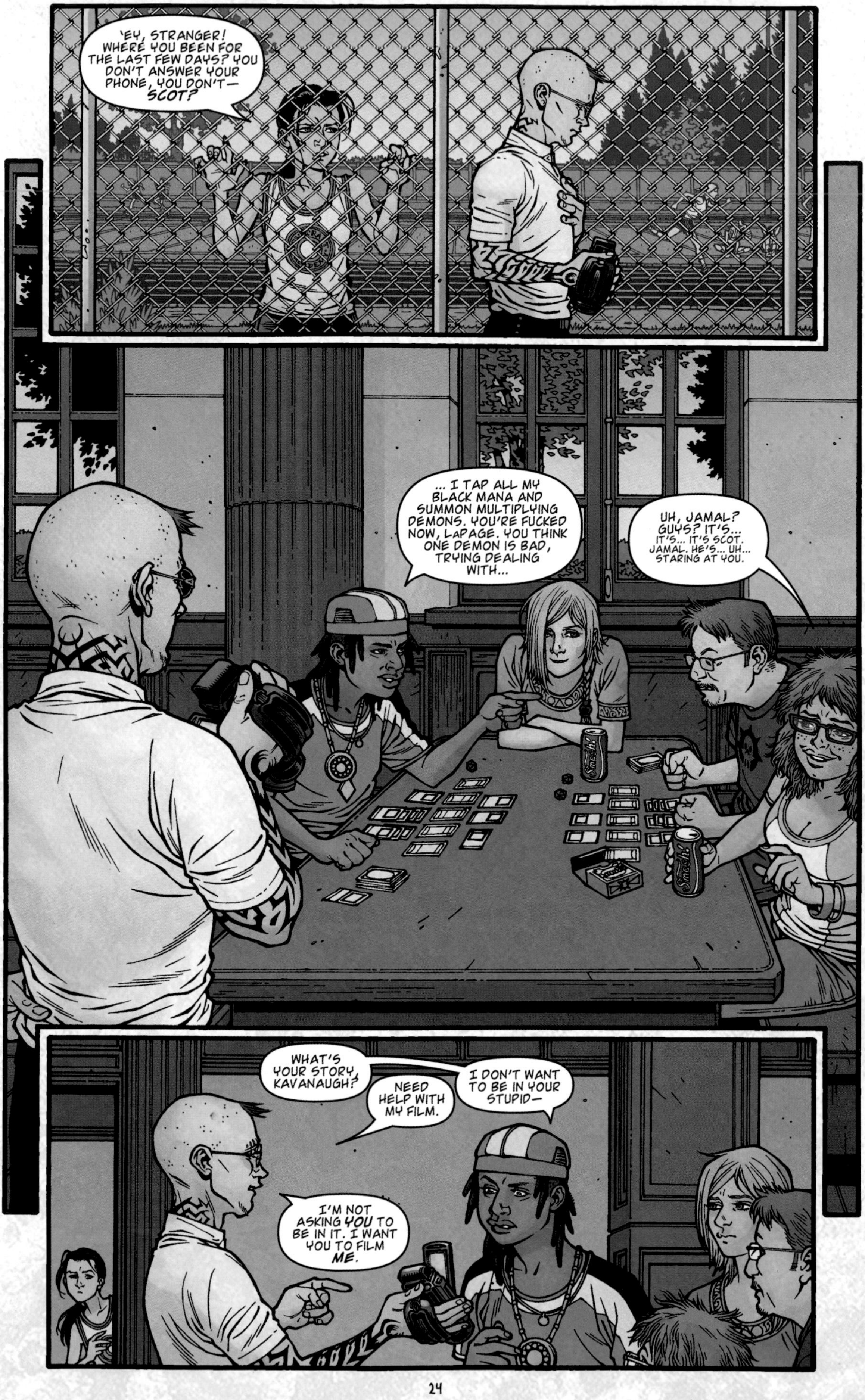
'EY, STRANGER! WHERE YOU BEEN FOR THE LAST FEW DAYS? YOU DON'T ANSWER YOUR PHONE, YOU DON'T— SCOT?
... I TAP ALL MY BLACK MANA AND SUMMON MULTIPLYING DEMONS. YOU'RE FUCKED NOW, LaPAGE. YOU THINK ONE DEMON IS BAD, TRYING DEALING WITH...
UH, JAMAL? GUYS? IT'S... IT'S... IT'S SCOT. JAMAL. HE'S... UH... STARING AT YOU.
WHAT'S YOUR STORY, KAVANAUGH?
NEED HELP WITH MY FILM.
I DON'T WANT TO BE IN YOUR STUPID—
I'M NOT ASKING YOU TO BE IN IT. I WANT YOU TO FILM ME.

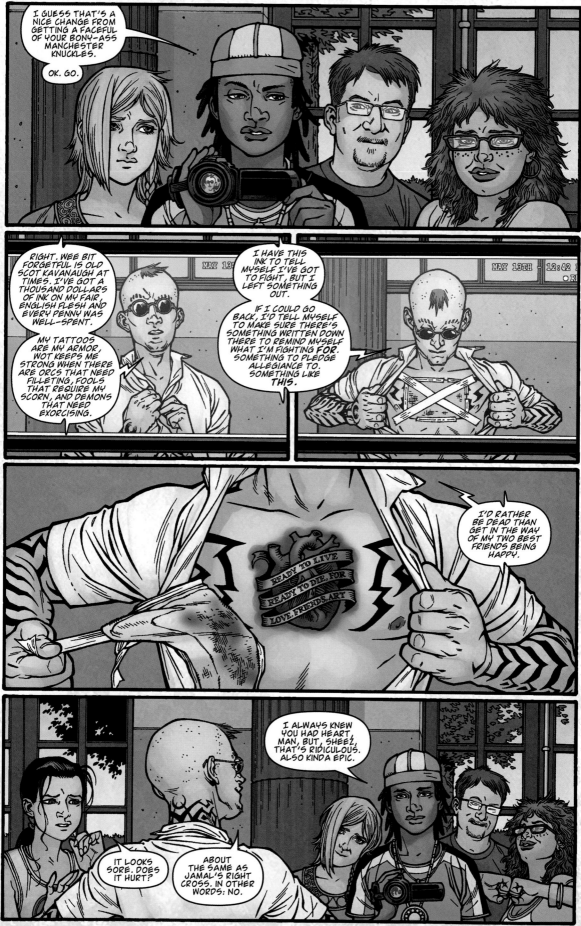

I GUESS THAT'S A NICE CHANGE FROM GETTING A FACEFUL OF YOUR BONY-ASS MANCHESTER KNUCKLES.

OK. GO.

RIGHT. WEE BIT FORGETFUL IS OLD SCOT KAVANAUGH AT TIMES. I'VE GOT A THOUSAND DOLLARS OF INK ON MY FAIR, ENGLISH FLESH AND EVERY PENNY WAS WELL-SPENT.

MY TATTOOS ARE MY ARMOR, WOT KEEPS ME STRONG WHEN THERE ARE ORCS THAT NEED FILLETING, FOOLS THAT REQUIRE MY SCORN, AND DEMONS THAT NEED EXORCISING.

I HAVE THIS INK TO TELL MYSELF I'VE GOT TO FIGHT, BUT I LEFT SOMETHING OUT.

IF I COULD GO BACK, I'D TELL MYSELF TO MAKE SURE THERE'S SOMETHING WRITTEN DOWN THERE TO REMIND MYSELF WHAT I'M FIGHTING FOR. SOMETHING TO PLEDGE ALLEGIANCE TO. SOMETHING LIKE THIS.

MAY 13TH - 12:42

I'D RATHER BE DEAD THAN GET IN THE WAY OF MY TWO BEST FRIENDS BEING HAPPY.

READY TO LIVE READY TO DIE, FOR LOVE, FRIENDS, ART

I ALWAYS KNEW YOU HAD HEART, MAN, BUT, SHEEZ, THAT'S RIDICULOUS. ALSO KINDA EPIC.

IT LOOKS SORE. DOES IT HURT?

ABOUT THE SAME AS JAMAL'S RIGHT CROSS. IN OTHER WORDS: NO.

25

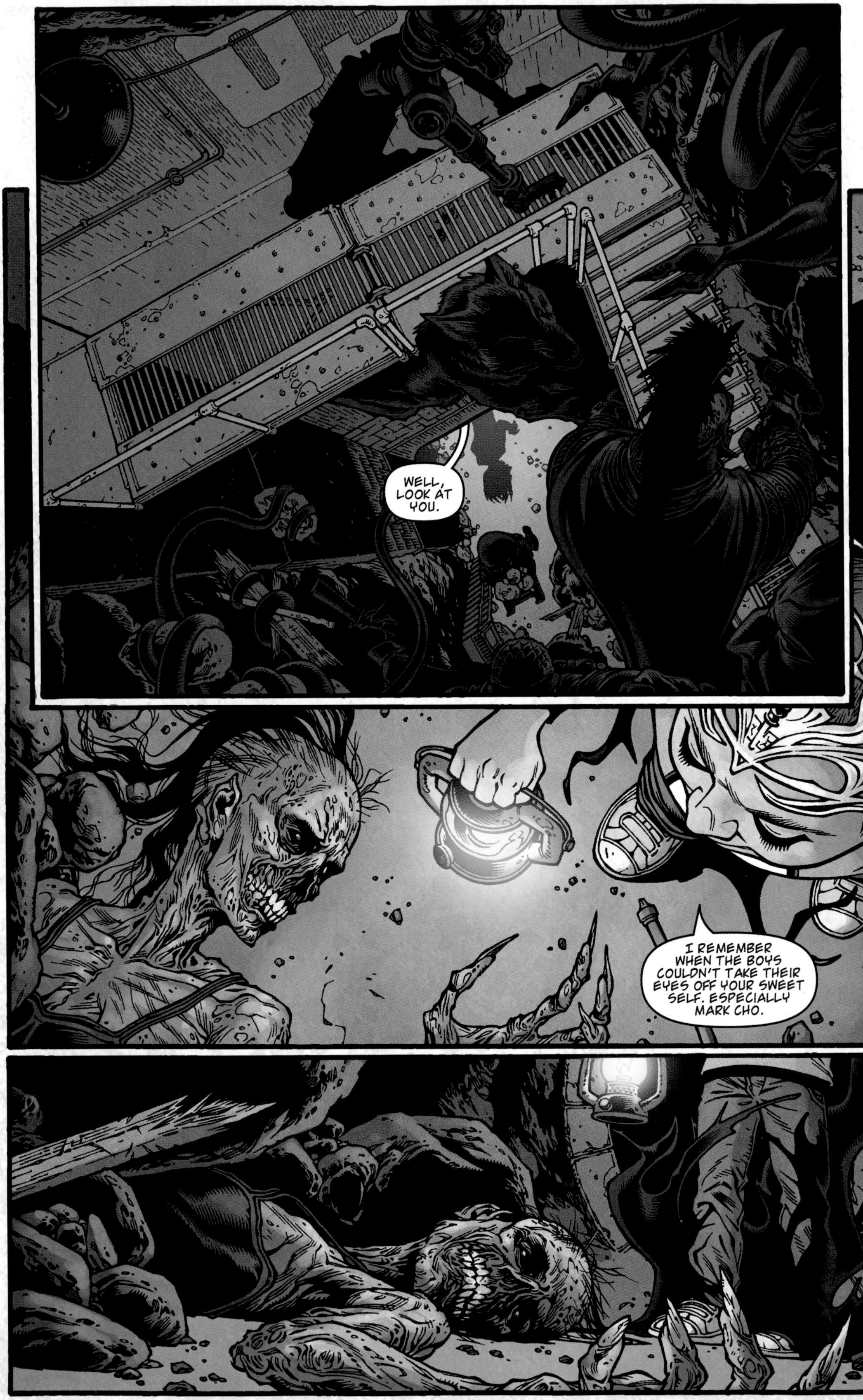
WELL, LOOK AT YOU.
I REMEMBER WHEN THE BOYS COULDN'T TAKE THEIR EYES OFF YOUR SWEET SELF. ESPECIALLY MARK CHO.

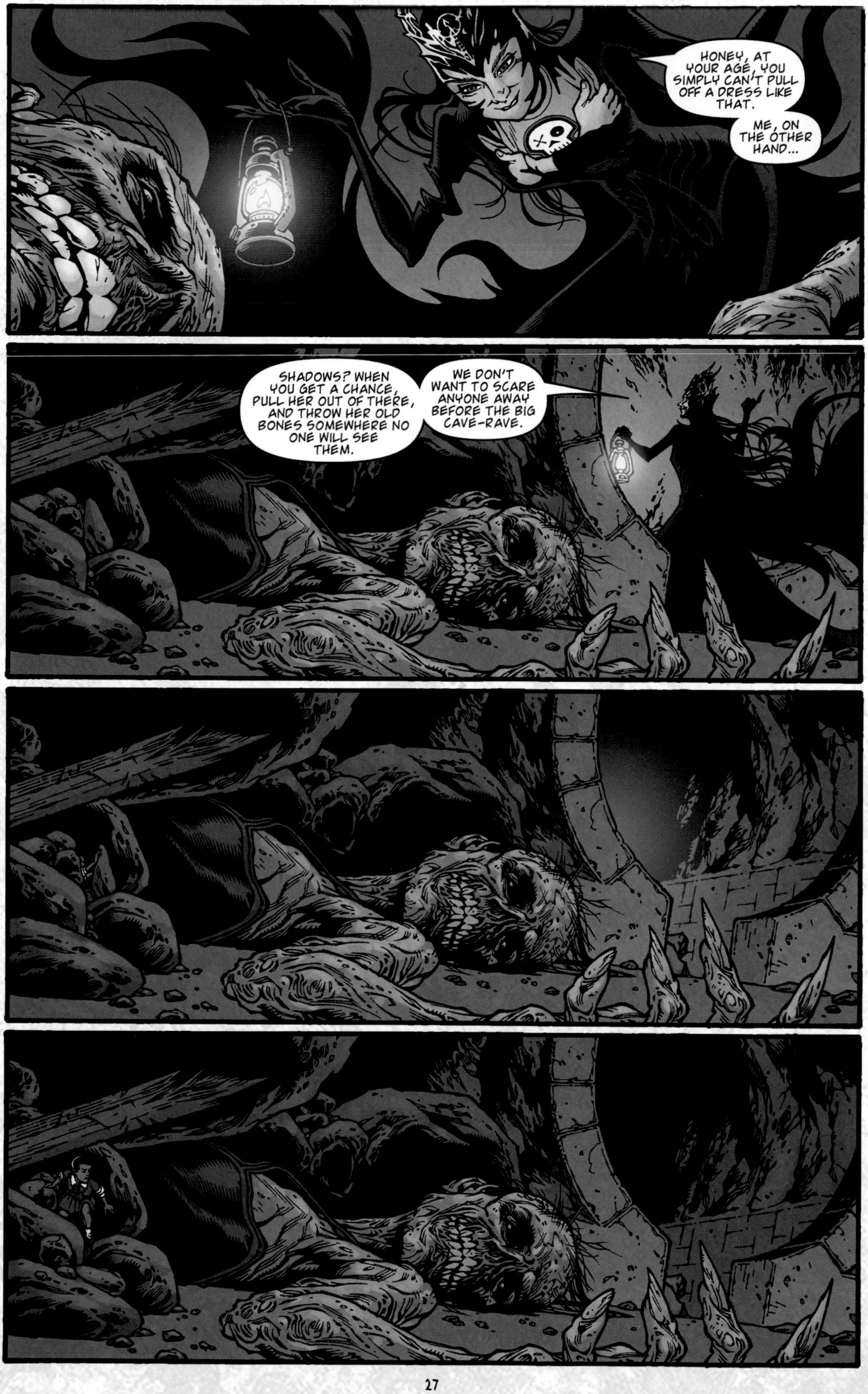
HONEY, AT YOUR AGE, YOU SIMPLY CAN'T PULL OFF A DRESS LIKE THAT.
ME, ON THE OTHER HAND...
SHADOWS? WHEN YOU GET A CHANCE, PULL HER OUT OF THERE, AND THROW HER OLD BONES SOMEWHERE NO ONE WILL SEE THEM.
WE DON'T WANT TO SCARE ANYONE AWAY BEFORE THE BIG CAVE-RAVE.

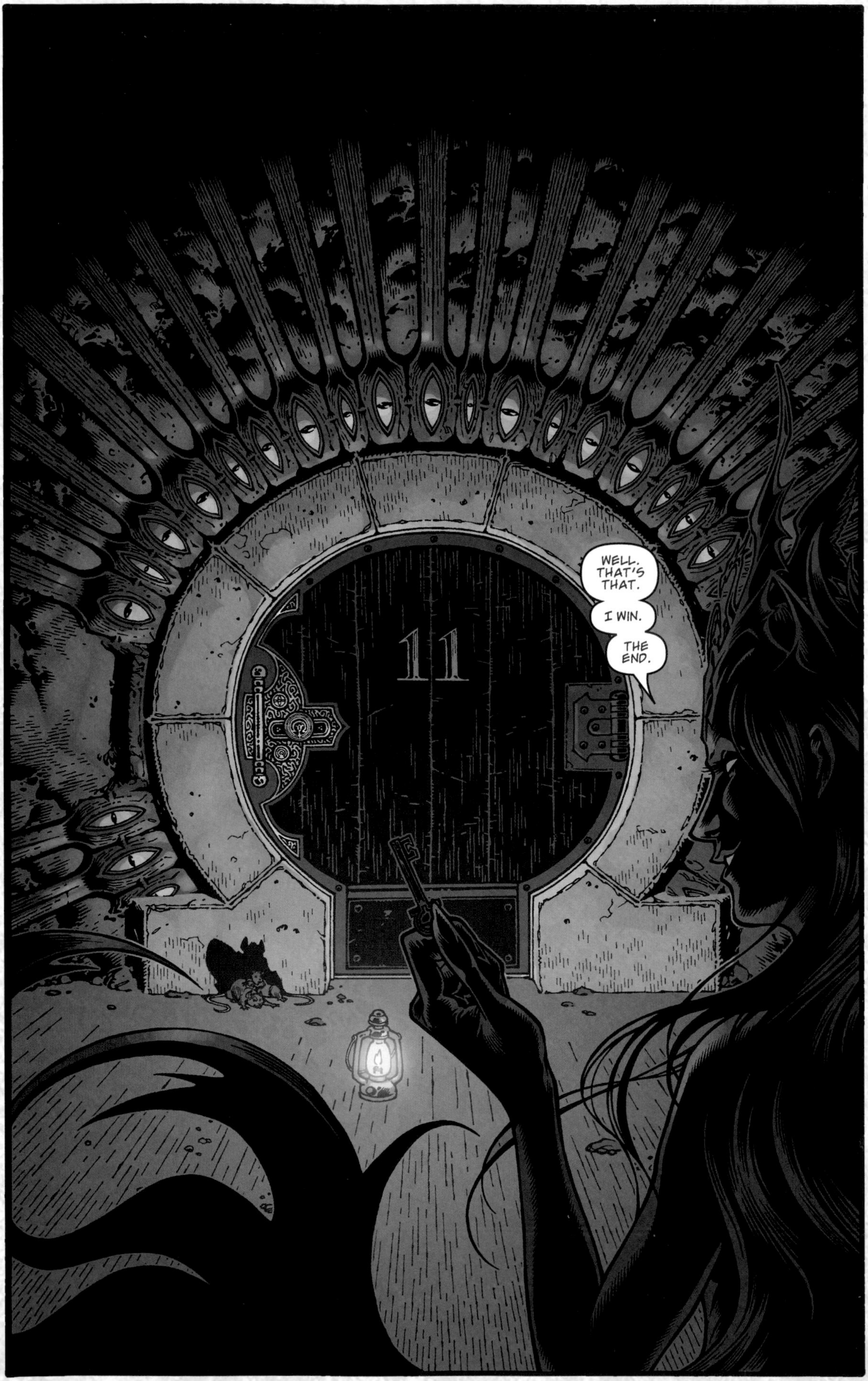
WELL. THAT'S THAT.
I WIN.
THE END.
11

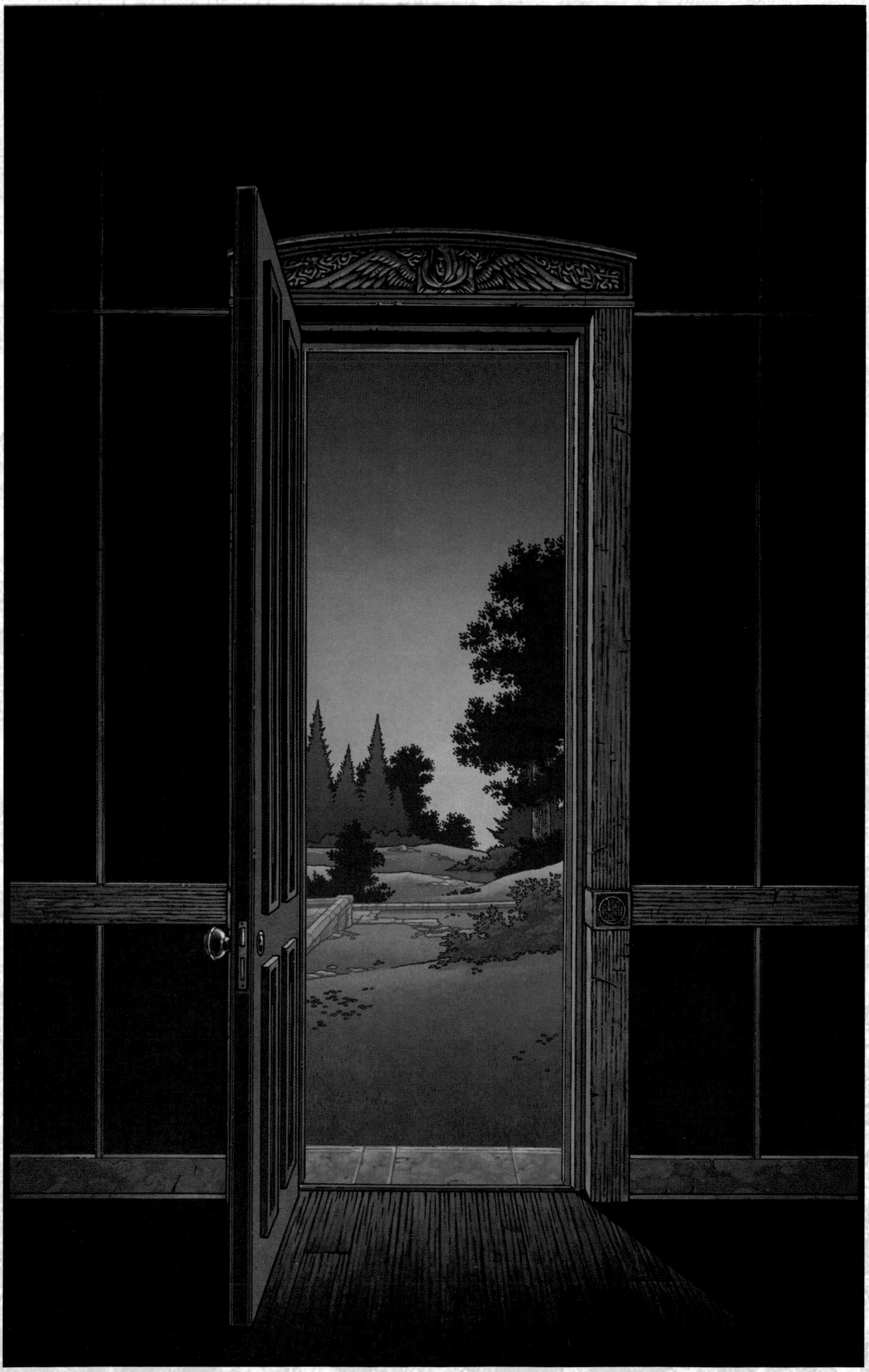

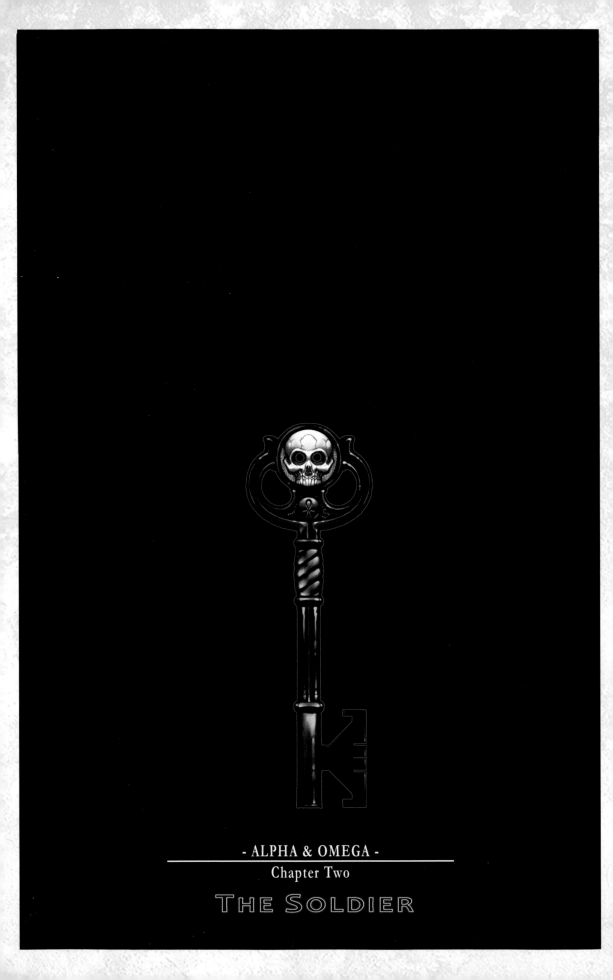

- ALPHA & OMEGA -

Chapter Two

THE SOLDIER

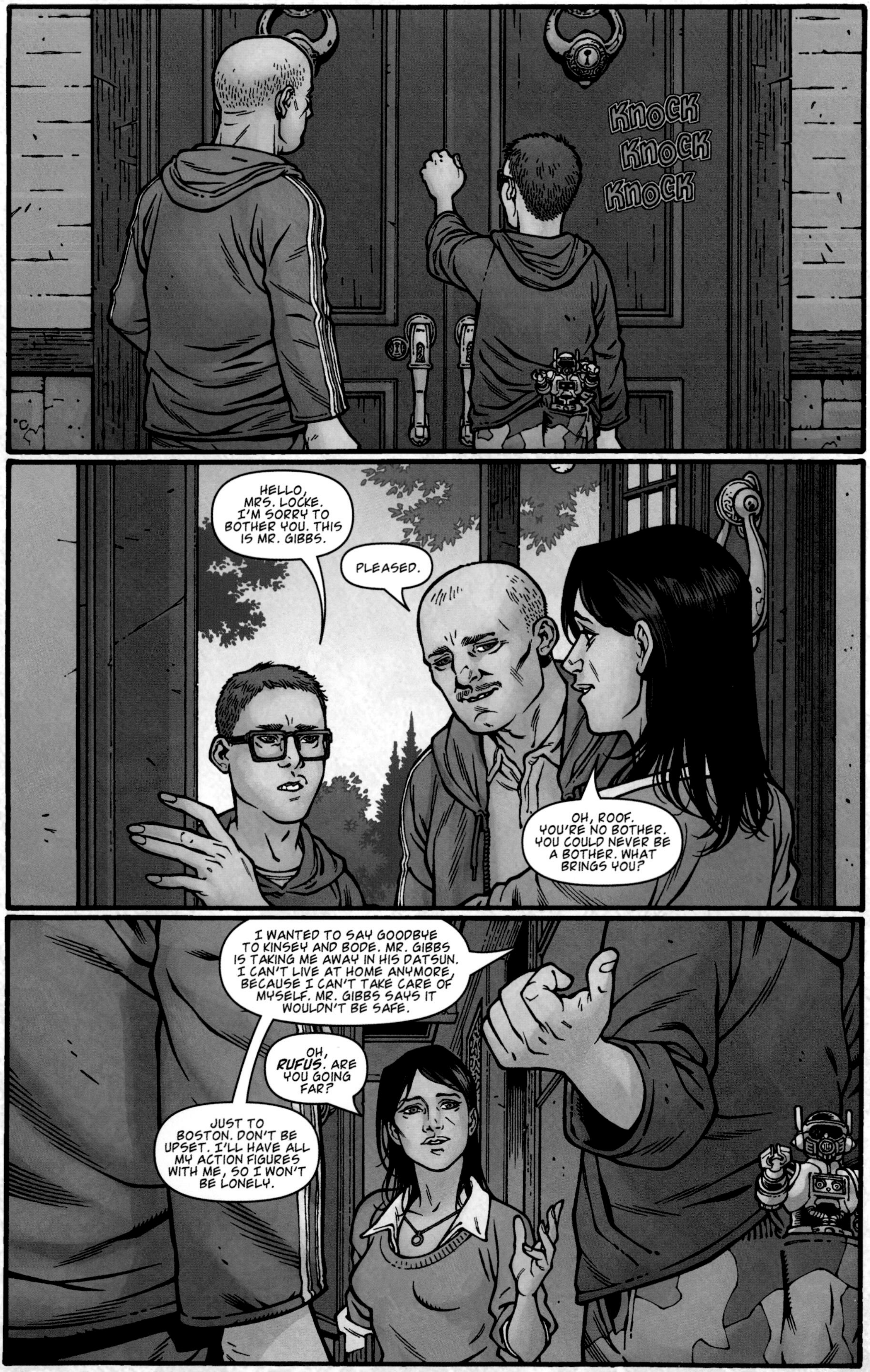
KNOCK
KNOCK
KNOCK
HELLO, MRS. LOCKE. I'M SORRY TO BOTHER YOU. THIS IS MR. GIBBS.
PLEASED.
OH, ROOF. YOU'RE NO BOTHER. YOU COULD NEVER BE A BOTHER. WHAT BRINGS YOU?
I WANTED TO SAY GOODBYE TO KINSEY AND BODE. MR. GIBBS IS TAKING ME AWAY IN HIS DATSUN. I CAN'T LIVE AT HOME ANYMORE, BECAUSE I CAN'T TAKE CARE OF MYSELF. MR. GIBBS SAYS IT WOULDN'T BE SAFE.
OH, ***RUFUS***. ARE YOU GOING FAR?
JUST TO BOSTON. DON'T BE UPSET. I'LL HAVE ALL MY ACTION FIGURES WITH ME, SO I WON'T BE LONELY.

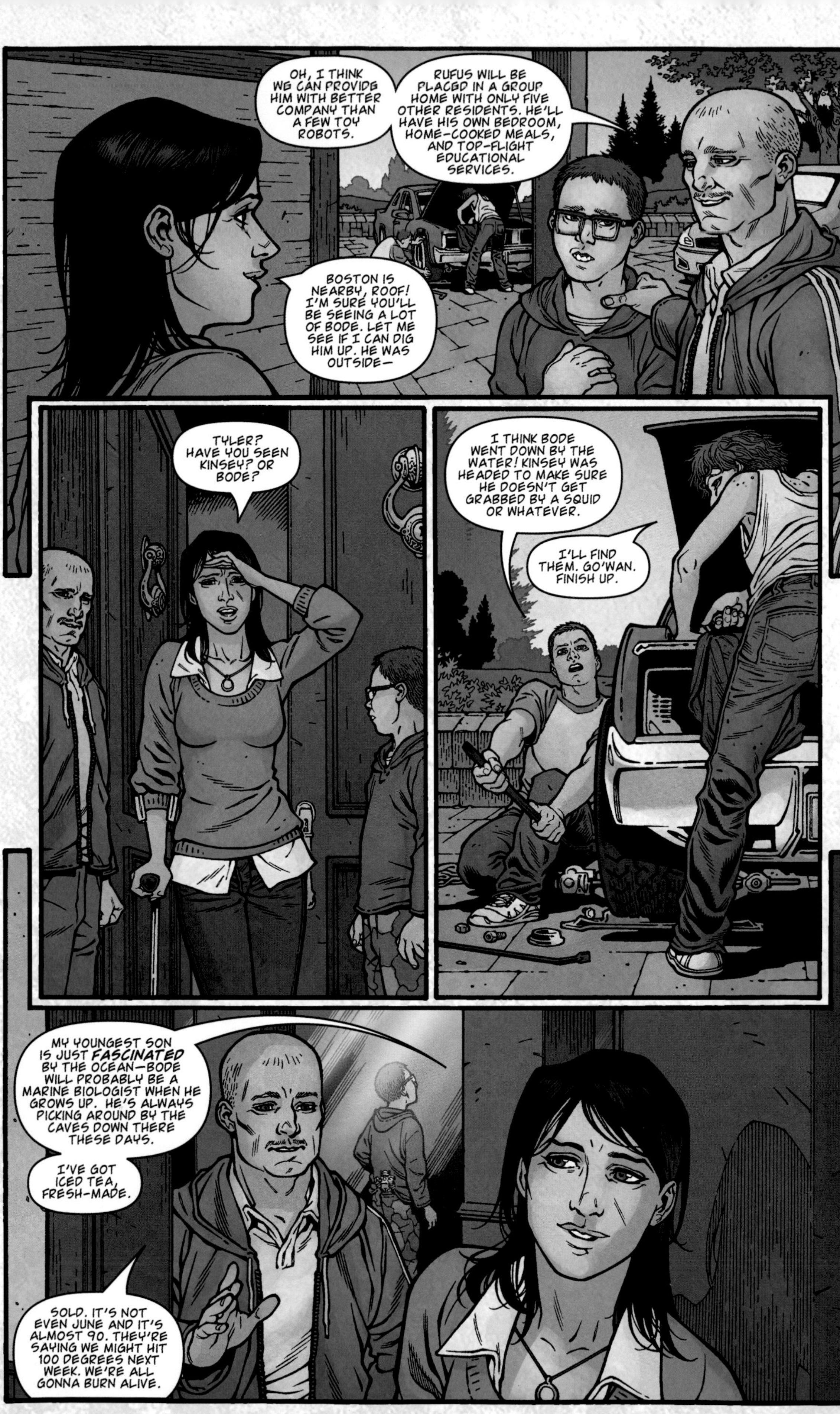
OH, I THINK WE CAN PROVIDE HIM WITH BETTER COMPANY THAN A FEW TOY ROBOTS.
RUFUS WILL BE PLACED IN A GROUP HOME WITH ONLY FIVE OTHER RESIDENTS. HE'LL HAVE HIS OWN BEDROOM, HOME-COOKED MEALS, AND TOP-FLIGHT EDUCATIONAL SERVICES.
BOSTON IS NEARBY, ROOF! I'M SURE YOU'LL BE SEEING A LOT OF BODE. LET ME SEE IF I CAN DIG HIM UP. HE WAS OUTSIDE—
TYLER? HAVE YOU SEEN KINSEY? OR BODE?
I THINK BODE WENT DOWN BY THE WATER! KINSEY WAS HEADED TO MAKE SURE HE DOESN'T GET GRABBED BY A SQUID OR WHATEVER.
I'LL FIND THEM. GO'WAN. FINISH UP.
MY YOUNGEST SON IS JUST FASCINATED BY THE OCEAN—BODE WILL PROBABLY BE A MARINE BIOLOGIST WHEN HE GROWS UP. HE'S ALWAYS PICKING AROUND BY THE CAVES DOWN THERE THESE DAYS.
I'VE GOT ICED TEA, FRESH-MADE.
SOLD. IT'S NOT EVEN JUNE AND IT'S ALMOST 90. THEY'RE SAYING WE MIGHT HIT 100 DEGREES NEXT WEEK. WE'RE ALL GONNA BURN ALIVE.

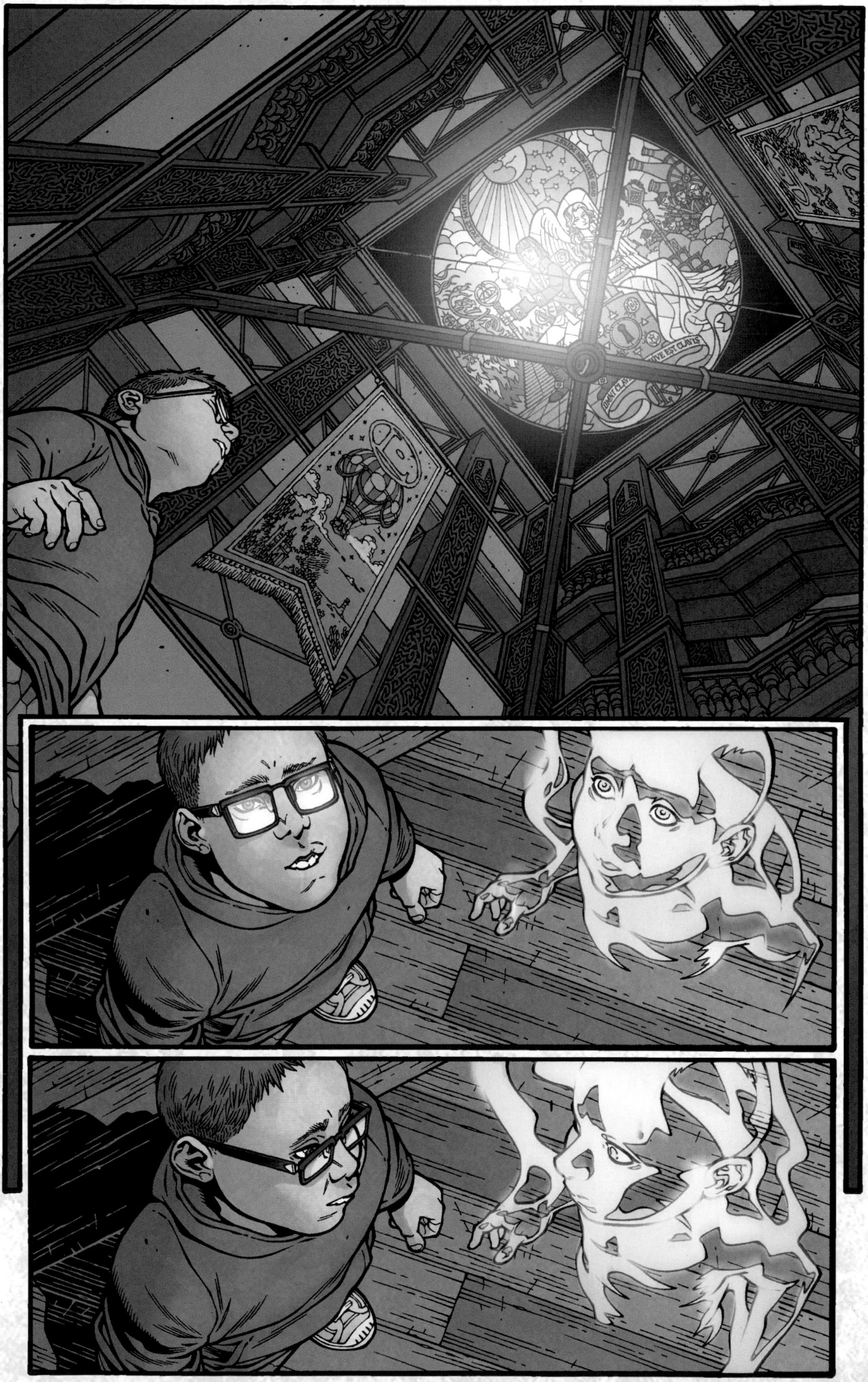

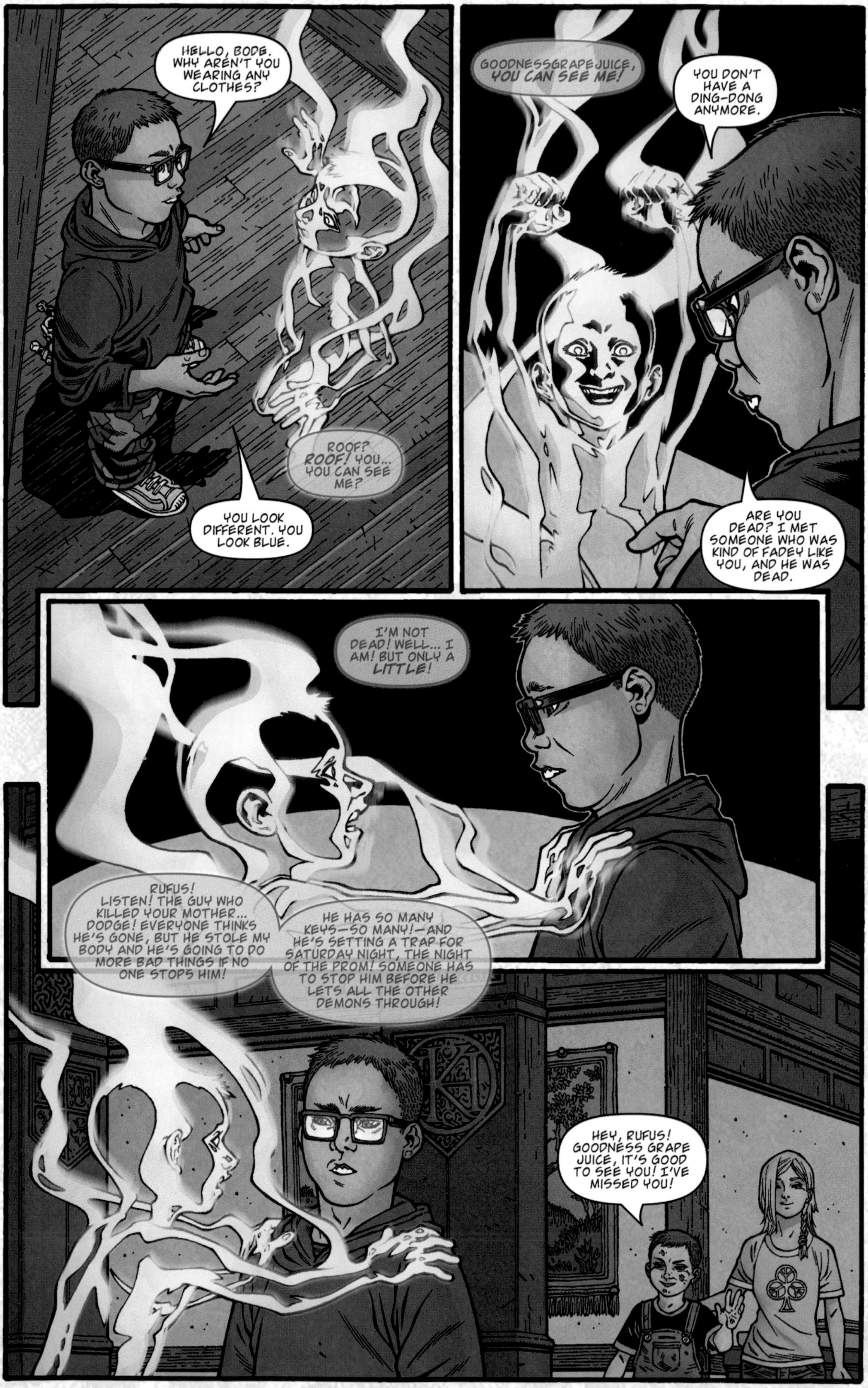
HELLO, BODE. WHY AREN'T YOU WEARING ANY CLOTHES?
ROOF? ROOF! YOU... YOU CAN SEE ME?
YOU LOOK DIFFERENT. YOU LOOK BLUE.
GOODNESSGRAPEJUICE, YOU CAN SEE ME!
YOU DON'T HAVE A DING-DONG ANYMORE.
ARE YOU DEAD? I MET SOMEONE WHO WAS KIND OF FADEY LIKE YOU, AND HE WAS DEAD.
I'M NOT DEAD! WELL... I AM! BUT ONLY A LITTLE!
RUFUS! LISTEN! THE GUY WHO KILLED YOUR MOTHER... DODGE! EVERYONE THINKS HE'S GONE, BUT HE STOLE MY BODY AND HE'S GOING TO DO MORE BAD THINGS IF NO ONE STOPS HIM!
HE HAS SO MANY KEYS—SO MANY!—AND HE'S SETTING A TRAP FOR SATURDAY NIGHT, THE NIGHT OF THE PROM! SOMEONE HAS TO STOP HIM BEFORE HE LETS ALL THE OTHER DEMONS THROUGH!
HEY, RUFUS! GOODNESS GRAPE JUICE, IT'S GOOD TO SEE YOU! I'VE MISSED YOU!

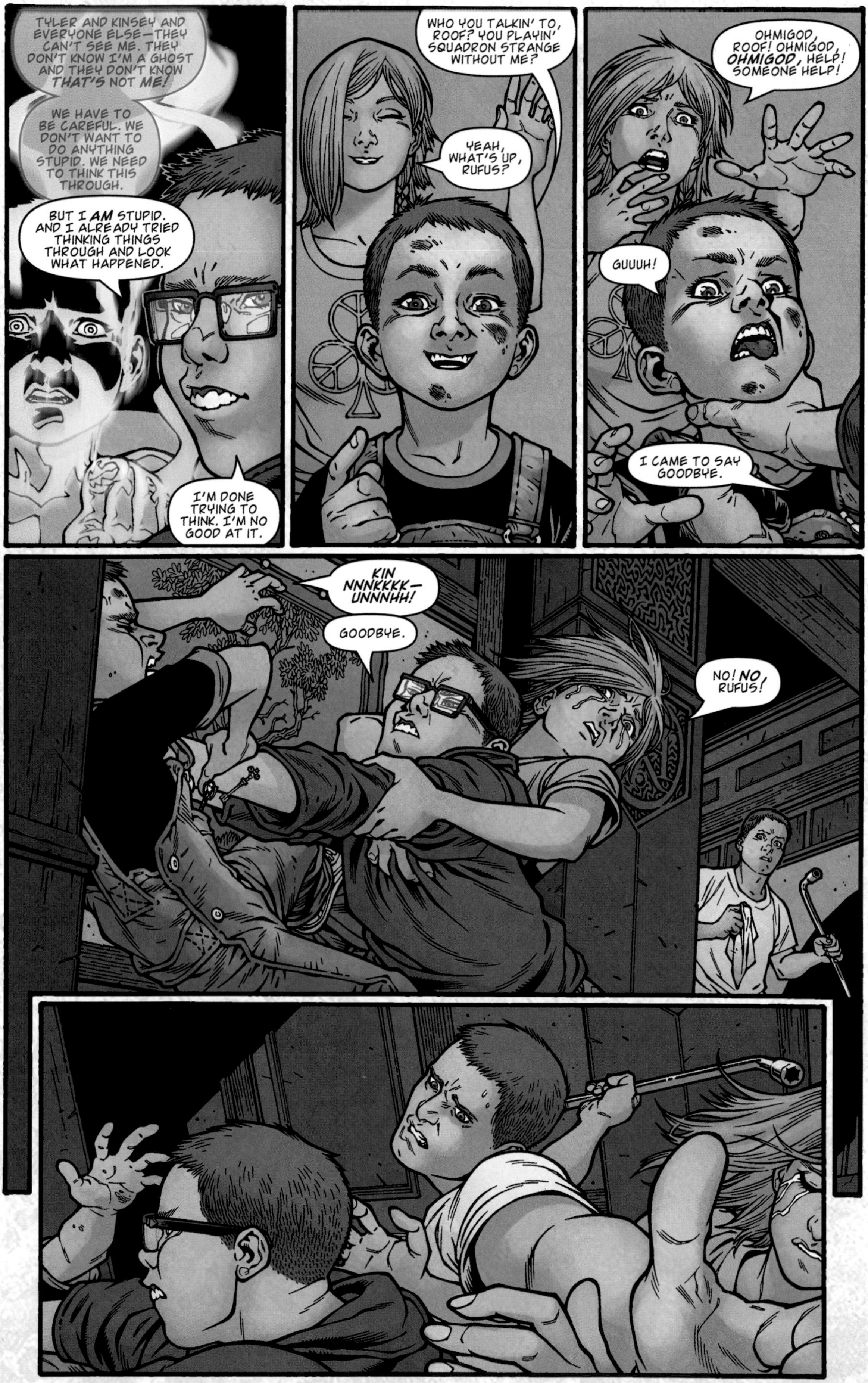
TYLER AND KINSEY AND EVERYONE ELSE—THEY CAN'T SEE ME. THEY DON'T KNOW I'M A GHOST AND THEY DON'T KNOW THAT'S NOT ME!
WE HAVE TO BE CAREFUL. WE DON'T WANT TO DO ANYTHING STUPID. WE NEED TO THINK THIS THROUGH.
BUT I AM STUPID. AND I ALREADY TRIED THINKING THINGS THROUGH AND LOOK WHAT HAPPENED.
I'M DONE TRYING TO THINK. I'M NO GOOD AT IT.
WHO YOU TALKIN' TO, ROOF? YOU PLAYIN' SQUADRON STRANGE WITHOUT ME?
YEAH, WHAT'S UP, RUFUS?
OHMIGOD, ROOF! OHMIGOD, OHMIGOD, HELP! SOMEONE HELP!
GUUUH!
I CAME TO SAY GOODBYE.
KIN NNNKKKK—UNNNHH!
GOODBYE.
NO! NO RUFUS!

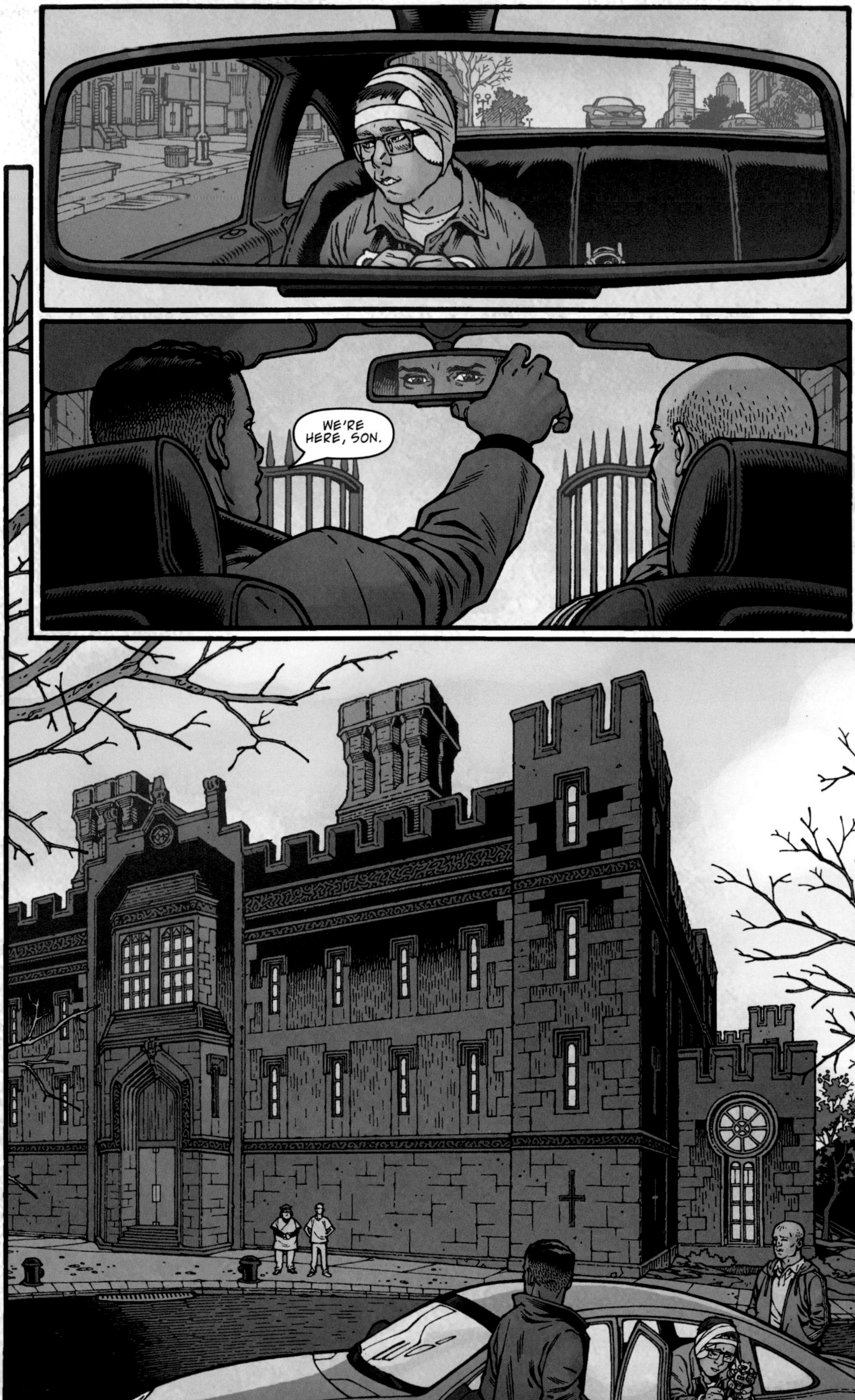
WE'RE HERE, SON.

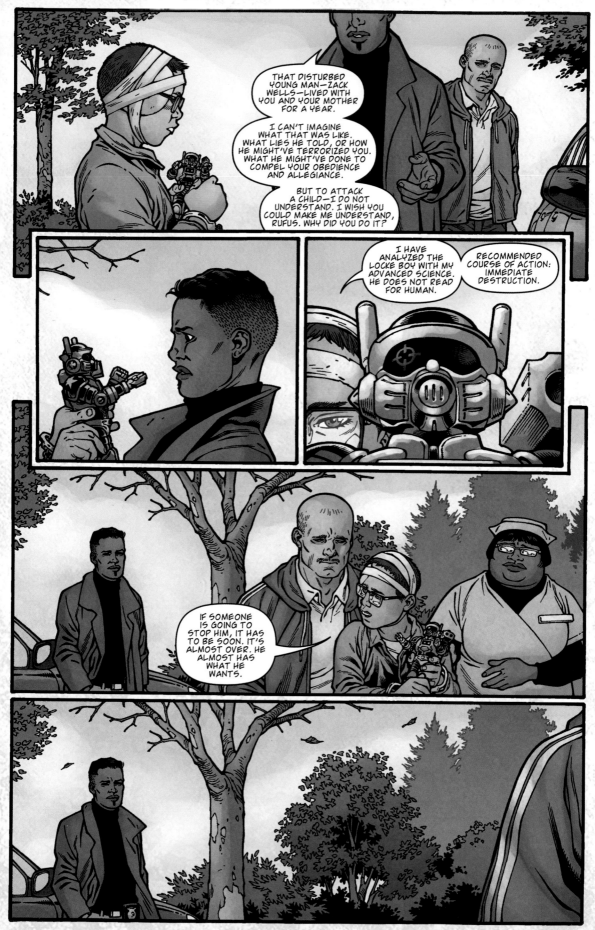

THAT DISTURBED YOUNG MAN—ZACK WELLS—LIVED WITH YOU AND YOUR MOTHER FOR A YEAR.

I CAN'T IMAGINE WHAT THAT WAS LIKE. WHAT LIES HE TOLD, OR HOW HE MIGHT'VE TERRORIZED YOU. WHAT HE MIGHT'VE DONE TO COMPEL YOUR OBEDIENCE AND ALLEGIANCE.

BUT TO ATTACK A CHILD—I DO NOT UNDERSTAND. I WISH YOU COULD MAKE ME UNDERSTAND, RUFUS. WHY DID YOU DO IT?

I HAVE ANALYZED THE LOCKE BOY WITH MY ADVANCED SCIENCE. HE DOES NOT READ FOR HUMAN.

RECOMMENDED COURSE OF ACTION: IMMEDIATE DESTRUCTION.

IF SOMEONE IS GOING TO STOP HIM, IT HAS TO BE SOON. IT'S ALMOST OVER. HE ALMOST HAS WHAT HE WANTS.

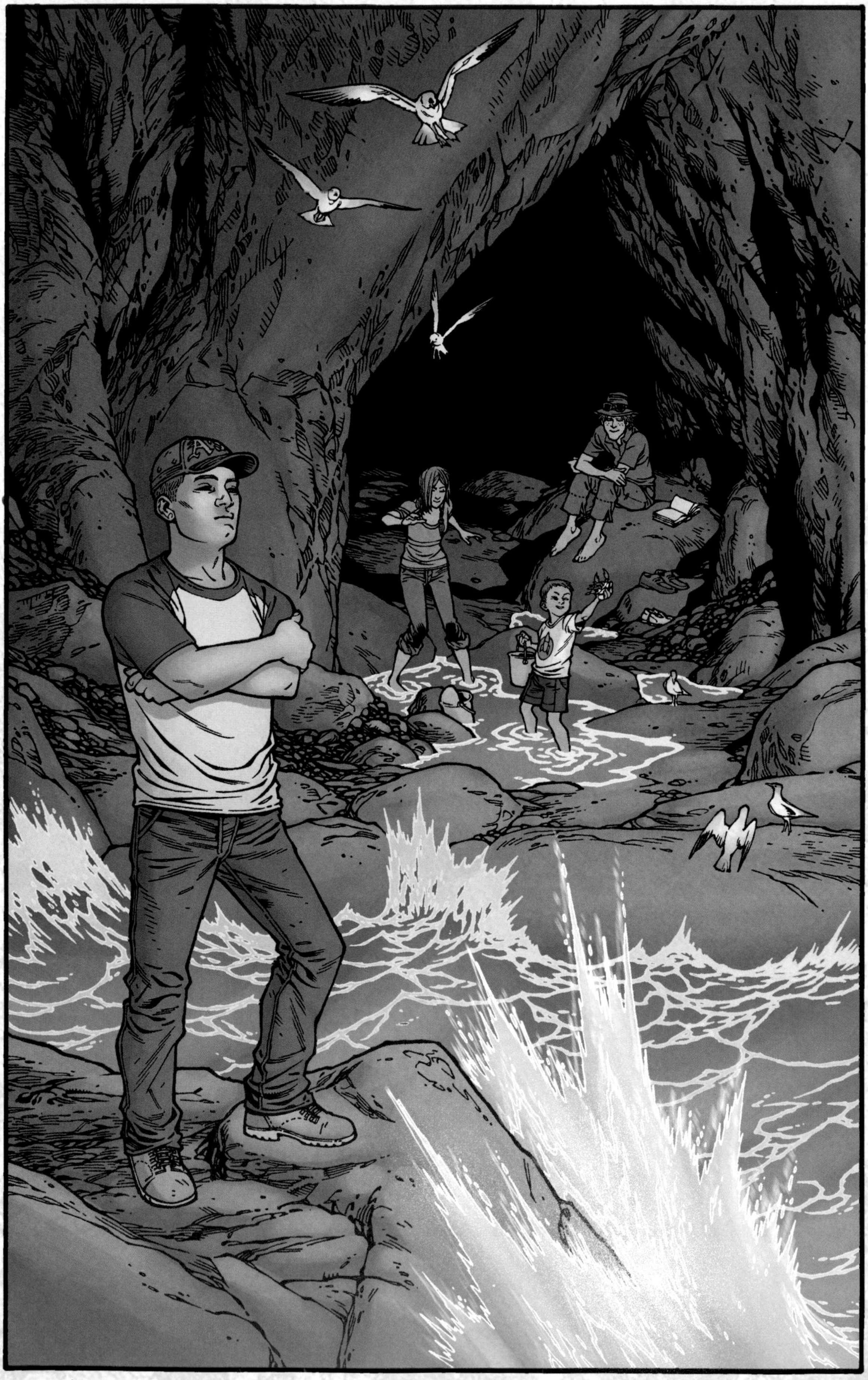

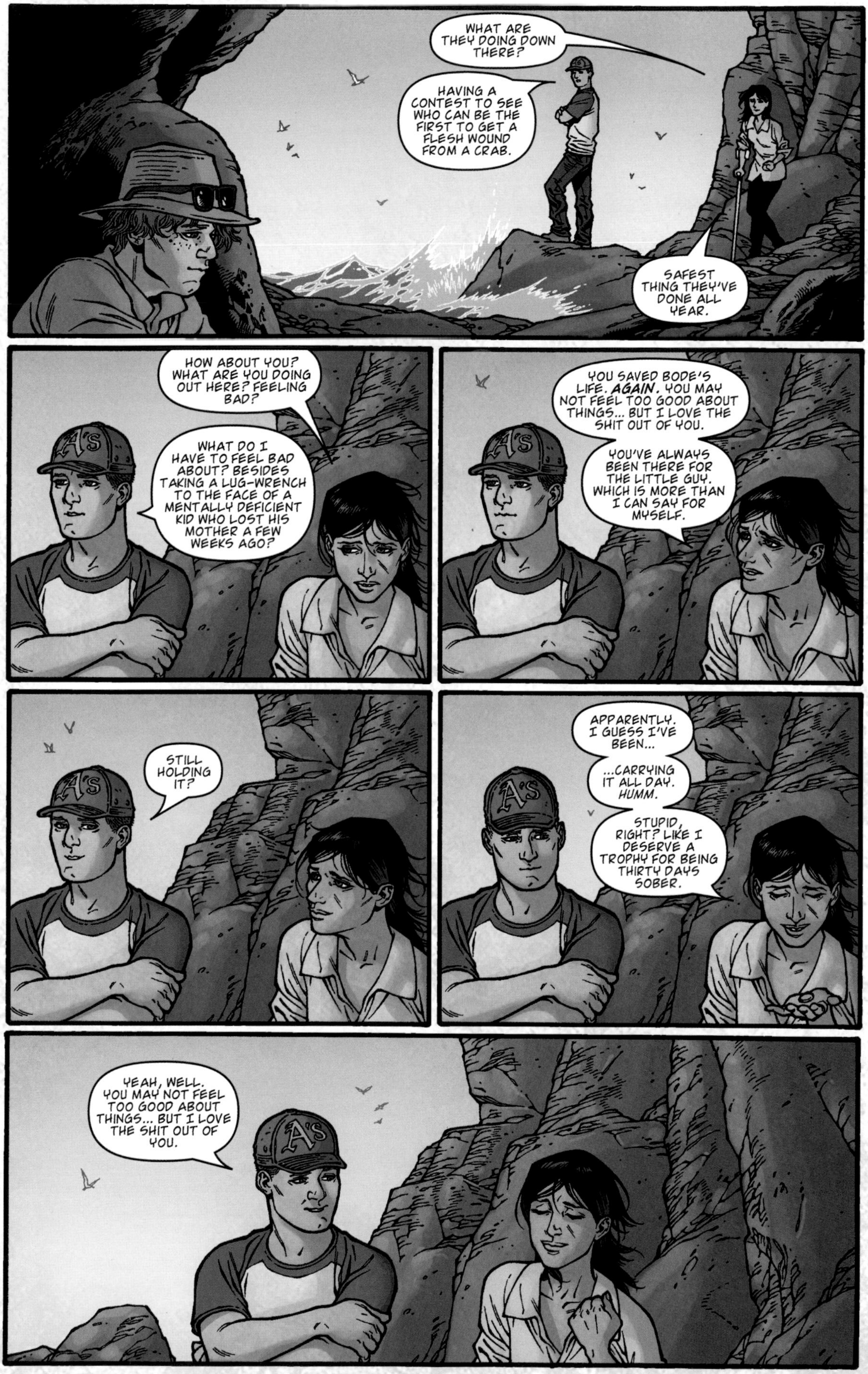
WHAT ARE THEY DOING DOWN THERE?
HAVING A CONTEST TO SEE WHO CAN BE THE FIRST TO GET A FLESH WOUND FROM A CRAB.
SAFEST THING THEY'VE DONE ALL YEAR.
HOW ABOUT YOU? WHAT ARE YOU DOING OUT HERE? FEELING BAD?
WHAT DO I HAVE TO FEEL BAD ABOUT? BESIDES TAKING A LUG-WRENCH TO THE FACE OF A MENTALLY DEFICIENT KID WHO LOST HIS MOTHER A FEW WEEKS AGO?
YOU SAVED BODE'S LIFE. AGAIN. YOU MAY NOT FEEL TOO GOOD ABOUT THINGS... BUT I LOVE THE SHIT OUT OF YOU.
YOU'VE ALWAYS BEEN THERE FOR THE LITTLE GUY. WHICH IS MORE THAN I CAN SAY FOR MYSELF.
STILL HOLDING IT?
APPARENTLY. I GUESS I'VE BEEN...
...CARRYING IT ALL DAY. HUMM.
STUPID, RIGHT? LIKE I DESERVE A TROPHY FOR BEING THIRTY DAYS SOBER.
YEAH, WELL. YOU MAY NOT FEEL TOO GOOD ABOUT THINGS... BUT I LOVE THE SHIT OUT OF YOU.

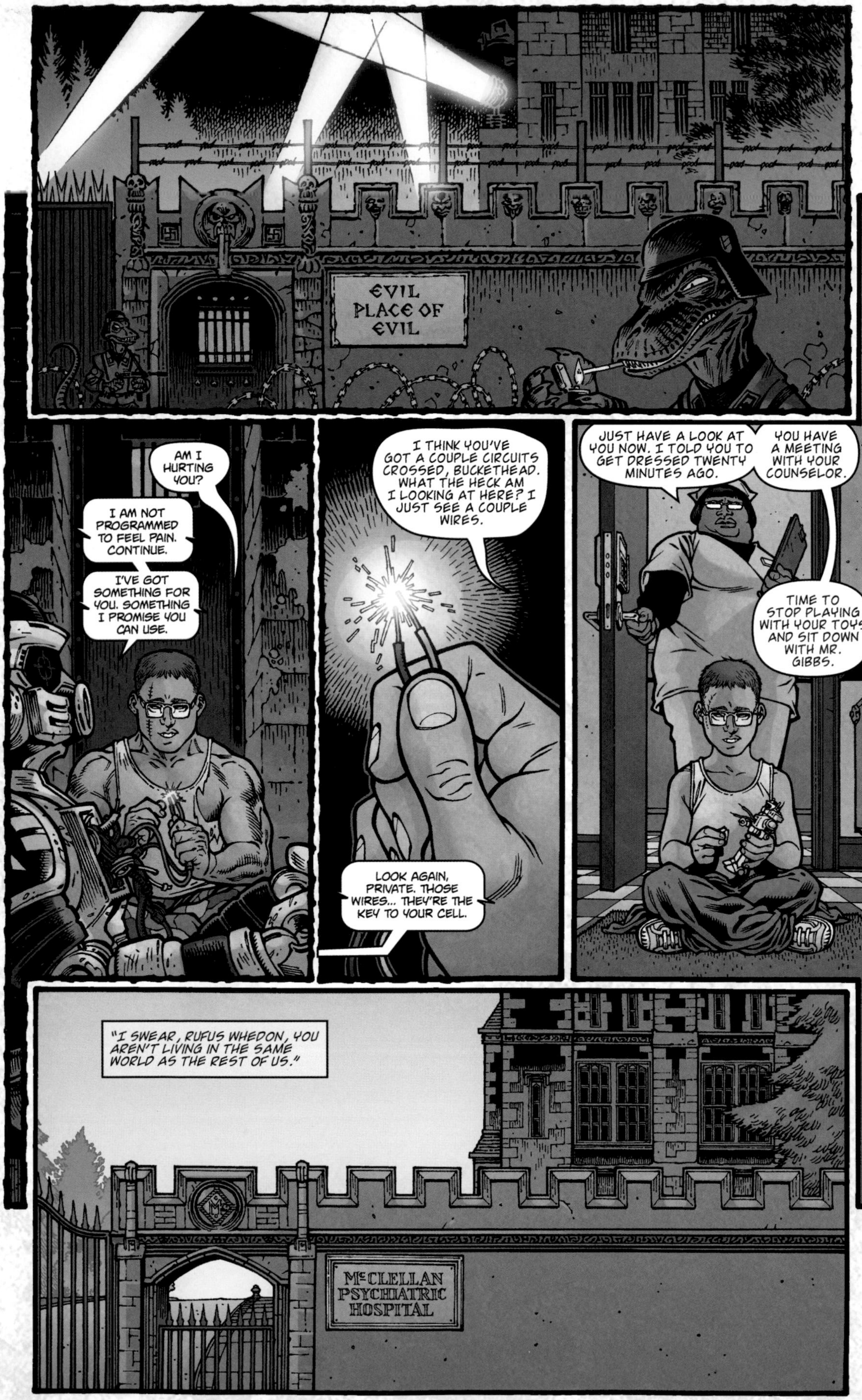
EVIL PLACE OF EVIL
AM I HURTING YOU?
I AM NOT PROGRAMMED TO FEEL PAIN. CONTINUE.
I'VE GOT SOMETHING FOR YOU. SOMETHING I PROMISE YOU CAN USE.
I THINK YOU'VE GOT A COUPLE CIRCUITS CROSSED, BUCKETHEAD. WHAT THE HECK AM I LOOKING AT HERE? I JUST SEE A COUPLE WIRES.
LOOK AGAIN, PRIVATE. THOSE WIRES... THEY'RE THE KEY TO YOUR CELL.
JUST HAVE A LOOK AT YOU NOW. I TOLD YOU TO GET DRESSED TWENTY MINUTES AGO.
YOU HAVE A MEETING WITH YOUR COUNSELOR.
TIME TO STOP PLAYING WITH YOUR TOYS AND SIT DOWN WITH MR. GIBBS.
"I SWEAR, RUFUS WHEDON, YOU AREN'T LIVING IN THE SAME WORLD AS THE REST OF US."
McCLELLAN PSYCHIATRIC HOSPITAL

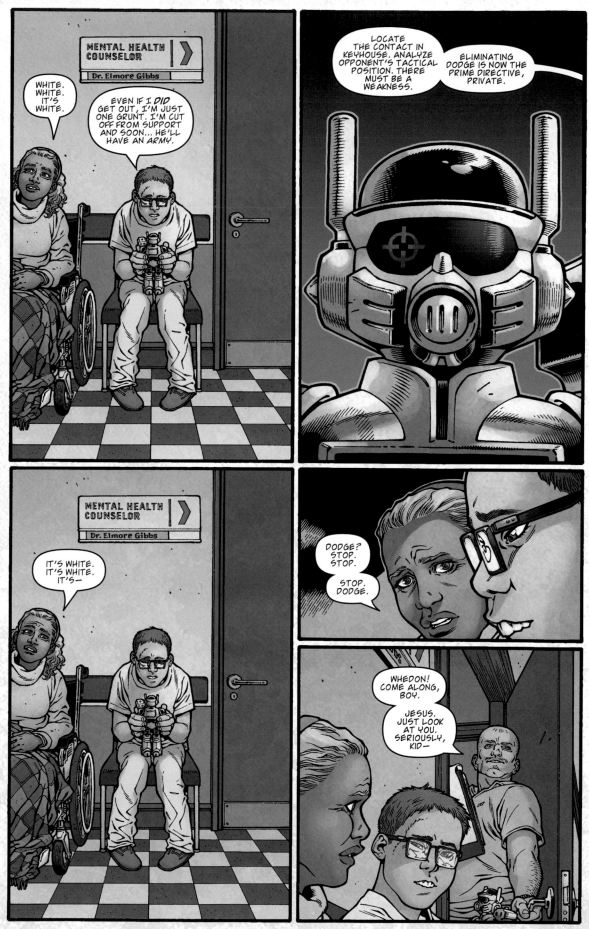

MENTAL HEALTH COUNSELOR ▶

Dr. Elmore Gibbs

WHITE. WHITE. IT'S WHITE.

EVEN IF I *DID* GET OUT, I'M JUST ONE GRUNT. I'M CUT OFF FROM SUPPORT AND SOON... HE'LL HAVE AN ARMY.

LOCATE THE CONTACT IN KEYHOUSE. ANALYZE OPPONENT'S TACTICAL POSITION. THERE MUST BE A WEAKNESS.

ELIMINATING DODGE IS NOW THE PRIME DIRECTIVE, PRIVATE.

MENTAL HEALTH COUNSELOR ▶

Dr. Elmore Gibbs

IT'S WHITE. IT'S WHITE. IT'S—

DODGE? STOP. STOP.

STOP. DODGE.

WHEDON! COME ALONG, BOY.

JESUS. JUST LOOK AT YOU. SERIOUSLY, KID—

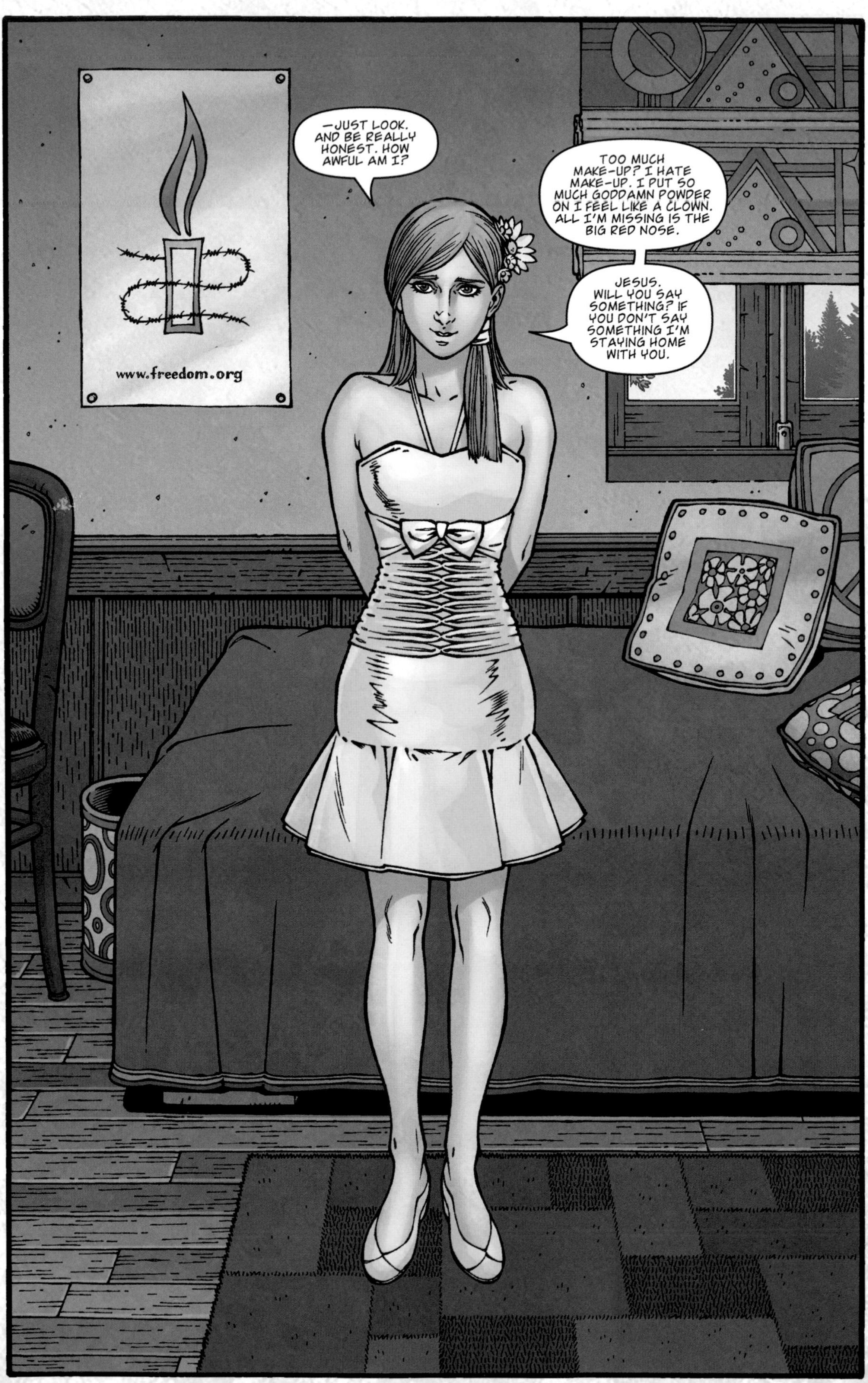
www.freedom.org
—JUST LOOK. AND BE REALLY HONEST. HOW AWFUL AM I?
TOO MUCH MAKE-UP? I HATE MAKE-UP. I PUT SO MUCH GODDAMN POWDER ON I FEEL LIKE A CLOWN. ALL I'M MISSING IS THE BIG RED NOSE.
JESUS. WILL YOU SAY SOMETHING? IF YOU DON'T SAY SOMETHING I'M STAYING HOME WITH YOU.

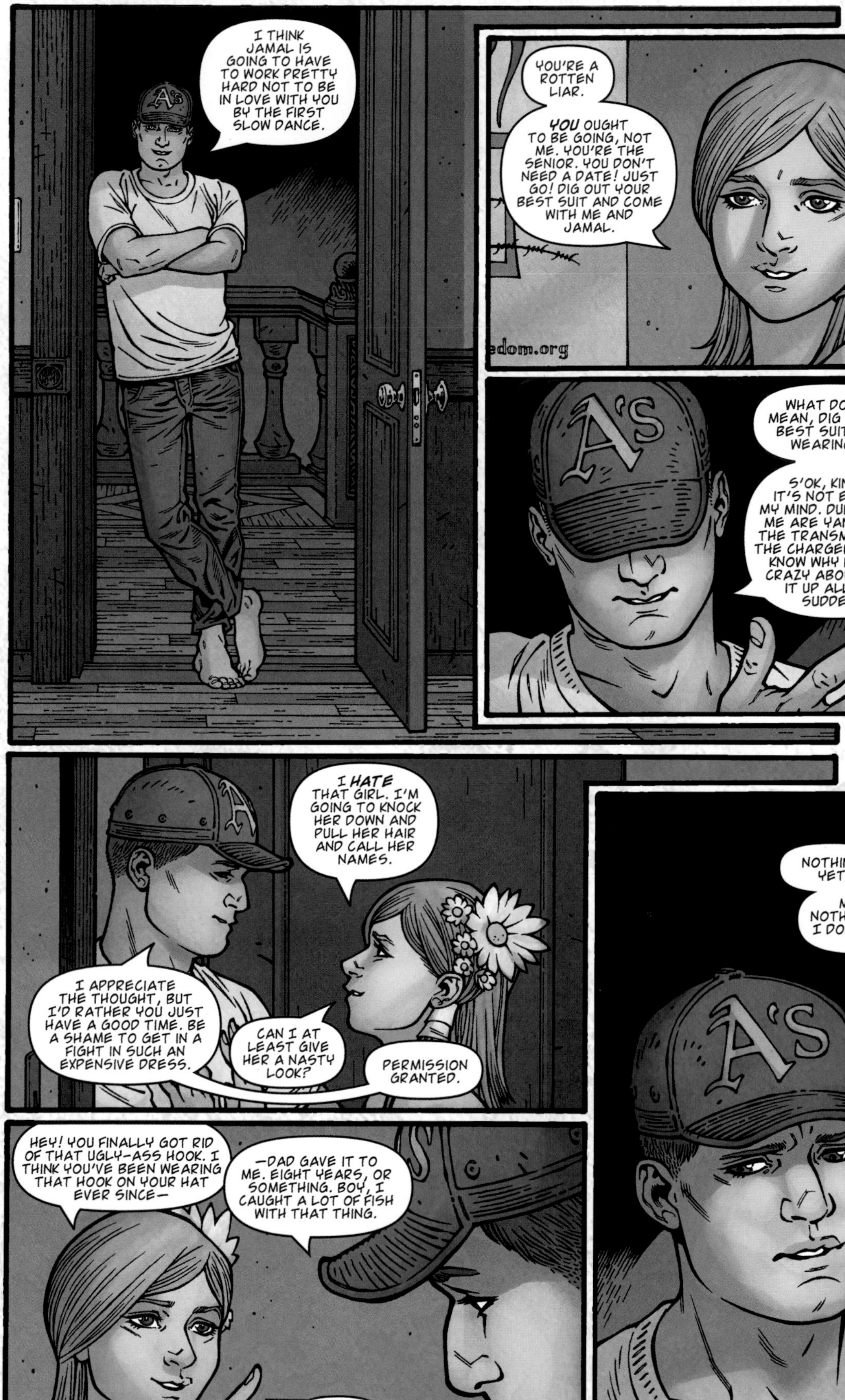
I THINK JAMAL IS GOING TO HAVE TO WORK PRETTY HARD NOT TO BE IN LOVE WITH YOU BY THE FIRST SLOW DANCE.
YOU'RE A ROTTEN LIAR.
YOU OUGHT TO BE GOING, NOT ME. YOU'RE THE SENIOR. YOU DON'T NEED A DATE! JUST GO! DIG OUT YOUR BEST SUIT AND COME WITH ME AND JAMAL.
edom.org
WHAT DO YOU MEAN, DIG OUT MY BEST SUIT? I'M WEARING IT.
S'OK, KINSEY. IT'S NOT EVEN ON MY MIND. DUNCAN AND ME ARE YANKIN' OUT THE TRANSMISSION IN THE CHARGER. I DON'T KNOW WHY HE'S SO CRAZY ABOUT FIXING IT UP ALL OF A SUDDEN—
I *HATE* THAT GIRL. I'M GOING TO KNOCK HER DOWN AND PULL HER HAIR AND CALL HER NAMES.
I APPRECIATE THE THOUGHT, BUT I'D RATHER YOU JUST HAVE A GOOD TIME. BE A SHAME TO GET IN A FIGHT IN SUCH AN EXPENSIVE DRESS.
CAN I AT LEAST GIVE HER A NASTY LOOK?
PERMISSION GRANTED.
HEY! YOU FINALLY GOT RID OF THAT UGLY-ASS HOOK. I THINK YOU'VE BEEN WEARING THAT HOOK ON YOUR HAT EVER SINCE—
—DAD GAVE IT TO ME. EIGHT YEARS, OR SOMETHING. BOY, I CAUGHT A LOT OF FISH WITH THAT THING.
WHAT'D YOU DO WITH IT?
NOTHING. YET.
MAYBE NOTHING EVER. I DON'T KNOW.

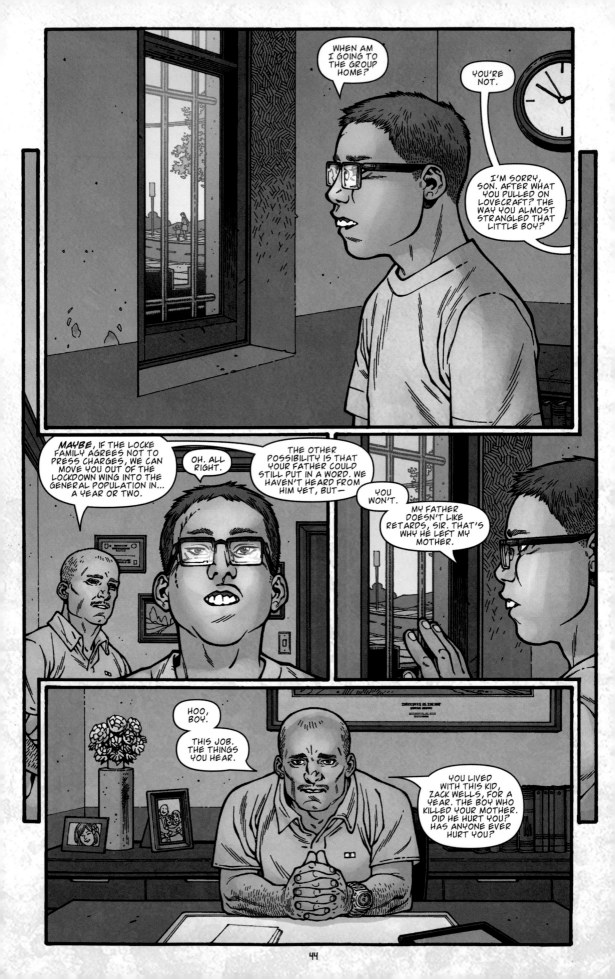

WHEN AM I GOING TO THE GROUP HOME?

YOU'RE NOT.

I'M SORRY, SON. AFTER WHAT YOU PULLED ON LOVECRAFT? THE WAY YOU ALMOST STRANGLED THAT LITTLE BOY?

MAYBE, IF THE LOCKE FAMILY AGREES NOT TO PRESS CHARGES, WE CAN MOVE YOU OUT OF THE LOCKDOWN WING INTO THE GENERAL POPULATION IN... A YEAR OR TWO.

OH. ALL RIGHT.

THE OTHER POSSIBILITY IS THAT YOUR FATHER COULD STILL PUT IN A WORD. WE HAVEN'T HEARD FROM HIM YET, BUT—

YOU WON'T.

MY FATHER DOESN'T LIKE RETARDS, SIR. THAT'S WHY HE LEFT MY MOTHER.

HOO, BOY.

THIS JOB. THE THINGS YOU HEAR.

YOU LIVED WITH THIS KID, ZACK WELLS, FOR A YEAR. THE BOY WHO KILLED YOUR MOTHER. DID HE HURT YOU? HAS ANYONE EVER HURT YOU?

44

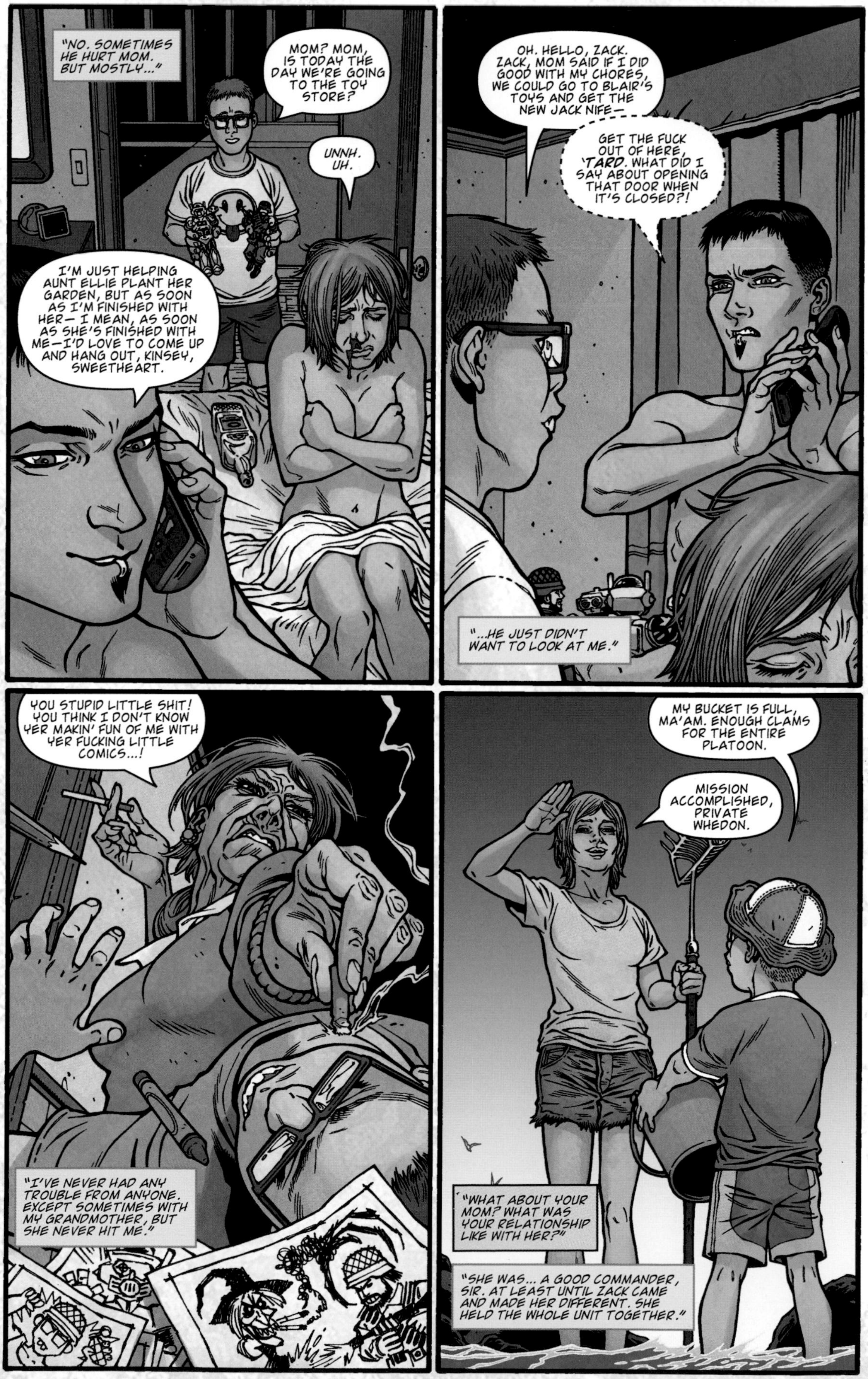
"NO. SOMETIMES HE HURT MOM. BUT MOSTLY..."
MOM? MOM, IS TODAY THE DAY WE'RE GOING TO THE TOY STORE?
UNNH. UH.
I'M JUST HELPING AUNT ELLIE PLANT HER GARDEN, BUT AS SOON AS I'M FINISHED WITH HER— I MEAN, AS SOON AS SHE'S FINISHED WITH ME—I'D LOVE TO COME UP AND HANG OUT, KINSEY, SWEETHEART.
OH. HELLO, ZACK. ZACK, MOM SAID IF I DID GOOD WITH MY CHORES, WE COULD GO TO BLAIR'S TOYS AND GET THE NEW JACK NIFE—
GET THE FUCK OUT OF HERE, 'TARD. WHAT DID I SAY ABOUT OPENING THAT DOOR WHEN IT'S CLOSED?!
"...HE JUST DIDN'T WANT TO LOOK AT ME."
YOU STUPID LITTLE SHIT! YOU THINK I DON'T KNOW YER MAKIN' FUN OF ME WITH YER FUCKING LITTLE COMICS...!
"I'VE NEVER HAD ANY TROUBLE FROM ANYONE. EXCEPT SOMETIMES WITH MY GRANDMOTHER, BUT SHE NEVER HIT ME."
MY BUCKET IS FULL, MA'AM. ENOUGH CLAMS FOR THE ENTIRE PLATOON.
MISSION ACCOMPLISHED, PRIVATE WHEDON.
"WHAT ABOUT YOUR MOM? WHAT WAS YOUR RELATIONSHIP LIKE WITH HER?"
"SHE WAS... A GOOD COMMANDER, SIR. AT LEAST UNTIL ZACK CAME AND MADE HER DIFFERENT. SHE HELD THE WHOLE UNIT TOGETHER."

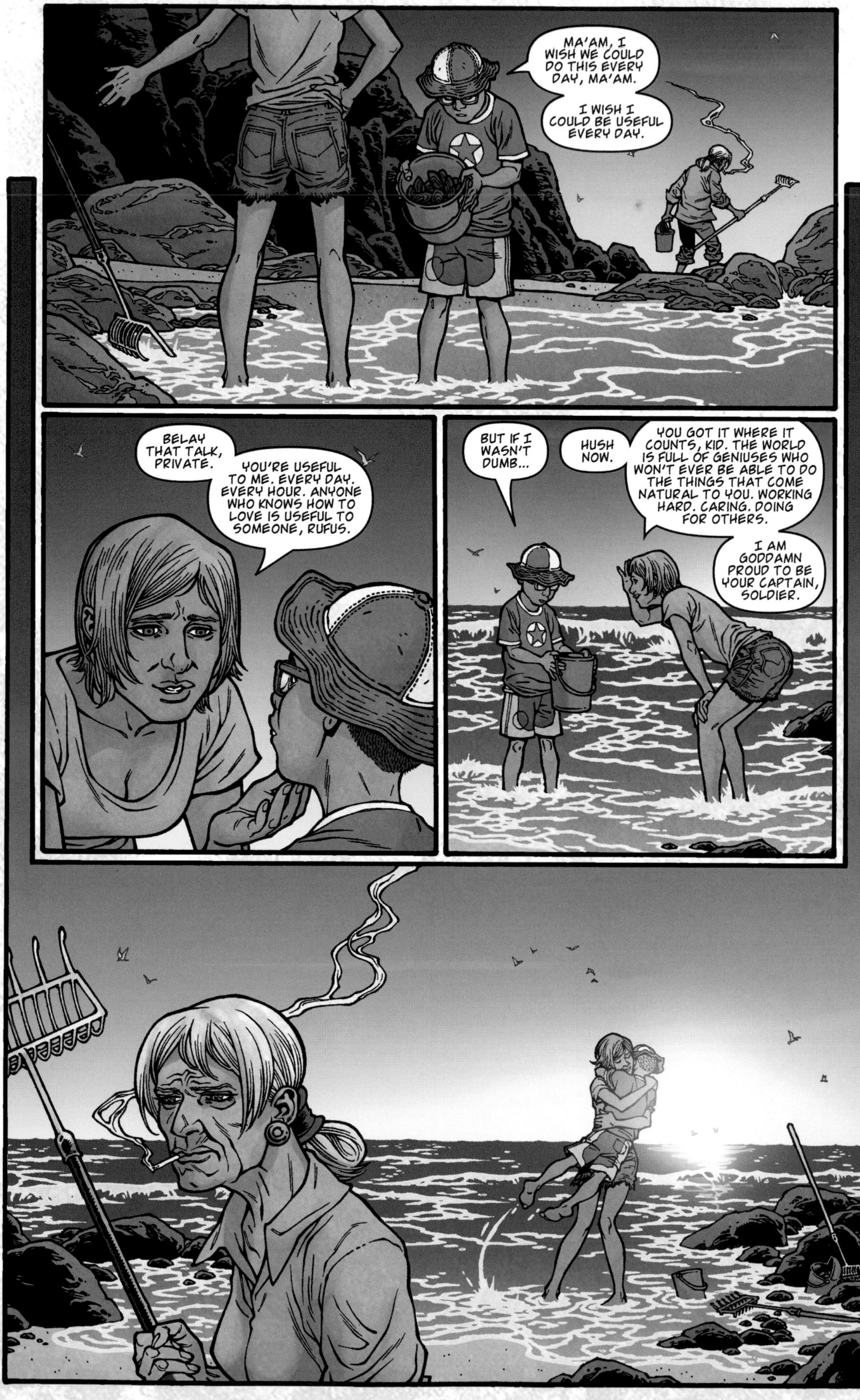
MA'AM, I WISH WE COULD DO THIS EVERY DAY, MA'AM.
I WISH I COULD BE USEFUL EVERY DAY.
BELAY THAT TALK, PRIVATE.
YOU'RE USEFUL TO ME. EVERY DAY. EVERY HOUR. ANYONE WHO KNOWS HOW TO LOVE IS USEFUL TO SOMEONE, RUFUS.
BUT IF I WASN'T DUMB...
HUSH NOW.
YOU GOT IT WHERE IT COUNTS, KID. THE WORLD IS FULL OF GENIUSES WHO WON'T EVER BE ABLE TO DO THE THINGS THAT COME NATURAL TO YOU. WORKING HARD. CARING. DOING FOR OTHERS.
I AM GODDAMN PROUD TO BE YOUR CAPTAIN, SOLDIER.

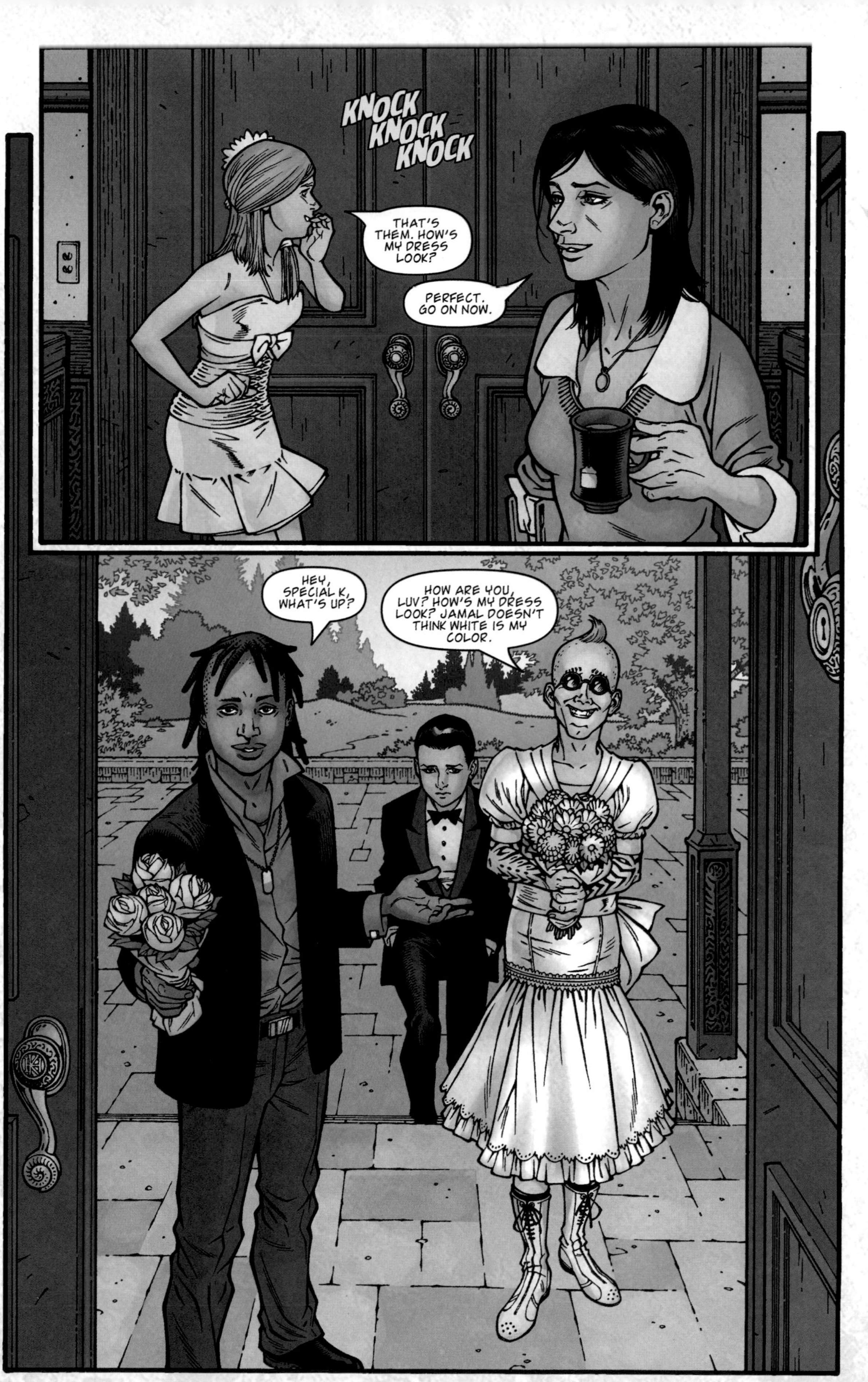

KNOCK KNOCK KNOCK
THAT'S THEM. HOW'S MY DRESS LOOK?
PERFECT. GO ON NOW.
HEY, SPECIAL K, WHAT'S UP?
HOW ARE YOU, LUV? HOW'S MY DRESS LOOK? JAMAL DOESN'T THINK WHITE IS MY COLOR.

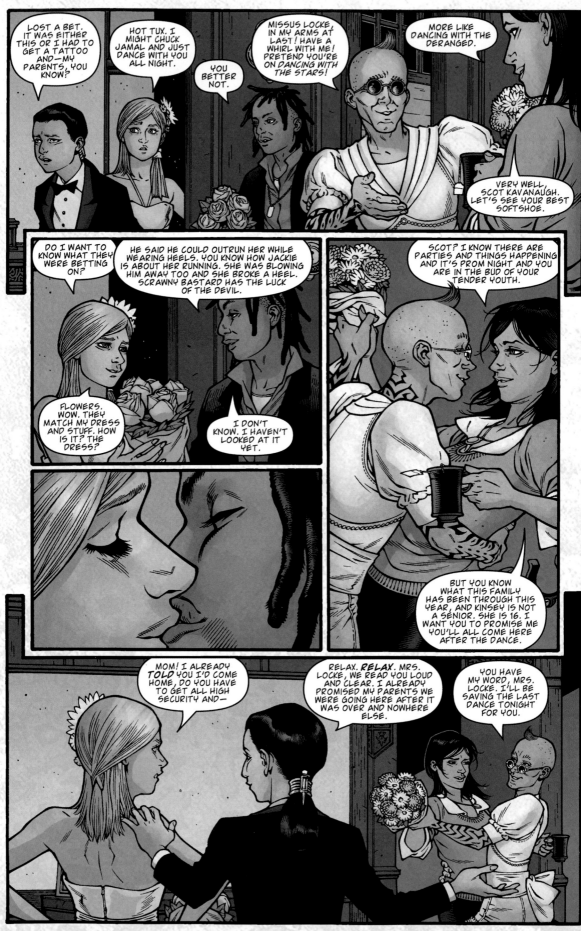

LOST A BET. IT WAS EITHER THIS OR I HAD TO GET A TATTOO AND—MY PARENTS, YOU KNOW?

HOT TUX. I MIGHT CHUCK JAMAL AND JUST DANCE WITH YOU ALL NIGHT.

YOU BETTER NOT.

MISSUS LOCKE, IN MY ARMS AT LAST! HAVE A WHIRL WITH ME! PRETEND YOU'RE ON DANCING WITH THE STARS!

MORE LIKE DANCING WITH THE DERANGED.

VERY WELL, SCOT KAVANAUGH. LET'S SEE YOUR BEST SOFTSHOE.

DO I WANT TO KNOW WHAT THEY WERE BETTING ON?

HE SAID HE COULD OUTRUN HER WHILE WEARING HEELS. YOU KNOW HOW JACKIE IS ABOUT HER RUNNING. SHE WAS BLOWING HIM AWAY TOO AND SHE BROKE A HEEL. SCRAWNY BASTARD HAS THE LUCK OF THE DEVIL.

FLOWERS. WOW. THEY MATCH MY DRESS AND STUFF. HOW IS IT? THE DRESS?

I DON'T KNOW. I HAVEN'T LOOKED AT IT YET.

SCOT? I KNOW THERE ARE PARTIES AND THINGS HAPPENING AND IT'S PROM NIGHT AND YOU ARE IN THE BUD OF YOUR TENDER YOUTH.

BUT YOU KNOW WHAT THIS FAMILY HAS BEEN THROUGH THIS YEAR, AND KINSEY IS NOT A SENIOR. SHE IS 16. I WANT YOU TO PROMISE ME YOU'LL ALL COME HERE AFTER THE DANCE.

MOM! I ALREADY *TOLD* YOU I'D COME HOME, DO YOU HAVE TO GET ALL HIGH SECURITY AND—

RELAX. *RELAX.* MRS. LOCKE, WE READ YOU LOUD AND CLEAR. I ALREADY PROMISED MY PARENTS WE WERE GOING HERE AFTER IT WAS OVER AND NOWHERE ELSE.

YOU HAVE MY WORD, MRS. LOCKE. I'LL BE SAVING THE LAST DANCE TONIGHT FOR YOU.

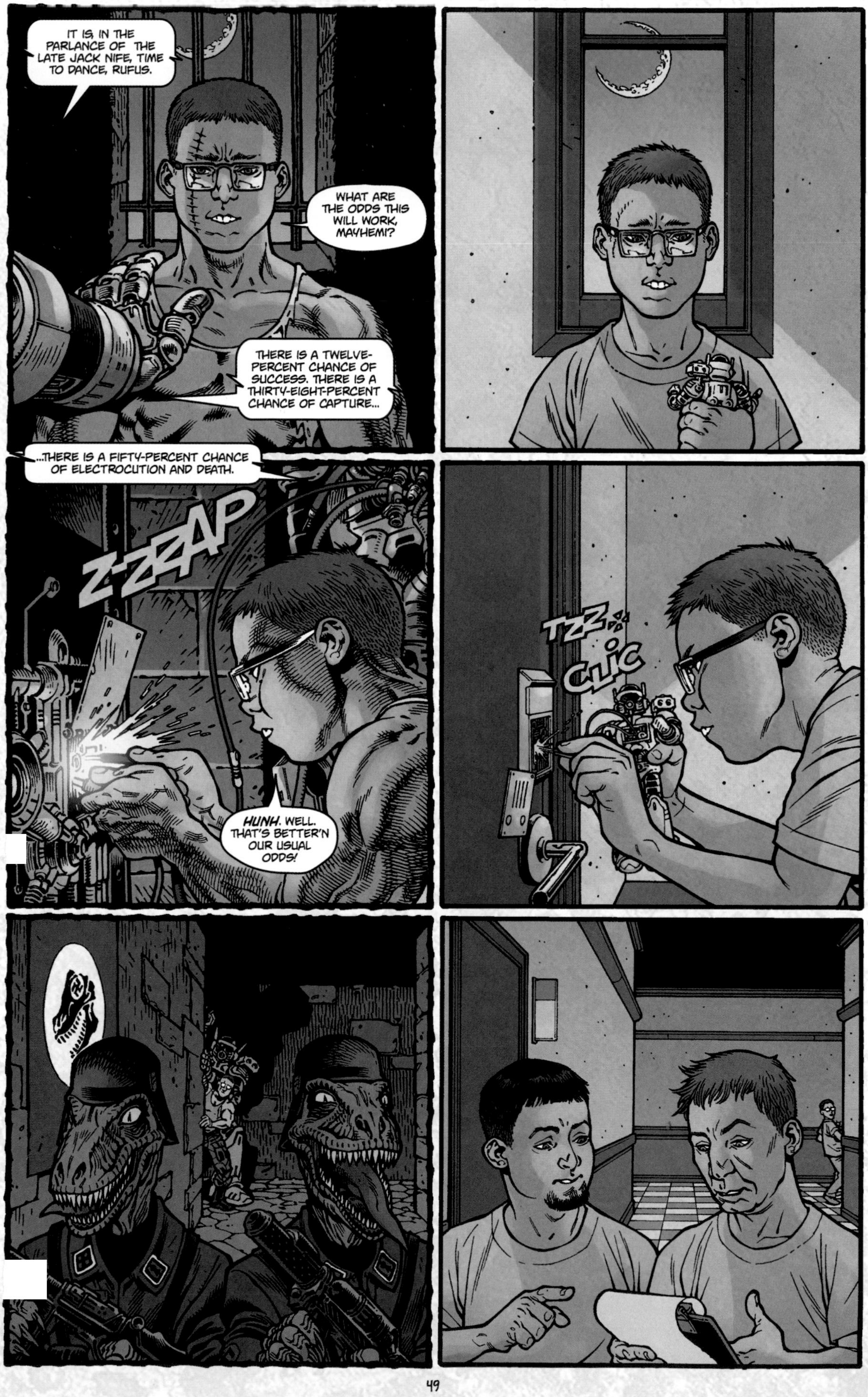
IT IS, IN THE PARLANCE OF THE LATE JACK NIFE, TIME TO DANCE, RUFUS.
WHAT ARE THE ODDS THIS WILL WORK, MAYHEM!?
THERE IS A TWELVE-PERCENT CHANCE OF SUCCESS. THERE IS A THIRTY-EIGHT-PERCENT CHANCE OF CAPTURE...
...THERE IS A FIFTY-PERCENT CHANCE OF ELECTROCUTION AND DEATH.
Z-ZRAP
HUNH. WELL. THAT'S BETTER'N OUR USUAL ODDS!
TZZ
CLIC

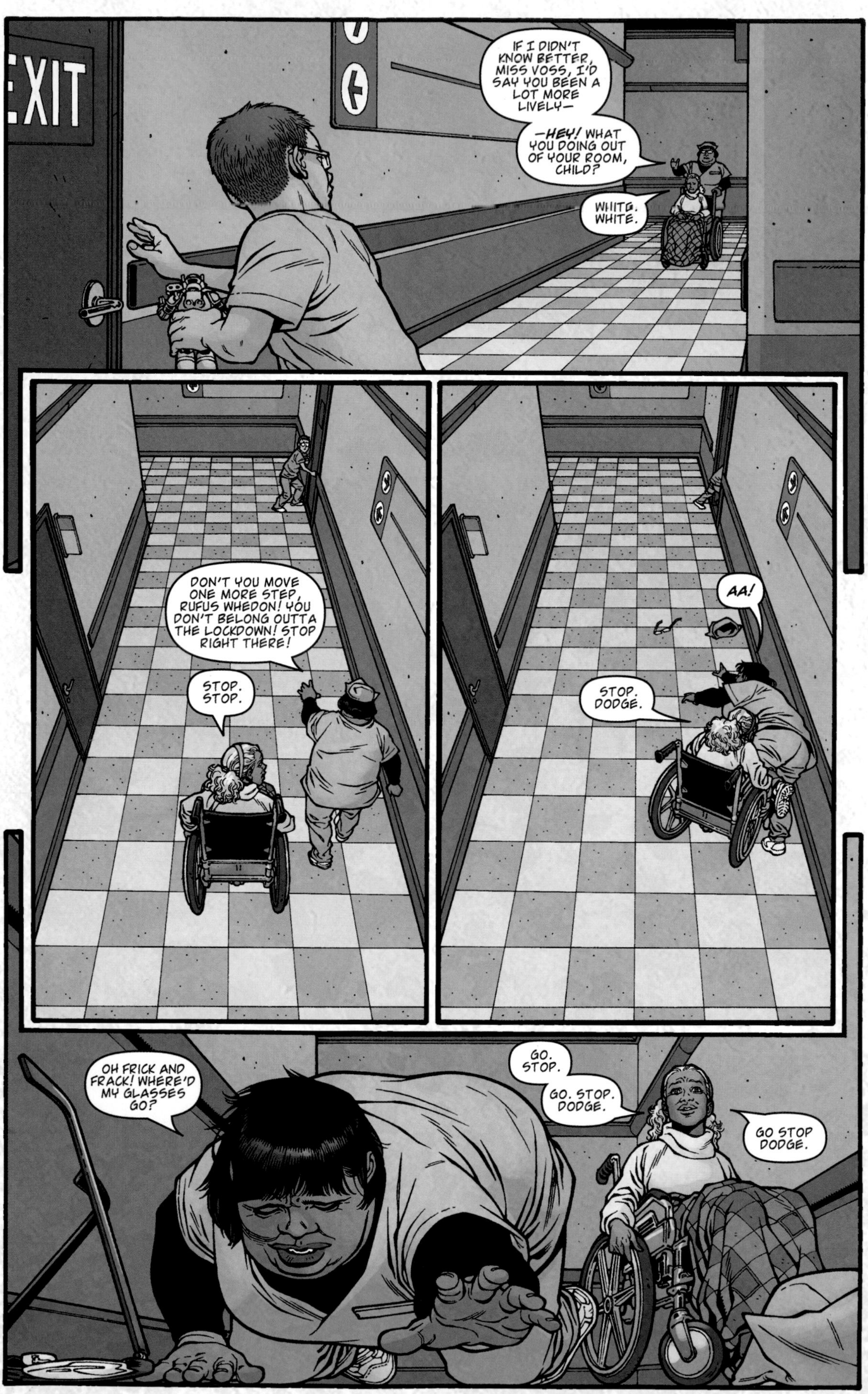
EXIT
IF I DIDN'T KNOW BETTER, MISS VOSS, I'D SAY YOU BEEN A LOT MORE LIVELY—
—HEY! WHAT YOU DOING OUT OF YOUR ROOM, CHILD?
WHITE. WHITE.
DON'T YOU MOVE ONE MORE STEP, RUFUS WHEDON! YOU DON'T BELONG OUTTA THE LOCKDOWN! STOP RIGHT THERE!
STOP. STOP.
AA!
STOP. DODGE.
OH FRICK AND FRACK! WHERE'D MY GLASSES GO?
GO. STOP.
GO. STOP. DODGE.
GO STOP DODGE.

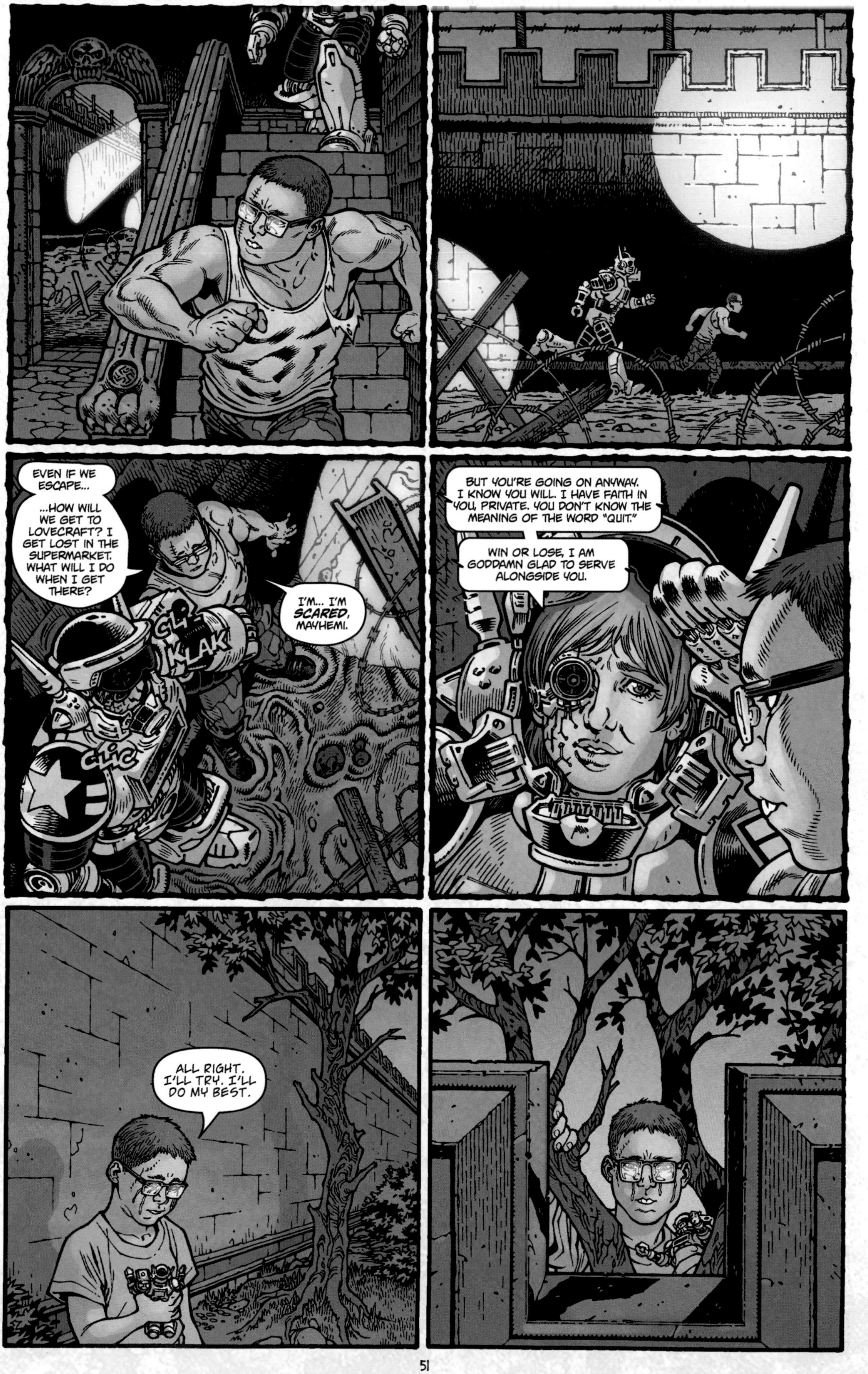
EVEN IF WE ESCAPE...
...HOW WILL WE GET TO LOVECRAFT? I GET LOST IN THE SUPERMARKET. WHAT WILL I DO WHEN I GET THERE?
CLIC KLAK
I'M... I'M SCARED, MAYHEM!
CLIC
BUT YOU'RE GOING ON ANYWAY. I KNOW YOU WILL. I HAVE FAITH IN YOU, PRIVATE. YOU DON'T KNOW THE MEANING OF THE WORD "QUIT."
WIN OR LOSE, I AM GODDAMN GLAD TO SERVE ALONGSIDE YOU.
ALL RIGHT. I'LL TRY. I'LL DO MY BEST.

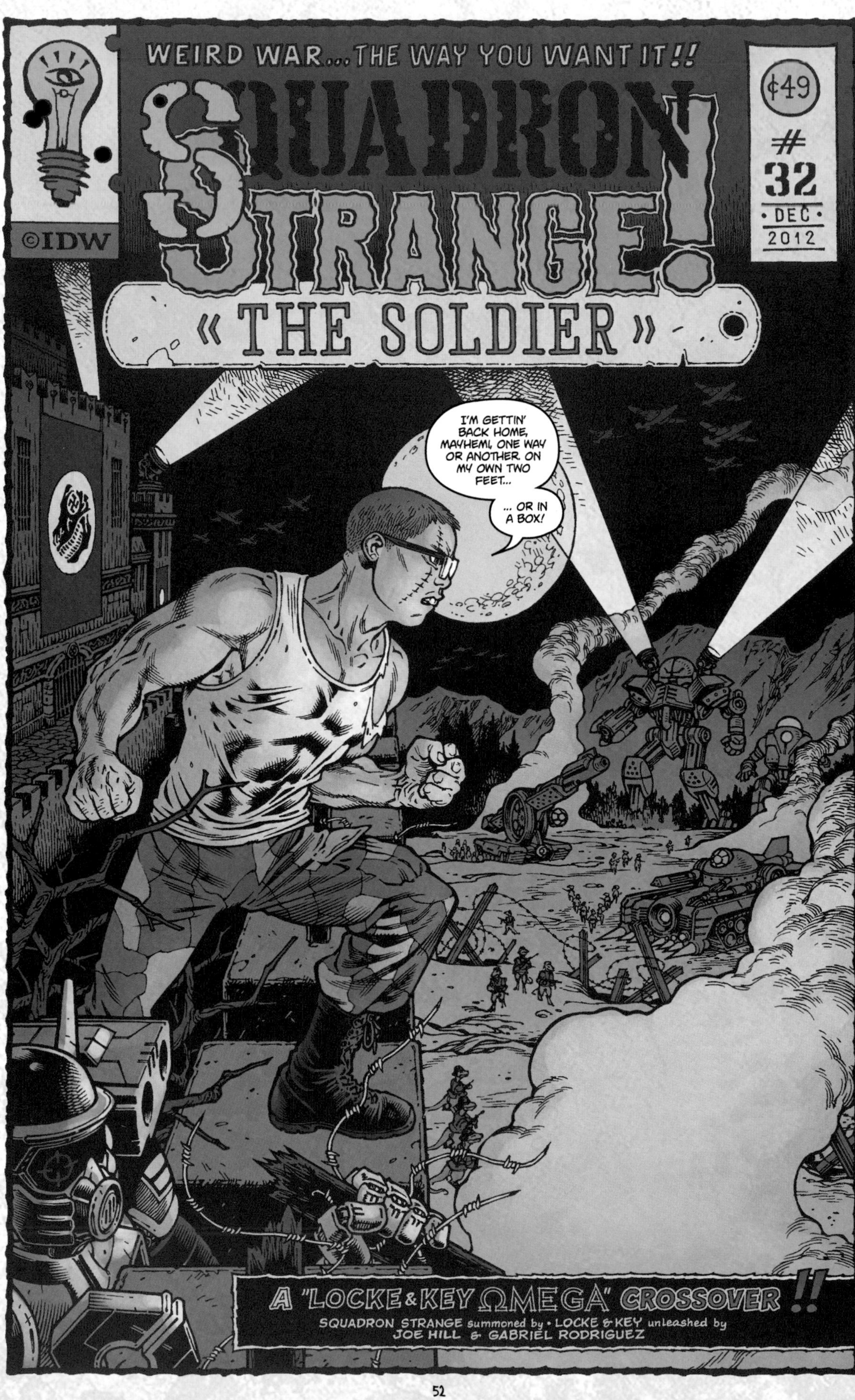
WEIRD WAR... THE WAY YOU WANT IT!!
SQUADRON STRANGE!
¢49
32
• DEC •
2012
©IDW
« THE SOLDIER »
I'M GETTIN' BACK HOME, MAYHEM, ONE WAY OR ANOTHER. ON MY OWN TWO FEET...
... OR IN A BOX!
A "LOCKE & KEY ΩMEGA" CROSSOVER!!
SQUADRON STRANGE summoned by • LOCKE & KEY unleashed by
JOE HILL & GABRIEL RODRIGUEZ

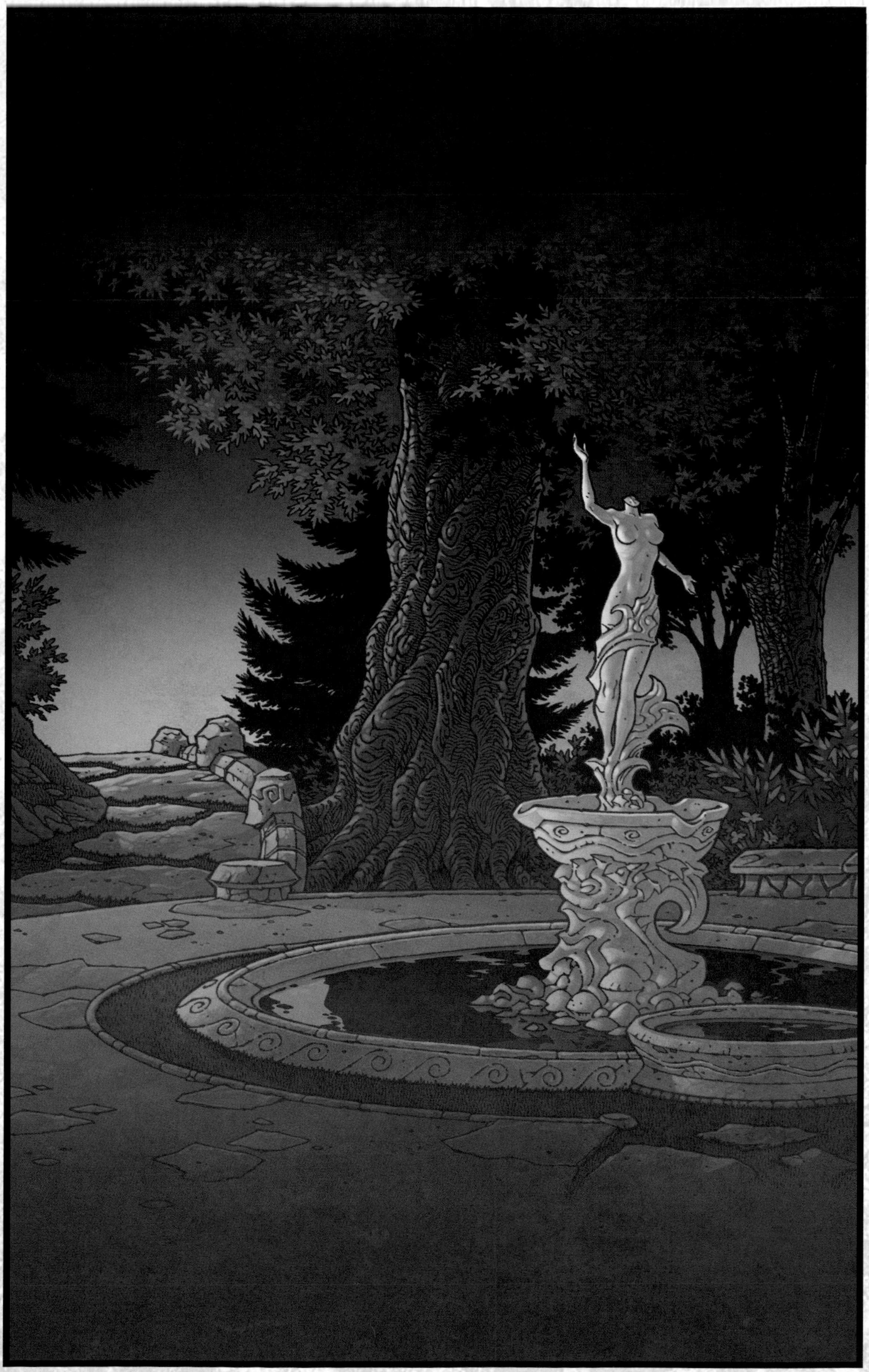

- ALPHA & OMEGA -

Chapter Three

LAST DANCE

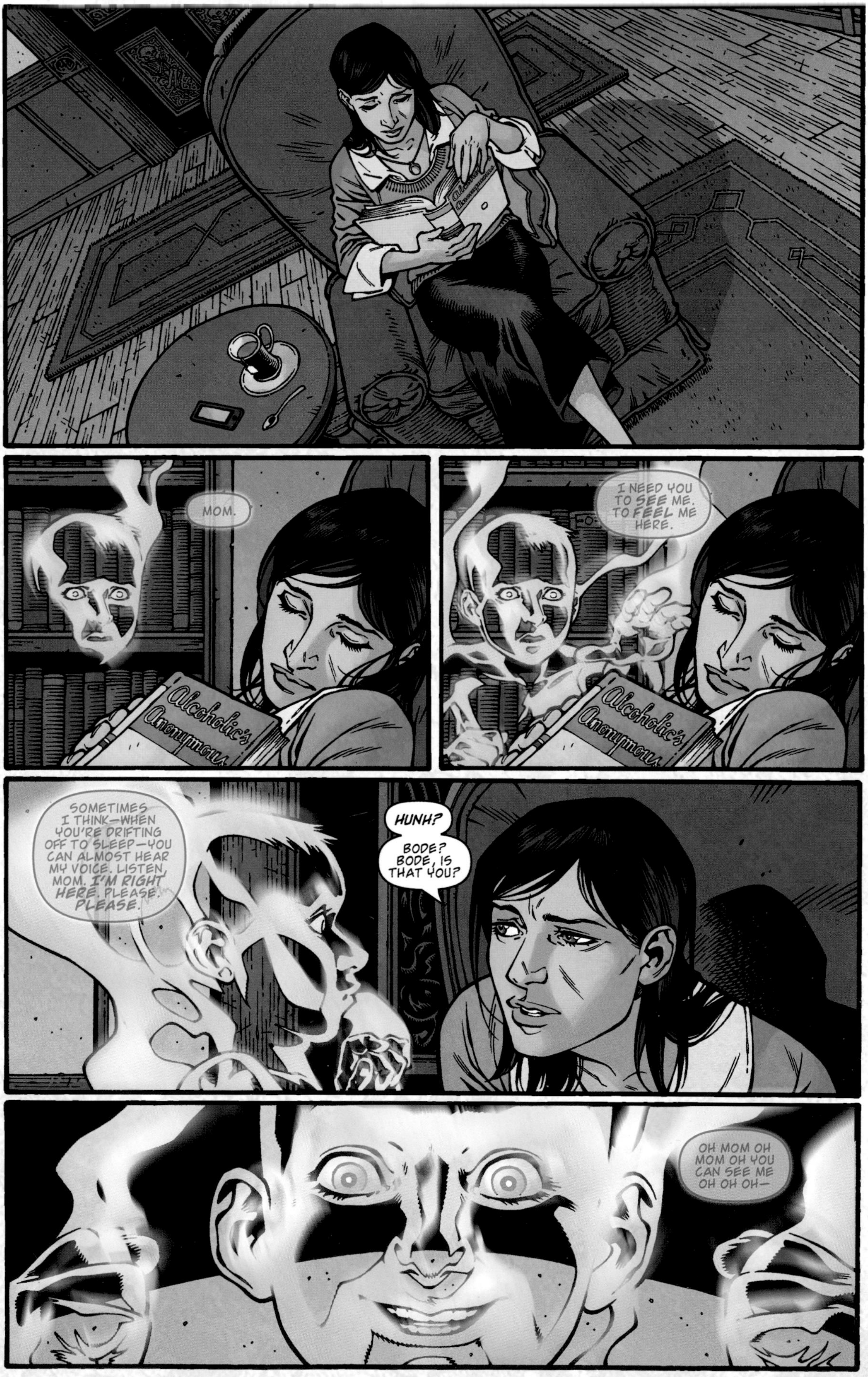
Alcoholic's Anonymous
MOM.
I NEED YOU TO SEE ME. TO FEEL ME HERE.
SOMETIMES I THINK—WHEN YOU'RE DRIFTING OFF TO SLEEP—YOU CAN ALMOST HEAR MY VOICE. LISTEN, MOM. I'M RIGHT HERE. PLEASE. PLEASE.
HUNH?
BODE? BODE, IS THAT YOU?
OH MOM OH MOM OH YOU CAN SEE ME OH OH OH—

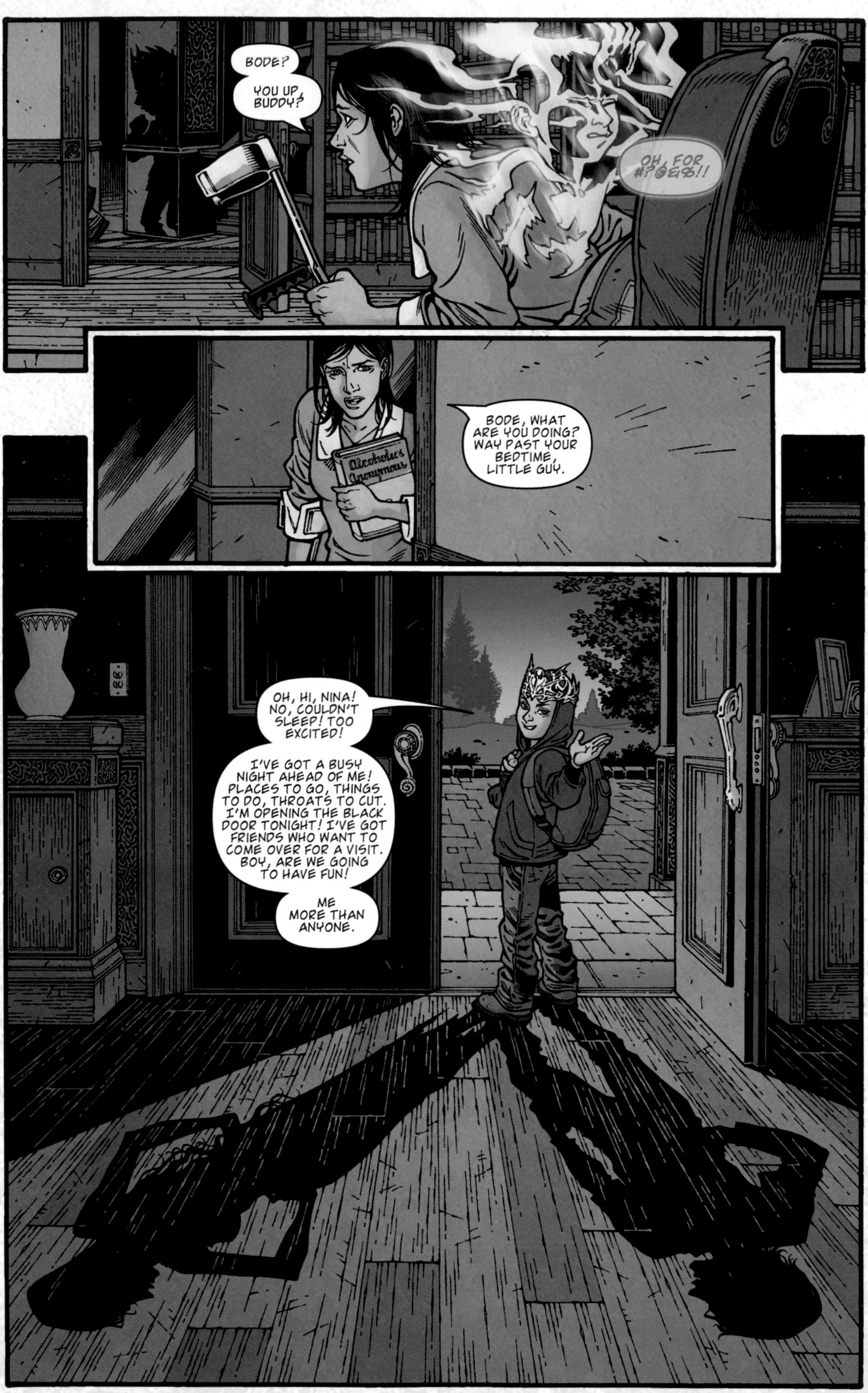
BODE?
YOU UP, BUDDY?
OH, FOR #?@&%!!
BODE, WHAT ARE YOU DOING? WAY PAST YOUR BEDTIME, LITTLE GUY.
Alcoholics Anonymous
OH, HI, NINA! NO, COULDN'T SLEEP! TOO EXCITED!
I'VE GOT A BUSY NIGHT AHEAD OF ME! PLACES TO GO, THINGS TO DO, THROATS TO CUT. I'M OPENING THE BLACK DOOR TONIGHT! I'VE GOT FRIENDS WHO WANT TO COME OVER FOR A VISIT. BOY, ARE WE GOING TO HAVE FUN!
ME MORE THAN ANYONE.

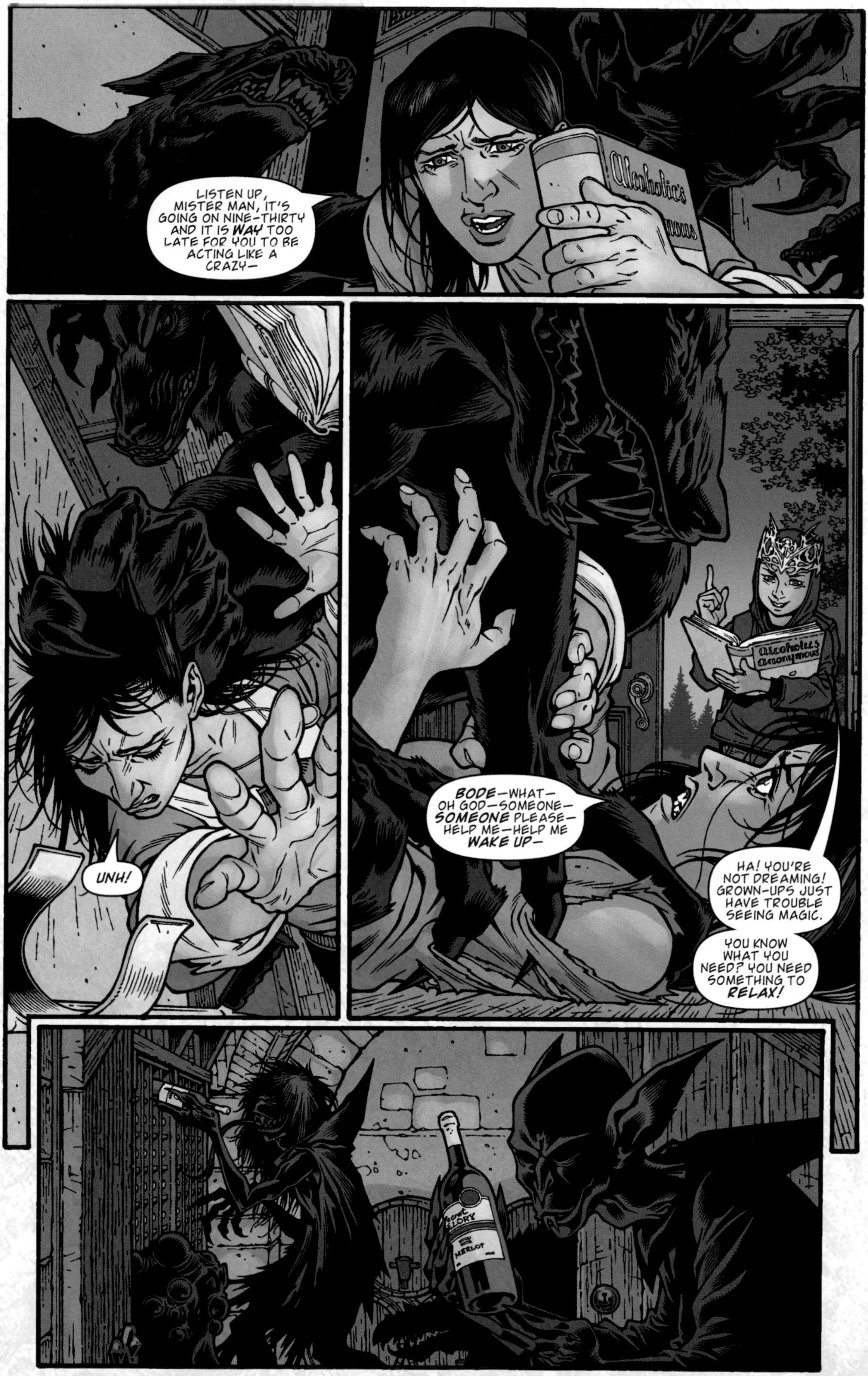
LISTEN UP, MISTER MAN, IT'S GOING ON NINE-THIRTY AND IT IS WAY TOO LATE FOR YOU TO BE ACTING LIKE A CRAZY—
UNH!
BODE—WHAT— OH GOD—SOMEONE— SOMEONE PLEASE— HELP ME—HELP ME WAKE UP—
HA! YOU'RE NOT DREAMING! GROWN-UPS JUST HAVE TROUBLE SEEING MAGIC.
YOU KNOW WHAT YOU NEED? YOU NEED SOMETHING TO RELAX!
MERLOT

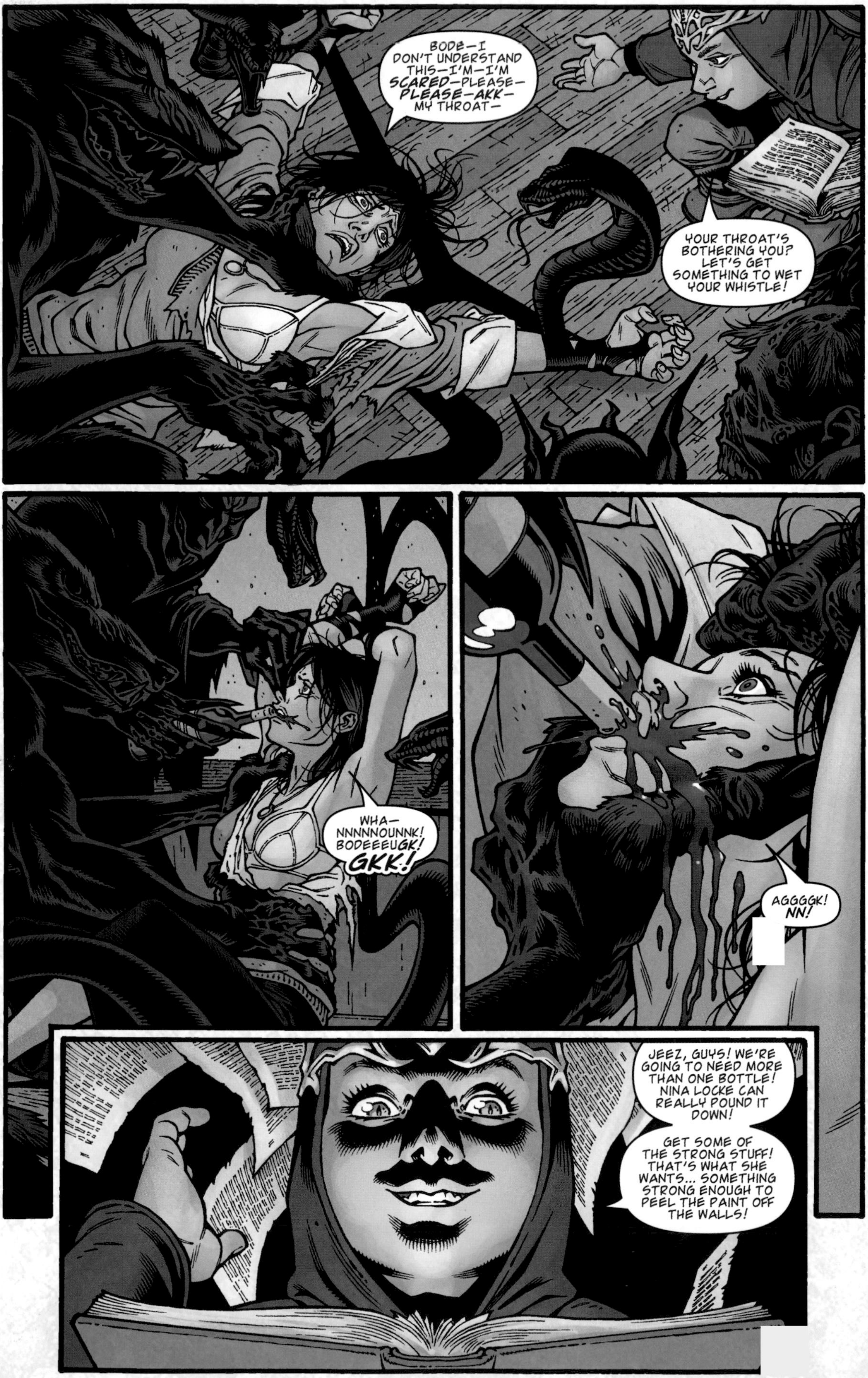
BODE—I DON'T UNDERSTAND THIS—I'M—I'M SCARED—PLEASE—PLEASE—AKK— MY THROAT—
YOUR THROAT'S BOTHERING YOU? LET'S GET SOMETHING TO WET YOUR WHISTLE!
WHA— NNNNNOUNNK! BODEEEUGK! GKK!
AGGGGK! NN!
JEEZ, GUYS! WE'RE GOING TO NEED MORE THAN ONE BOTTLE! NINA LOCKE CAN REALLY POUND IT DOWN!
GET SOME OF THE STRONG STUFF! THAT'S WHAT SHE WANTS... SOMETHING STRONG ENOUGH TO PEEL THE PAINT OFF THE WALLS!

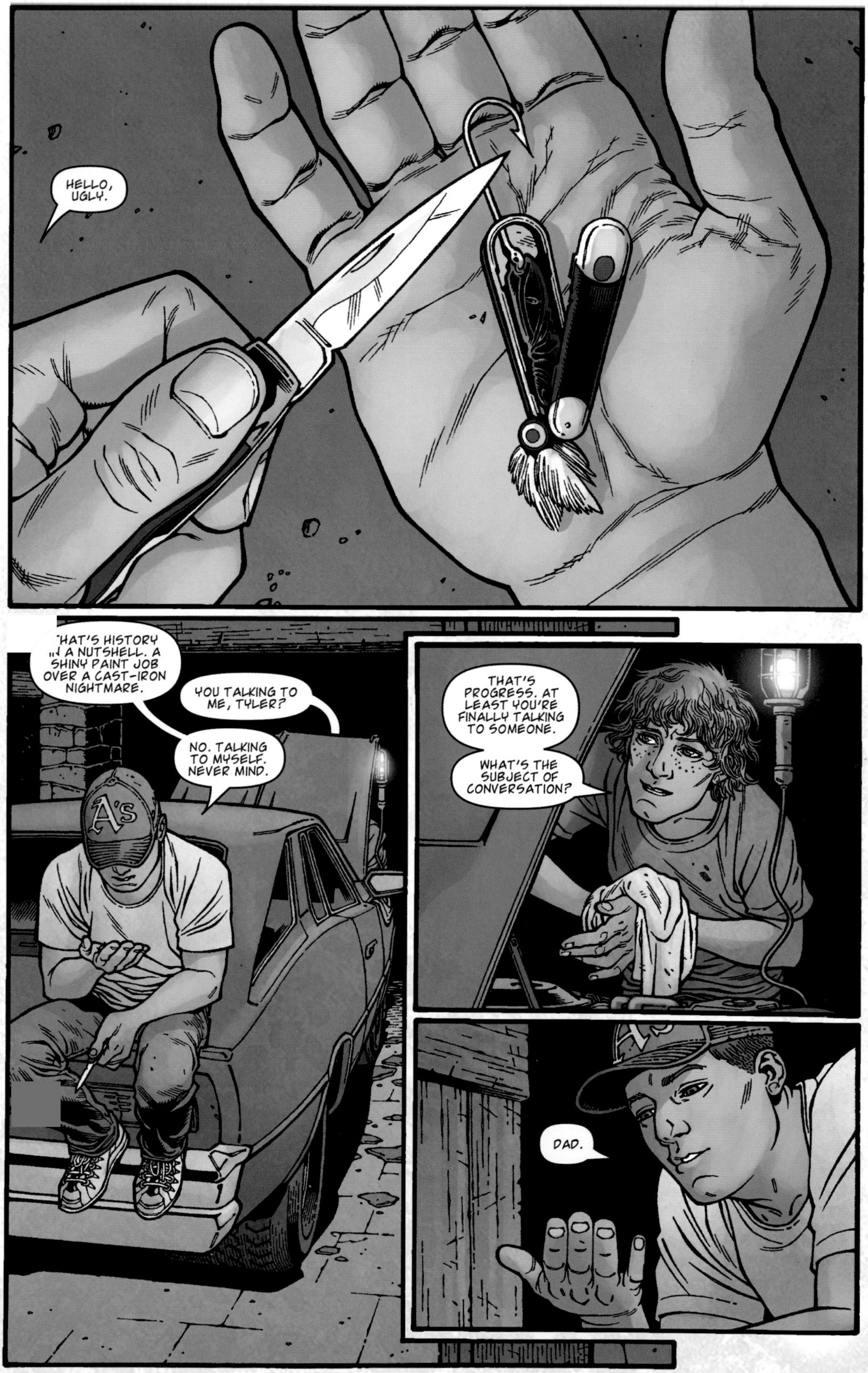
HELLO, UGLY.
THAT'S HISTORY IN A NUTSHELL. A SHINY PAINT JOB OVER A CAST-IRON NIGHTMARE.
YOU TALKING TO ME, TYLER?
NO. TALKING TO MYSELF. NEVER MIND.
THAT'S PROGRESS. AT LEAST YOU'RE FINALLY TALKING TO SOMEONE.
WHAT'S THE SUBJECT OF CONVERSATION?
DAD.

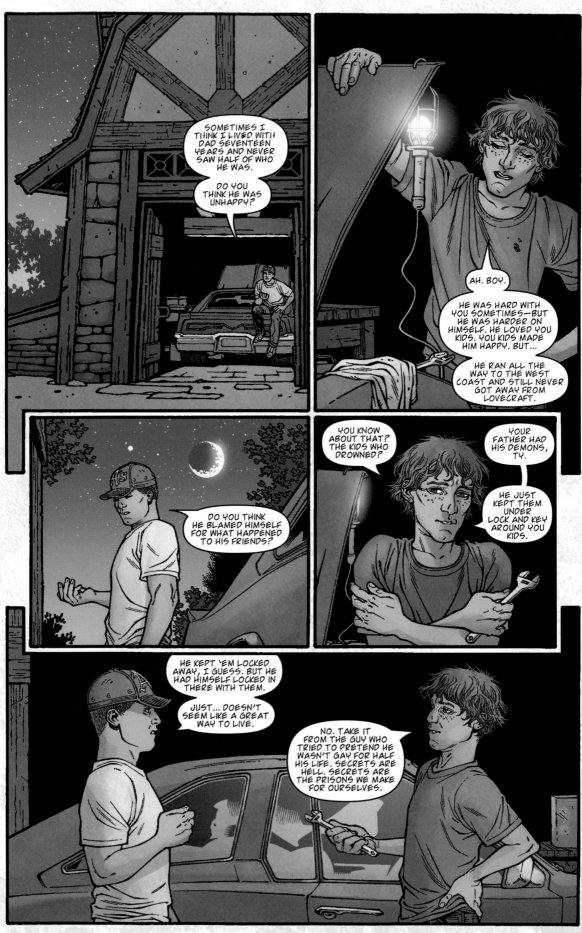

SOMETIMES I THINK I LIVED WITH DAD SEVENTEEN YEARS AND NEVER SAW HALF OF WHO HE WAS.

DO YOU THINK HE WAS UNHAPPY?

AH. BOY.

HE WAS HARD WITH YOU SOMETIMES—BUT HE WAS HARDER ON HIMSELF. HE LOVED YOU KIDS. YOU KIDS MADE HIM HAPPY. BUT...

HE RAN ALL THE WAY TO THE WEST COAST AND STILL NEVER GOT AWAY FROM LOVECRAFT.

DO YOU THINK HE BLAMED HIMSELF FOR WHAT HAPPENED TO HIS FRIENDS?

YOU KNOW ABOUT THAT? THE KIDS WHO DROWNED?

YOUR FATHER HAD HIS DEMONS, TY.

HE JUST KEPT THEM UNDER LOCK AND KEY AROUND YOU KIDS.

HE KEPT 'EM LOCKED AWAY, I GUESS. BUT HE HAD HIMSELF LOCKED IN THERE WITH THEM.

JUST... DOESN'T SEEM LIKE A GREAT WAY TO LIVE.

NO. TAKE IT FROM THE GUY WHO TRIED TO PRETEND HE WASN'T GAY FOR HALF HIS LIFE. SECRETS ARE HELL. SECRETS ARE THE PRISONS WE MAKE FOR OURSELVES.

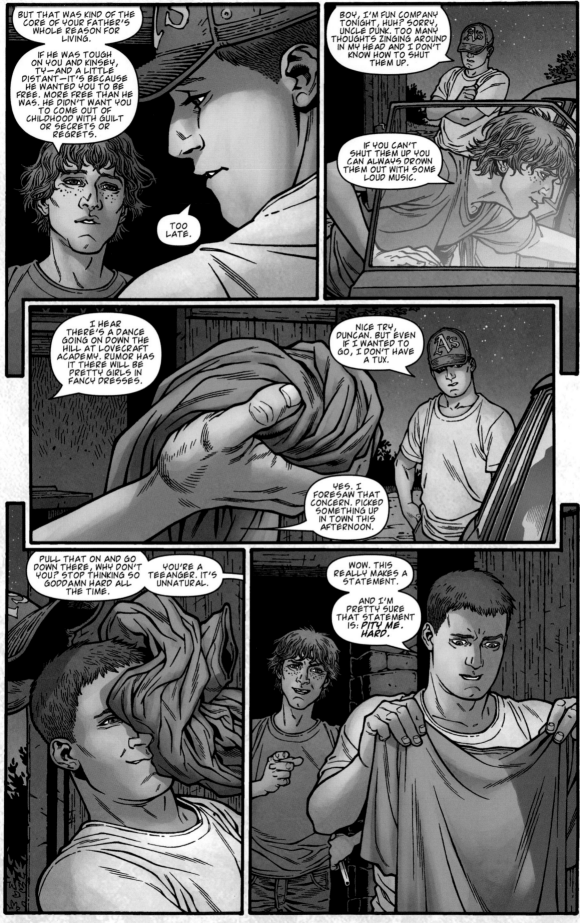

BUT THAT WAS KIND OF THE CORE OF YOUR FATHER'S WHOLE REASON FOR LIVING.

IF HE WAS TOUGH ON YOU AND KINSEY, TY—AND A LITTLE DISTANT—IT'S BECAUSE HE WANTED YOU TO BE FREE. MORE FREE THAN HE WAS. HE DIDN'T WANT YOU TO COME OUT OF CHILDHOOD WITH GUILT OR SECRETS OR REGRETS.

TOO LATE.

BOY, I'M FUN COMPANY TONIGHT, HUH? SORRY, UNCLE DUNK. TOO MANY THOUGHTS ZINGING AROUND IN MY HEAD AND I DON'T KNOW HOW TO SHUT THEM UP.

IF YOU CAN'T SHUT THEM UP YOU CAN ALWAYS DROWN THEM OUT WITH SOME LOUD MUSIC.

I HEAR THERE'S A DANCE GOING ON DOWN THE HILL AT LOVECRAFT ACADEMY. RUMOR HAS IT THERE WILL BE PRETTY GIRLS IN FANCY DRESSES.

NICE TRY, DUNCAN. BUT EVEN IF I WANTED TO GO, I DON'T HAVE A TUX.

YES. I FORESAW THAT CONCERN. PICKED SOMETHING UP IN TOWN THIS AFTERNOON.

PULL THAT ON AND GO DOWN THERE, WHY DON'T YOU? STOP THINKING SO GODDAMN HARD ALL THE TIME.

YOU'RE A TEENAGER. IT'S UNNATURAL.

WOW. THIS REALLY MAKES A STATEMENT.

AND I'M PRETTY SURE THAT STATEMENT IS: *PITY ME. HARD.*

61

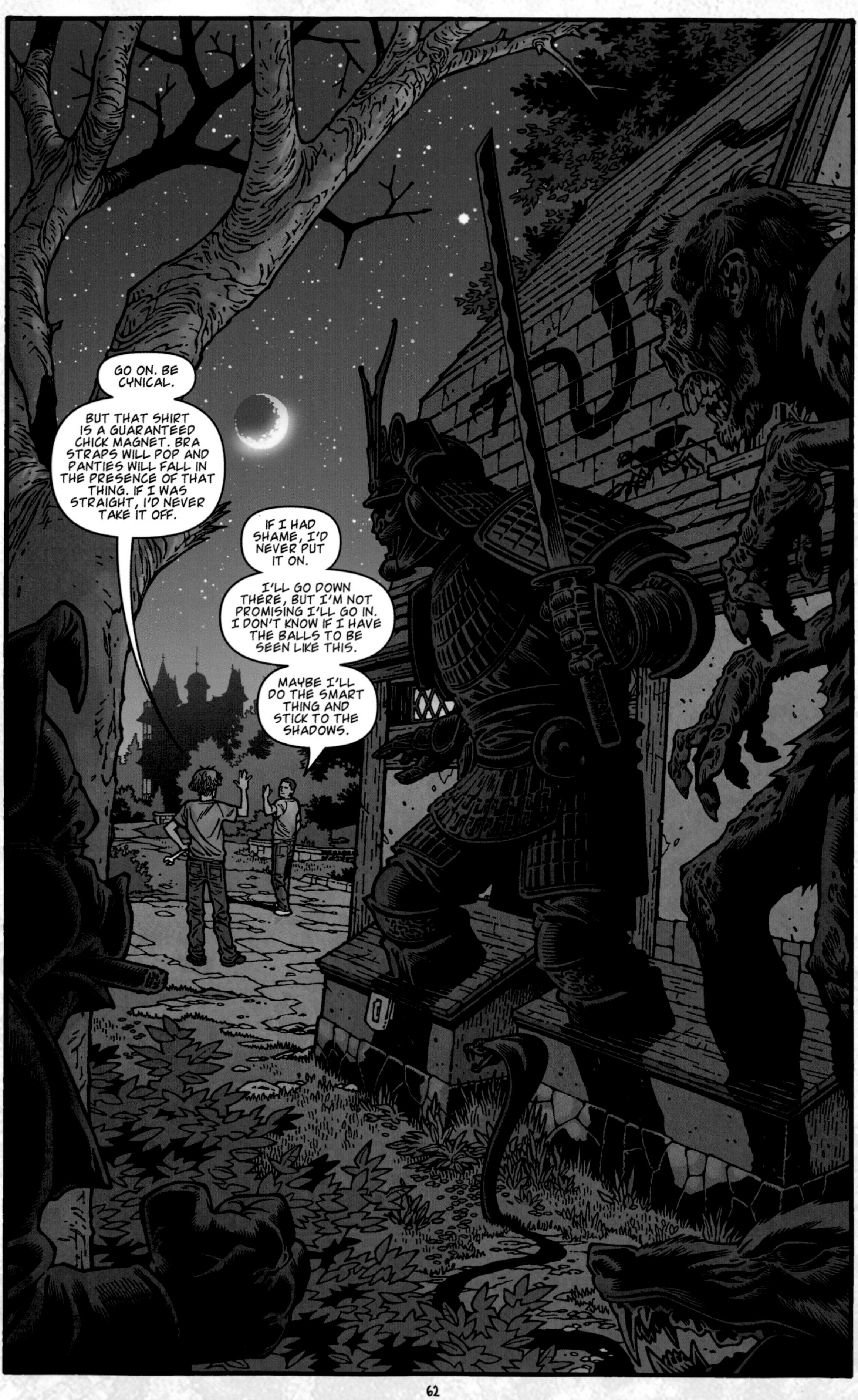
GO ON. BE CYNICAL.
BUT THAT SHIRT IS A GUARANTEED CHICK MAGNET. BRA STRAPS WILL POP AND PANTIES WILL FALL IN THE PRESENCE OF THAT THING. IF I WAS STRAIGHT, I'D NEVER TAKE IT OFF.
IF I HAD SHAME, I'D NEVER PUT IT ON.
I'LL GO DOWN THERE, BUT I'M NOT PROMISING I'LL GO IN. I DON'T KNOW IF I HAVE THE BALLS TO BE SEEN LIKE THIS.
MAYBE I'LL DO THE SMART THING AND STICK TO THE SHADOWS.

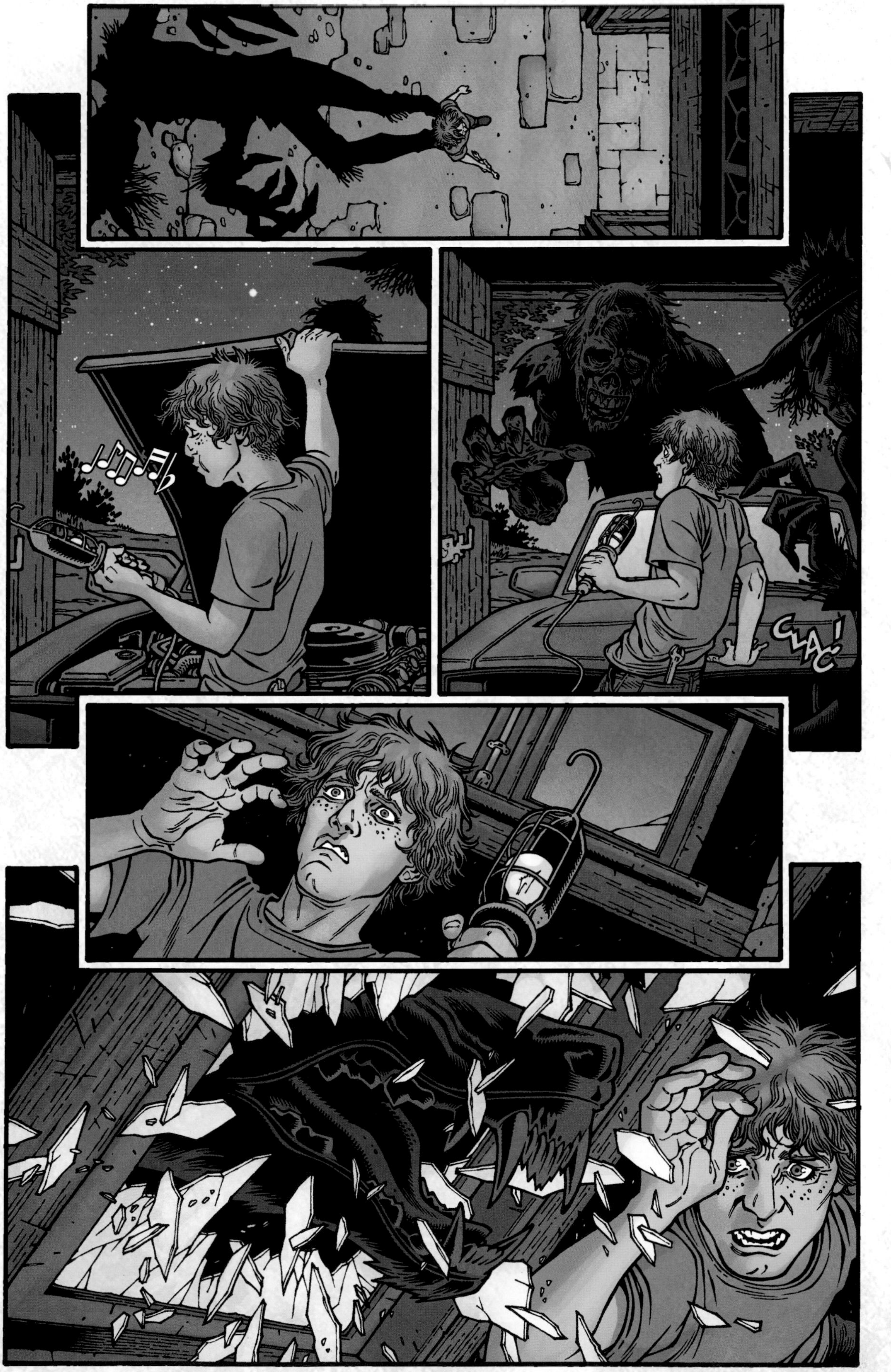
CLAC!

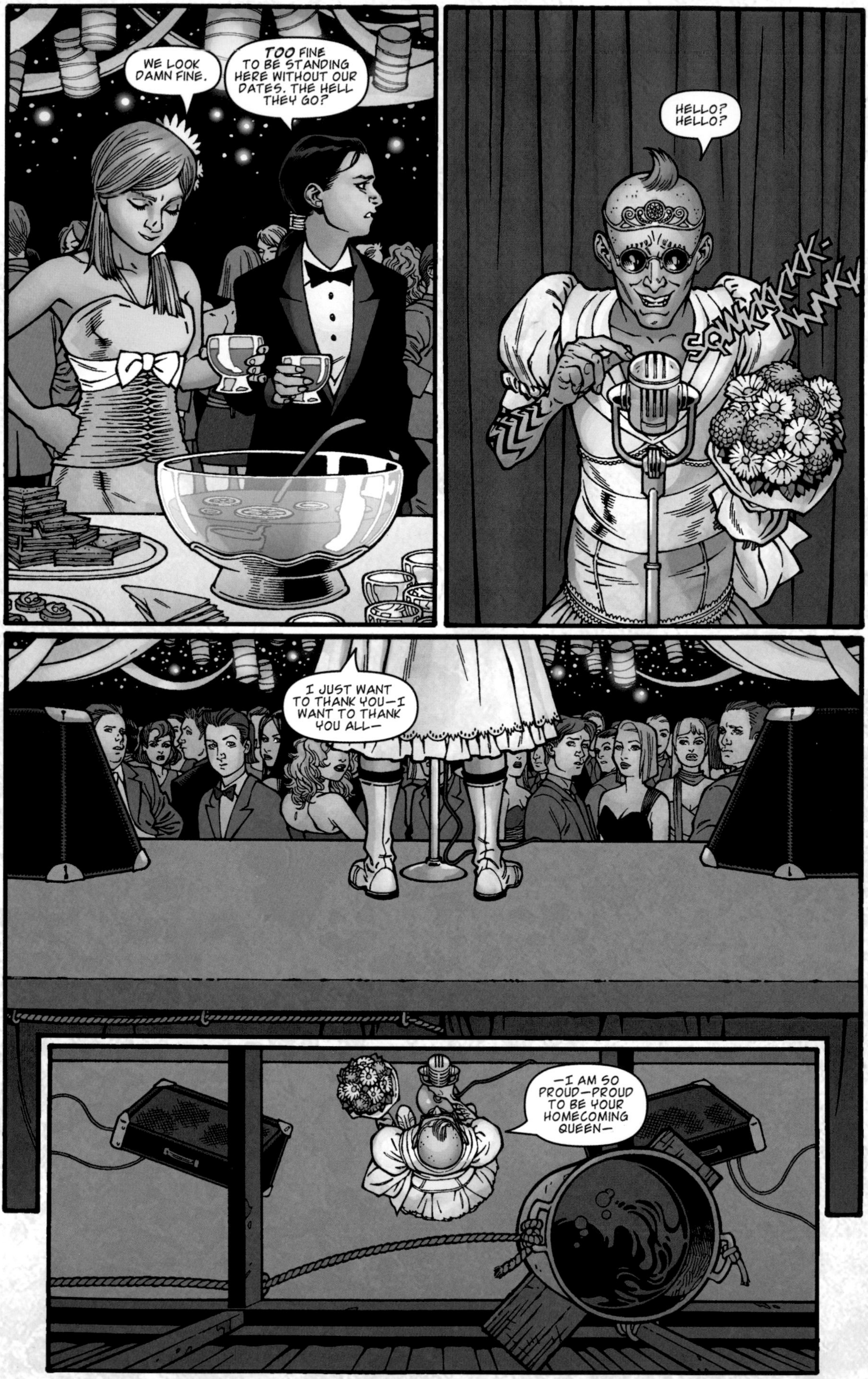
WE LOOK DAMN FINE.
TOO FINE TO BE STANDING HERE WITHOUT OUR DATES. THE HELL THEY GO?
HELLO? HELLO?
SQWKKKKK-NNNKKK
I JUST WANT TO THANK YOU—I WANT TO THANK YOU ALL—
—I AM SO PROUD—PROUD TO BE YOUR HOMECOMING QUEEN—

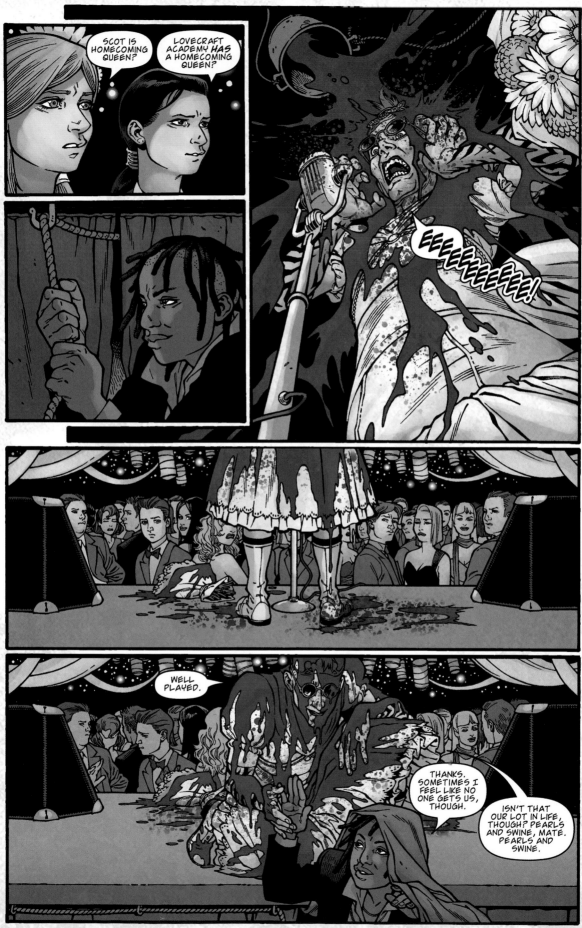

SCOT IS HOMECOMING QUEEN?

LOVECRAFT ACADEMY *HAS* A HOMECOMING QUEEN?

EEEEEEEEEEE!

WELL PLAYED.

THANKS. SOMETIMES I FEEL LIKE NO ONE GETS US, THOUGH.

ISN'T THAT OUR LOT IN LIFE, THOUGH? PEARLS AND SWINE, MATE. PEARLS AND SWINE.

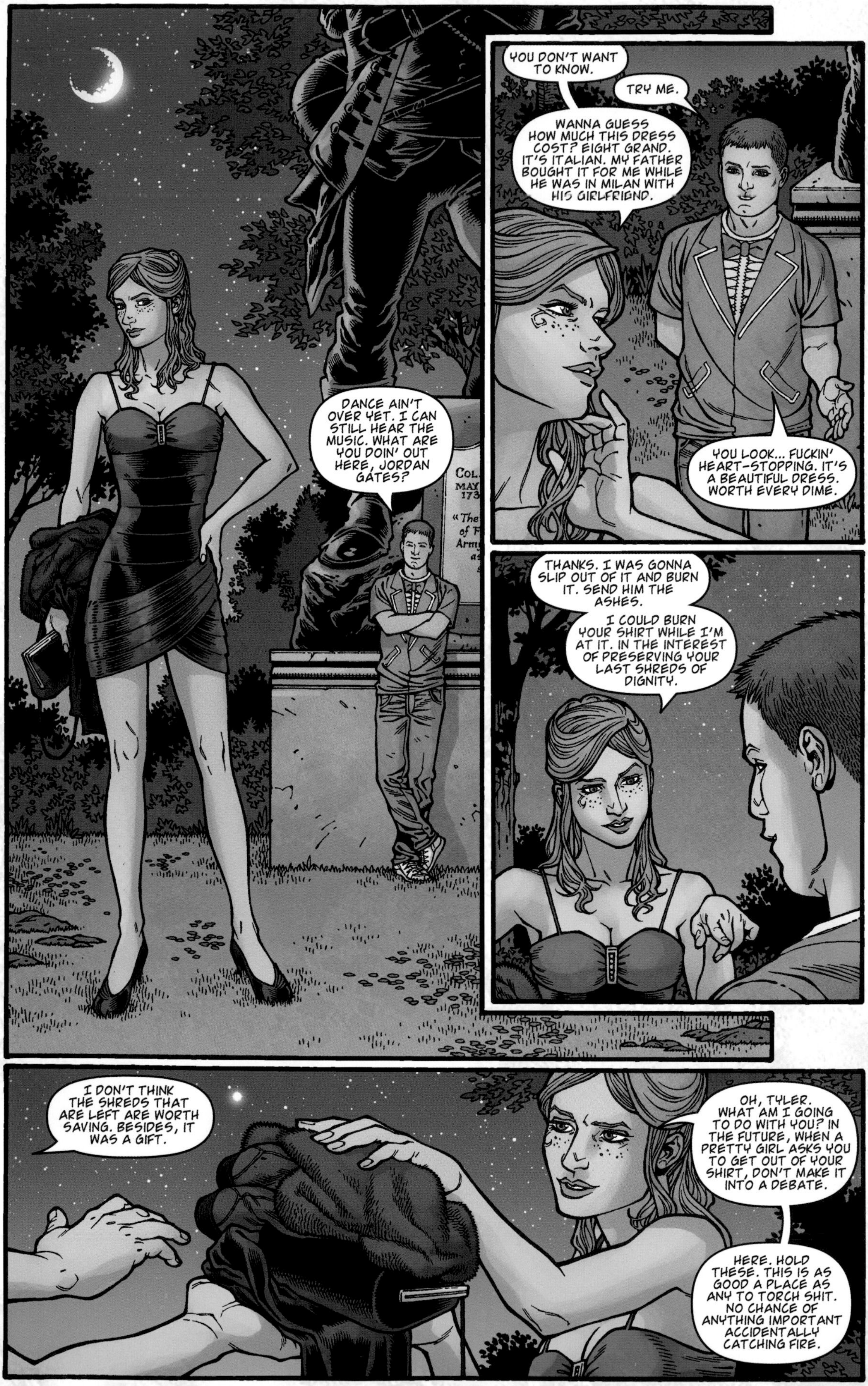
DANCE AIN'T OVER YET. I CAN STILL HEAR THE MUSIC. WHAT ARE YOU DOIN' OUT HERE, JORDAN GATES?
YOU DON'T WANT TO KNOW.
TRY ME.
WANNA GUESS HOW MUCH THIS DRESS COST? EIGHT GRAND. IT'S ITALIAN. MY FATHER BOUGHT IT FOR ME WHILE HE WAS IN MILAN WITH HIS GIRLFRIEND.
YOU LOOK... FUCKIN' HEART-STOPPING. IT'S A BEAUTIFUL DRESS. WORTH EVERY DIME.
THANKS. I WAS GONNA SLIP OUT OF IT AND BURN IT. SEND HIM THE ASHES.
I COULD BURN YOUR SHIRT WHILE I'M AT IT. IN THE INTEREST OF PRESERVING YOUR LAST SHREDS OF DIGNITY.
I DON'T THINK THE SHREDS THAT ARE LEFT ARE WORTH SAVING. BESIDES, IT WAS A GIFT.
OH, TYLER. WHAT AM I GOING TO DO WITH YOU? IN THE FUTURE, WHEN A PRETTY GIRL ASKS YOU TO GET OUT OF YOUR SHIRT, DON'T MAKE IT INTO A DEBATE.
HERE. HOLD THESE. THIS IS AS GOOD A PLACE AS ANY TO TORCH SHIT. NO CHANCE OF ANYTHING IMPORTANT ACCIDENTALLY CATCHING FIRE.

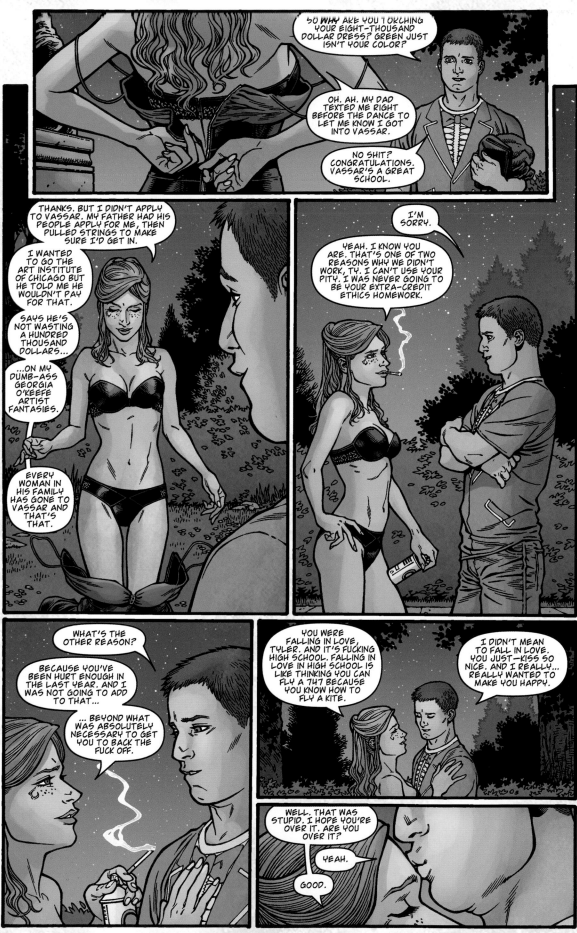

SO **WHY** ARE YOU TORCHING YOUR EIGHT-THOUSAND DOLLAR DRESS? GREEN JUST ISN'T YOUR COLOR?

OH. AH. MY DAD TEXTED ME RIGHT BEFORE THE DANCE TO LET ME KNOW I GOT INTO VASSAR.

NO SHIT? CONGRATULATIONS. VASSAR'S A GREAT SCHOOL.

THANKS. BUT I DIDN'T APPLY TO VASSAR. MY FATHER HAD HIS PEOPLE APPLY FOR ME, THEN PULLED STRINGS TO MAKE SURE I'D GET IN.

I WANTED TO GO THE ART INSTITUTE OF CHICAGO BUT HE TOLD ME HE WOULDN'T PAY FOR THAT.

SAYS HE'S NOT WASTING A HUNDRED THOUSAND DOLLARS...

...ON MY DUMB-ASS GEORGIA O'KEEFE ARTIST FANTASIES.

EVERY WOMAN IN HIS FAMILY HAS GONE TO VASSAR AND THAT'S THAT.

I'M SORRY.

YEAH. I KNOW YOU ARE. THAT'S ONE OF TWO REASONS WHY WE DIDN'T WORK, TY. I CAN'T USE YOUR PITY. I WAS NEVER GOING TO BE YOUR EXTRA-CREDIT ETHICS HOMEWORK.

WHAT'S THE OTHER REASON?

BECAUSE YOU'VE BEEN HURT ENOUGH IN THE LAST YEAR. AND I WAS NOT GOING TO ADD TO THAT...

... BEYOND WHAT WAS ABSOLUTELY NECESSARY TO GET YOU TO BACK THE FUCK OFF.

YOU WERE FALLING IN LOVE, TYLER. AND IT'S FUCKING HIGH SCHOOL. FALLING IN LOVE IN HIGH SCHOOL IS LIKE THINKING YOU CAN FLY A 747 BECAUSE YOU KNOW HOW TO FLY A KITE.

I DIDN'T MEAN TO FALL IN LOVE. YOU JUST—KISS SO NICE. AND I REALLY... REALLY WANTED TO MAKE YOU HAPPY.

WELL. THAT WAS STUPID. I HOPE YOU'RE OVER IT. ARE YOU OVER IT?

YEAH.

GOOD.

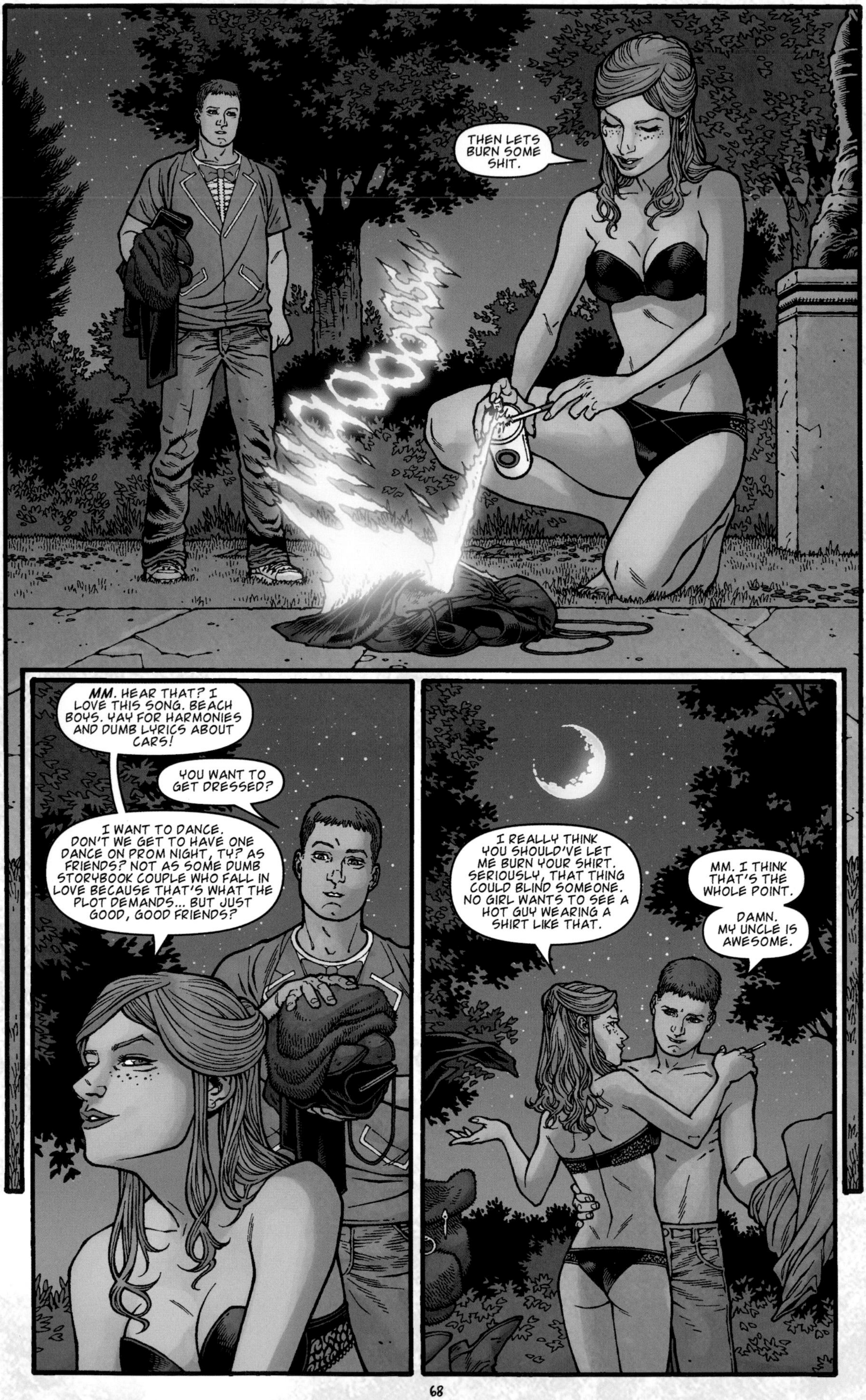
THEN LETS BURN SOME SHIT.
WHOOSH!
MM. HEAR THAT? I LOVE THIS SONG. BEACH BOYS. YAY FOR HARMONIES AND DUMB LYRICS ABOUT CARS!
YOU WANT TO GET DRESSED?
I WANT TO DANCE. DON'T WE GET TO HAVE ONE DANCE ON PROM NIGHT, TY? AS FRIENDS? NOT AS SOME DUMB STORYBOOK COUPLE WHO FALL IN LOVE BECAUSE THAT'S WHAT THE PLOT DEMANDS... BUT JUST GOOD, GOOD FRIENDS?
I REALLY THINK YOU SHOULD'VE LET ME BURN YOUR SHIRT. SERIOUSLY, THAT THING COULD BLIND SOMEONE. NO GIRL WANTS TO SEE A HOT GUY WEARING A SHIRT LIKE THAT.
MM. I THINK THAT'S THE WHOLE POINT.
DAMN. MY UNCLE IS AWESOME.

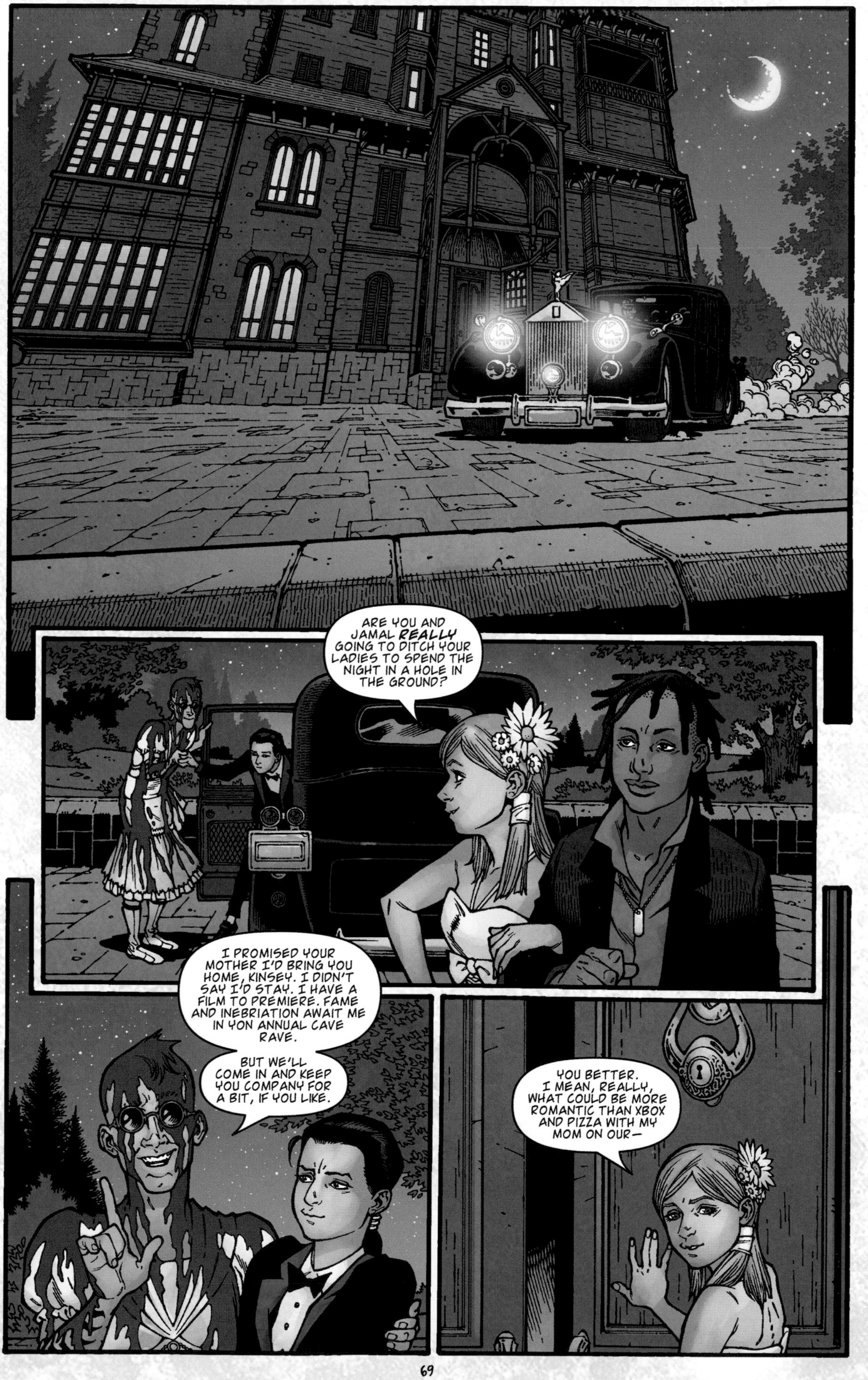
ARE YOU AND JAMAL REALLY GOING TO DITCH YOUR LADIES TO SPEND THE NIGHT IN A HOLE IN THE GROUND?
I PROMISED YOUR MOTHER I'D BRING YOU HOME, KINSEY. I DIDN'T SAY I'D STAY. I HAVE A FILM TO PREMIERE. FAME AND INEBRIATION AWAIT ME IN YON ANNUAL CAVE RAVE.
BUT WE'LL COME IN AND KEEP YOU COMPANY FOR A BIT, IF YOU LIKE.
YOU BETTER. I MEAN, REALLY, WHAT COULD BE MORE ROMANTIC THAN XBOX AND PIZZA WITH MY MOM ON OUR—

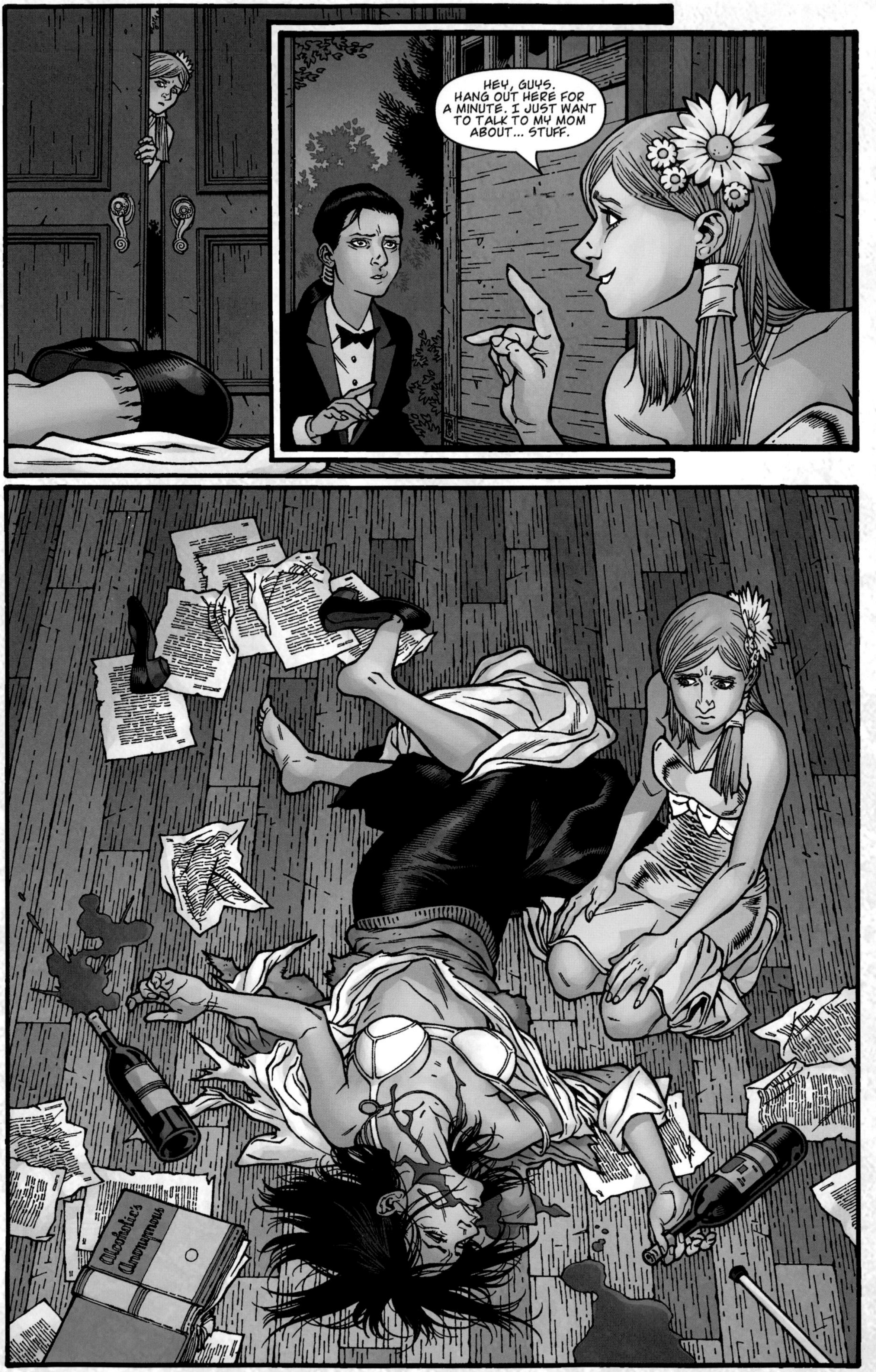
HEY, GUYS. HANG OUT HERE FOR A MINUTE. I JUST WANT TO TALK TO MY MOM ABOUT... STUFF.

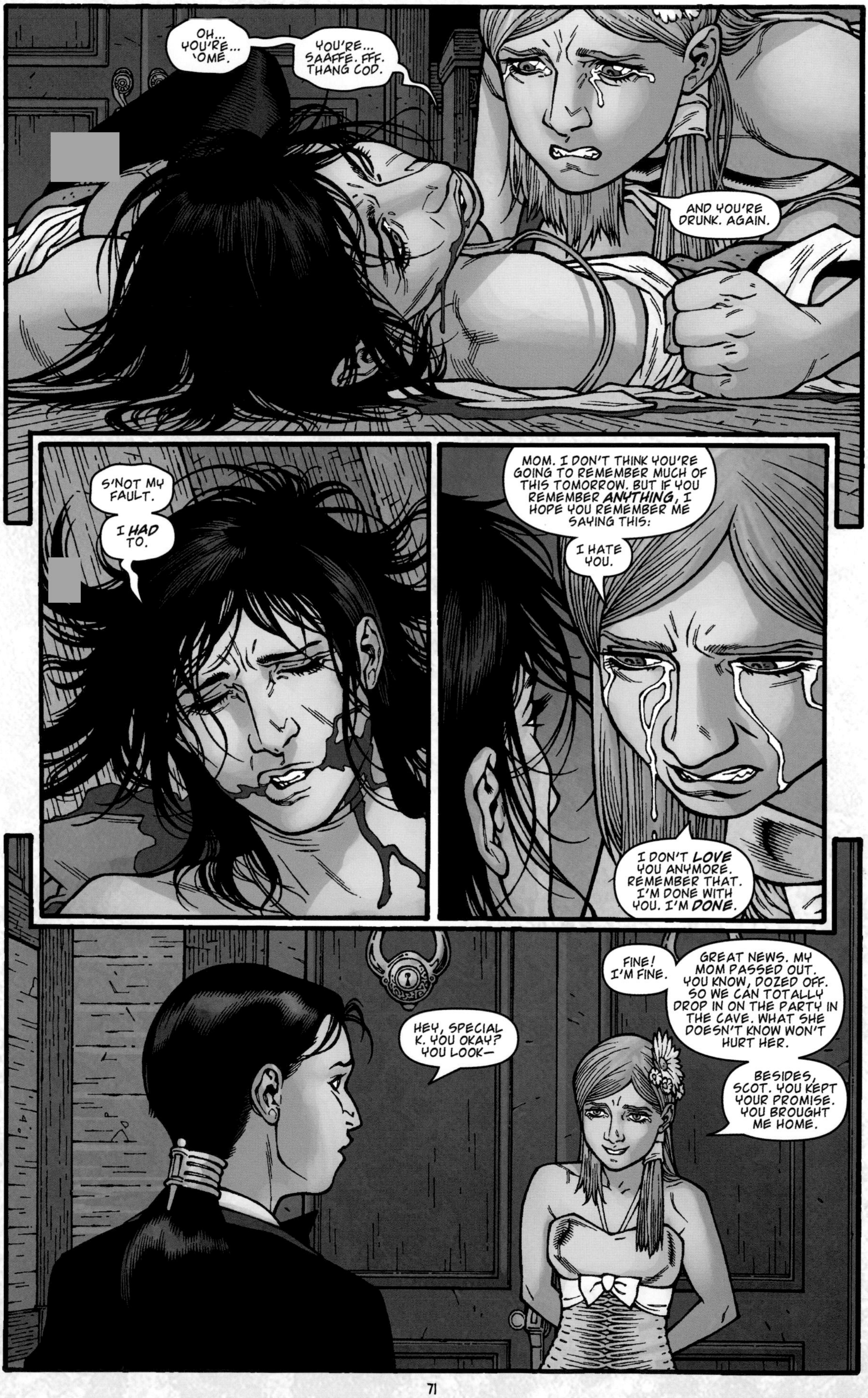
OH... YOU'RE... 'OME.
YOU'RE... SAAFFE. FFF. THANG COD.
AND YOU'RE DRUNK. AGAIN.
S'NOT MY FAULT.
I **HAD** TO.
MOM. I DON'T THINK YOU'RE GOING TO REMEMBER MUCH OF THIS TOMORROW. BUT IF YOU REMEMBER **ANYTHING**, I HOPE YOU REMEMBER ME SAYING THIS:
I HATE YOU.
I DON'T **LOVE** YOU ANYMORE. REMEMBER THAT. I'M DONE WITH YOU. I'M **DONE**.
HEY, SPECIAL K. YOU OKAY? YOU LOOK—
FINE! I'M FINE.
GREAT NEWS. MY MOM PASSED OUT. YOU KNOW, DOZED OFF. SO WE CAN TOTALLY DROP IN ON THE PARTY IN THE CAVE. WHAT SHE DOESN'T KNOW WON'T HURT HER.
BESIDES, SCOT. YOU KEPT YOUR PROMISE. YOU BROUGHT ME HOME.

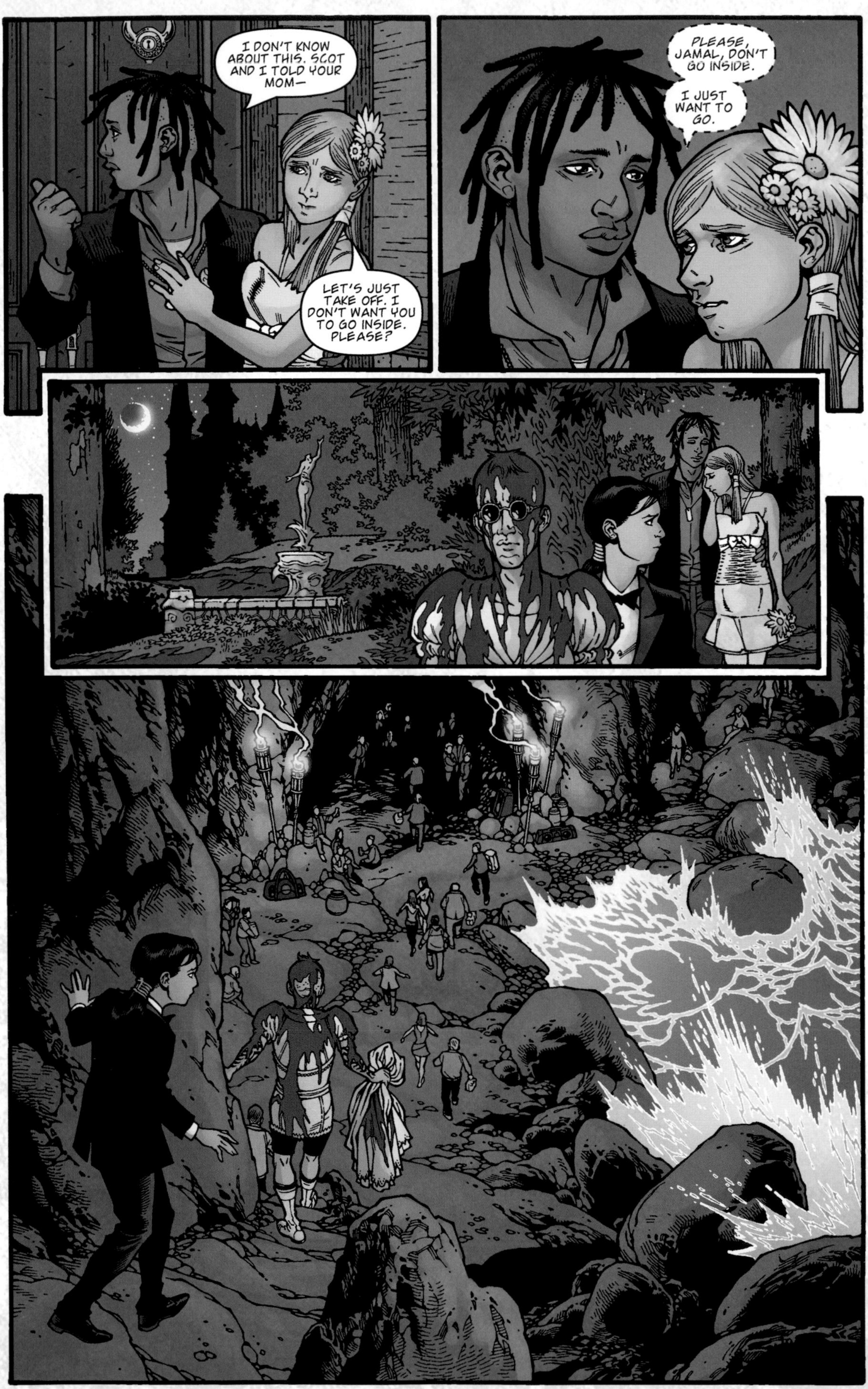
I DON'T KNOW ABOUT THIS. SCOT AND I TOLD YOUR MOM—
LET'S JUST TAKE OFF. I DON'T WANT YOU TO GO INSIDE. PLEASE?
PLEASE, JAMAL, DON'T GO INSIDE.
I JUST WANT TO GO.

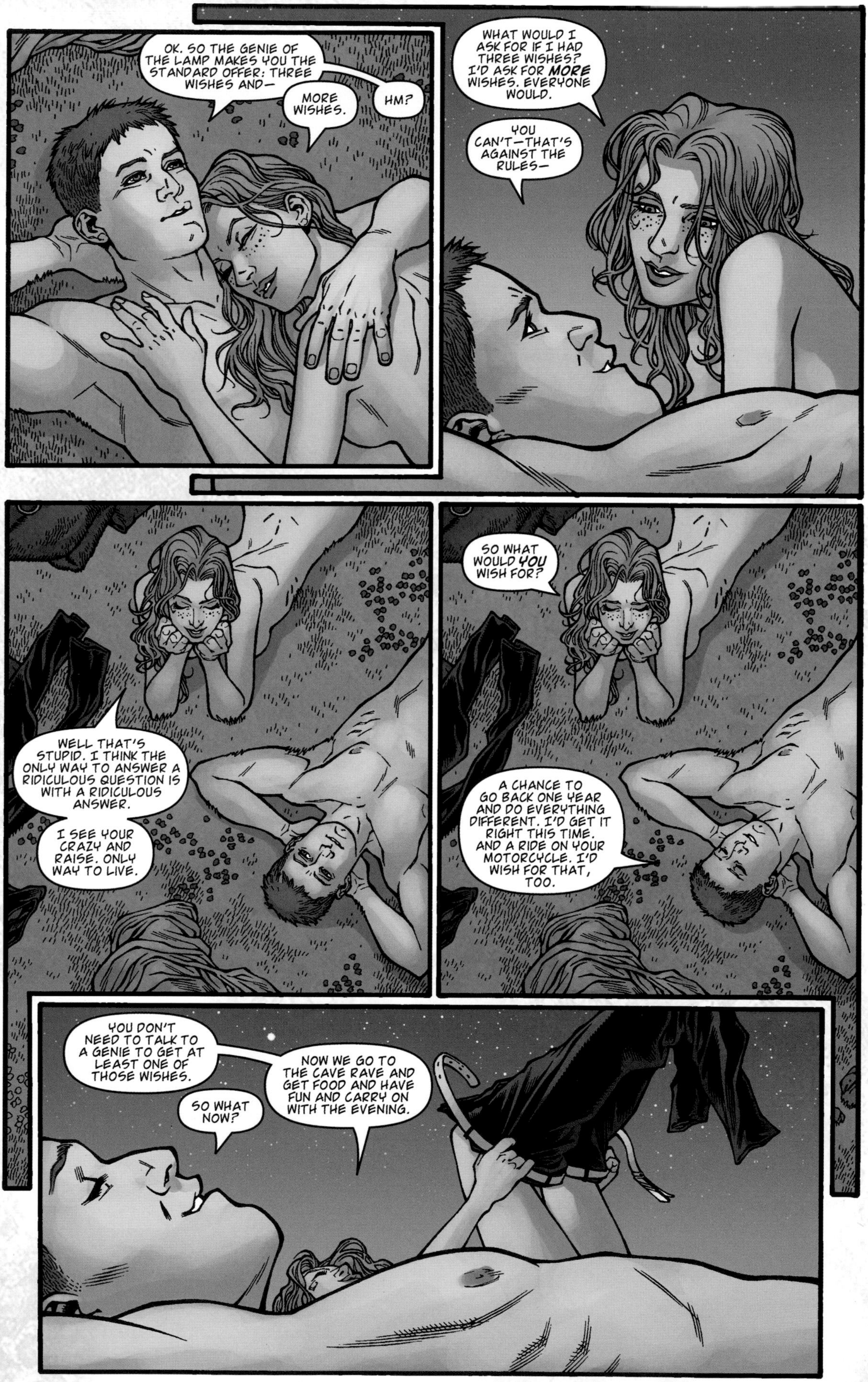
OK. SO THE GENIE OF THE LAMP MAKES YOU THE STANDARD OFFER: THREE WISHES AND—
MORE WISHES.
HM?
WHAT WOULD I ASK FOR IF I HAD THREE WISHES? I'D ASK FOR MORE WISHES. EVERYONE WOULD.
YOU CAN'T—THAT'S AGAINST THE RULES—
WELL THAT'S STUPID. I THINK THE ONLY WAY TO ANSWER A RIDICULOUS QUESTION IS WITH A RIDICULOUS ANSWER.
I SEE YOUR CRAZY AND RAISE. ONLY WAY TO LIVE.
SO WHAT WOULD YOU WISH FOR?
A CHANCE TO GO BACK ONE YEAR AND DO EVERYTHING DIFFERENT. I'D GET IT RIGHT THIS TIME. AND A RIDE ON YOUR MOTORCYCLE. I'D WISH FOR THAT, TOO.
YOU DON'T NEED TO TALK TO A GENIE TO GET AT LEAST ONE OF THOSE WISHES.
SO WHAT NOW?
NOW WE GO TO THE CAVE RAVE AND GET FOOD AND HAVE FUN AND CARRY ON WITH THE EVENING.

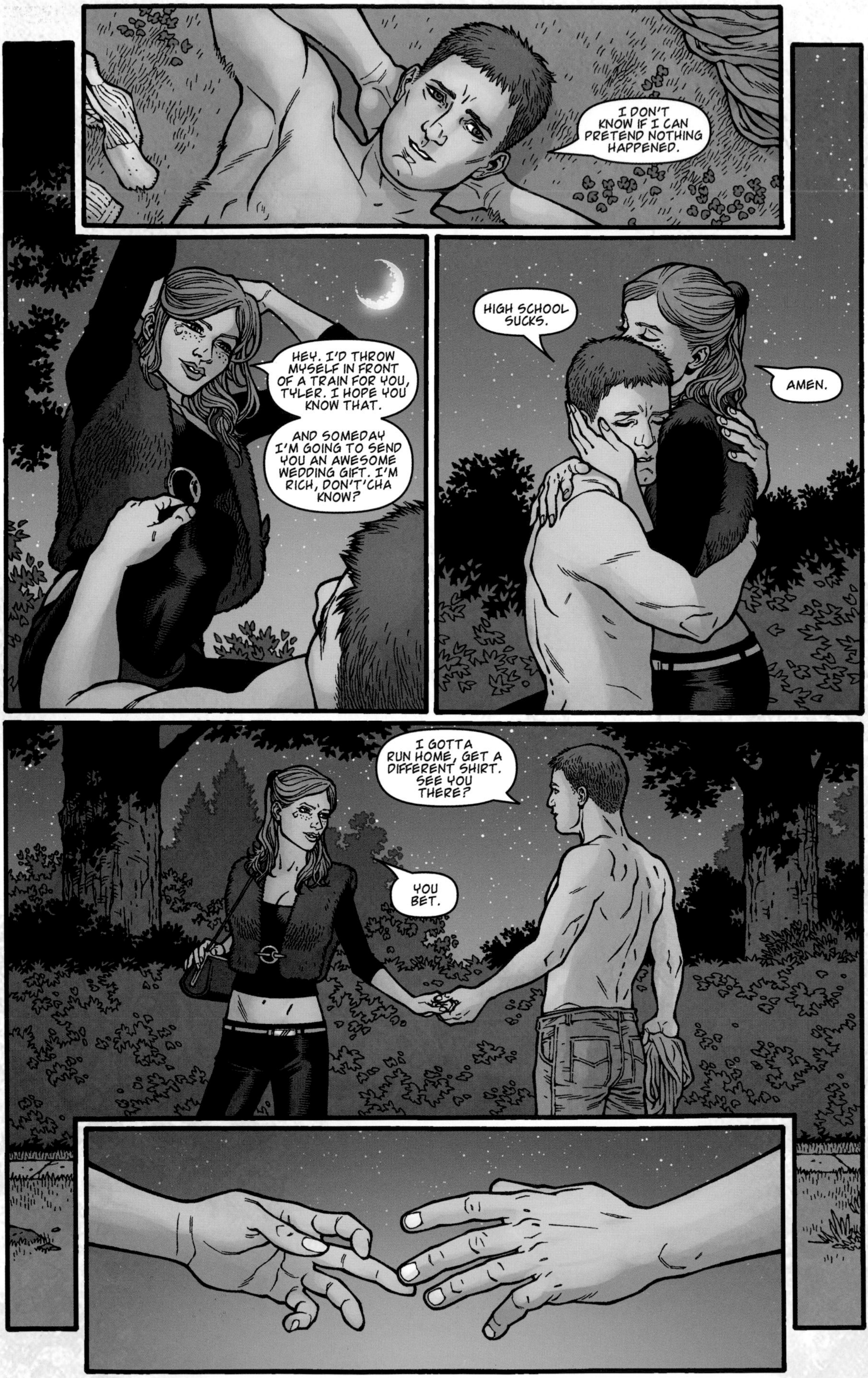
I DON'T KNOW IF I CAN PRETEND NOTHING HAPPENED.
HEY. I'D THROW MYSELF IN FRONT OF A TRAIN FOR YOU, TYLER. I HOPE YOU KNOW THAT.
AND SOMEDAY I'M GOING TO SEND YOU AN AWESOME WEDDING GIFT. I'M RICH, DON'T'CHA KNOW?
HIGH SCHOOL SUCKS.
AMEN.
I GOTTA RUN HOME, GET A DIFFERENT SHIRT. SEE YOU THERE?
YOU BET.

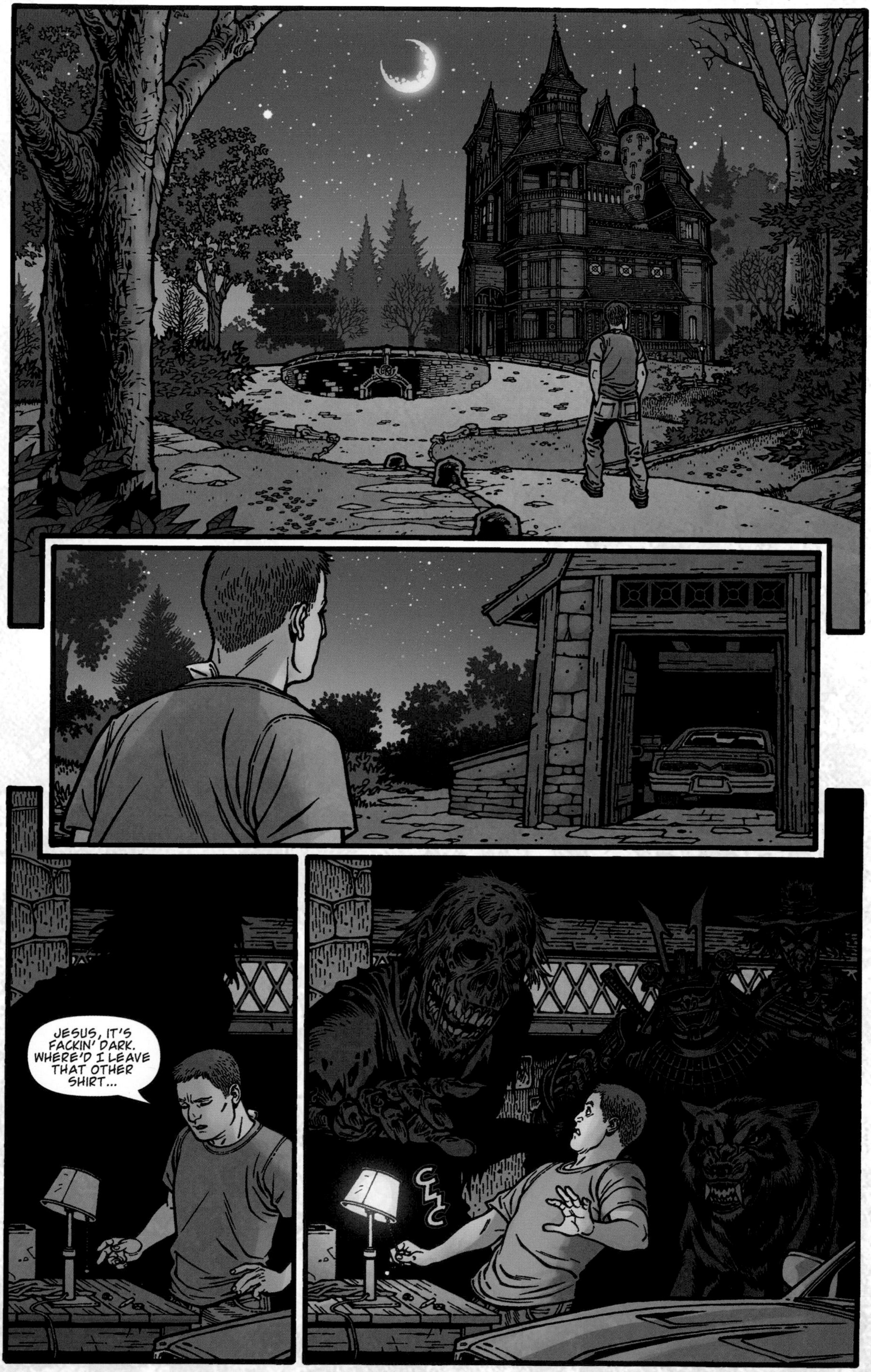
JESUS, IT'S FACKIN' DARK. WHERE'D I LEAVE THAT OTHER SHIRT...
CLIC

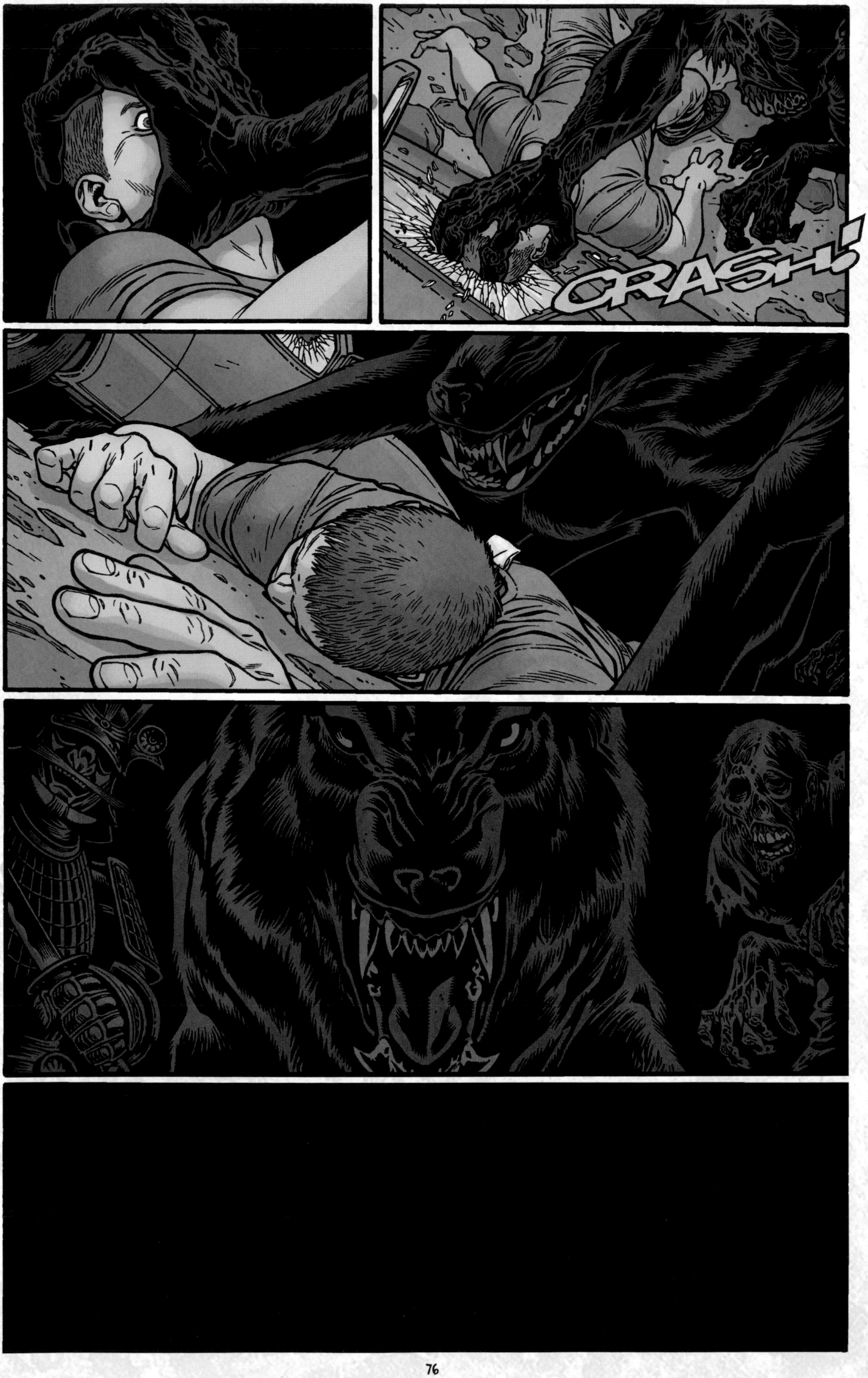
CRASH!

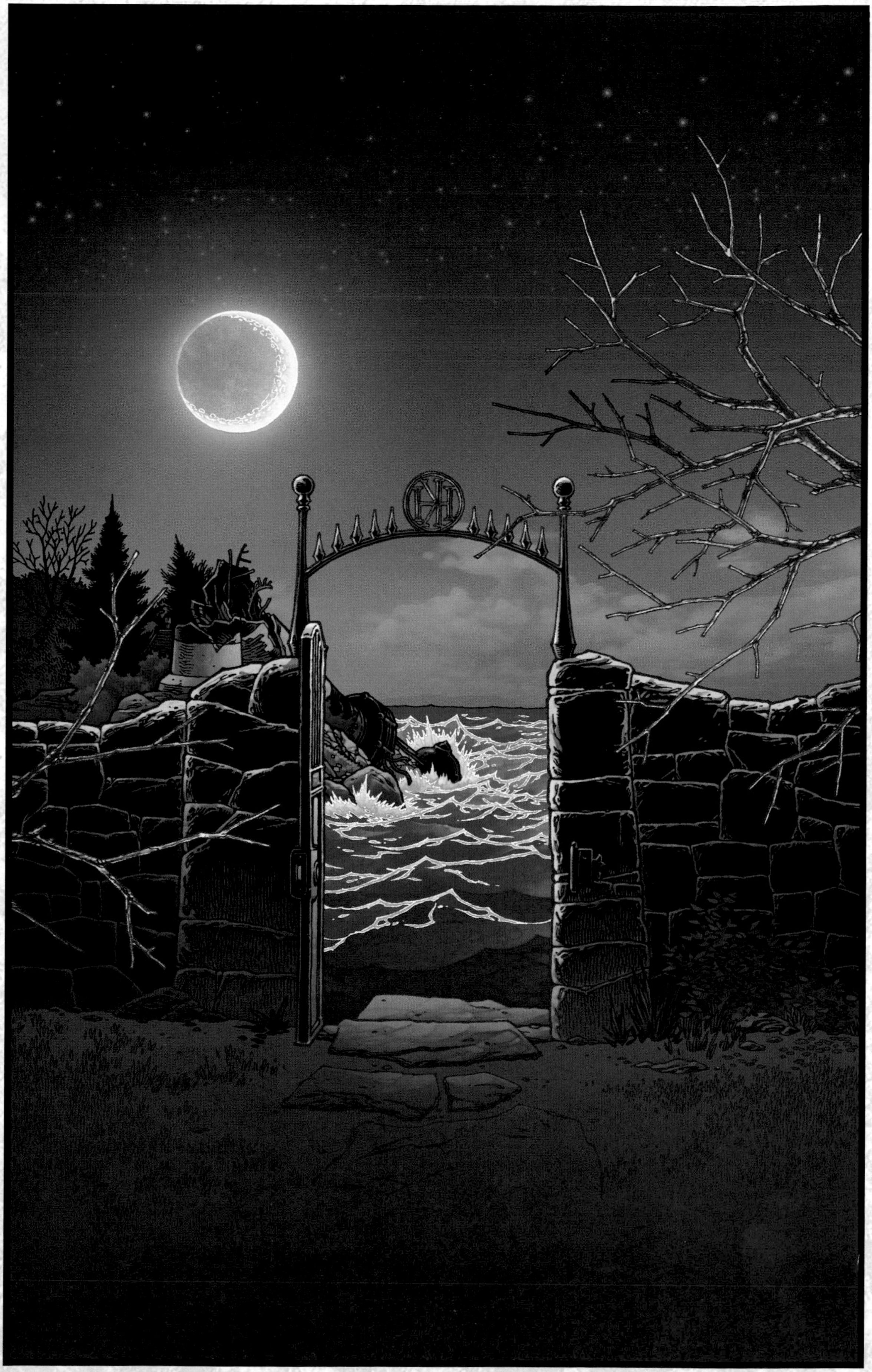

- ALPHA & OMEGA -

Chapter Four

HUMAN SACRIFICES

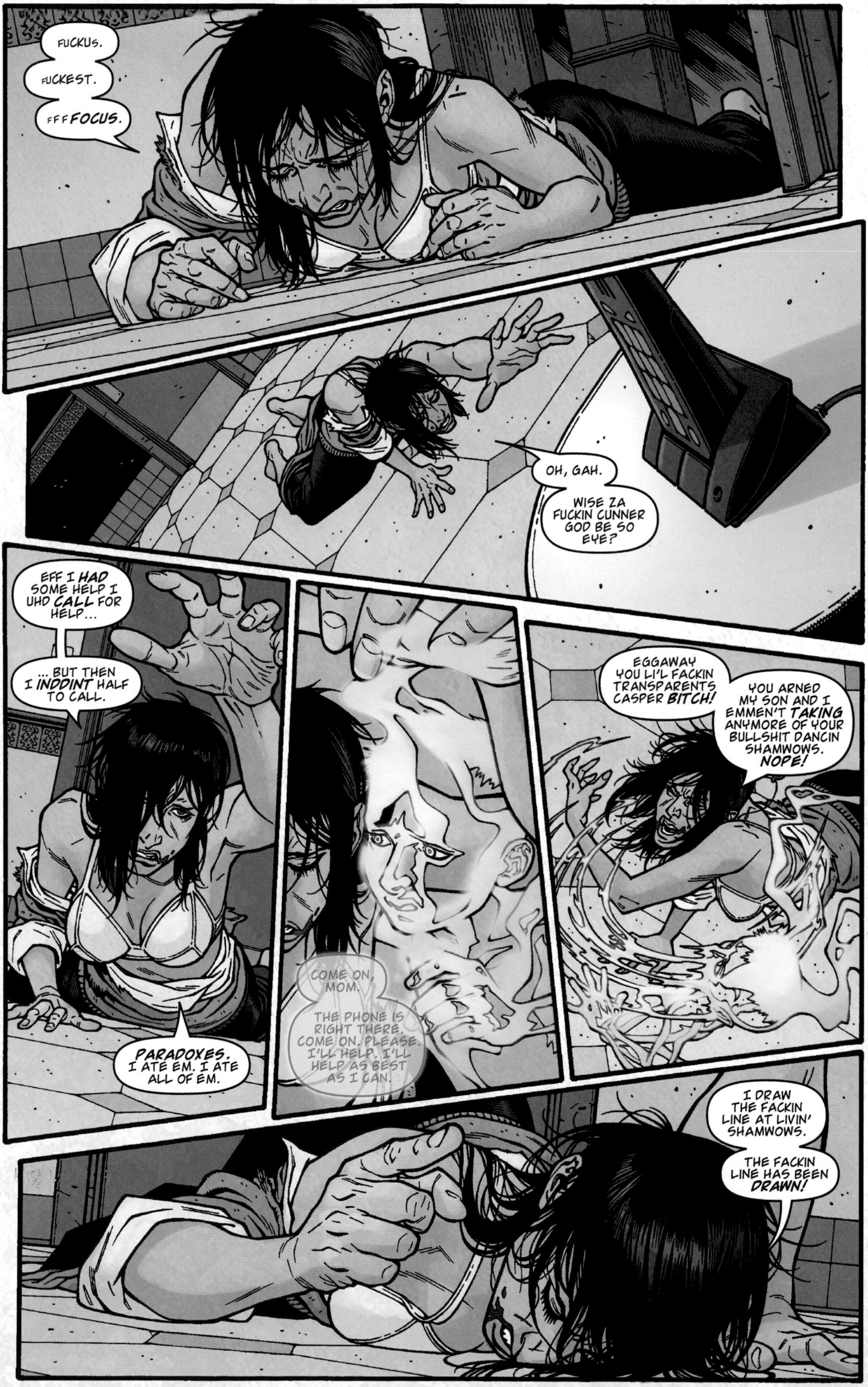
FUCKUS.
FUCKEST.
FFF FOCUS.
OH, GAH.
WISE ZA FUCKIN CUNNER GOD BE SO EYE?
EFF I HAD SOME HELP I UHD CALL FOR HELP...
... BUT THEN I INDDINT HALF TO CALL.
PARADOXES. I ATE EM. I ATE ALL OF EM.
COME ON, MOM.
THE PHONE IS RIGHT THERE. COME ON. PLEASE. I'LL HELP. I'LL HELP AS BEST AS I CAN.
EGGAWAY YOU LI'L FACKIN TRANSPARENTS CASPER BITCH!
YOU ARNED MY SON AND I EMMEN'T TAKING ANYMORE OF YOUR BULLSHIT DANCIN SHAMWOWS. NOPE!
I DRAW THE FACKIN LINE AT LIVIN' SHAMWOWS.
THE FACKIN LINE HAS BEEN DRAWN!

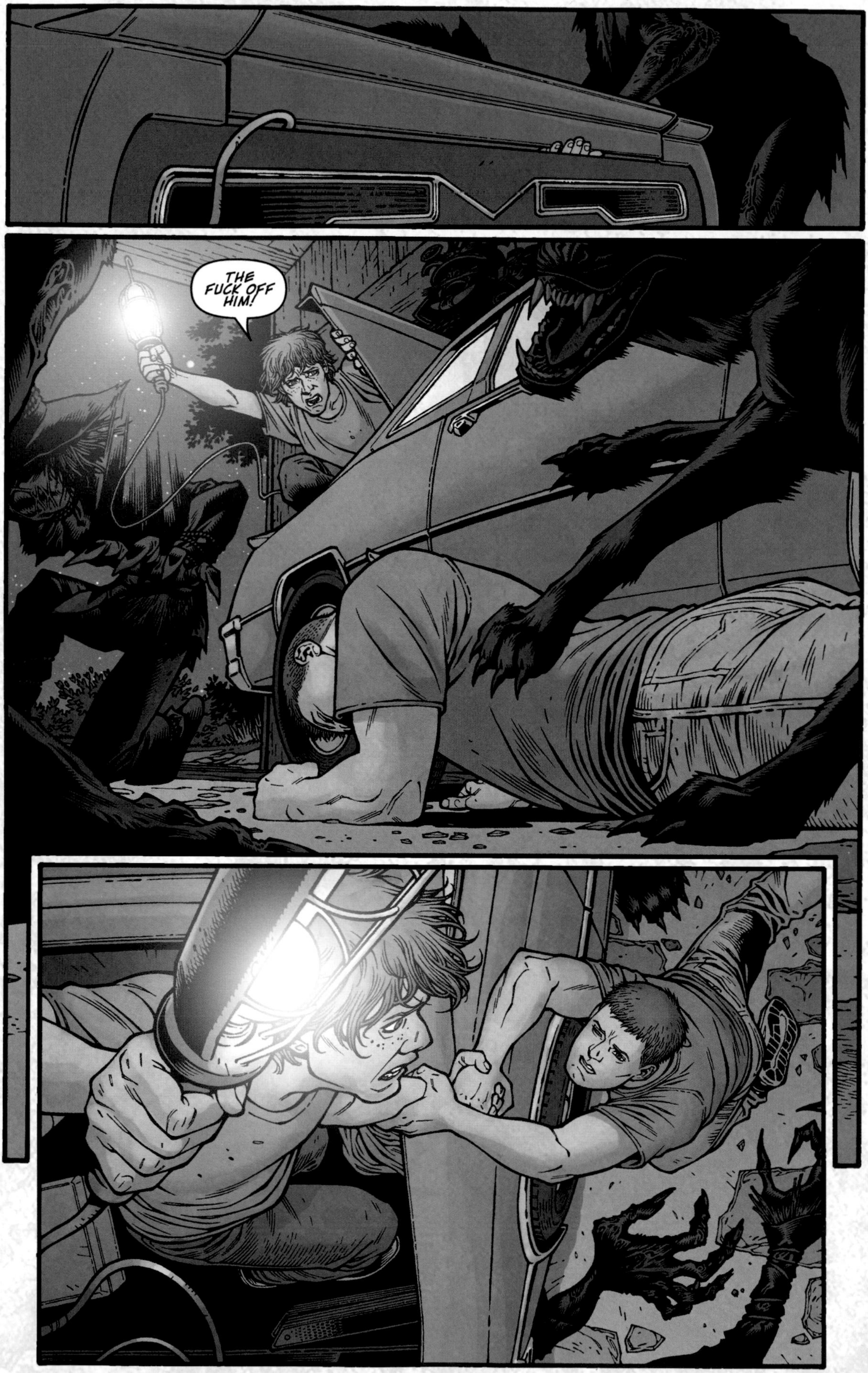
THE FUCK OFF HIM!

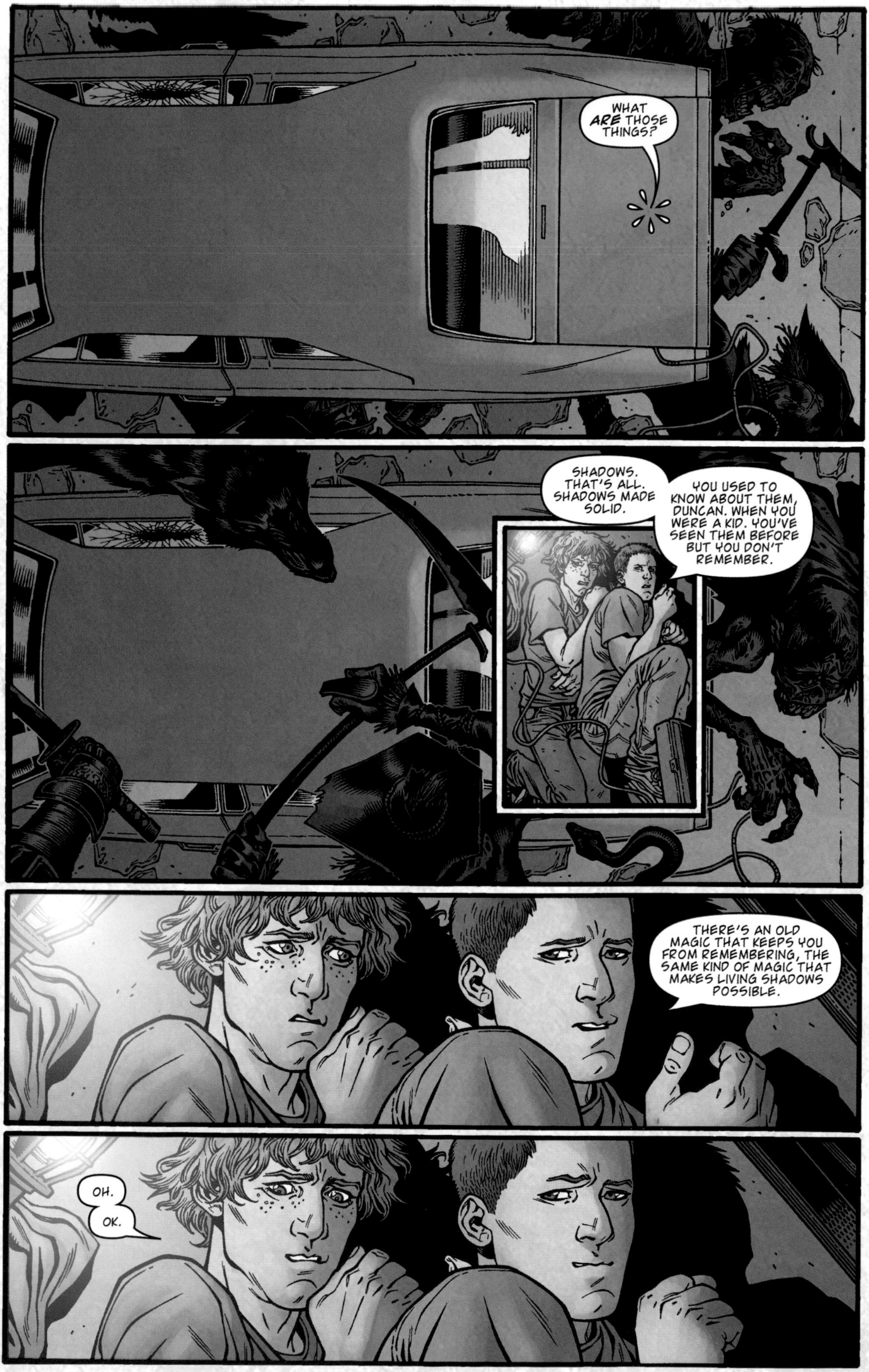
WHAT ARE THOSE THINGS?
SHADOWS. THAT'S ALL. SHADOWS MADE SOLID.
YOU USED TO KNOW ABOUT THEM, DUNCAN. WHEN YOU WERE A KID. YOU'VE SEEN THEM BEFORE BUT YOU DON'T REMEMBER.
THERE'S AN OLD MAGIC THAT KEEPS YOU FROM REMEMBERING, THE SAME KIND OF MAGIC THAT MAKES LIVING SHADOWS POSSIBLE.
OH.
OK.

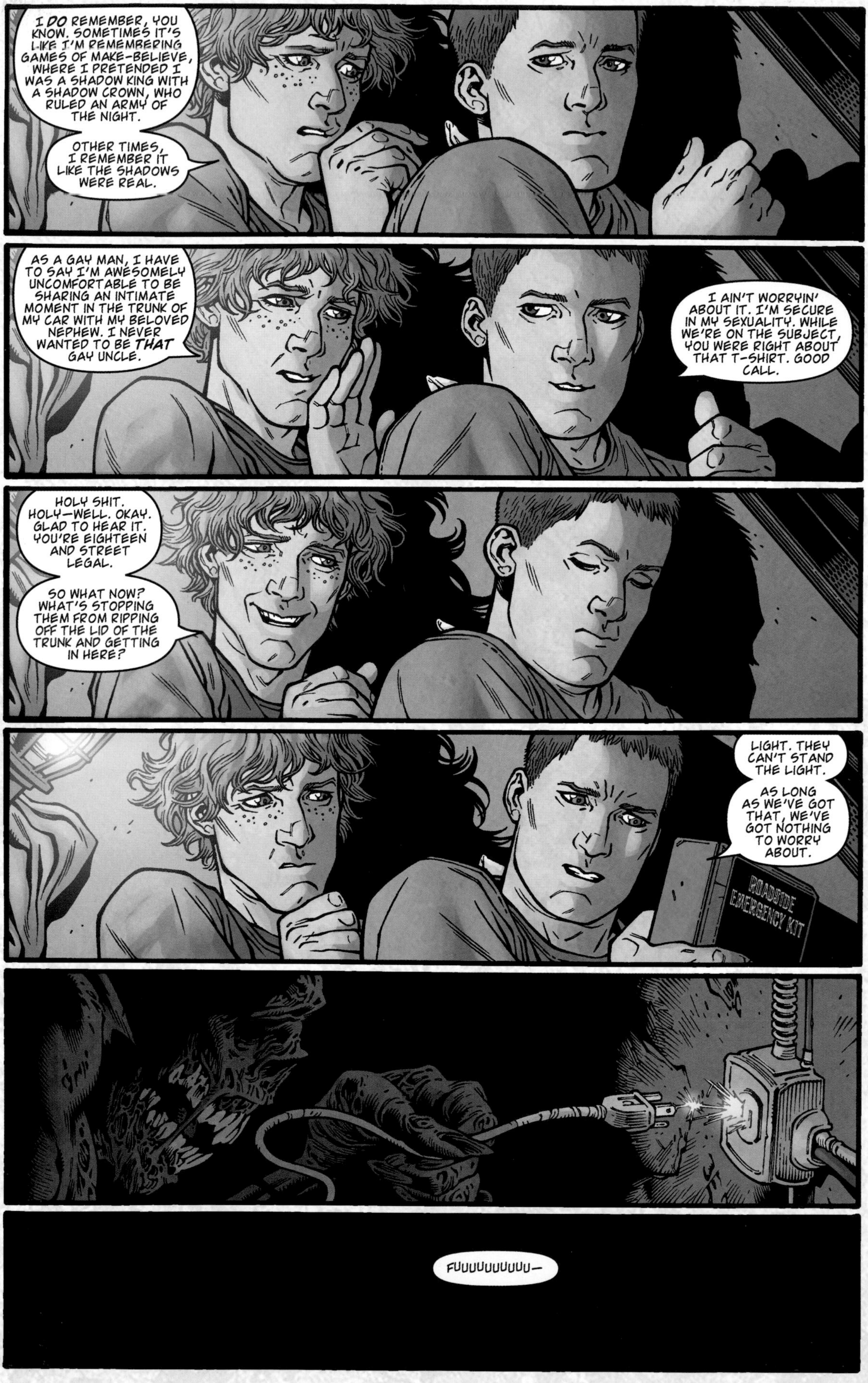
I DO REMEMBER, YOU KNOW. SOMETIMES IT'S LIKE I'M REMEMBERING GAMES OF MAKE-BELIEVE, WHERE I PRETENDED I WAS A SHADOW KING WITH A SHADOW CROWN, WHO RULED AN ARMY OF THE NIGHT.
OTHER TIMES, I REMEMBER IT LIKE THE SHADOWS WERE REAL.
AS A GAY MAN, I HAVE TO SAY I'M AWESOMELY UNCOMFORTABLE TO BE SHARING AN INTIMATE MOMENT IN THE TRUNK OF MY CAR WITH MY BELOVED NEPHEW. I NEVER WANTED TO BE THAT GAY UNCLE.
I AIN'T WORRYIN' ABOUT IT. I'M SECURE IN MY SEXUALITY. WHILE WE'RE ON THE SUBJECT, YOU WERE RIGHT ABOUT THAT T-SHIRT. GOOD CALL.
HOLY SHIT. HOLY—WELL. OKAY. GLAD TO HEAR IT. YOU'RE EIGHTEEN AND STREET LEGAL.
SO WHAT NOW? WHAT'S STOPPING THEM FROM RIPPING OFF THE LID OF THE TRUNK AND GETTING IN HERE?
LIGHT. THEY CAN'T STAND THE LIGHT.
AS LONG AS WE'VE GOT THAT, WE'VE GOT NOTHING TO WORRY ABOUT.
ROADSIDE EMERGENCY KIT
FUUUUUUUUUU—

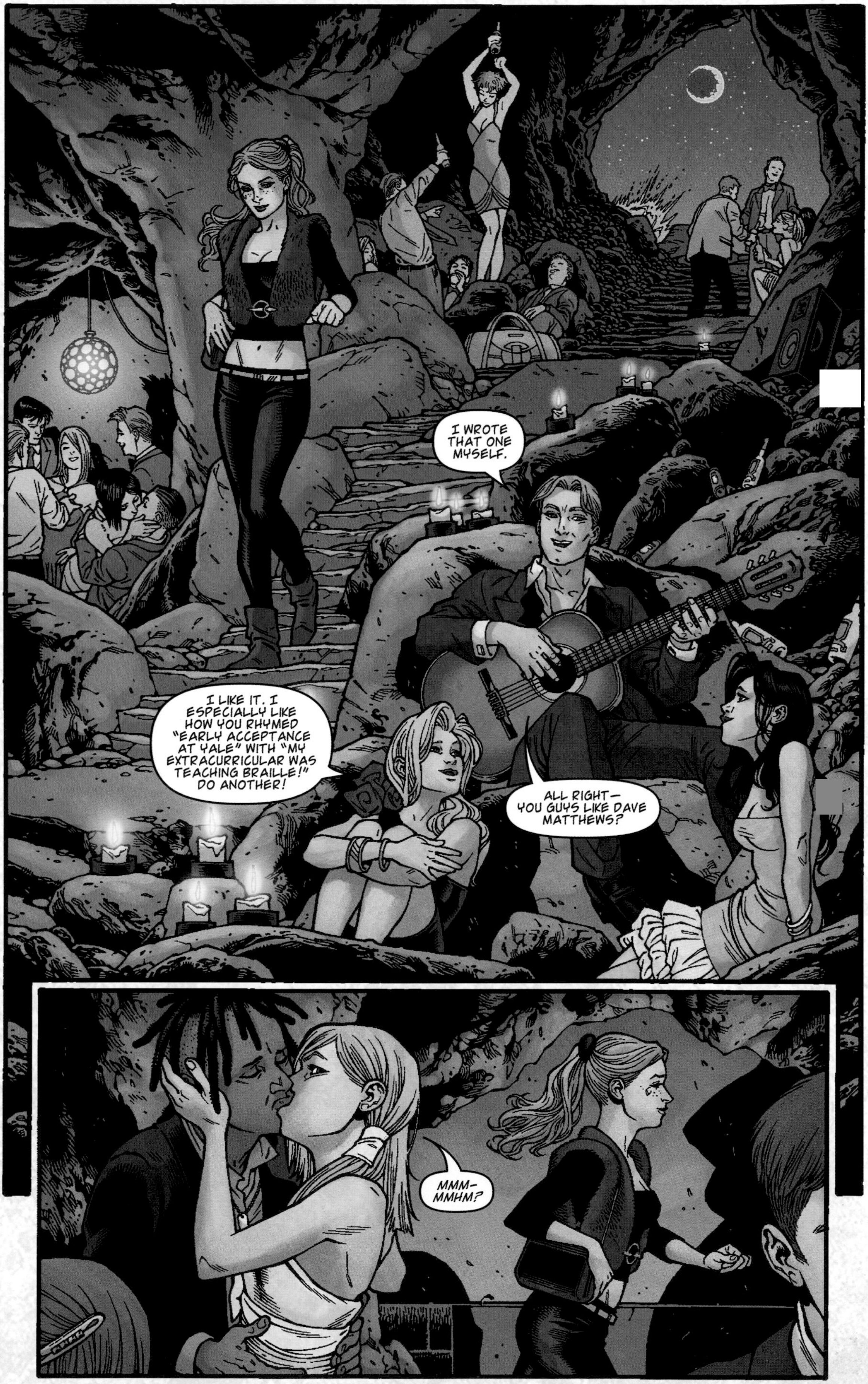
I WROTE THAT ONE MYSELF.
I LIKE IT. I ESPECIALLY LIKE HOW YOU RHYMED "EARLY ACCEPTANCE AT YALE" WITH "MY EXTRACURRICULAR WAS TEACHING BRAILLE!" DO ANOTHER!
ALL RIGHT— YOU GUYS LIKE DAVE MATTHEWS?
MMM-MMHM?

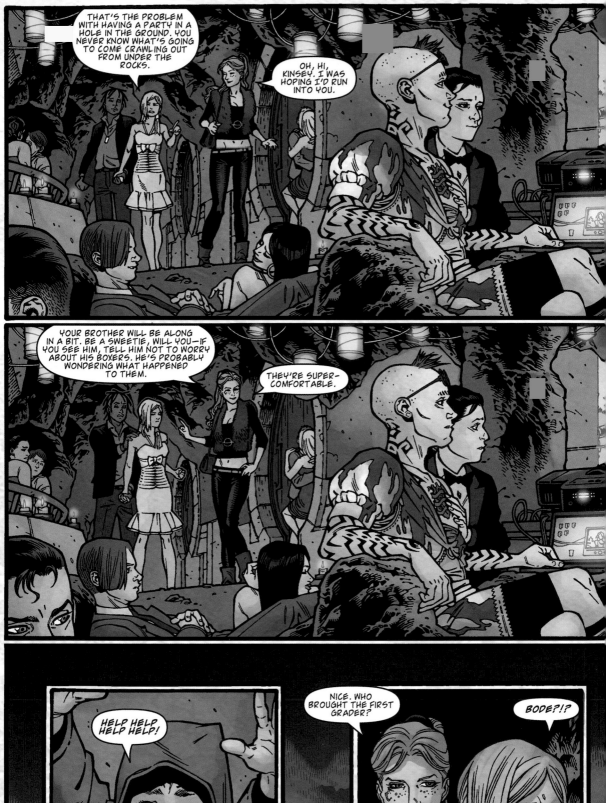

THAT'S THE PROBLEM WITH HAVING A PARTY IN A HOLE IN THE GROUND. YOU NEVER KNOW WHAT'S GOING TO COME CRAWLING OUT FROM UNDER THE ROCKS.

OH, HI, KINSEY. I WAS HOPING I'D RUN INTO YOU.

YOUR BROTHER WILL BE ALONG IN A BIT. BE A SWEETIE, WILL YOU—IF YOU SEE HIM, TELL HIM NOT TO WORRY ABOUT HIS BOXERS. HE'S PROBABLY WONDERING WHAT HAPPENED TO THEM.

THEY'RE SUPER-COMFORTABLE.

HELP HELP HELP HELP!

NICE. WHO BROUGHT THE FIRST GRADER?

BODE?!?

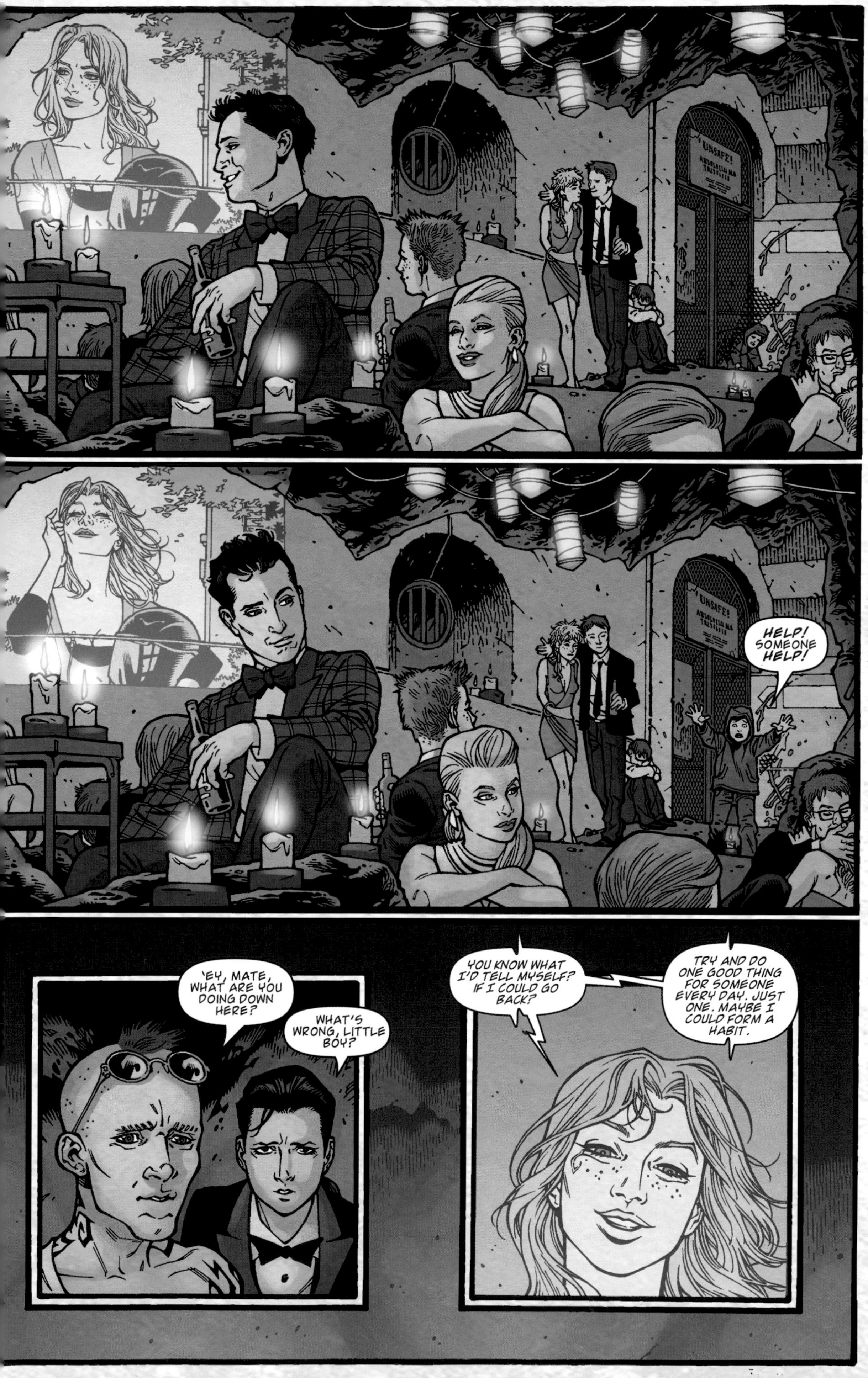
UNSAFE!
UNSAFE!
HELP! SOMEONE HELP!
'EY, MATE, WHAT ARE YOU DOING DOWN HERE?
WHAT'S WRONG, LITTLE BOY?
YOU KNOW WHAT I'D TELL MYSELF? IF I COULD GO BACK?
TRY AND DO ONE GOOD THING FOR SOMEONE EVERY DAY. JUST ONE. MAYBE I COULD FORM A HABIT.

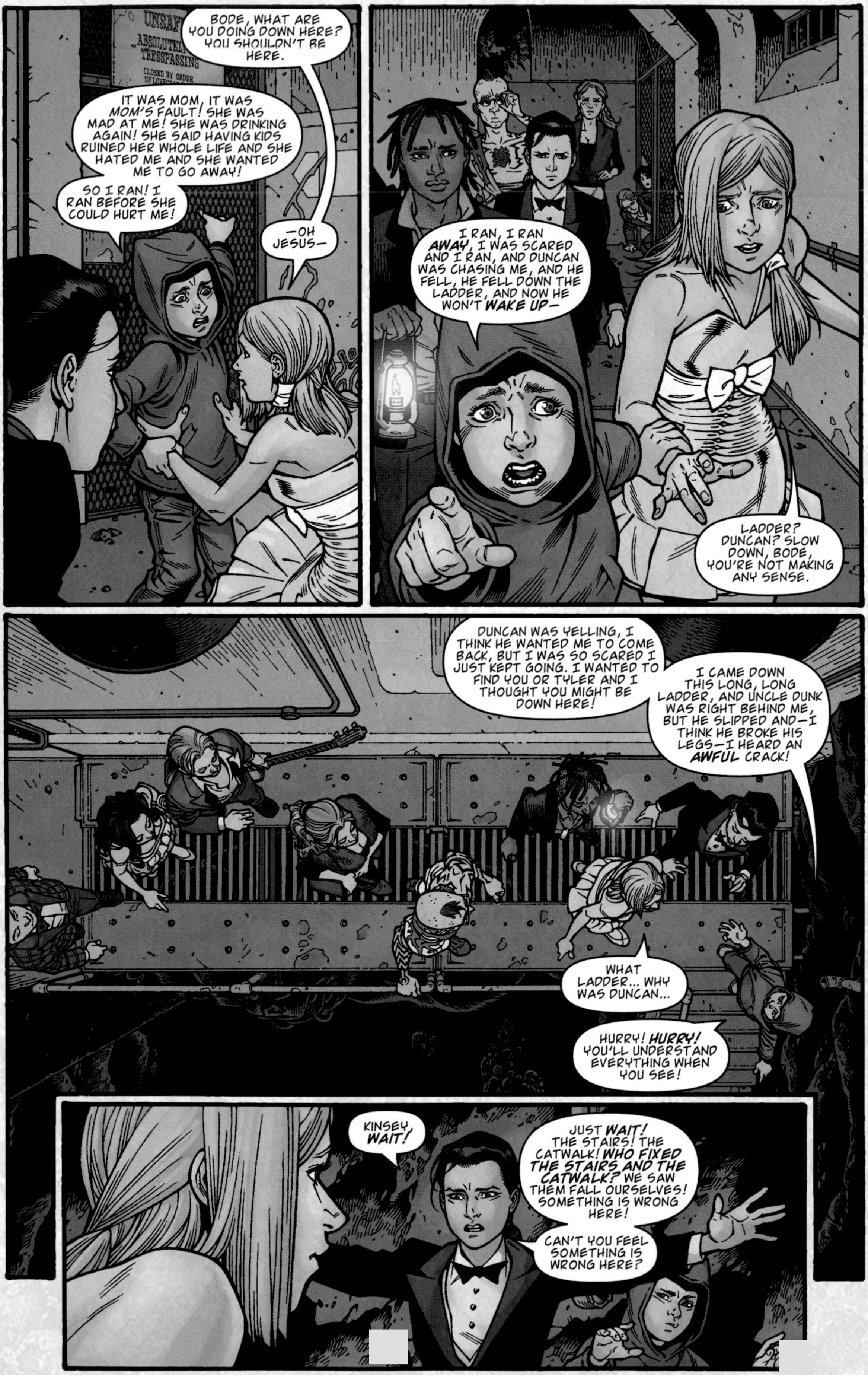
BODE, WHAT ARE YOU DOING DOWN HERE? YOU SHOULDN'T BE HERE.
IT WAS MOM, IT WAS MOM'S FAULT! SHE WAS MAD AT ME! SHE WAS DRINKING AGAIN! SHE SAID HAVING KIDS RUINED HER WHOLE LIFE AND SHE HATED ME AND SHE WANTED ME TO GO AWAY!
SO I RAN! I RAN BEFORE SHE COULD HURT ME!
—OH JESUS—
TRESSPASSING
CLOSED BY ORDER
I RAN, I RAN AWAY, I WAS SCARED AND I RAN, AND DUNCAN WAS CHASING ME, AND HE FELL, HE FELL DOWN THE LADDER, AND NOW HE WON'T WAKE UP—
LADDER? DUNCAN? SLOW DOWN, BODE, YOU'RE NOT MAKING ANY SENSE.
DUNCAN WAS YELLING, I THINK HE WANTED ME TO COME BACK, BUT I WAS SO SCARED I JUST KEPT GOING. I WANTED TO FIND YOU OR TYLER AND I THOUGHT YOU MIGHT BE DOWN HERE!
I CAME DOWN THIS LONG, LONG LADDER, AND UNCLE DUNK WAS RIGHT BEHIND ME, BUT HE SLIPPED AND—I THINK HE BROKE HIS LEGS—I HEARD AN AWFUL CRACK!
WHAT LADDER... WHY WAS DUNCAN...
HURRY! HURRY! YOU'LL UNDERSTAND EVERYTHING WHEN YOU SEE!
KINSEY, WAIT!
JUST WAIT! THE STAIRS! THE CATWALK! WHO FIXED THE STAIRS AND THE CATWALK? WE SAW THEM FALL OURSELVES! SOMETHING IS WRONG HERE!
CAN'T YOU FEEL SOMETHING IS WRONG HERE?

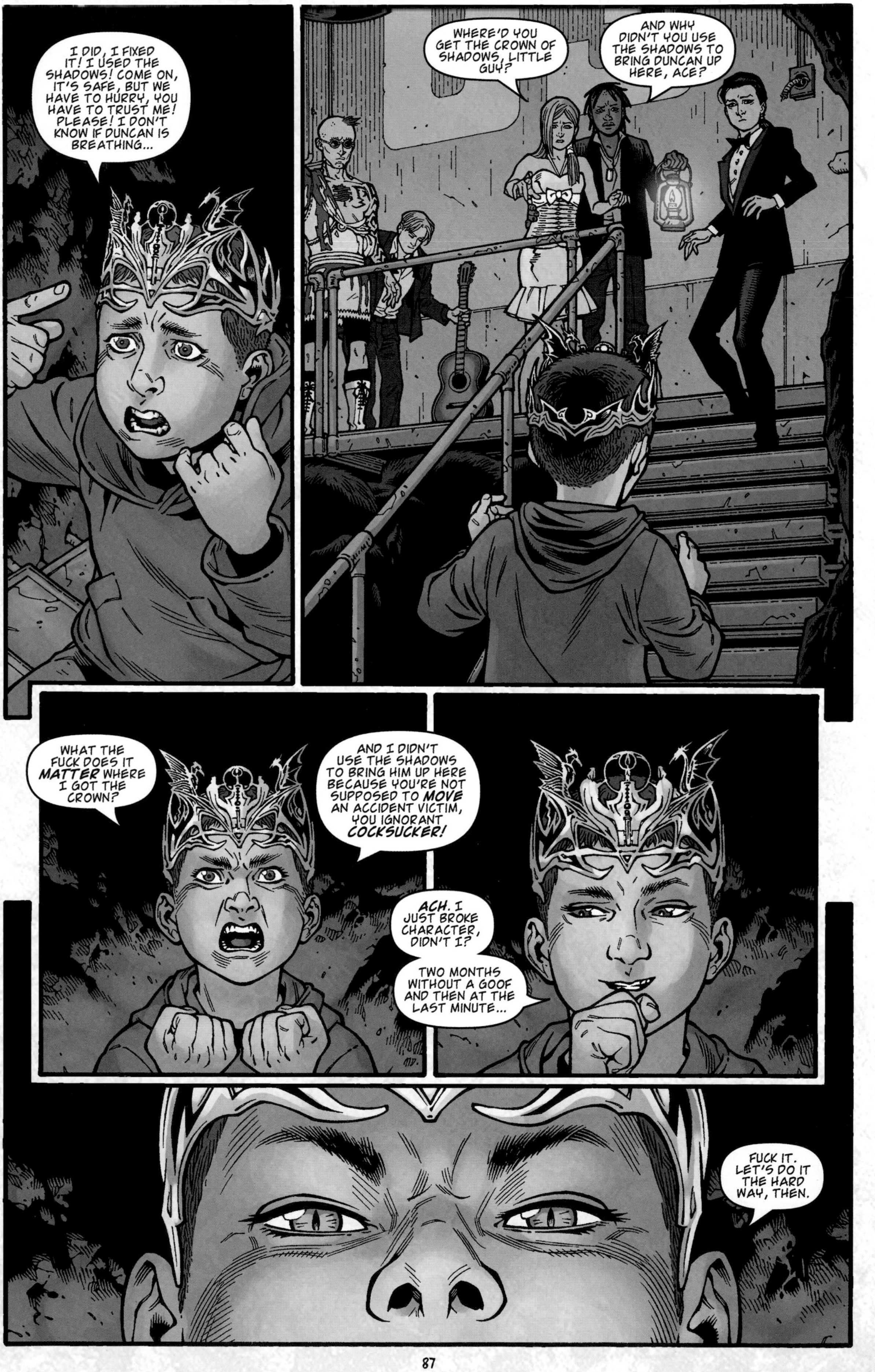
I DID, I FIXED IT! I USED THE SHADOWS! COME ON, IT'S SAFE, BUT WE HAVE TO HURRY, YOU HAVE TO TRUST ME! PLEASE! I DON'T KNOW IF DUNCAN IS BREATHING...
WHERE'D YOU GET THE CROWN OF SHADOWS, LITTLE GUY?
AND WHY DIDN'T YOU USE THE SHADOWS TO BRING DUNCAN UP HERE, ACE?
WHAT THE FUCK DOES IT MATTER WHERE I GOT THE CROWN?
AND I DIDN'T USE THE SHADOWS TO BRING HIM UP HERE BECAUSE YOU'RE NOT SUPPOSED TO MOVE AN ACCIDENT VICTIM, YOU IGNORANT COCKSUCKER!
ACH. I JUST BROKE CHARACTER, DIDN'T I?
TWO MONTHS WITHOUT A GOOF AND THEN AT THE LAST MINUTE...
FUCK IT. LET'S DO IT THE HARD WAY, THEN.

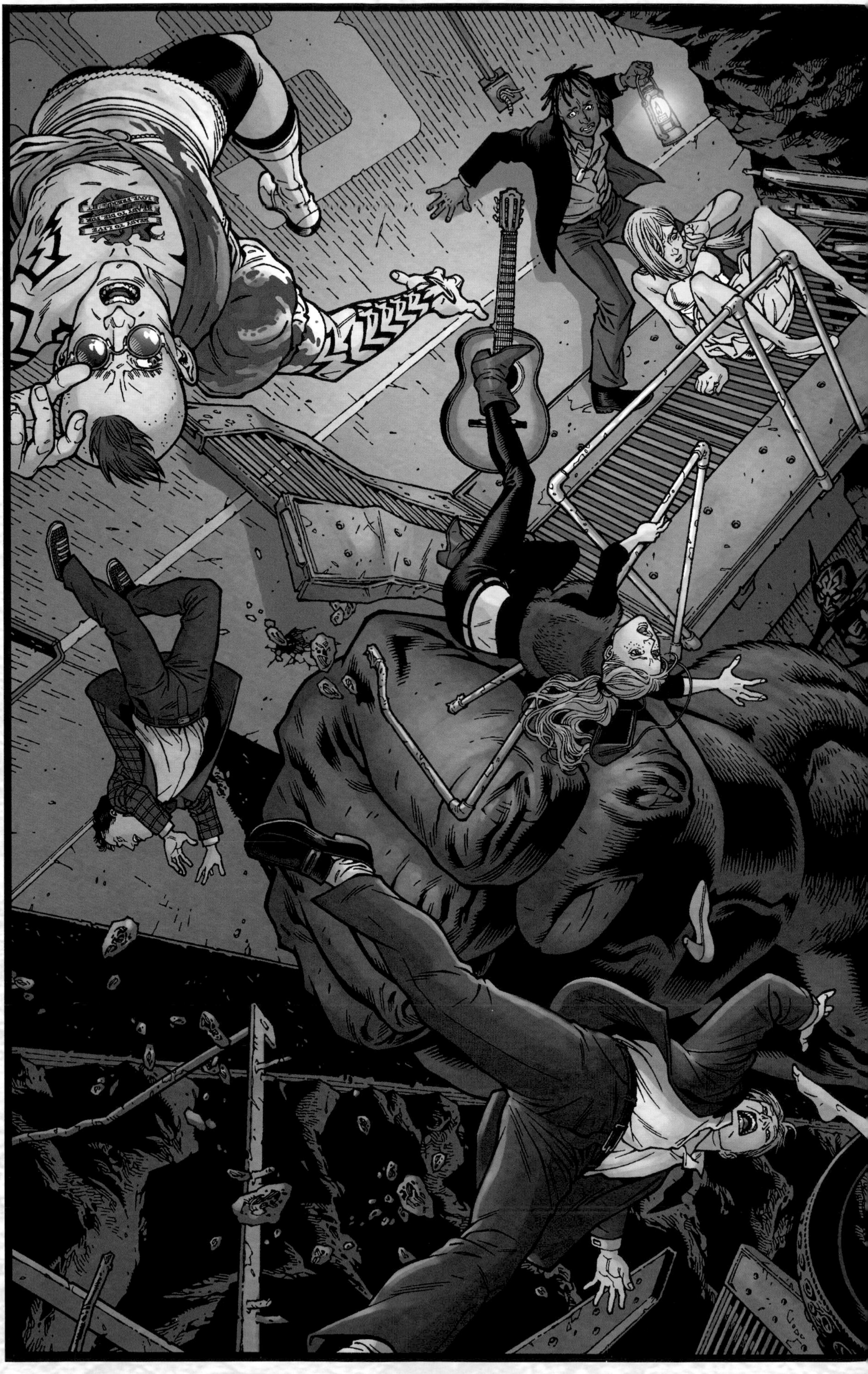

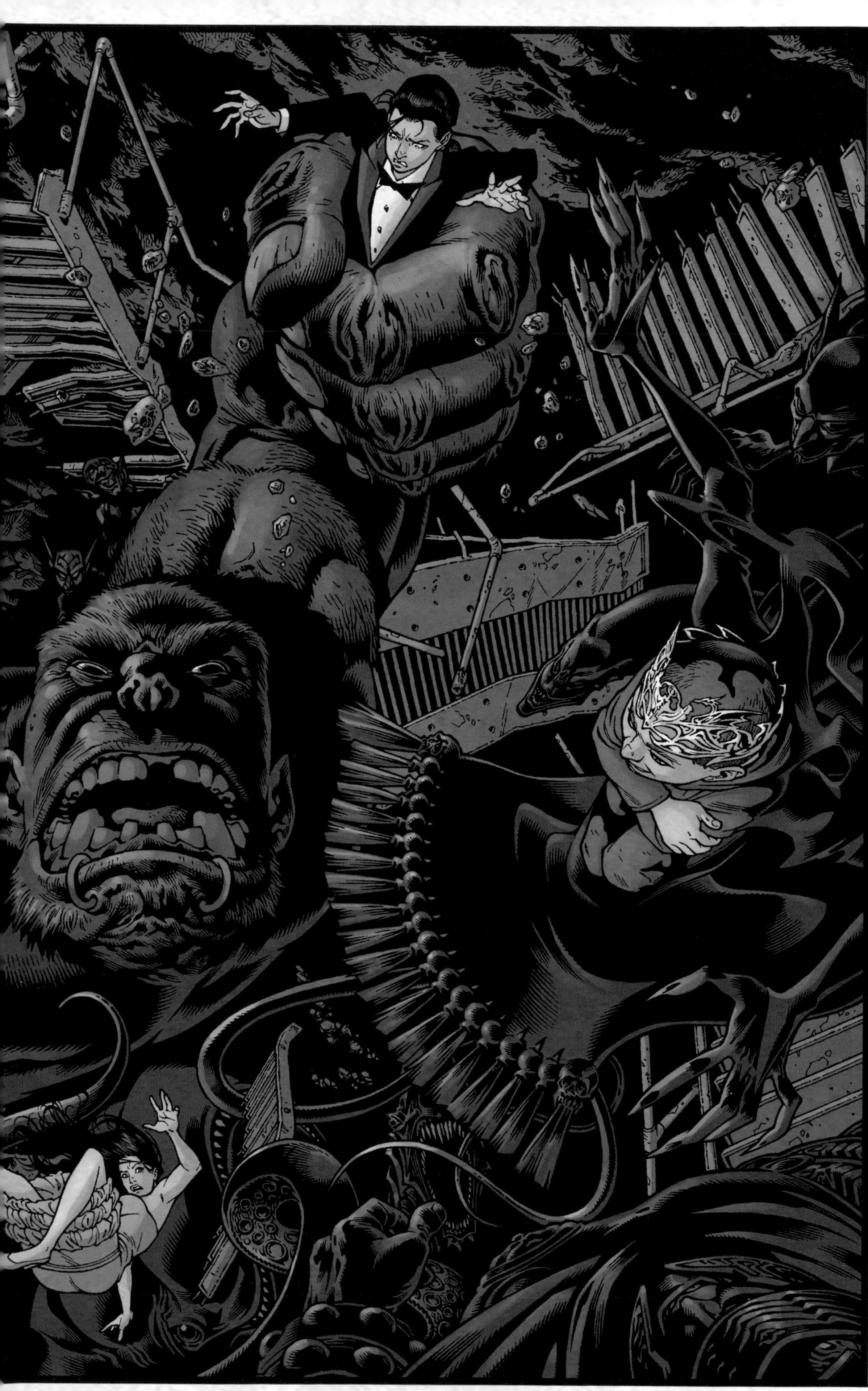

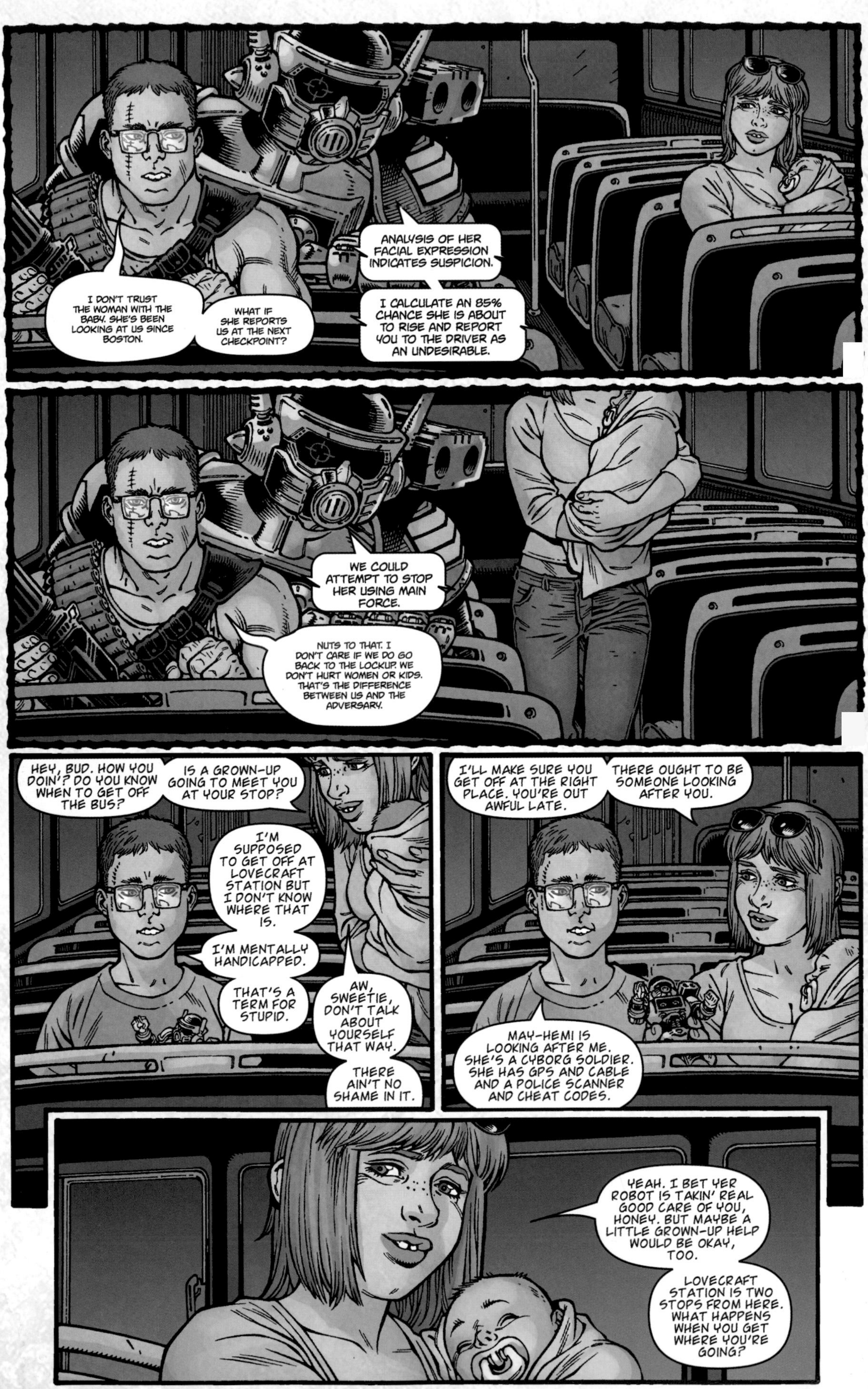
I DON'T TRUST THE WOMAN WITH THE BABY. SHE'S BEEN LOOKING AT US SINCE BOSTON.
WHAT IF SHE REPORTS US AT THE NEXT CHECKPOINT?
ANALYSIS OF HER FACIAL EXPRESSION INDICATES SUSPICION.
I CALCULATE AN 85% CHANCE SHE IS ABOUT TO RISE AND REPORT YOU TO THE DRIVER AS AN UNDESIRABLE.
WE COULD ATTEMPT TO STOP HER USING MAIN FORCE.
NUTS TO THAT. I DON'T CARE IF WE DO GO BACK TO THE LOCKUP. WE DON'T HURT WOMEN OR KIDS. THAT'S THE DIFFERENCE BETWEEN US AND THE ADVERSARY.
HEY, BUD. HOW YOU DOIN'? DO YOU KNOW WHEN TO GET OFF THE BUS?
IS A GROWN-UP GOING TO MEET YOU AT YOUR STOP?
I'M SUPPOSED TO GET OFF AT LOVECRAFT STATION BUT I DON'T KNOW WHERE THAT IS.
I'M MENTALLY HANDICAPPED.
THAT'S A TERM FOR STUPID.
AW, SWEETIE, DON'T TALK ABOUT YOURSELF THAT WAY.
THERE AIN'T NO SHAME IN IT.
I'LL MAKE SURE YOU GET OFF AT THE RIGHT PLACE. YOU'RE OUT AWFUL LATE.
THERE OUGHT TO BE SOMEONE LOOKING AFTER YOU.
MAY-HEMI IS LOOKING AFTER ME. SHE'S A CYBORG SOLDIER. SHE HAS GPS AND CABLE AND A POLICE SCANNER AND CHEAT CODES.
YEAH. I BET YER ROBOT IS TAKIN' REAL GOOD CARE OF YOU, HONEY. BUT MAYBE A LITTLE GROWN-UP HELP WOULD BE OKAY, TOO.
LOVECRAFT STATION IS TWO STOPS FROM HERE. WHAT HAPPENS WHEN YOU GET WHERE YOU'RE GOING?

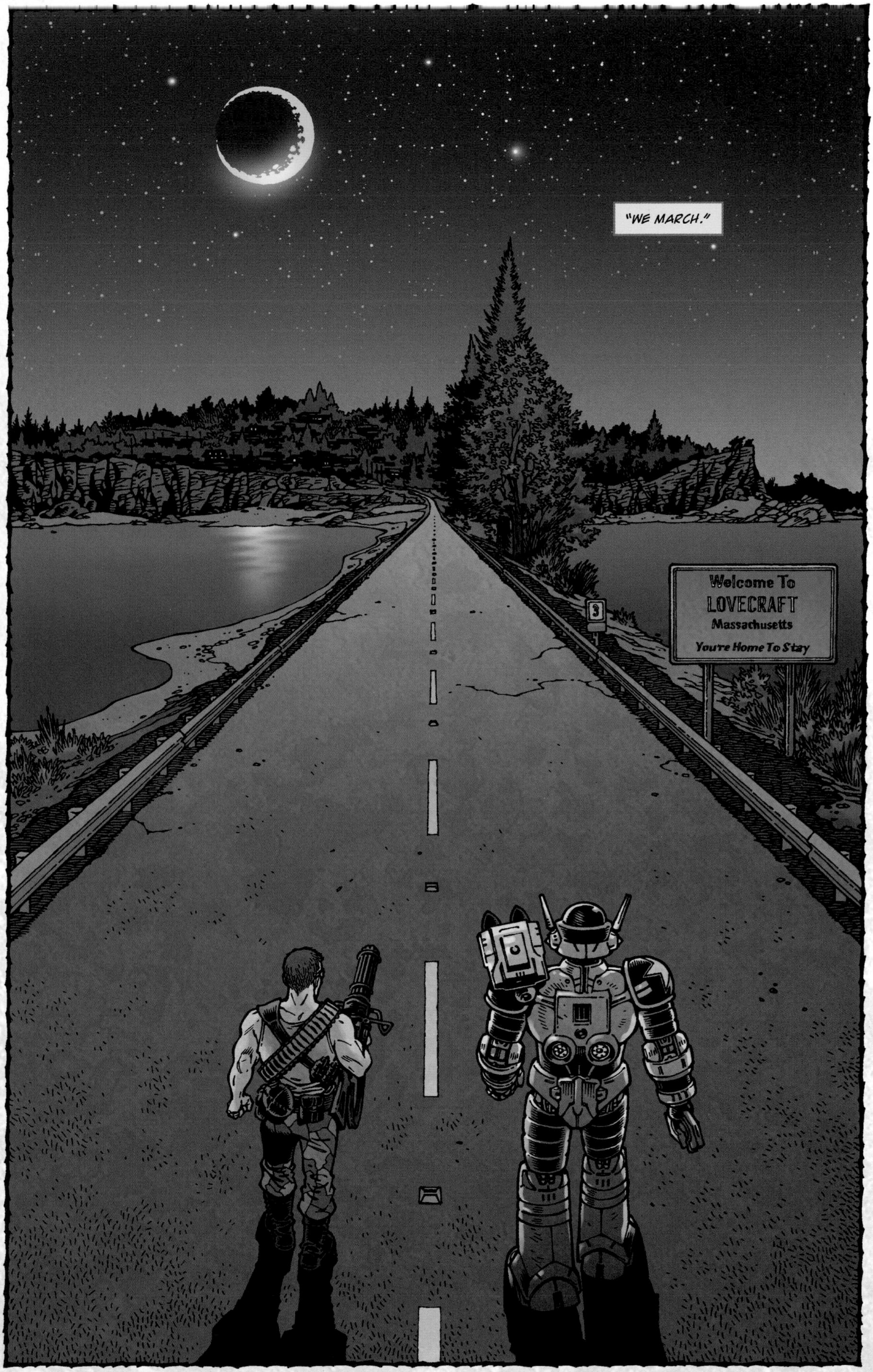
"WE MARCH."
Welcome To
LOVECRAFT
Massachusetts
You're Home To Stay
3

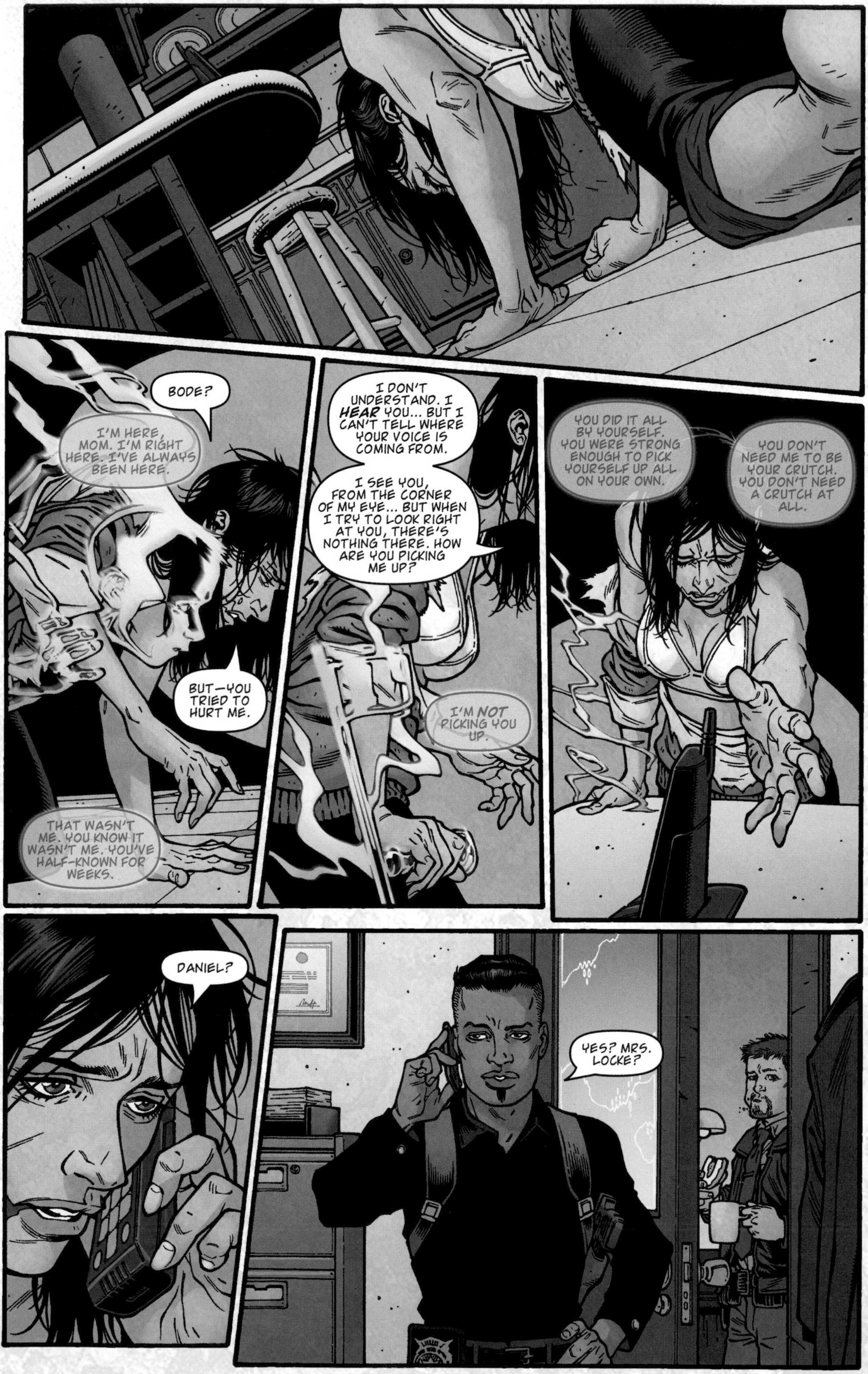
BODE?
I'M HERE, MOM. I'M RIGHT HERE. I'VE ALWAYS BEEN HERE.
BUT—YOU TRIED TO HURT ME.
THAT WASN'T ME. YOU KNOW IT WASN'T ME. YOU'VE HALF-KNOWN FOR WEEKS.
I DON'T UNDERSTAND. I HEAR YOU... BUT I CAN'T TELL WHERE YOUR VOICE IS COMING FROM.
I SEE YOU, FROM THE CORNER OF MY EYE... BUT WHEN I TRY TO LOOK RIGHT AT YOU, THERE'S NOTHING THERE. HOW ARE YOU PICKING ME UP?
I'M NOT PICKING YOU UP.
YOU DID IT ALL BY YOURSELF. YOU WERE STRONG ENOUGH TO PICK YOURSELF UP ALL ON YOUR OWN.
YOU DON'T NEED ME TO BE YOUR CRUTCH. YOU DON'T NEED A CRUTCH AT ALL.
DANIEL?
YES? MRS. LOCKE?

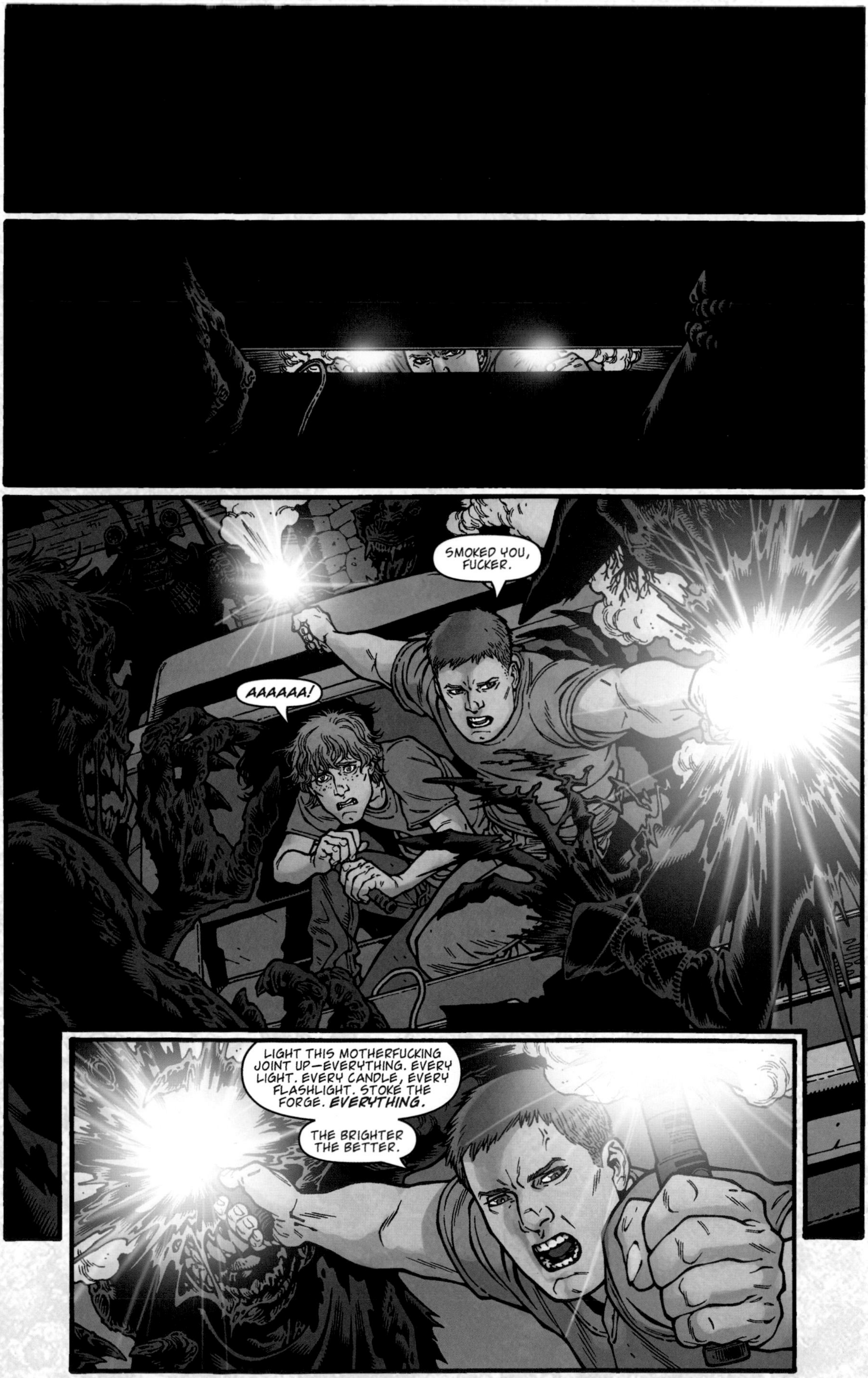
SMOKED YOU, FUCKER.
AAAAAA!
LIGHT THIS MOTHERFUCKING JOINT UP—EVERYTHING. EVERY LIGHT. EVERY CANDLE, EVERY FLASHLIGHT. STOKE THE FORGE. EVERYTHING.
THE BRIGHTER THE BETTER.

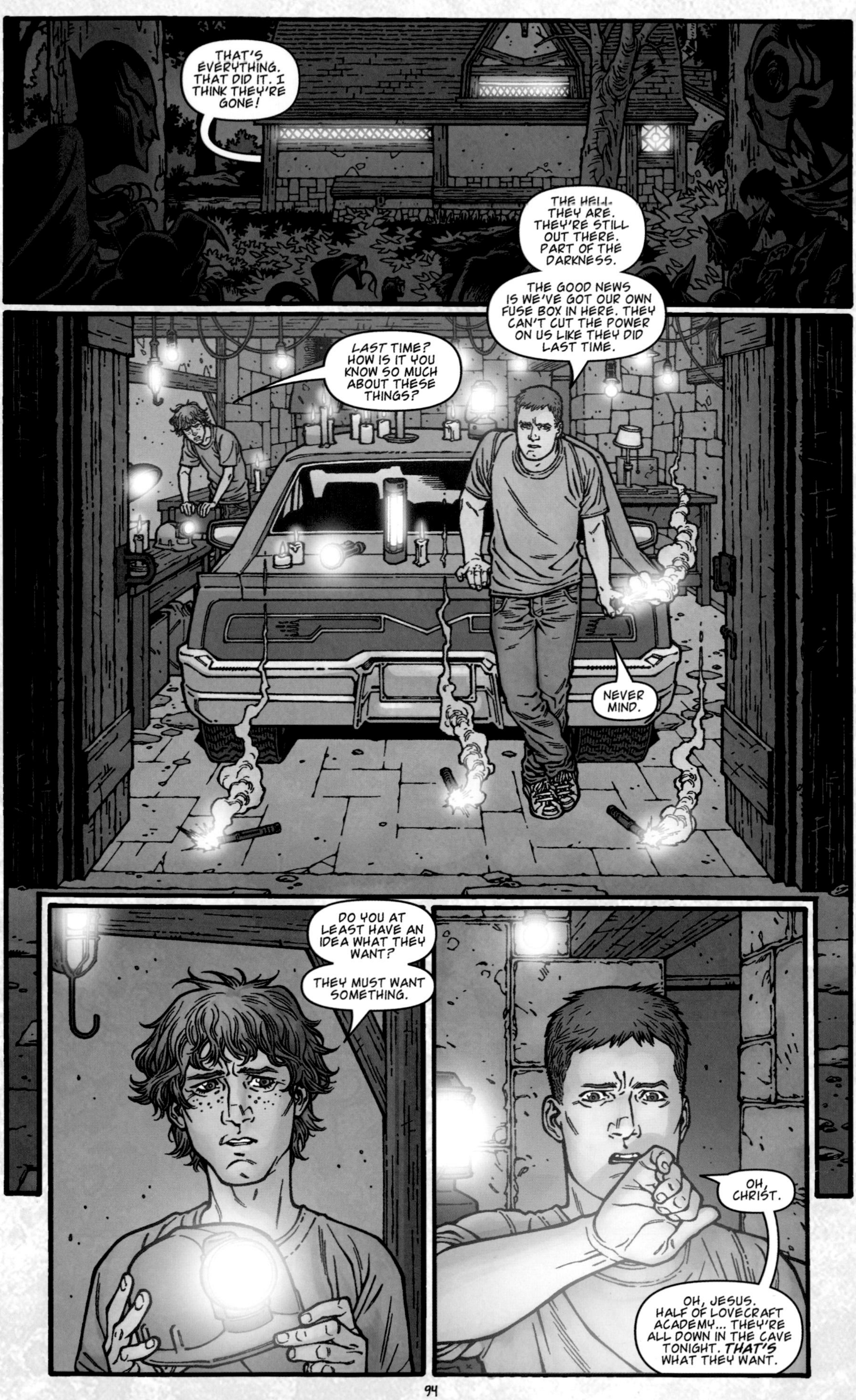
THAT'S EVERYTHING. THAT DID IT. I THINK THEY'RE GONE!
THE HELL THEY ARE. THEY'RE STILL OUT THERE. PART OF THE DARKNESS.
THE GOOD NEWS IS WE'VE GOT OUR OWN FUSE BOX IN HERE. THEY CAN'T CUT THE POWER ON US LIKE THEY DID LAST TIME.
LAST TIME? HOW IS IT YOU KNOW SO MUCH ABOUT THESE THINGS?
NEVER MIND.
DO YOU AT LEAST HAVE AN IDEA WHAT THEY WANT?
THEY MUST WANT SOMETHING.
OH, CHRIST.
OH, JESUS. HALF OF LOVECRAFT ACADEMY... THEY'RE ALL DOWN IN THE CAVE TONIGHT. *THAT'S* WHAT THEY WANT.

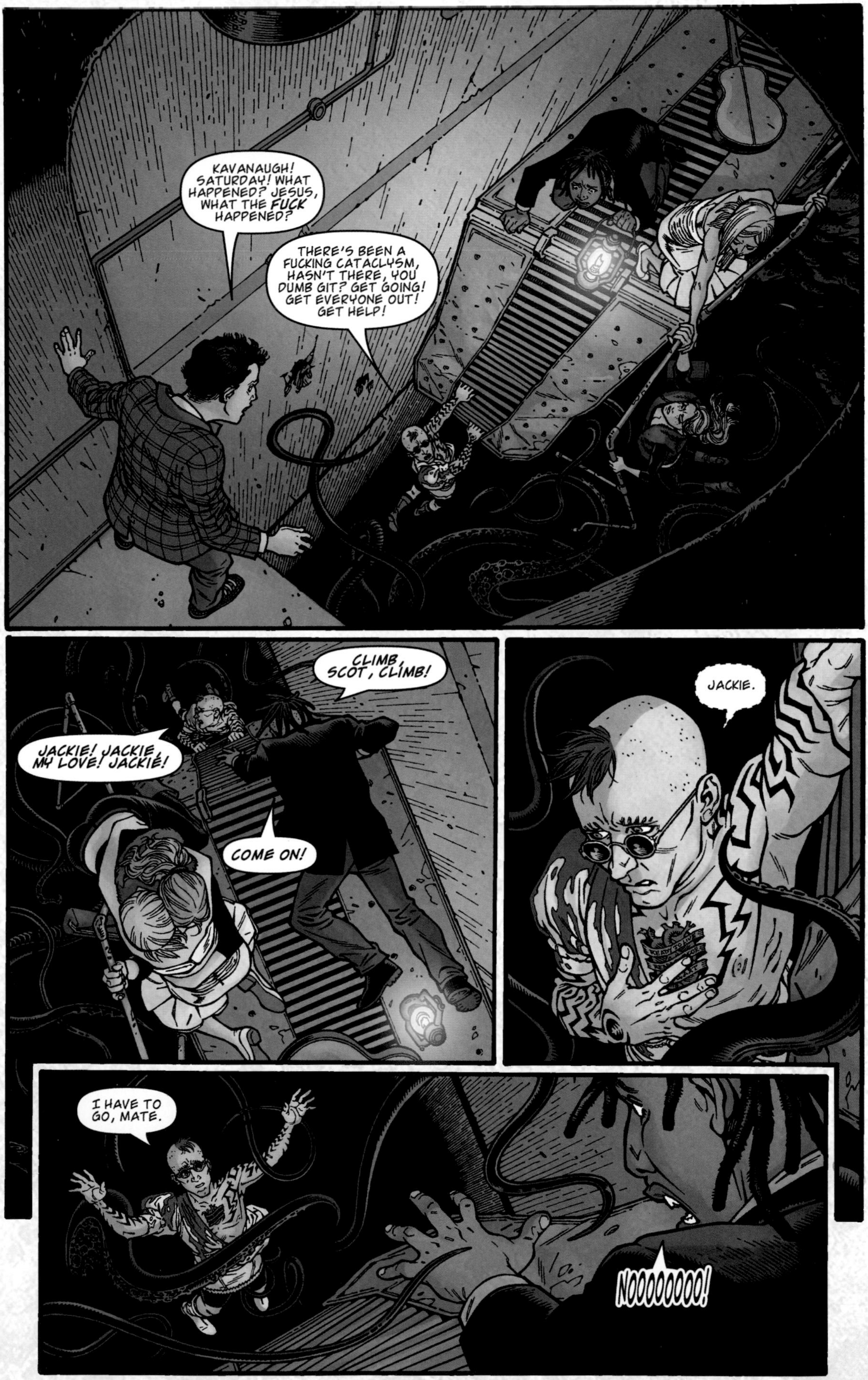
KAVANAUGH! SATURDAY! WHAT HAPPENED? JESUS, WHAT THE FUCK HAPPENED?
THERE'S BEEN A FUCKING CATACLYSM, HASN'T THERE, YOU DUMB GIT? GET GOING! GET EVERYONE OUT! GET HELP!
CLIMB, SCOT, CLIMB!
JACKIE! JACKIE, MY LOVE! JACKIE!
COME ON!
JACKIE.
I HAVE TO GO, MATE.
NOOOOOOOO!

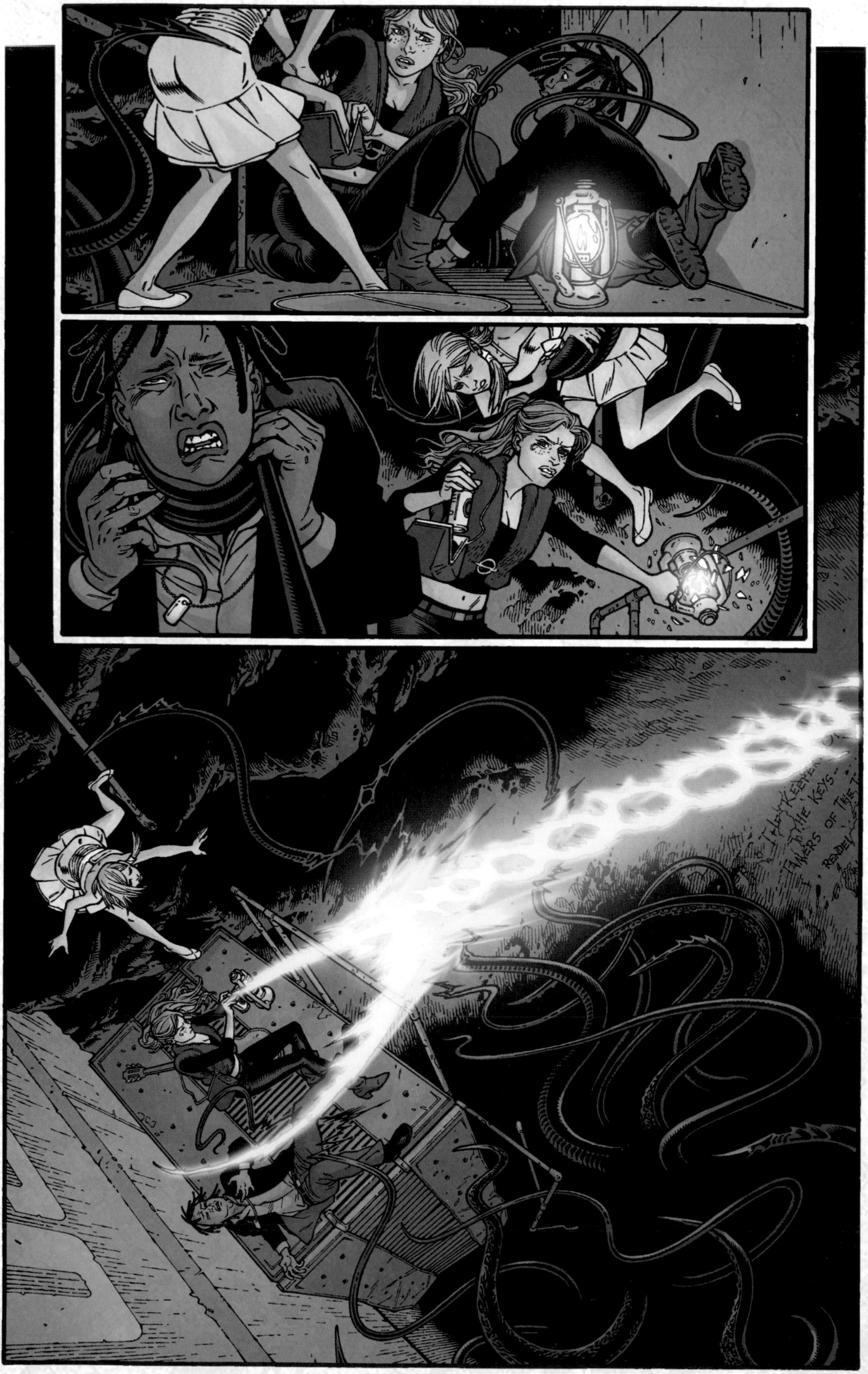
THE KEYS -
OF THE

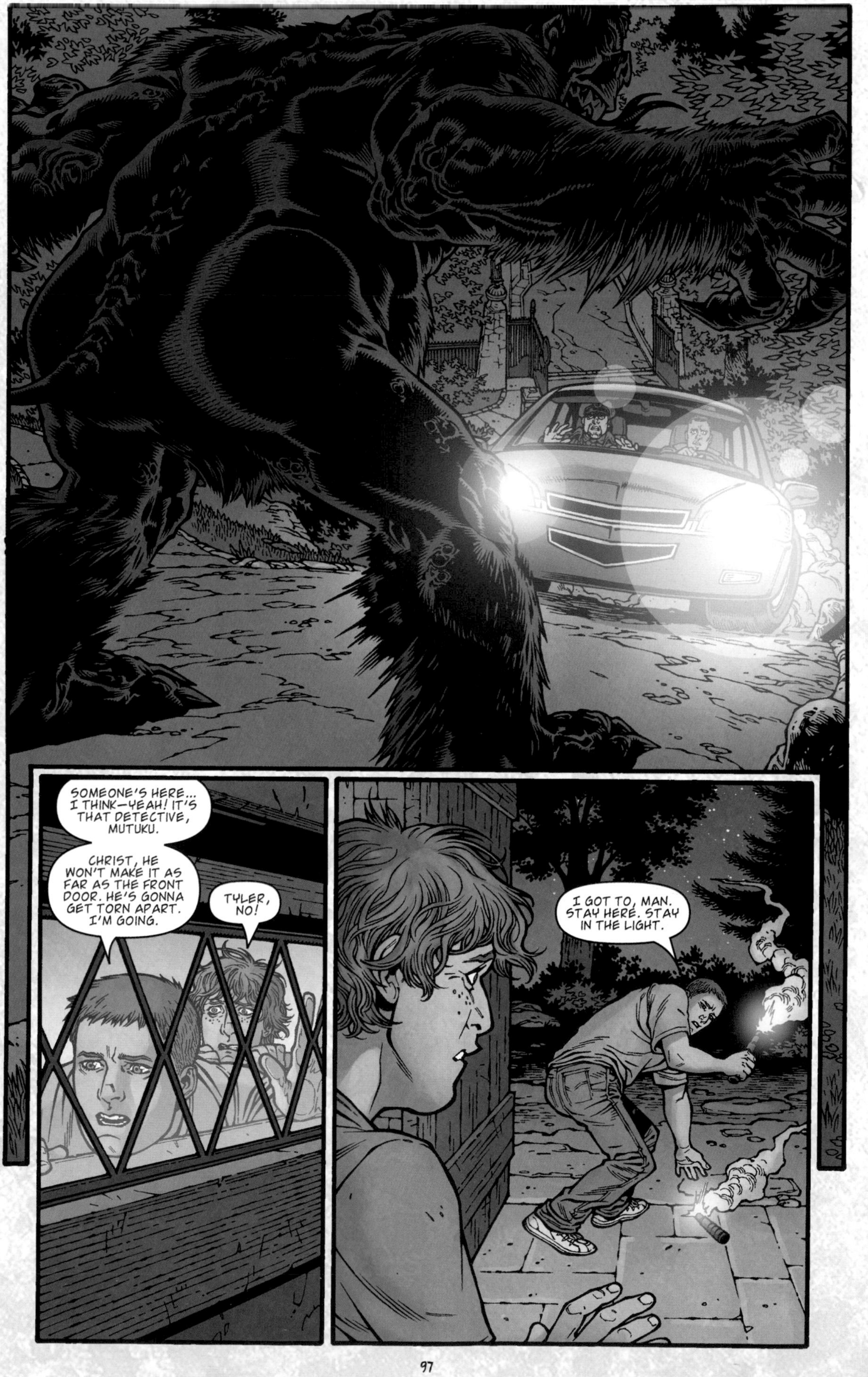
SOMEONE'S HERE... I THINK—YEAH! IT'S THAT DETECTIVE, MUTUKU.
CHRIST, HE WON'T MAKE IT AS FAR AS THE FRONT DOOR. HE'S GONNA GET TORN APART. I'M GOING.
TYLER, NO!
I GOT TO, MAN. STAY HERE. STAY IN THE LIGHT.

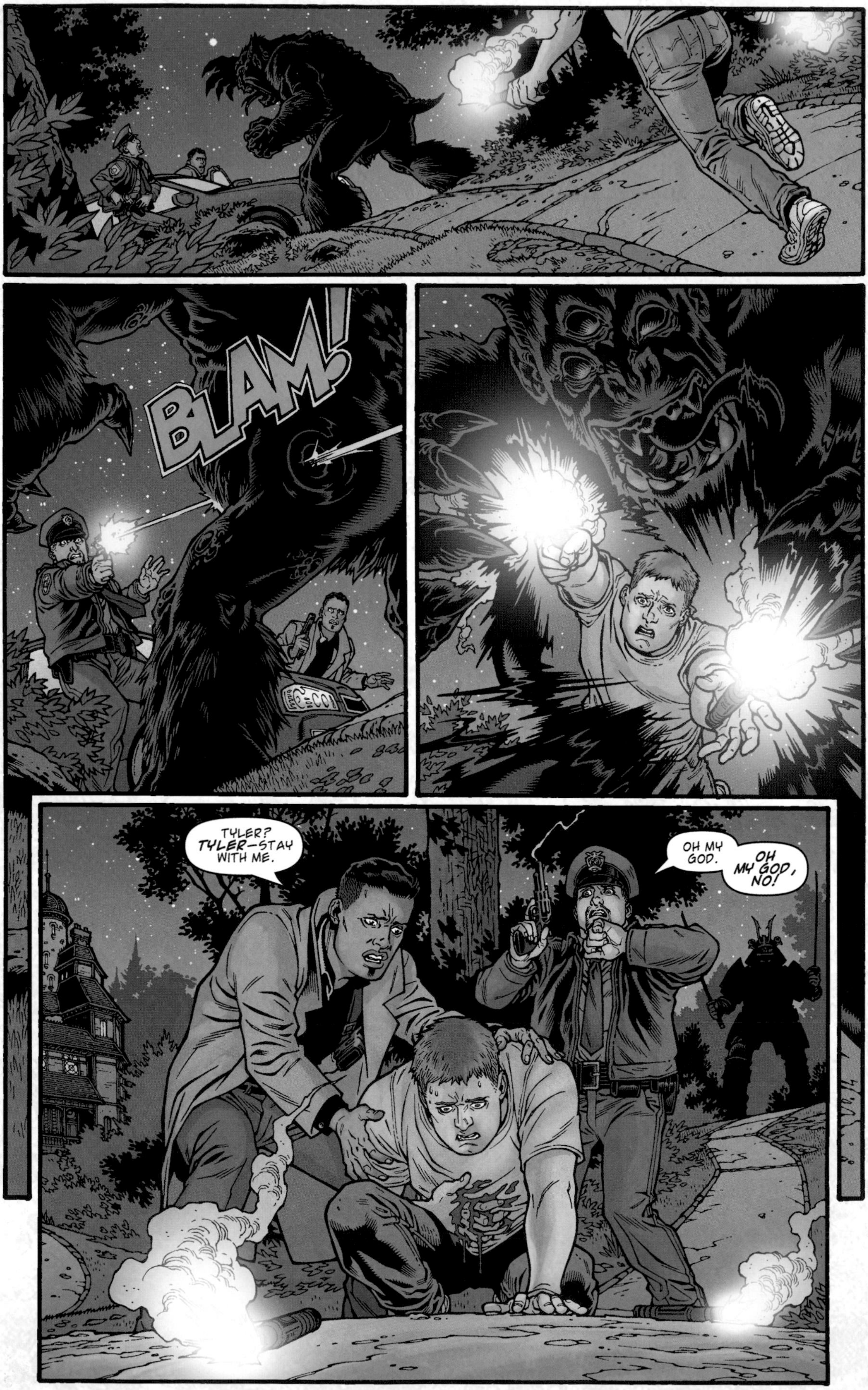
BLAM!
TYLER? TYLER—STAY WITH ME.
OH MY GOD.
OH MY GOD, NO!

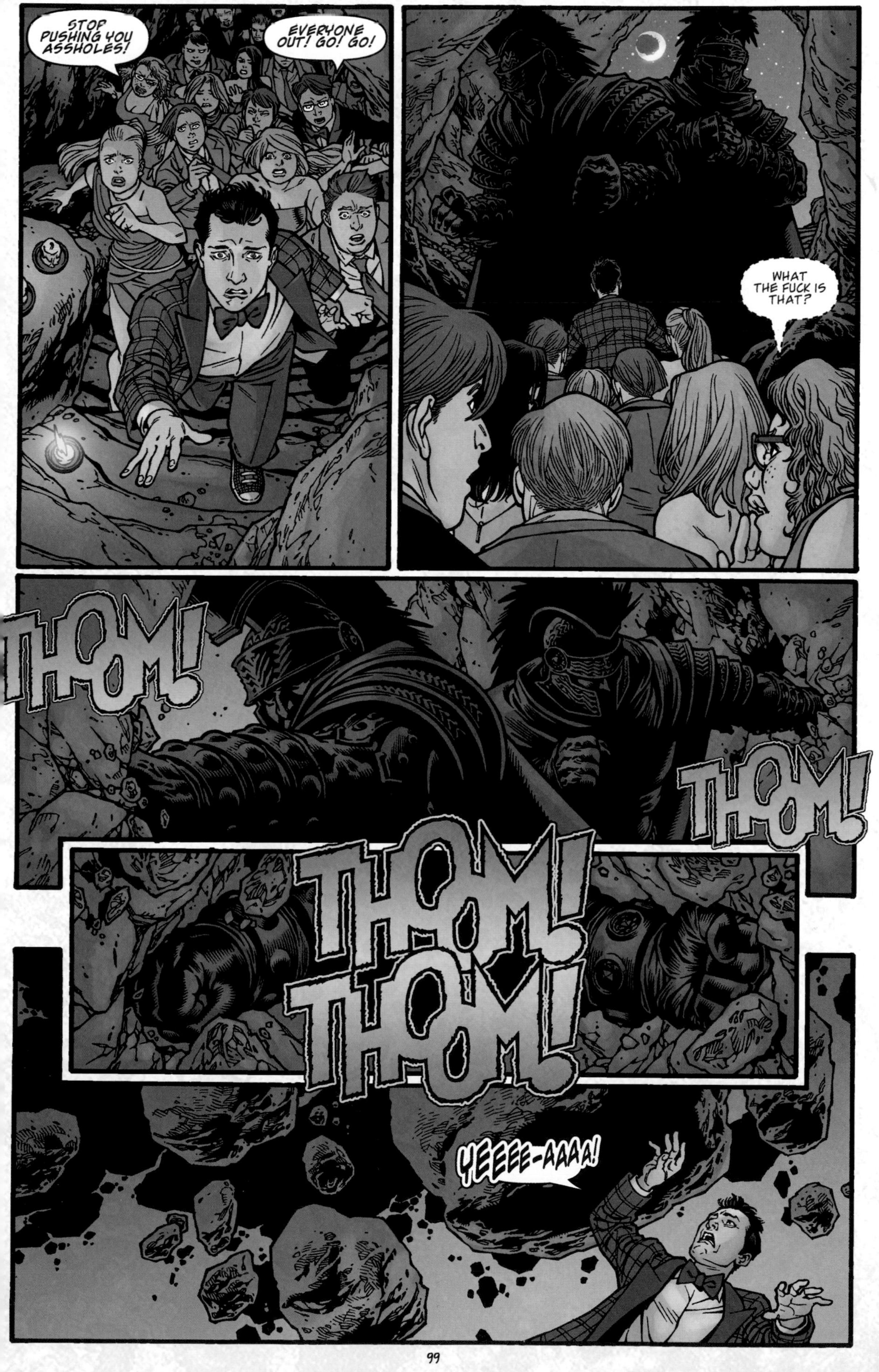
STOP PUSHING YOU ASSHOLES!
EVERYONE OUT! GO! GO!
WHAT THE FUCK IS THAT?
THOM!
THOM!
THOM!
THOM!
YEEEE-AAAA!

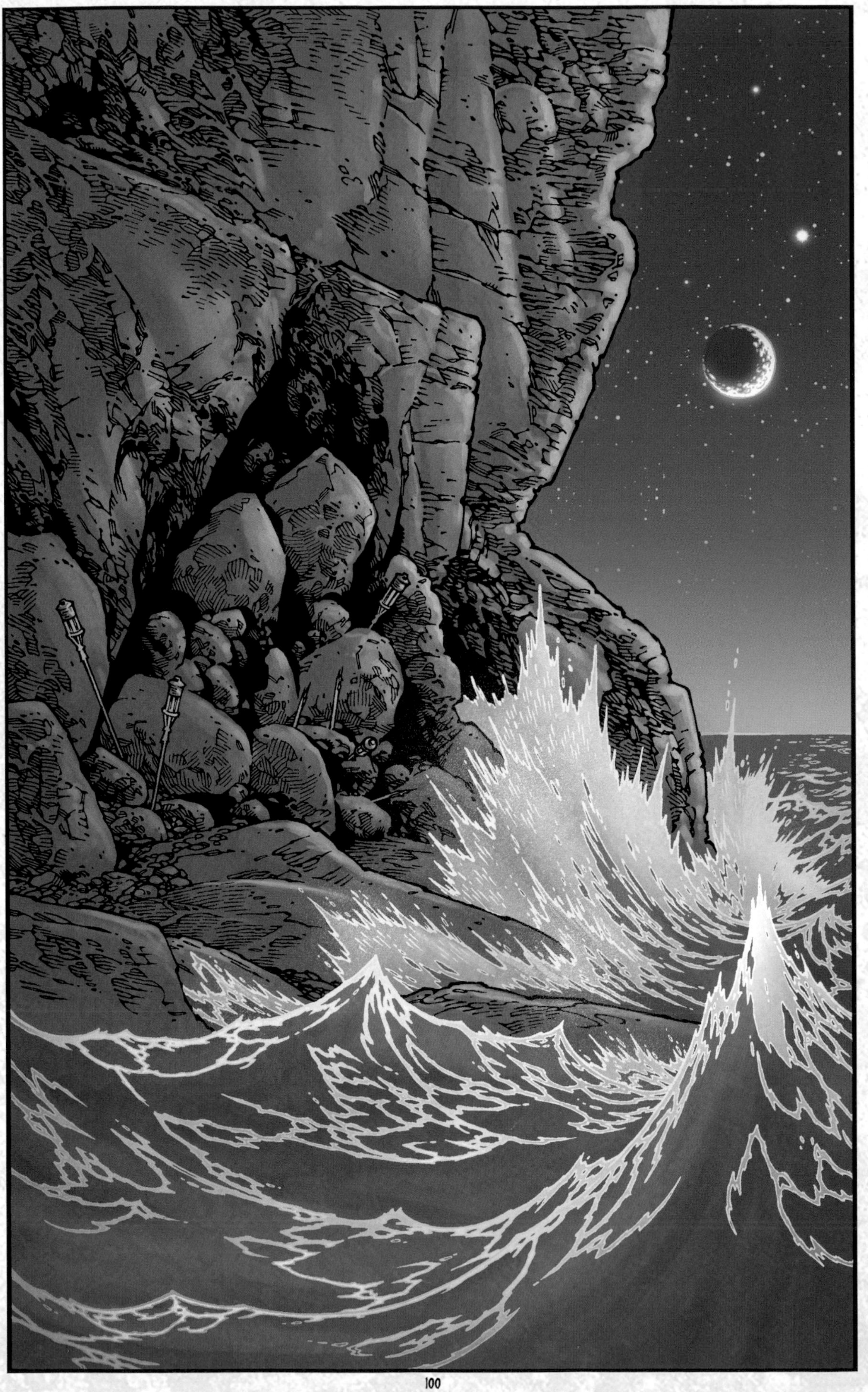

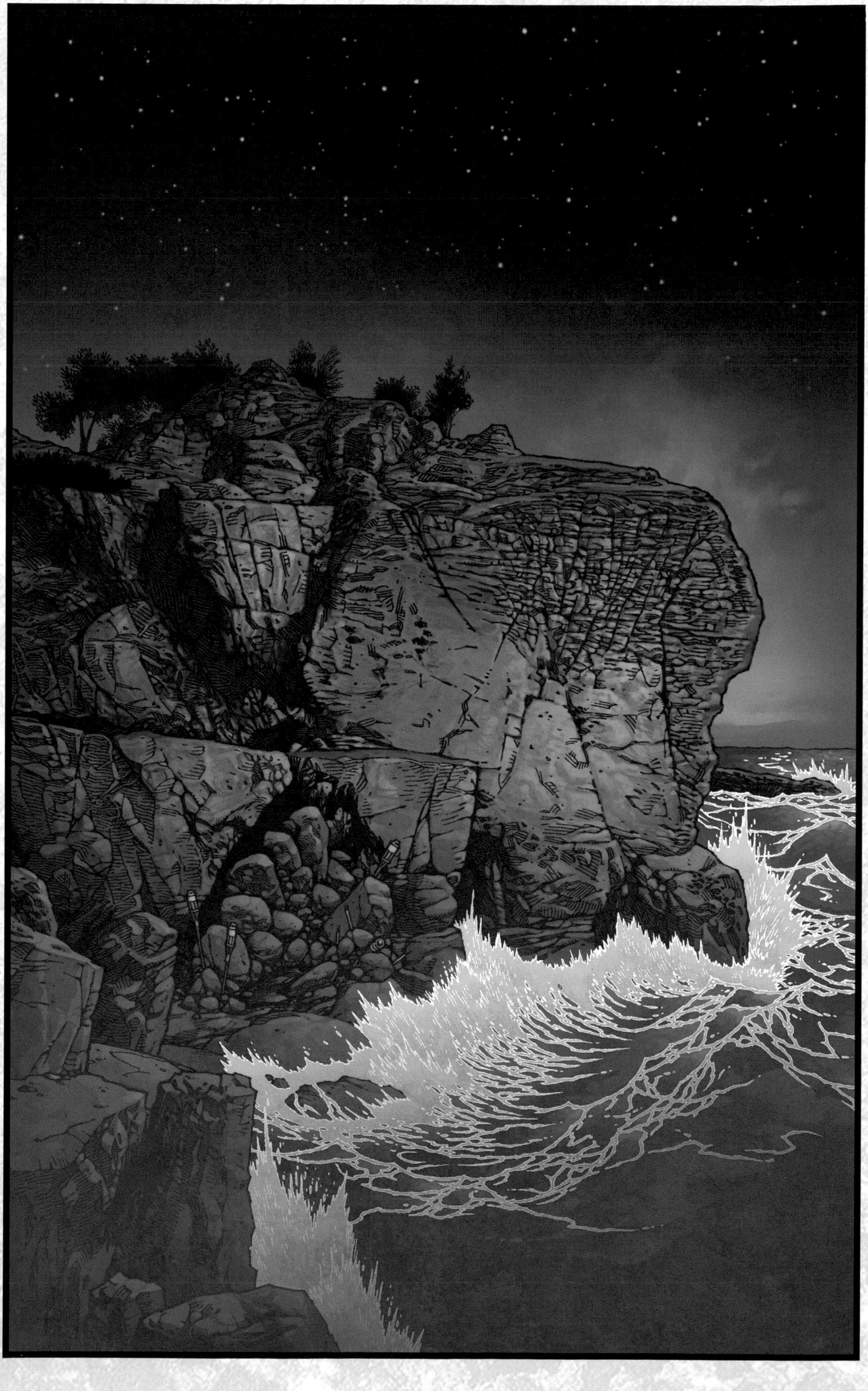

- ALPHA & OMEGA -

Chapter Five

THE FALL

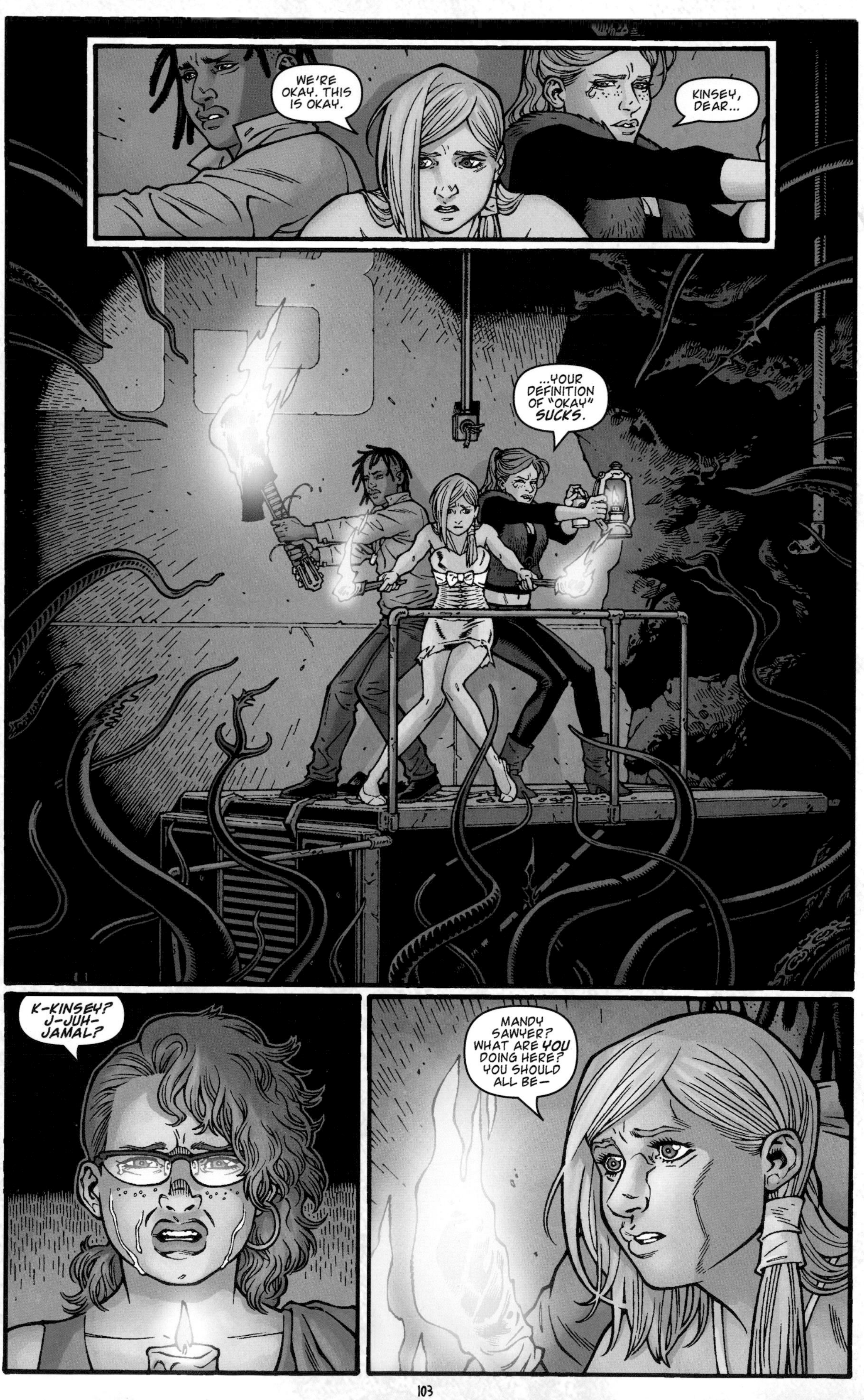
WE'RE OKAY. THIS IS OKAY.
KINSEY, DEAR...
...YOUR DEFINITION OF "OKAY" SUCKS.
K-KINSEY? J-JUH-JAMAL?
MANDY SAWYER? WHAT ARE YOU DOING HERE? YOU SHOULD ALL BE—

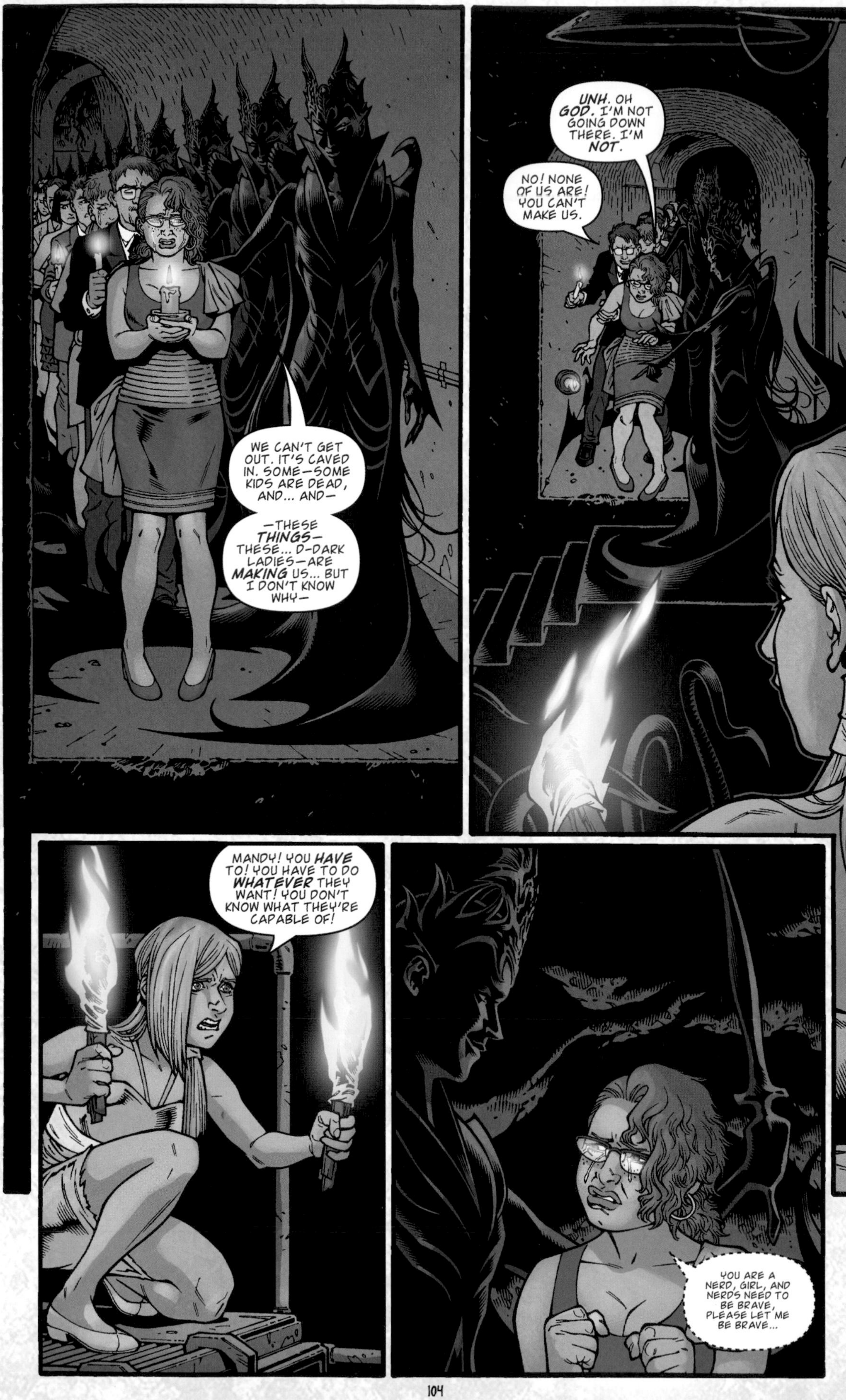

WE CAN'T GET OUT. IT'S CAVED IN. SOME—SOME KIDS ARE DEAD, AND... AND—
—THESE THINGS— THESE... D-DARK LADIES—ARE MAKING US... BUT I DON'T KNOW WHY—
UNH. OH GOD. I'M NOT GOING DOWN THERE. I'M NOT.
NO! NONE OF US ARE! YOU CAN'T MAKE US.
MANDY! YOU HAVE TO! YOU HAVE TO DO WHATEVER THEY WANT! YOU DON'T KNOW WHAT THEY'RE CAPABLE OF!
YOU ARE A NERD, GIRL, AND NERDS NEED TO BE BRAVE, PLEASE LET ME BE BRAVE...

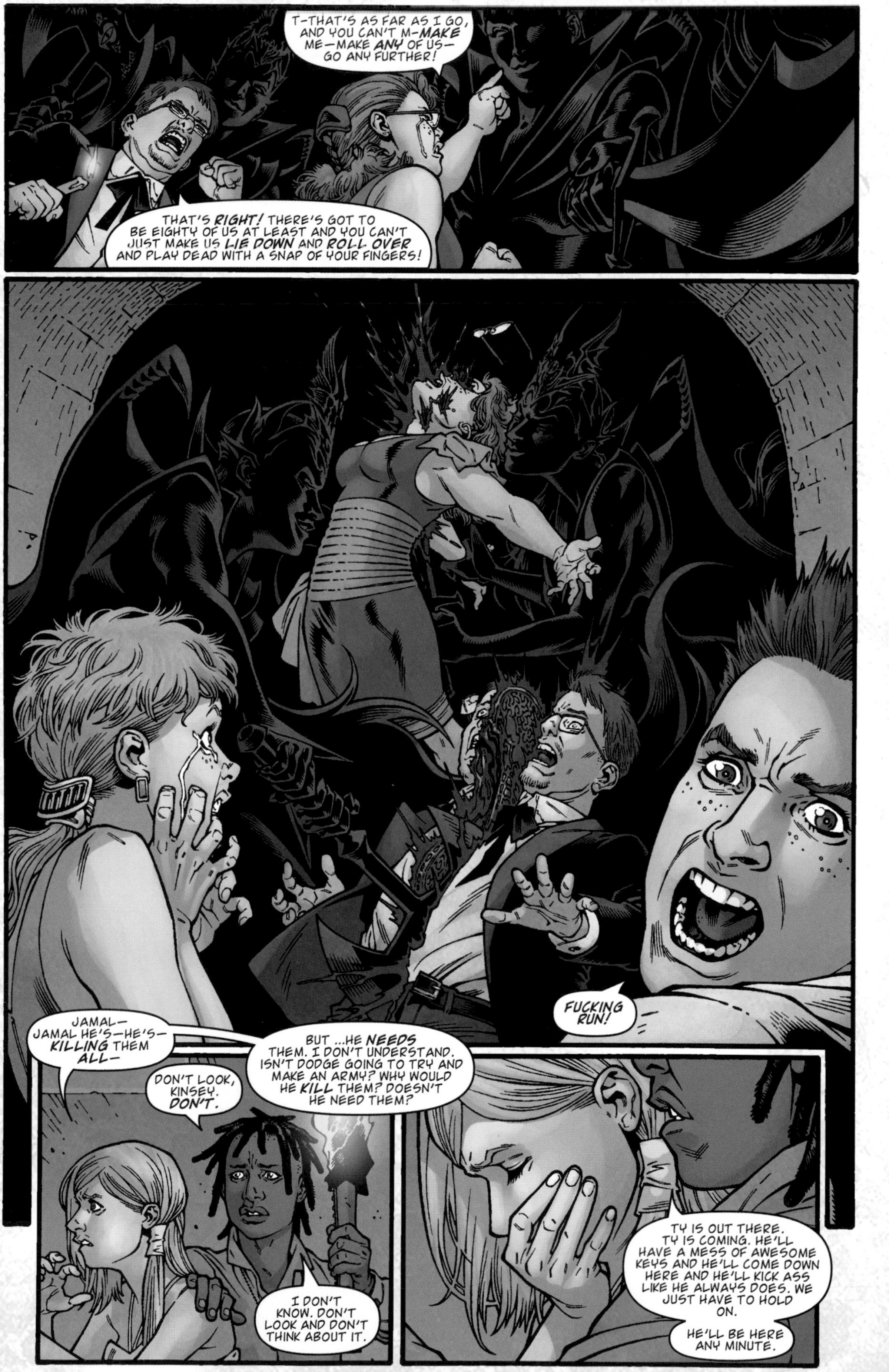

T-THAT'S AS FAR AS I GO, AND YOU CAN'T M-MAKE ME—MAKE ANY OF US—GO ANY FURTHER!
THAT'S RIGHT! THERE'S GOT TO BE EIGHTY OF US AT LEAST AND YOU CAN'T JUST MAKE US LIE DOWN AND ROLL OVER AND PLAY DEAD WITH A SNAP OF YOUR FINGERS!
FUCKING RUN!
JAMAL— JAMAL HE'S—HE'S—KILLING THEM ALL—
DON'T LOOK, KINSEY. DON'T.
BUT ...HE NEEDS THEM. I DON'T UNDERSTAND. ISN'T DODGE GOING TO TRY AND MAKE AN ARMY? WHY WOULD HE KILL THEM? DOESN'T HE NEED THEM?
I DON'T KNOW. DON'T LOOK AND DON'T THINK ABOUT IT.
TY IS OUT THERE. TY IS COMING. HE'LL HAVE A MESS OF AWESOME KEYS AND HE'LL COME DOWN HERE AND HE'LL KICK ASS LIKE HE ALWAYS DOES. WE JUST HAVE TO HOLD ON.
HE'LL BE HERE ANY MINUTE.

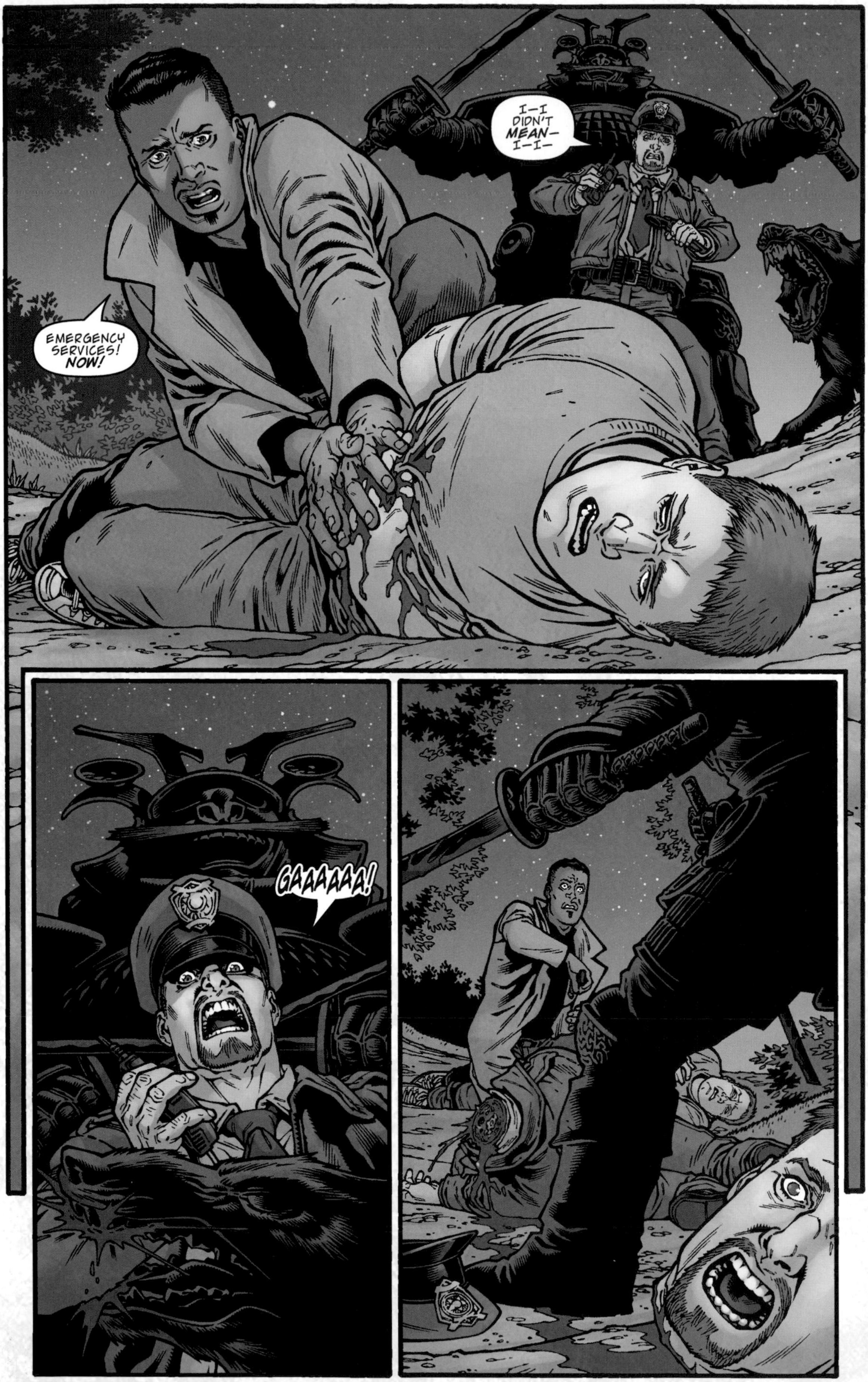
I—I DIDN'T MEAN— I—I—
EMERGENCY SERVICES! NOW!
GAAAAAA!

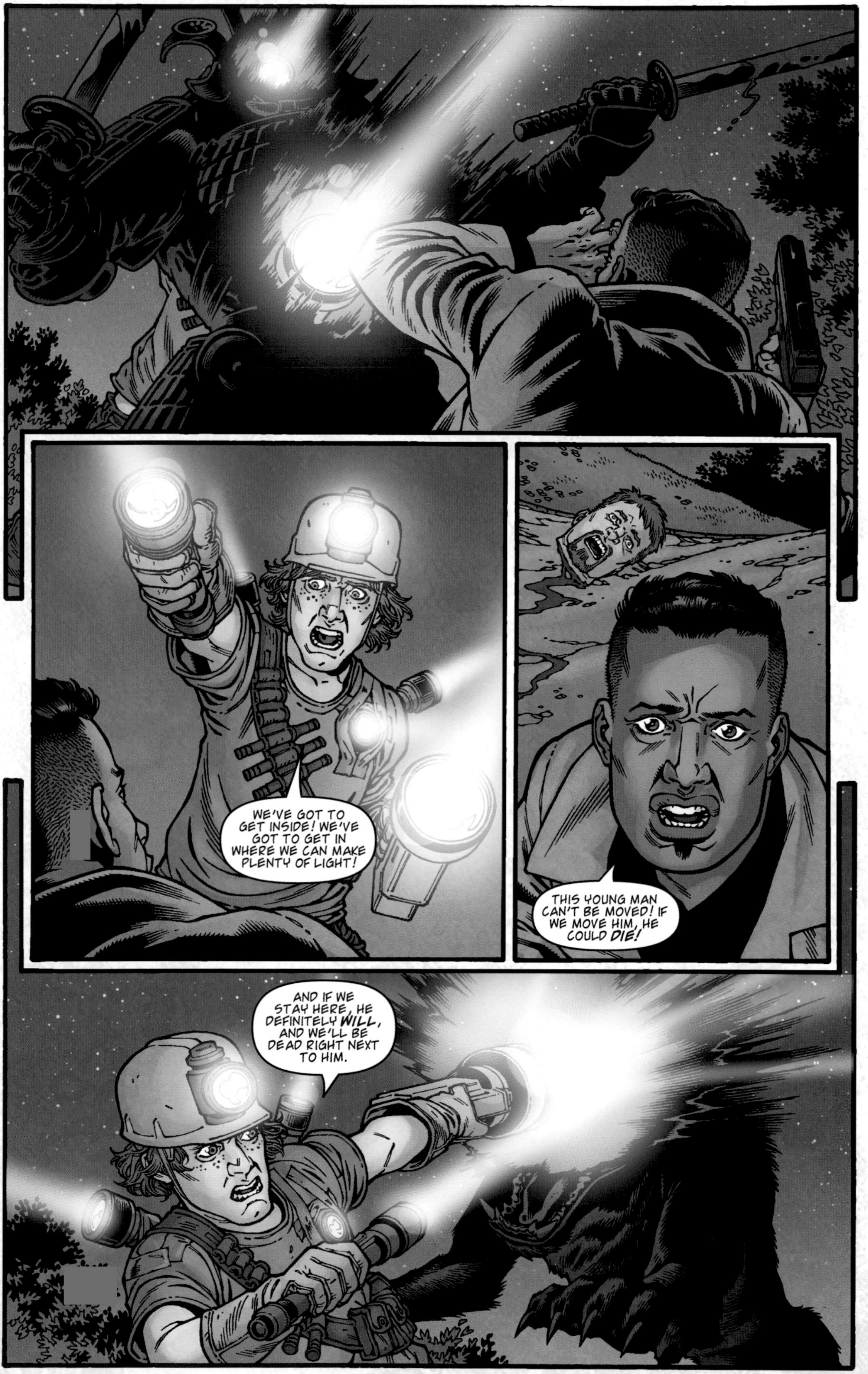
WE'VE GOT TO GET INSIDE! WE'VE GOT TO GET IN WHERE WE CAN MAKE PLENTY OF LIGHT!
THIS YOUNG MAN CAN'T BE MOVED! IF WE MOVE HIM, HE COULD DIE!
AND IF WE STAY HERE, HE DEFINITELY WILL, AND WE'LL BE DEAD RIGHT NEXT TO HIM.

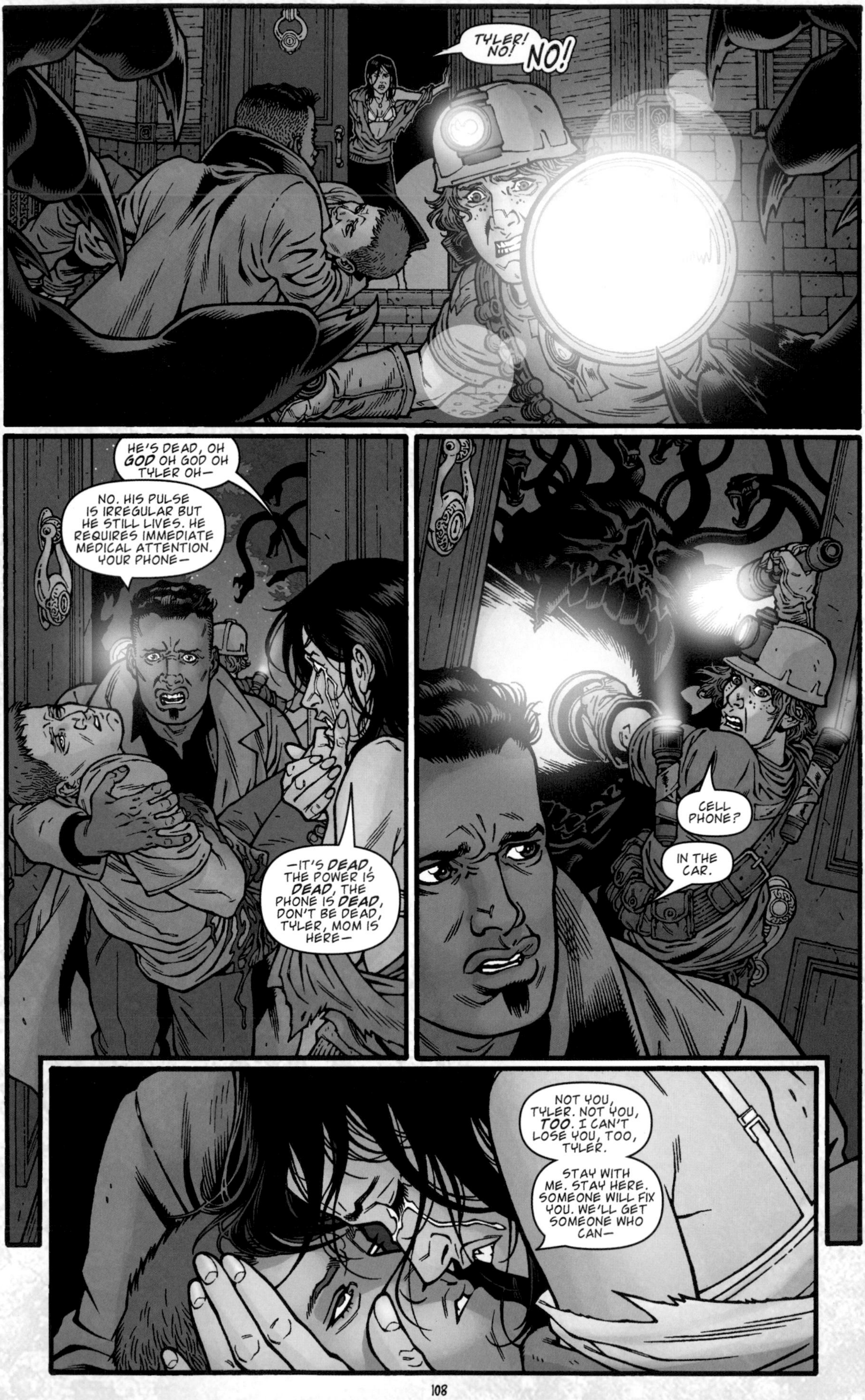
TYLER! NO! NO!
HE'S DEAD, OH GOD OH GOD OH TYLER OH—
NO. HIS PULSE IS IRREGULAR BUT HE STILL LIVES. HE REQUIRES IMMEDIATE MEDICAL ATTENTION. YOUR PHONE—
—IT'S DEAD, THE POWER IS DEAD, THE PHONE IS DEAD, DON'T BE DEAD, TYLER, MOM IS HERE—
CELL PHONE?
IN THE CAR.
NOT YOU, TYLER. NOT YOU, TOO. I CAN'T LOSE YOU, TOO, TYLER.
STAY WITH ME. STAY HERE. SOMEONE WILL FIX YOU. WE'LL GET SOMEONE WHO CAN—

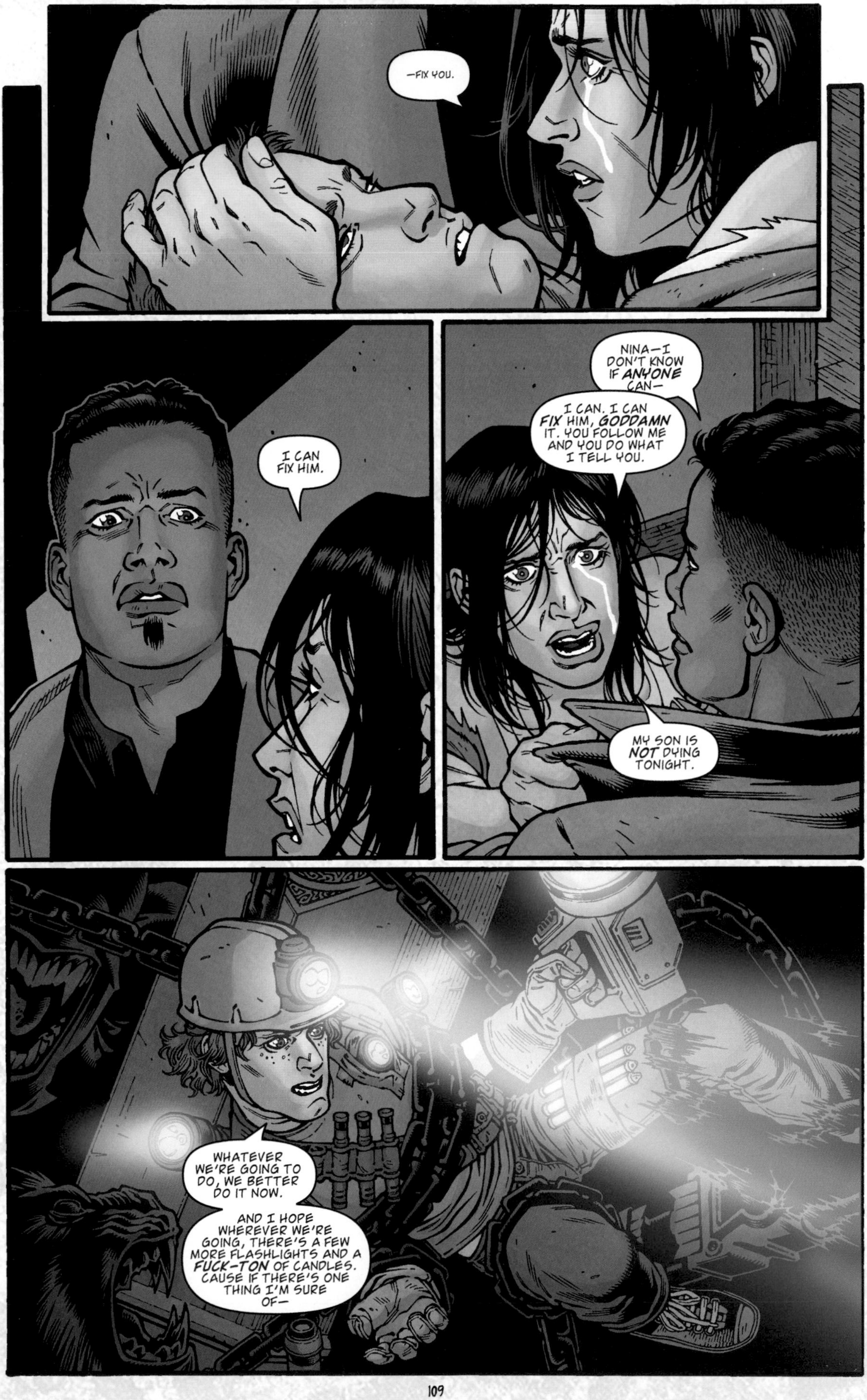
—FIX YOU.
I CAN FIX HIM.
NINA—I DON'T KNOW IF ANYONE CAN—
I CAN. I CAN FIX HIM, GODDAMN IT. YOU FOLLOW ME AND YOU DO WHAT I TELL YOU.
MY SON IS NOT DYING TONIGHT.
WHATEVER WE'RE GOING TO DO, WE BETTER DO IT NOW.
AND I HOPE WHEREVER WE'RE GOING, THERE'S A FEW MORE FLASHLIGHTS AND A FUCK-TON OF CANDLES. CAUSE IF THERE'S ONE THING I'M SURE OF—

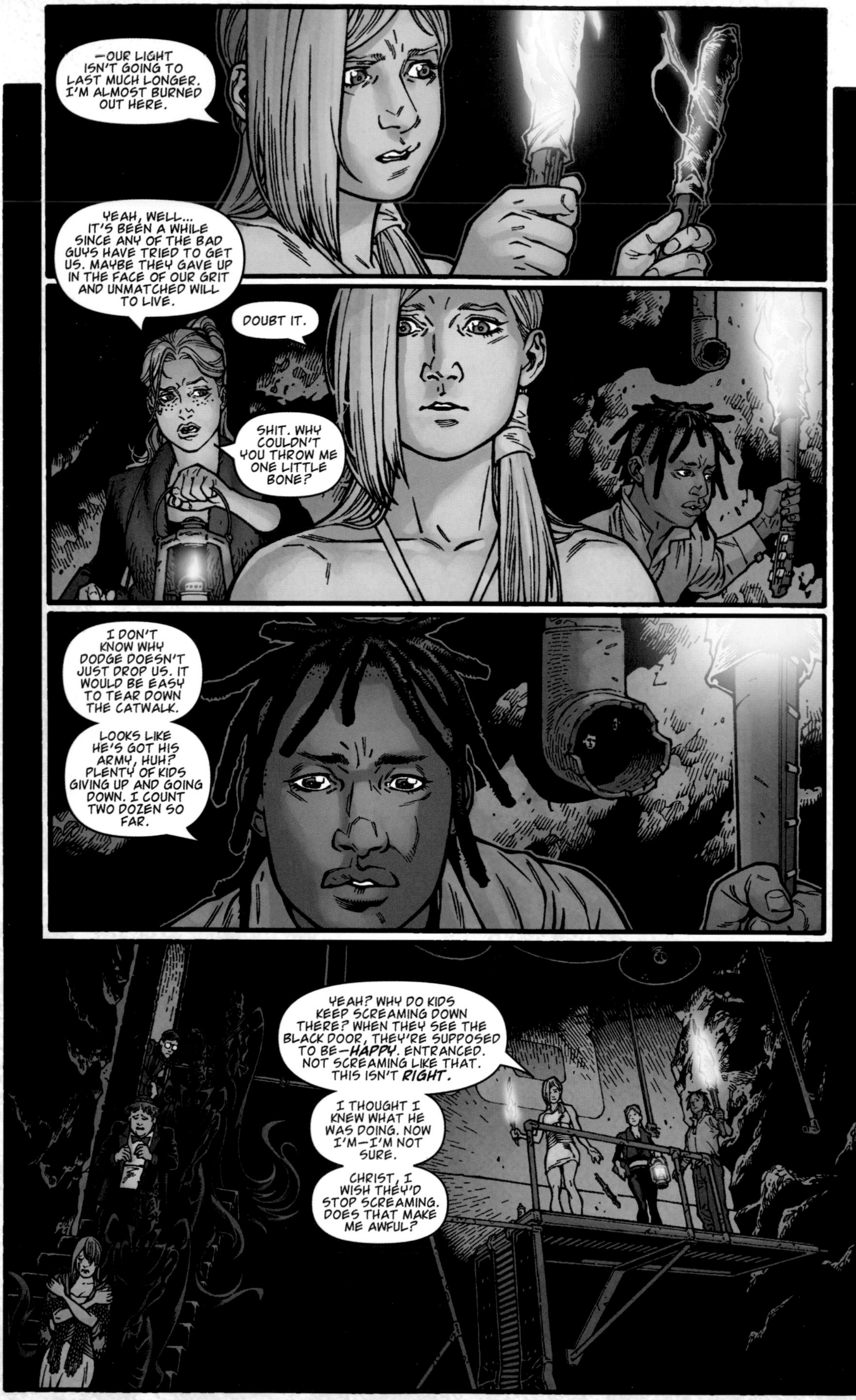
—OUR LIGHT ISN'T GOING TO LAST MUCH LONGER. I'M ALMOST BURNED OUT HERE.
YEAH, WELL... IT'S BEEN A WHILE SINCE ANY OF THE BAD GUYS HAVE TRIED TO GET US. MAYBE THEY GAVE UP IN THE FACE OF OUR GRIT AND UNMATCHED WILL TO LIVE.
DOUBT IT.
SHIT. WHY COULDN'T YOU THROW ME ONE LITTLE BONE?
I DON'T KNOW WHY DODGE DOESN'T JUST DROP US. IT WOULD BE EASY TO TEAR DOWN THE CATWALK.
LOOKS LIKE HE'S GOT HIS ARMY, HUH? PLENTY OF KIDS GIVING UP AND GOING DOWN. I COUNT TWO DOZEN SO FAR.
YEAH? WHY DO KIDS KEEP SCREAMING DOWN THERE? WHEN THEY SEE THE BLACK DOOR, THEY'RE SUPPOSED TO BE—*HAPPY*. ENTRANCED. NOT SCREAMING LIKE THAT. THIS ISN'T *RIGHT*.
I THOUGHT I KNEW WHAT HE WAS DOING. NOW I'M—I'M NOT SURE.
CHRIST, I WISH THEY'D STOP SCREAMING. DOES THAT MAKE ME AWFUL?

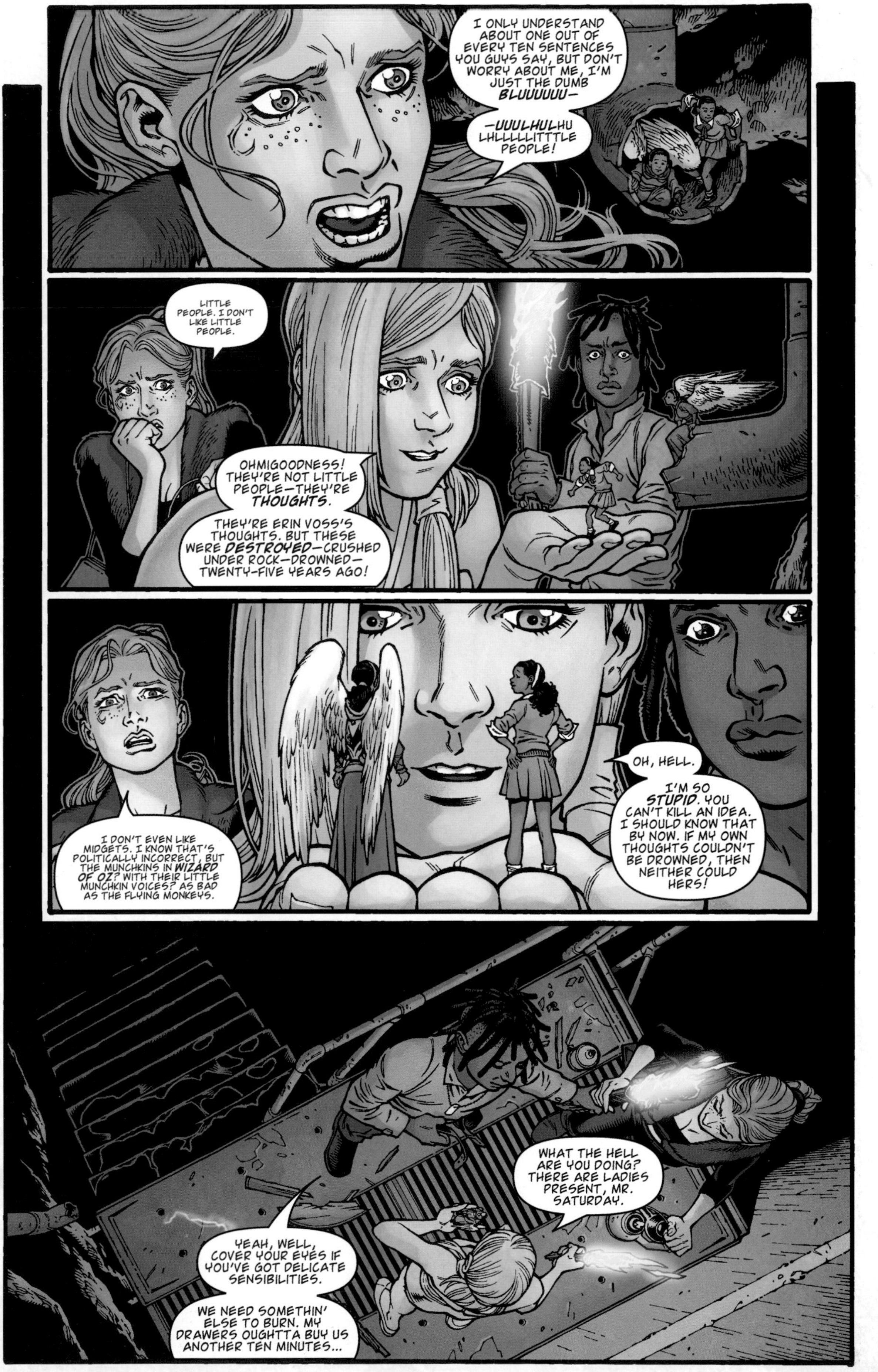
I ONLY UNDERSTAND ABOUT ONE OUT OF EVERY TEN SENTENCES YOU GUYS SAY, BUT DON'T WORRY ABOUT ME, I'M JUST THE DUMB BLUUUUUU—
—UUULHULHU LHLLLLLLITTTLE PEOPLE!
LITTLE PEOPLE. I DON'T LIKE LITTLE PEOPLE.
OHMIGOODNESS! THEY'RE NOT LITTLE PEOPLE—THEY'RE THOUGHTS.
THEY'RE ERIN VOSS'S THOUGHTS. BUT THESE WERE DESTROYED—CRUSHED UNDER ROCK—DROWNED—TWENTY-FIVE YEARS AGO!
I DON'T EVEN LIKE MIDGETS. I KNOW THAT'S POLITICALLY INCORRECT, BUT THE MUNCHKINS IN WIZARD OF OZ? WITH THEIR LITTLE MUNCHKIN VOICES? AS BAD AS THE FLYING MONKEYS.
OH, HELL.
I'M SO STUPID. YOU CAN'T KILL AN IDEA. I SHOULD KNOW THAT BY NOW. IF MY OWN THOUGHTS COULDN'T BE DROWNED, THEN NEITHER COULD HERS!
WHAT THE HELL ARE YOU DOING? THERE ARE LADIES PRESENT, MR. SATURDAY.
YEAH, WELL, COVER YOUR EYES IF YOU'VE GOT DELICATE SENSIBILITIES.
WE NEED SOMETHIN' ELSE TO BURN. MY DRAWERS OUGHTTA BUY US ANOTHER TEN MINUTES...

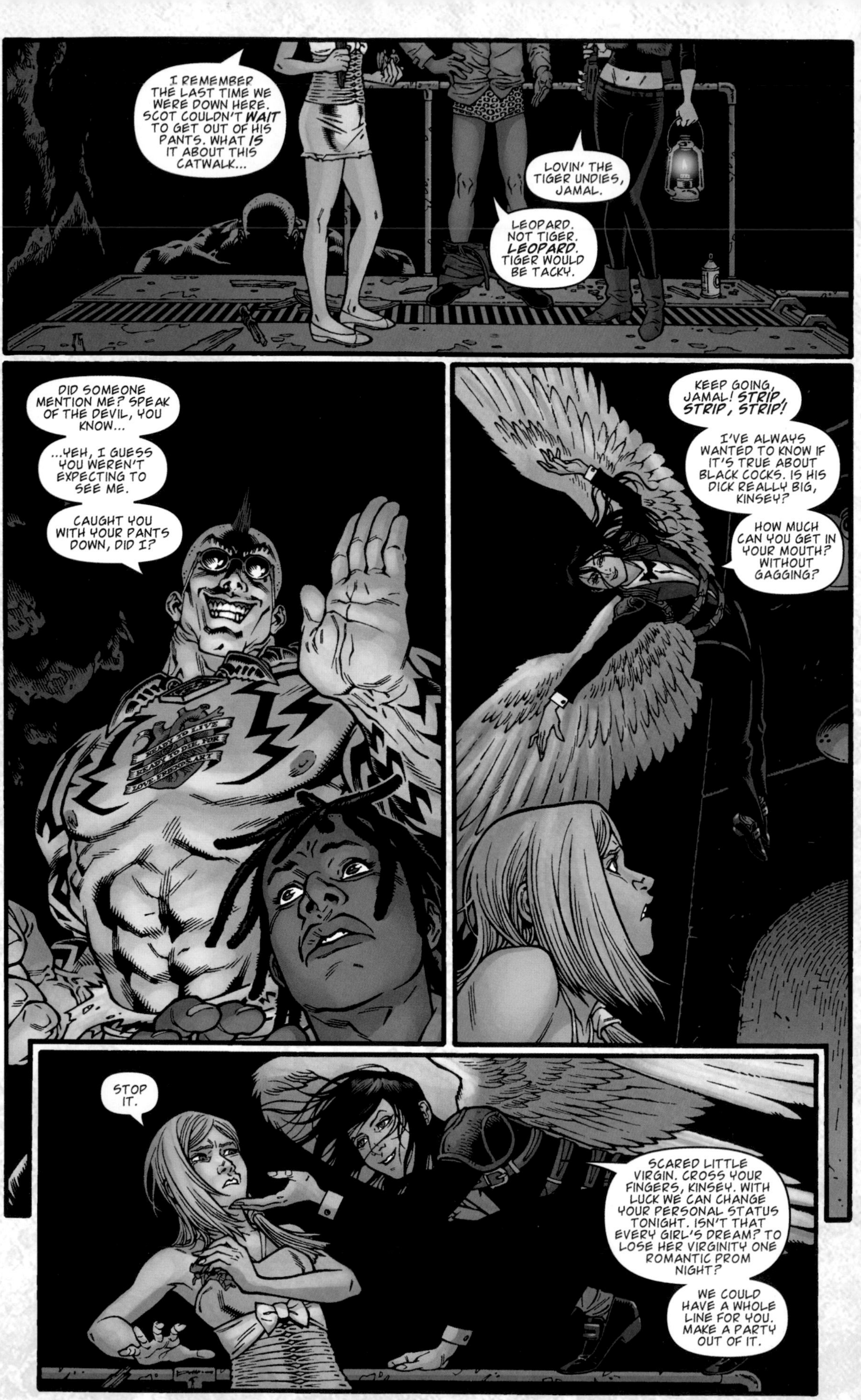

I REMEMBER THE LAST TIME WE WERE DOWN HERE. SCOT COULDN'T **WAIT** TO GET OUT OF HIS PANTS. WHAT **IS** IT ABOUT THIS CATWALK...
LOVIN' THE TIGER UNDIES, JAMAL.
LEOPARD. NOT TIGER. **LEOPARD.** TIGER WOULD BE TACKY.
DID SOMEONE MENTION ME? SPEAK OF THE DEVIL, YOU KNOW...
...YEH, I GUESS YOU WEREN'T EXPECTING TO SEE ME.
CAUGHT YOU WITH YOUR PANTS DOWN, DID I?
KEEP GOING, JAMAL! **STRIP, STRIP, STRIP!**
I'VE ALWAYS WANTED TO KNOW IF IT'S TRUE ABOUT BLACK COCKS. IS HIS DICK REALLY BIG, KINSEY?
HOW MUCH CAN YOU GET IN YOUR MOUTH? WITHOUT GAGGING?
STOP IT.
SCARED LITTLE VIRGIN. CROSS YOUR FINGERS, KINSEY. WITH LUCK WE CAN CHANGE YOUR PERSONAL STATUS TONIGHT. ISN'T THAT EVERY GIRL'S DREAM? TO LOSE HER VIRGINITY ONE ROMANTIC PROM NIGHT?
WE COULD HAVE A WHOLE LINE FOR YOU. MAKE A PARTY OUT OF IT.

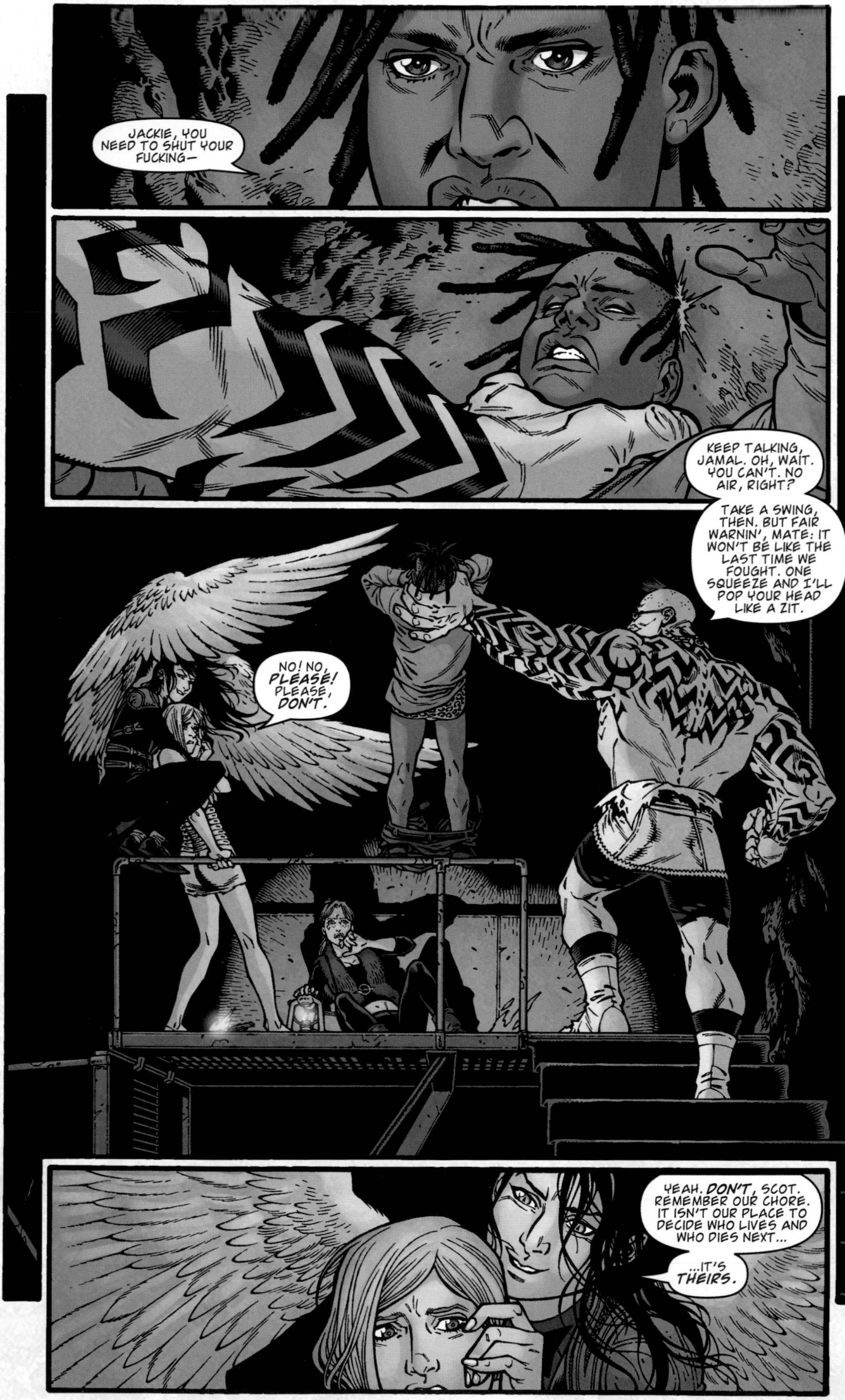
JACKIE, YOU NEED TO SHUT YOUR FUCKING—
KEEP TALKING, JAMAL. OH, WAIT. YOU CAN'T. NO AIR, RIGHT?
TAKE A SWING, THEN. BUT FAIR WARNIN', MATE: IT WON'T BE LIKE THE LAST TIME WE FOUGHT. ONE SQUEEZE AND I'LL POP YOUR HEAD LIKE A ZIT.
NO! NO, PLEASE! PLEASE, DON'T.
YEAH. DON'T, SCOT. REMEMBER OUR CHORE. IT ISN'T OUR PLACE TO DECIDE WHO LIVES AND WHO DIES NEXT...
...IT'S THEIRS.

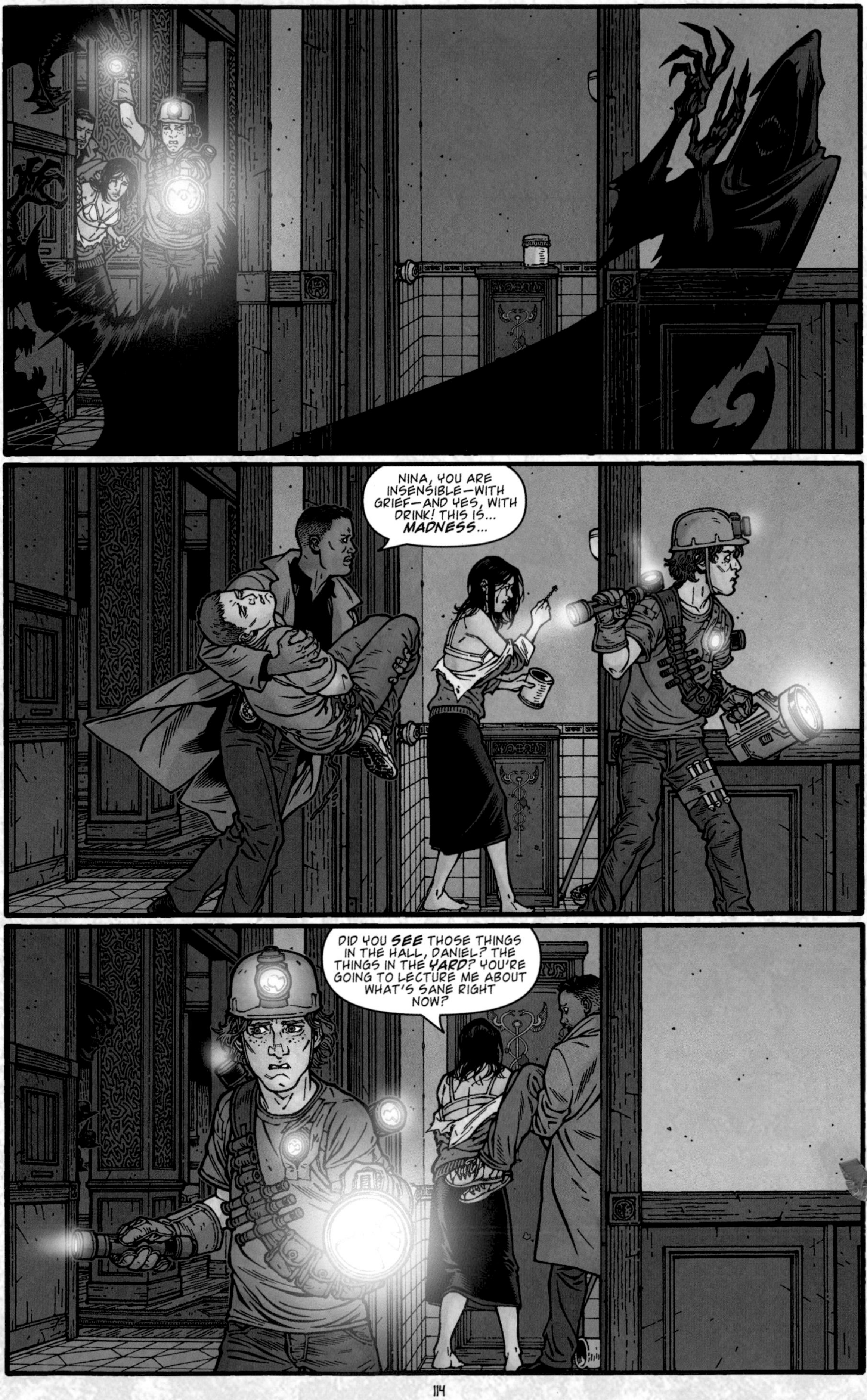
NINA, YOU ARE INSENSIBLE—WITH GRIEF—AND YES, WITH DRINK! THIS IS... MADNESS...
DID YOU SEE THOSE THINGS IN THE HALL, DANIEL? THE THINGS IN THE YARD? YOU'RE GOING TO LECTURE ME ABOUT WHAT'S SANE RIGHT NOW?

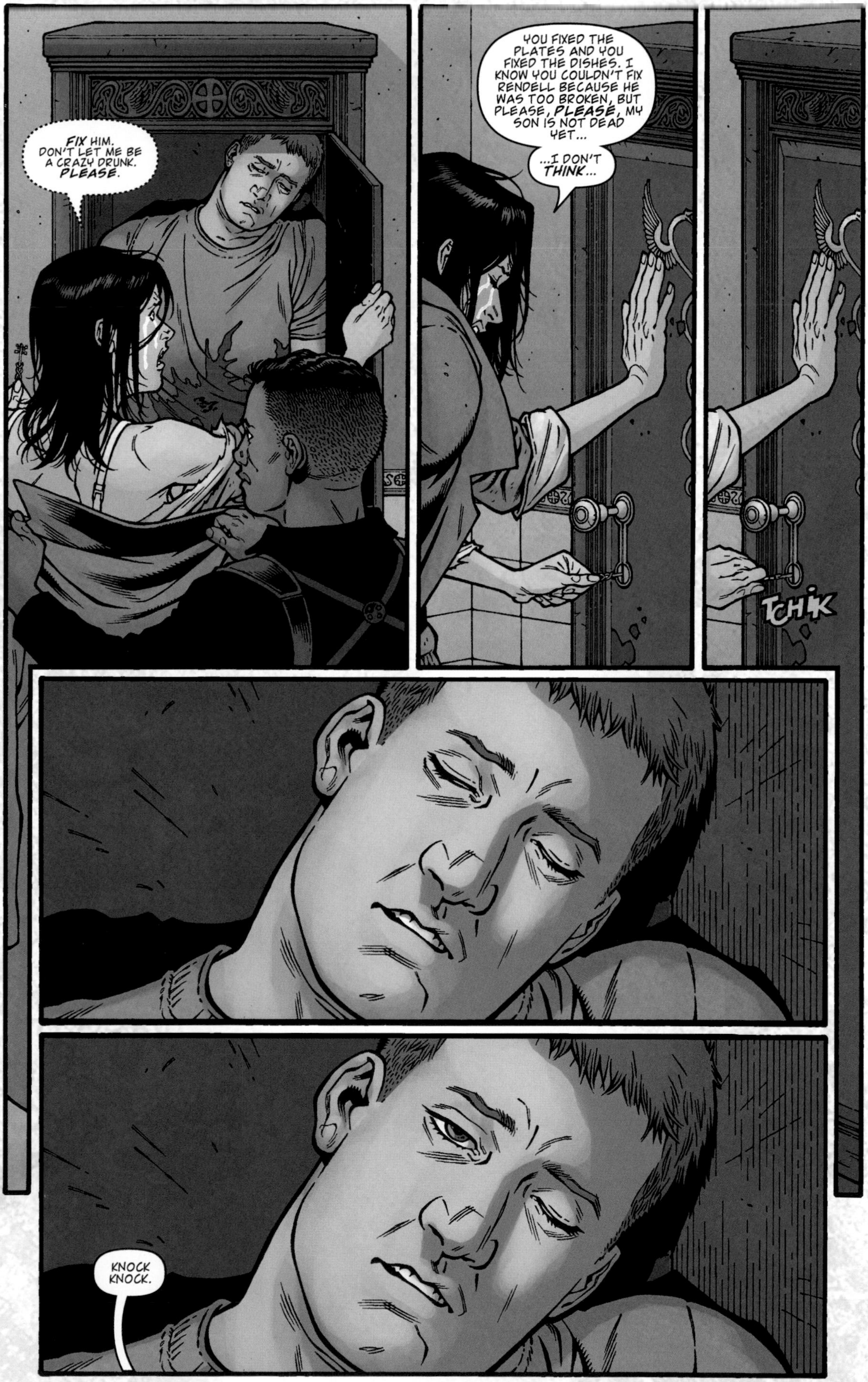
FIX HIM. DON'T LET ME BE A CRAZY DRUNK. PLEASE.
YOU FIXED THE PLATES AND YOU FIXED THE DISHES. I KNOW YOU COULDN'T FIX RENDELL BECAUSE HE WAS TOO BROKEN, BUT PLEASE, PLEASE, MY SON IS NOT DEAD YET...
...I DON'T THINK...
TCHIK
KNOCK KNOCK.

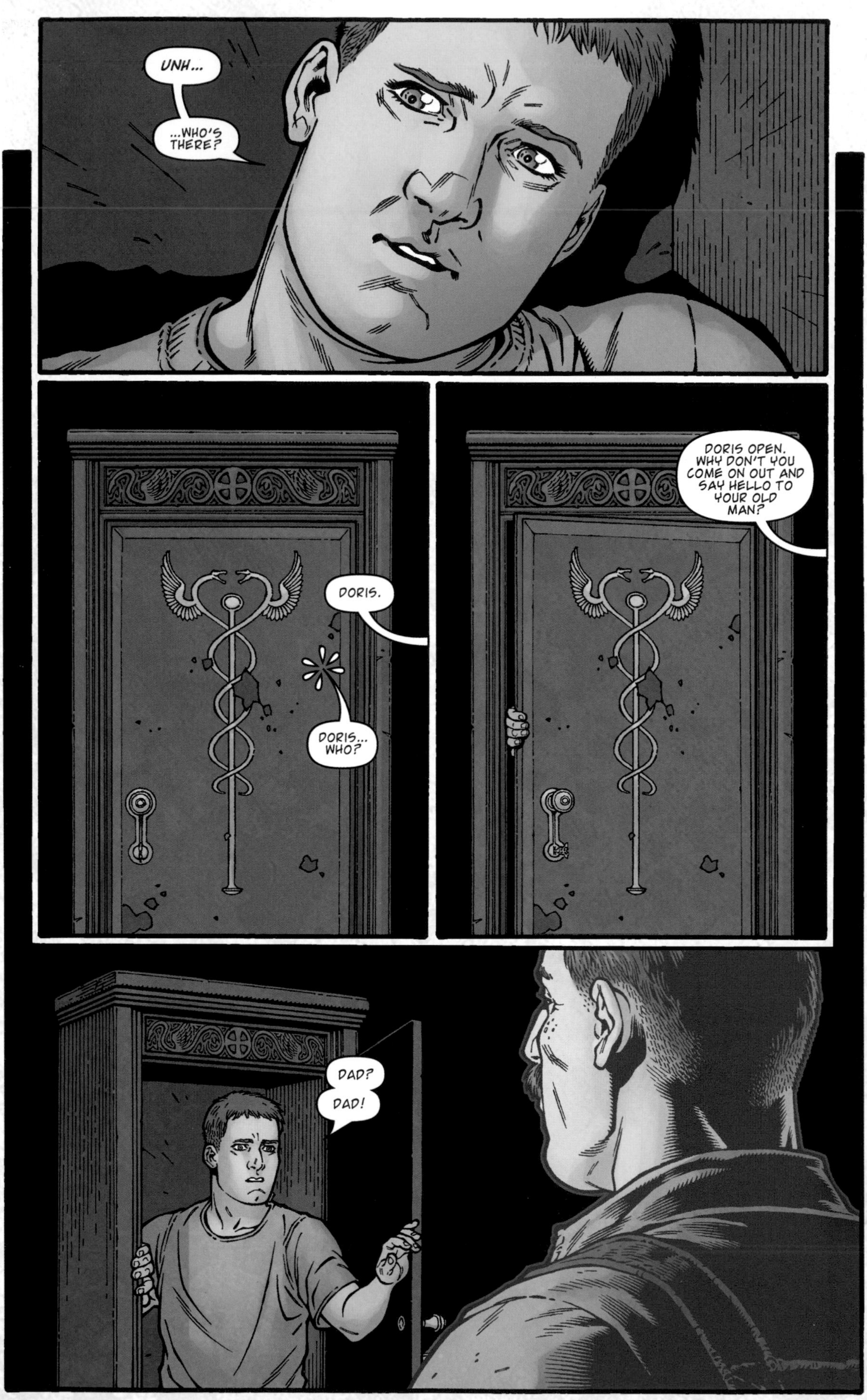
UNH...
...WHO'S THERE?
DORIS.
DORIS... WHO?
DORIS OPEN. WHY DON'T YOU COME ON OUT AND SAY HELLO TO YOUR OLD MAN?
DAD?
DAD!

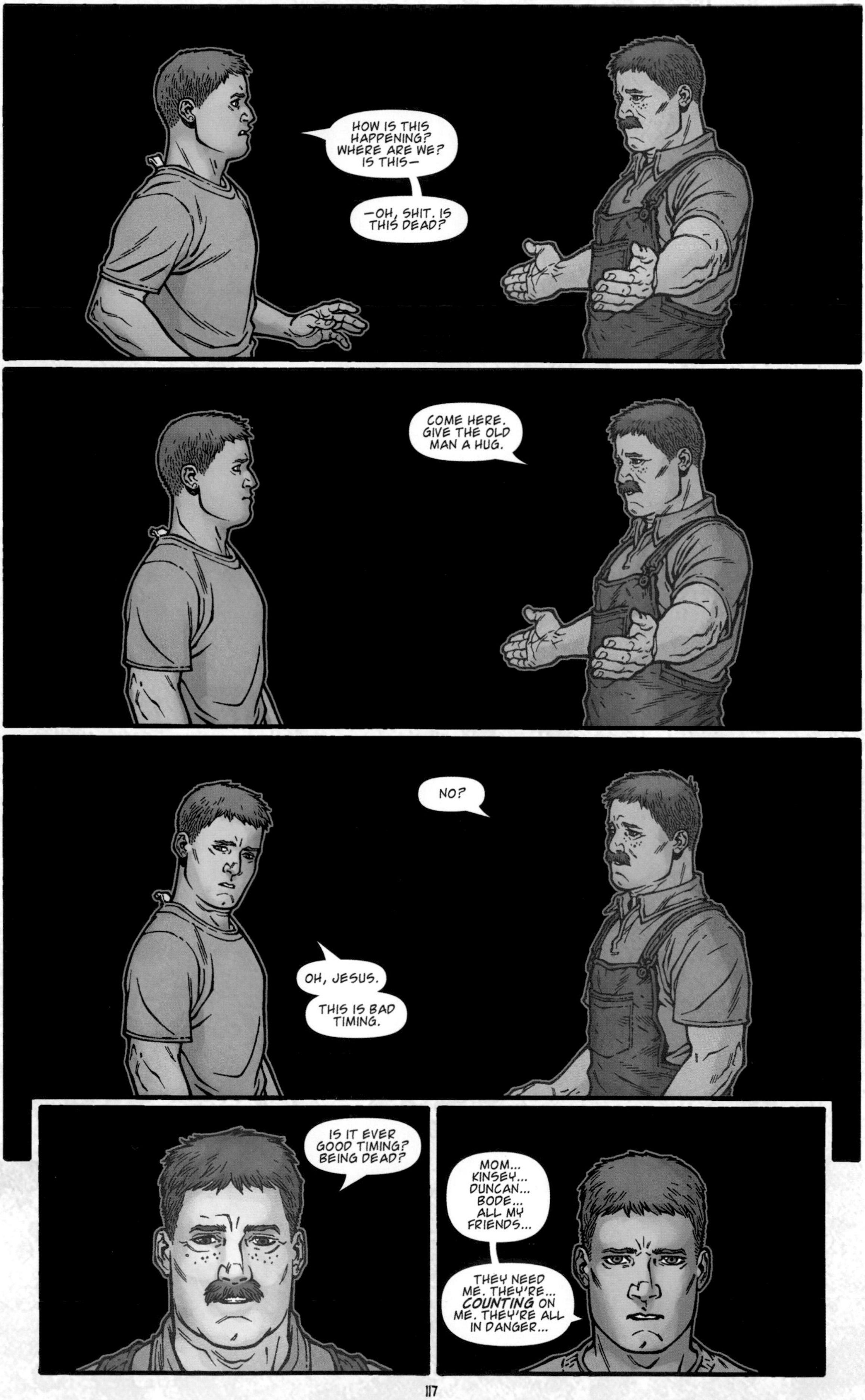
HOW IS THIS HAPPENING? WHERE ARE WE? IS THIS—
—OH, SHIT. IS THIS DEAD?
COME HERE. GIVE THE OLD MAN A HUG.
NO?
OH, JESUS.
THIS IS BAD TIMING.
IS IT EVER GOOD TIMING? BEING DEAD?
MOM... KINSEY... DUNCAN... BODE... ALL MY FRIENDS...
THEY NEED ME. THEY'RE... *COUNTING* ON ME. THEY'RE ALL IN DANGER...

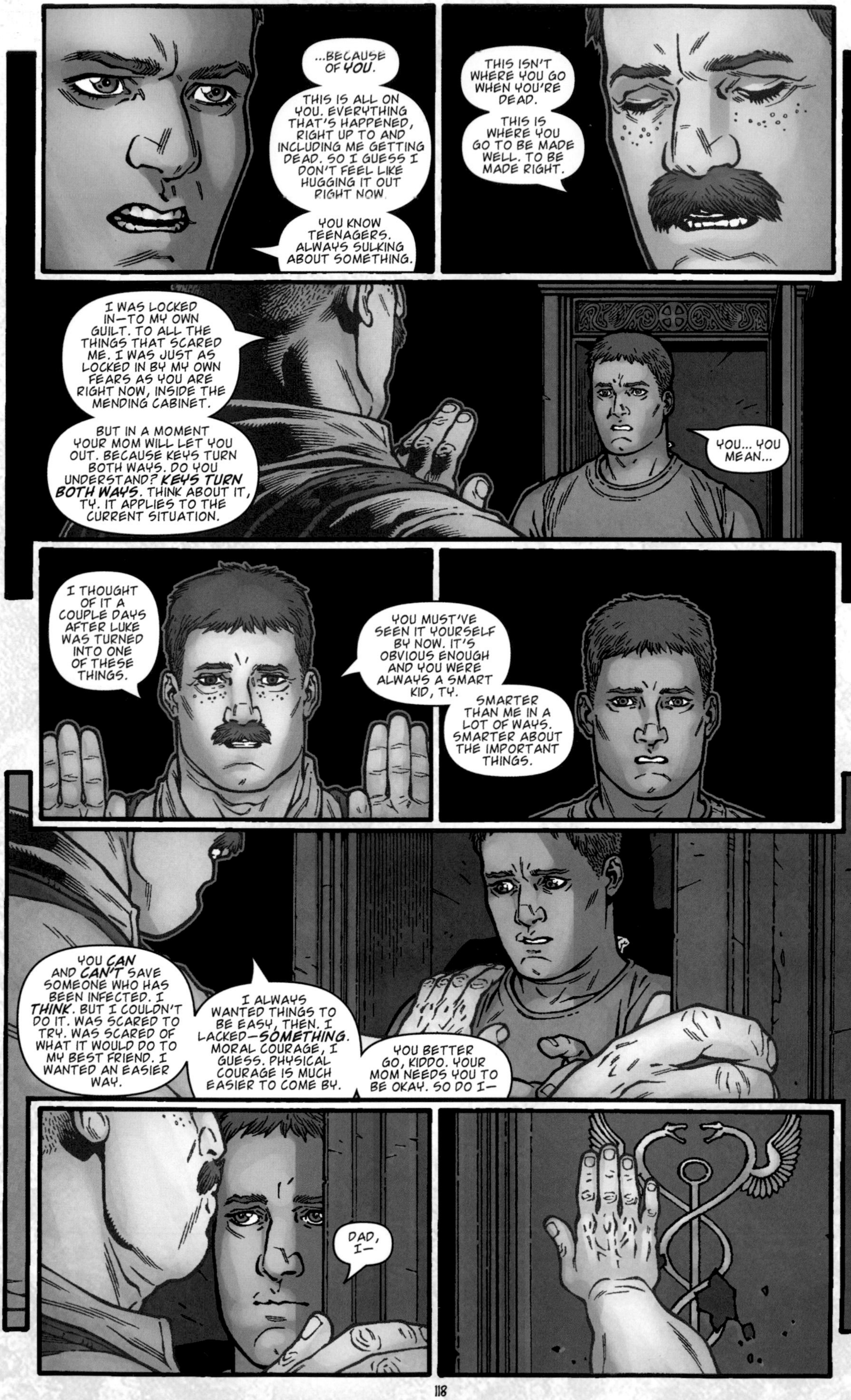
...BECAUSE OF YOU.
THIS IS ALL ON YOU. EVERYTHING THAT'S HAPPENED, RIGHT UP TO AND INCLUDING ME GETTING DEAD. SO I GUESS I DON'T FEEL LIKE HUGGING IT OUT RIGHT NOW.
YOU KNOW TEENAGERS. ALWAYS SULKING ABOUT SOMETHING.
THIS ISN'T WHERE YOU GO WHEN YOU'RE DEAD.
THIS IS WHERE YOU GO TO BE MADE WELL. TO BE MADE RIGHT.
I WAS LOCKED IN—TO MY OWN GUILT. TO ALL THE THINGS THAT SCARED ME. I WAS JUST AS LOCKED IN BY MY OWN FEARS AS YOU ARE RIGHT NOW, INSIDE THE MENDING CABINET.
BUT IN A MOMENT YOUR MOM WILL LET YOU OUT. BECAUSE KEYS TURN BOTH WAYS. DO YOU UNDERSTAND? KEYS TURN BOTH WAYS. THINK ABOUT IT, TY. IT APPLIES TO THE CURRENT SITUATION.
YOU... YOU MEAN...
I THOUGHT OF IT A COUPLE DAYS AFTER LUKE WAS TURNED INTO ONE OF THESE THINGS.
YOU MUST'VE SEEN IT YOURSELF BY NOW. IT'S OBVIOUS ENOUGH AND YOU WERE ALWAYS A SMART KID, TY.
SMARTER THAN ME IN A LOT OF WAYS. SMARTER ABOUT THE IMPORTANT THINGS.
YOU CAN AND CAN'T SAVE SOMEONE WHO HAS BEEN INFECTED. I THINK. BUT I COULDN'T DO IT. WAS SCARED TO TRY. WAS SCARED OF WHAT IT WOULD DO TO MY BEST FRIEND. I WANTED AN EASIER WAY.
I ALWAYS WANTED THINGS TO BE EASY, THEN. I LACKED—SOMETHING. MORAL COURAGE, I GUESS. PHYSICAL COURAGE IS MUCH EASIER TO COME BY.
YOU BETTER GO, KIDDO. YOUR MOM NEEDS YOU TO BE OKAY. SO DO I—
DAD, I—

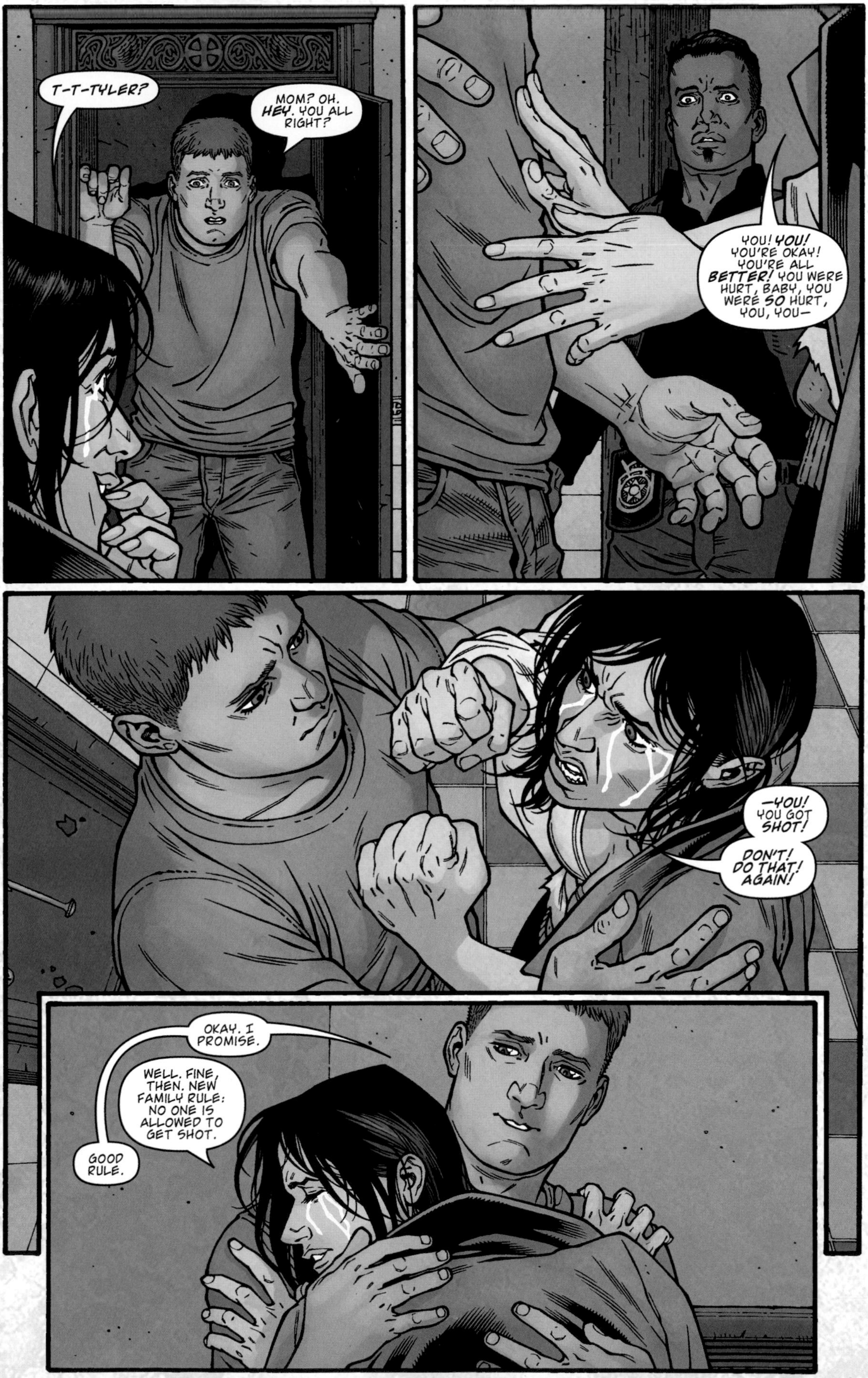
T-T-TYLER?
MOM? OH. HEY. YOU ALL RIGHT?
YOU! YOU! YOU'RE OKAY! YOU'RE ALL BETTER! YOU WERE HURT, BABY, YOU WERE SO HURT, YOU, YOU—
—YOU! YOU GOT SHOT!
DON'T! DO THAT! AGAIN!
OKAY. I PROMISE.
WELL. FINE, THEN. NEW FAMILY RULE: NO ONE IS ALLOWED TO GET SHOT.
GOOD RULE.

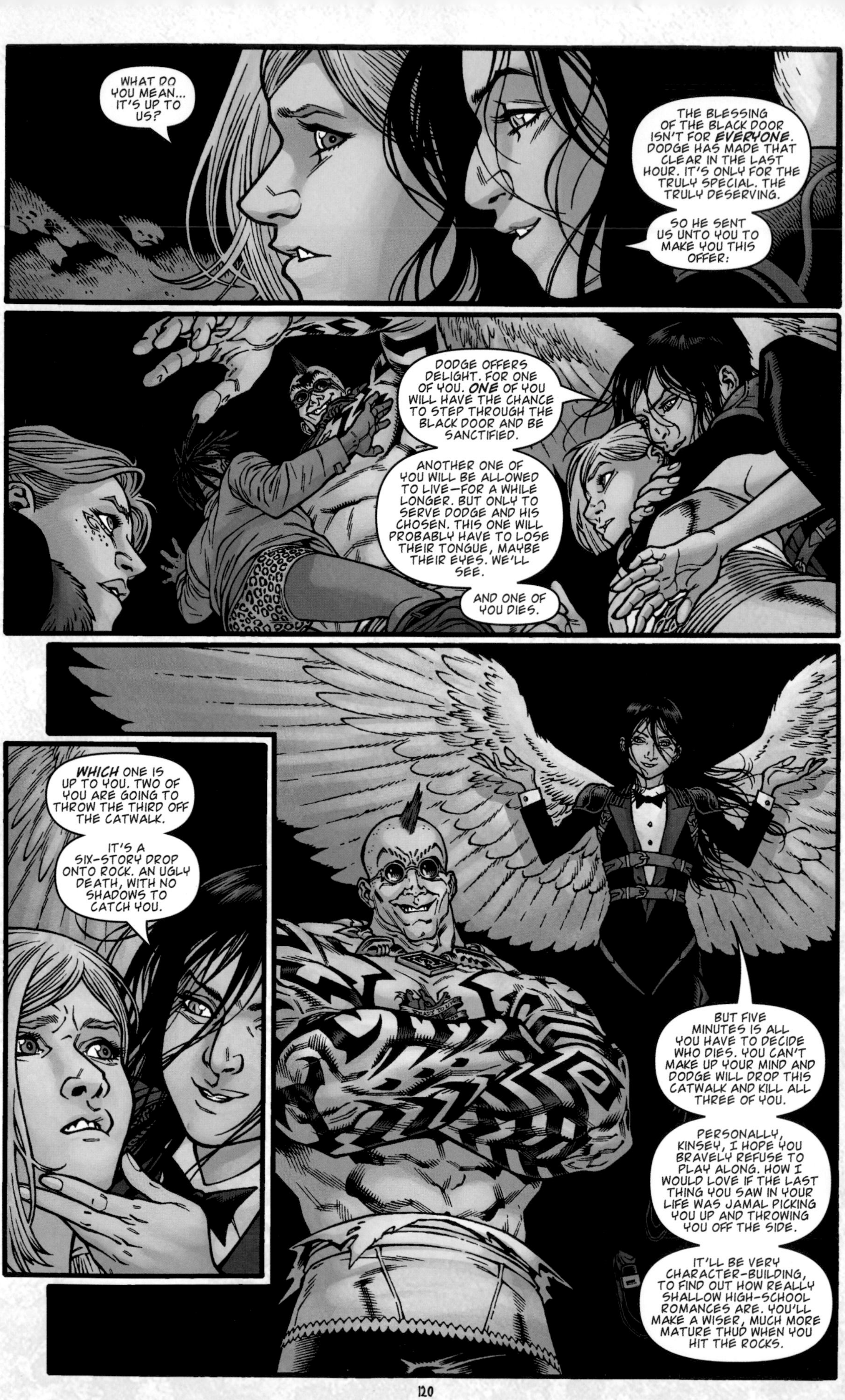
WHAT DO YOU MEAN... IT'S UP TO US?
THE BLESSING OF THE BLACK DOOR ISN'T FOR EVERYONE. DODGE HAS MADE THAT CLEAR IN THE LAST HOUR. IT'S ONLY FOR THE TRULY SPECIAL. THE TRULY DESERVING.
SO HE SENT US UNTO YOU TO MAKE YOU THIS OFFER:
DODGE OFFERS DELIGHT. FOR ONE OF YOU. ONE OF YOU WILL HAVE THE CHANCE TO STEP THROUGH THE BLACK DOOR AND BE SANCTIFIED.
ANOTHER ONE OF YOU WILL BE ALLOWED TO LIVE—FOR A WHILE LONGER. BUT ONLY TO SERVE DODGE AND HIS CHOSEN. THIS ONE WILL PROBABLY HAVE TO LOSE THEIR TONGUE, MAYBE THEIR EYES. WE'LL SEE.
AND ONE OF YOU DIES.
WHICH ONE IS UP TO YOU. TWO OF YOU ARE GOING TO THROW THE THIRD OFF THE CATWALK.
IT'S A SIX-STORY DROP ONTO ROCK. AN UGLY DEATH, WITH NO SHADOWS TO CATCH YOU.
BUT FIVE MINUTES IS ALL YOU HAVE TO DECIDE WHO DIES. YOU CAN'T MAKE UP YOUR MIND AND DODGE WILL DROP THIS CATWALK AND KILL ALL THREE OF YOU.
PERSONALLY, KINSEY, I HOPE YOU BRAVELY REFUSE TO PLAY ALONG. HOW I WOULD LOVE IF THE LAST THING YOU SAW IN YOUR LIFE WAS JAMAL PICKING YOU UP AND THROWING YOU OFF THE SIDE.
IT'LL BE VERY CHARACTER-BUILDING, TO FIND OUT HOW REALLY SHALLOW HIGH-SCHOOL ROMANCES ARE. YOU'LL MAKE A WISER, MUCH MORE MATURE THUD WHEN YOU HIT THE ROCKS.

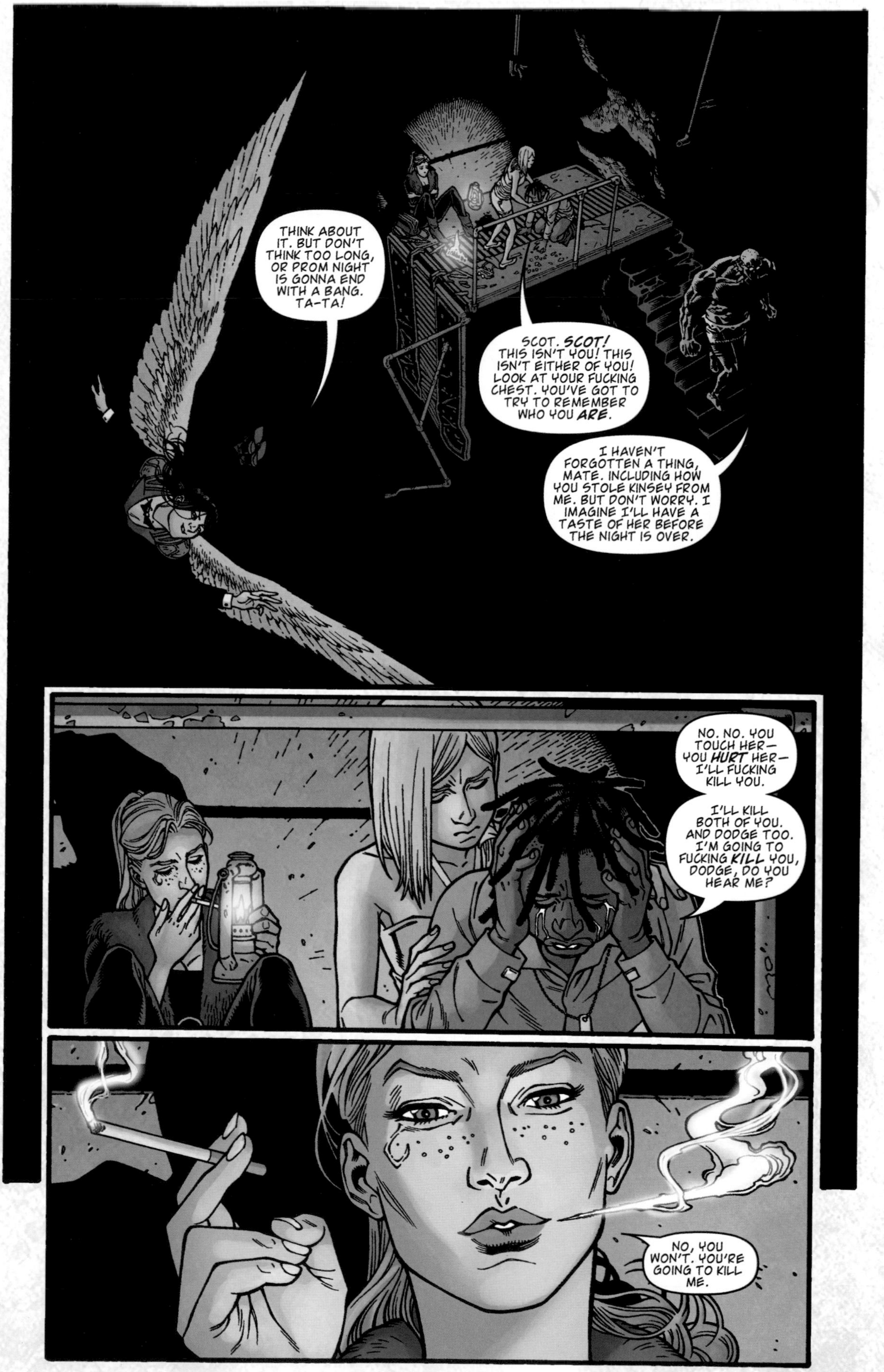
THINK ABOUT IT. BUT DON'T THINK TOO LONG, OR PROM NIGHT IS GONNA END WITH A BANG. TA-TA!
SCOT. SCOT! THIS ISN'T YOU! THIS ISN'T EITHER OF YOU! LOOK AT YOUR FUCKING CHEST. YOU'VE GOT TO TRY TO REMEMBER WHO YOU ARE.
I HAVEN'T FORGOTTEN A THING, MATE. INCLUDING HOW YOU STOLE KINSEY FROM ME. BUT DON'T WORRY. I IMAGINE I'LL HAVE A TASTE OF HER BEFORE THE NIGHT IS OVER.
NO. NO. YOU TOUCH HER— YOU HURT HER— I'LL FUCKING KILL YOU.
I'LL KILL BOTH OF YOU. AND DODGE TOO. I'M GOING TO FUCKING KILL YOU, DODGE, DO YOU HEAR ME?
NO, YOU WON'T. YOU'RE GOING TO KILL ME.

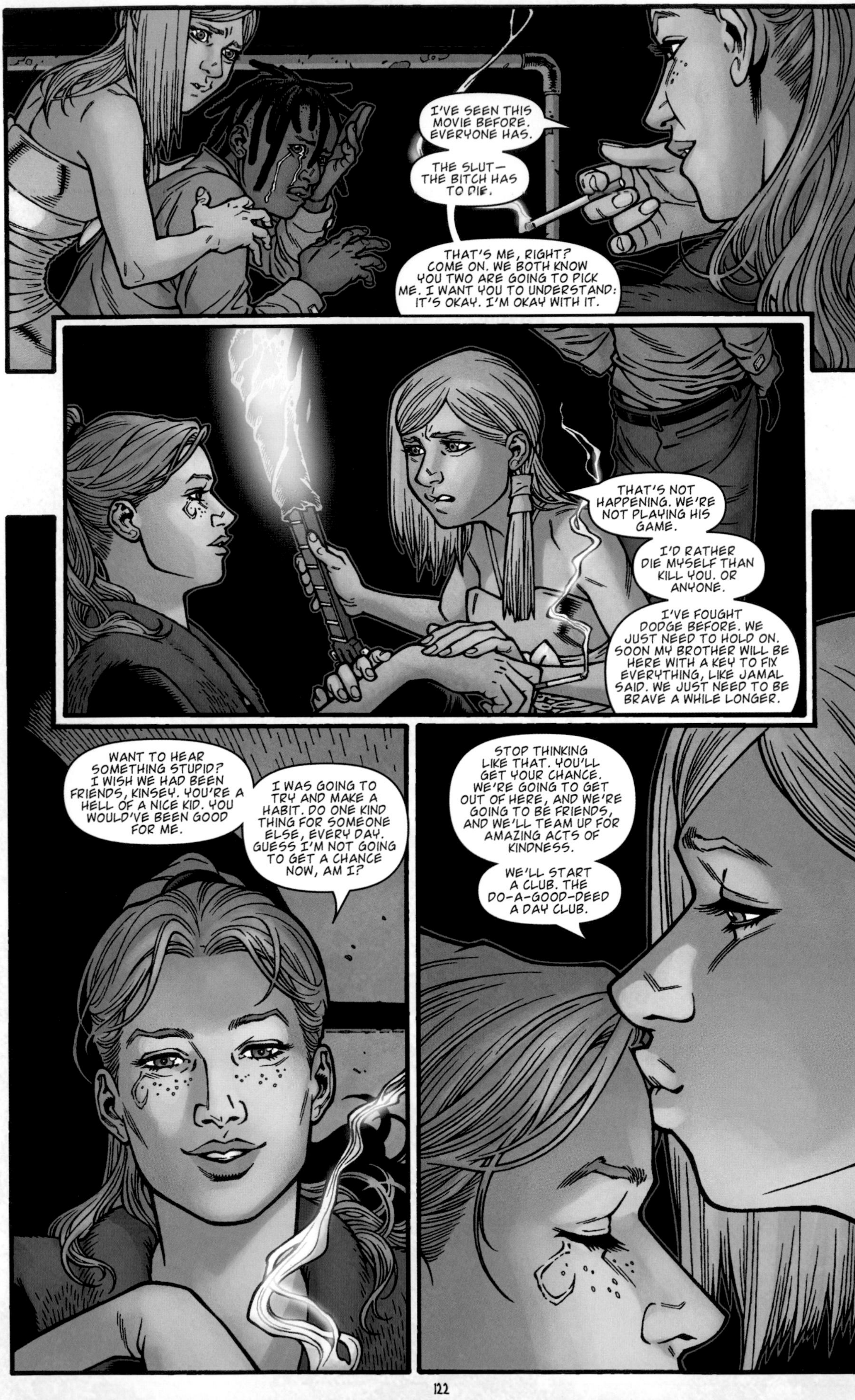

I'VE SEEN THIS MOVIE BEFORE. EVERYONE HAS.
THE SLUT—THE BITCH HAS TO DIE.
THAT'S ME, RIGHT? COME ON. WE BOTH KNOW YOU TWO ARE GOING TO PICK ME. I WANT YOU TO UNDERSTAND: IT'S OKAY. I'M OKAY WITH IT.
THAT'S NOT HAPPENING. WE'RE NOT PLAYING HIS GAME.
I'D RATHER DIE MYSELF THAN KILL YOU. OR ANYONE.
I'VE FOUGHT DODGE BEFORE. WE JUST NEED TO HOLD ON. SOON MY BROTHER WILL BE HERE WITH A KEY TO FIX EVERYTHING, LIKE JAMAL SAID. WE JUST NEED TO BE BRAVE A WHILE LONGER.
WANT TO HEAR SOMETHING STUPID? I WISH WE HAD BEEN FRIENDS, KINSEY. YOU'RE A HELL OF A NICE KID. YOU WOULD'VE BEEN GOOD FOR ME.
I WAS GOING TO TRY AND MAKE A HABIT. DO ONE KIND THING FOR SOMEONE ELSE, EVERY DAY. GUESS I'M NOT GOING TO GET A CHANCE NOW, AM I?
STOP THINKING LIKE THAT. YOU'LL GET YOUR CHANCE. WE'RE GOING TO GET OUT OF HERE, AND WE'RE GOING TO BE FRIENDS, AND WE'LL TEAM UP FOR AMAZING ACTS OF KINDNESS.
WE'LL START A CLUB. THE DO-A-GOOD-DEED A DAY CLUB.

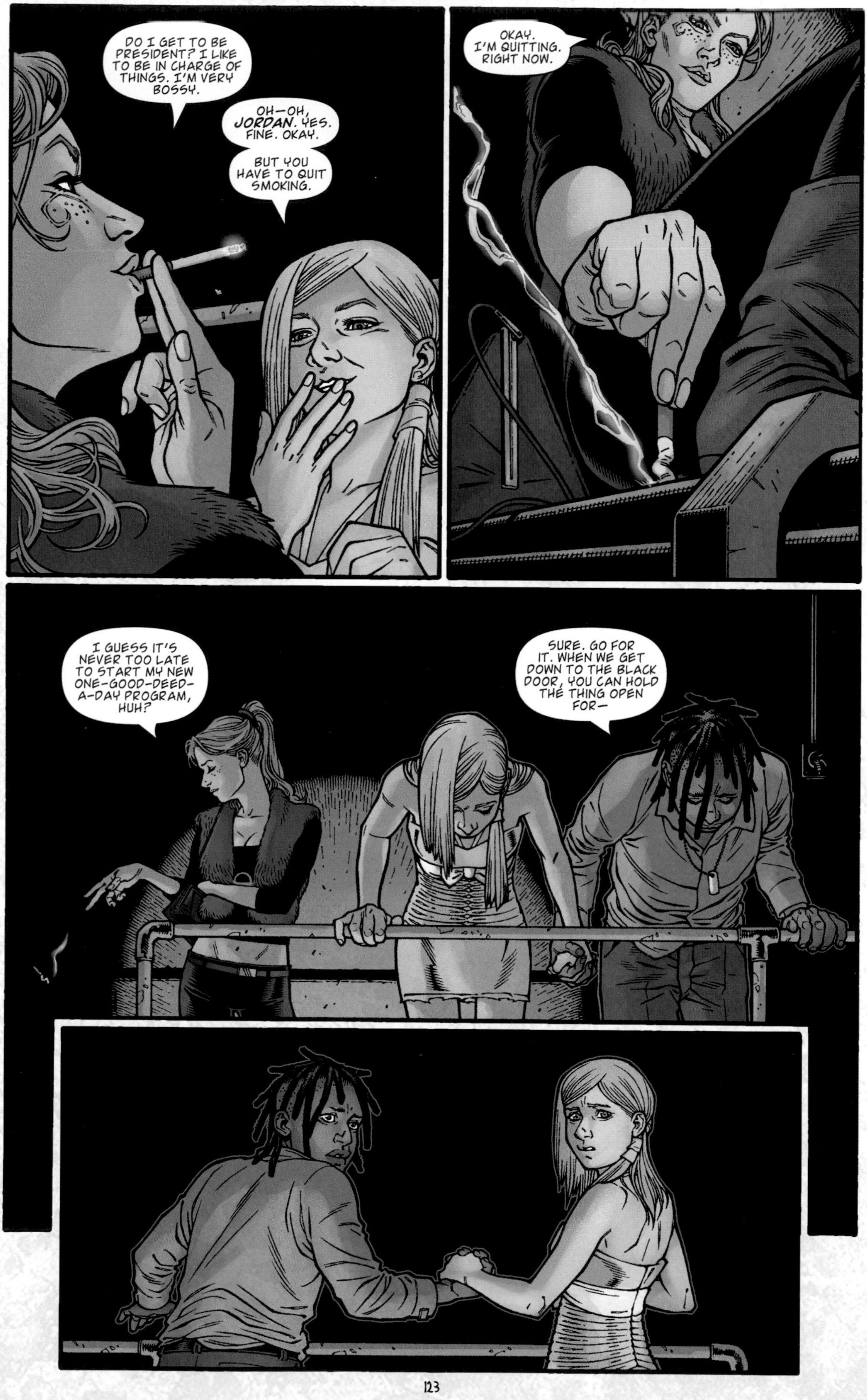
DO I GET TO BE PRESIDENT? I LIKE TO BE IN CHARGE OF THINGS. I'M VERY BOSSY.
OH—OH, JORDAN. YES. FINE. OKAY.
BUT YOU HAVE TO QUIT SMOKING.
OKAY. I'M QUITTING. RIGHT NOW.
I GUESS IT'S NEVER TOO LATE TO START MY NEW ONE-GOOD-DEED-A-DAY PROGRAM, HUH?
SURE. GO FOR IT. WHEN WE GET DOWN TO THE BLACK DOOR, YOU CAN HOLD THE THING OPEN FOR—

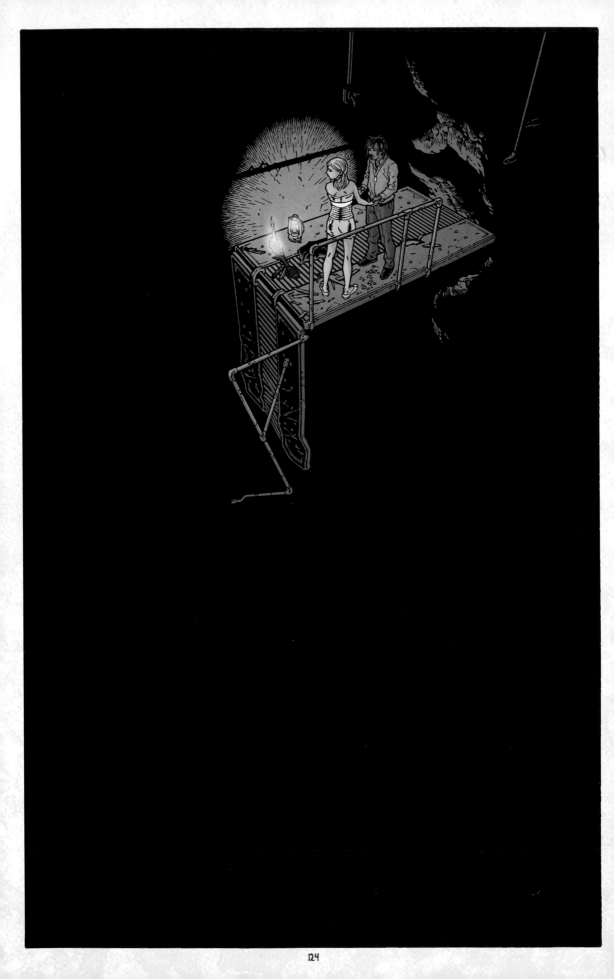

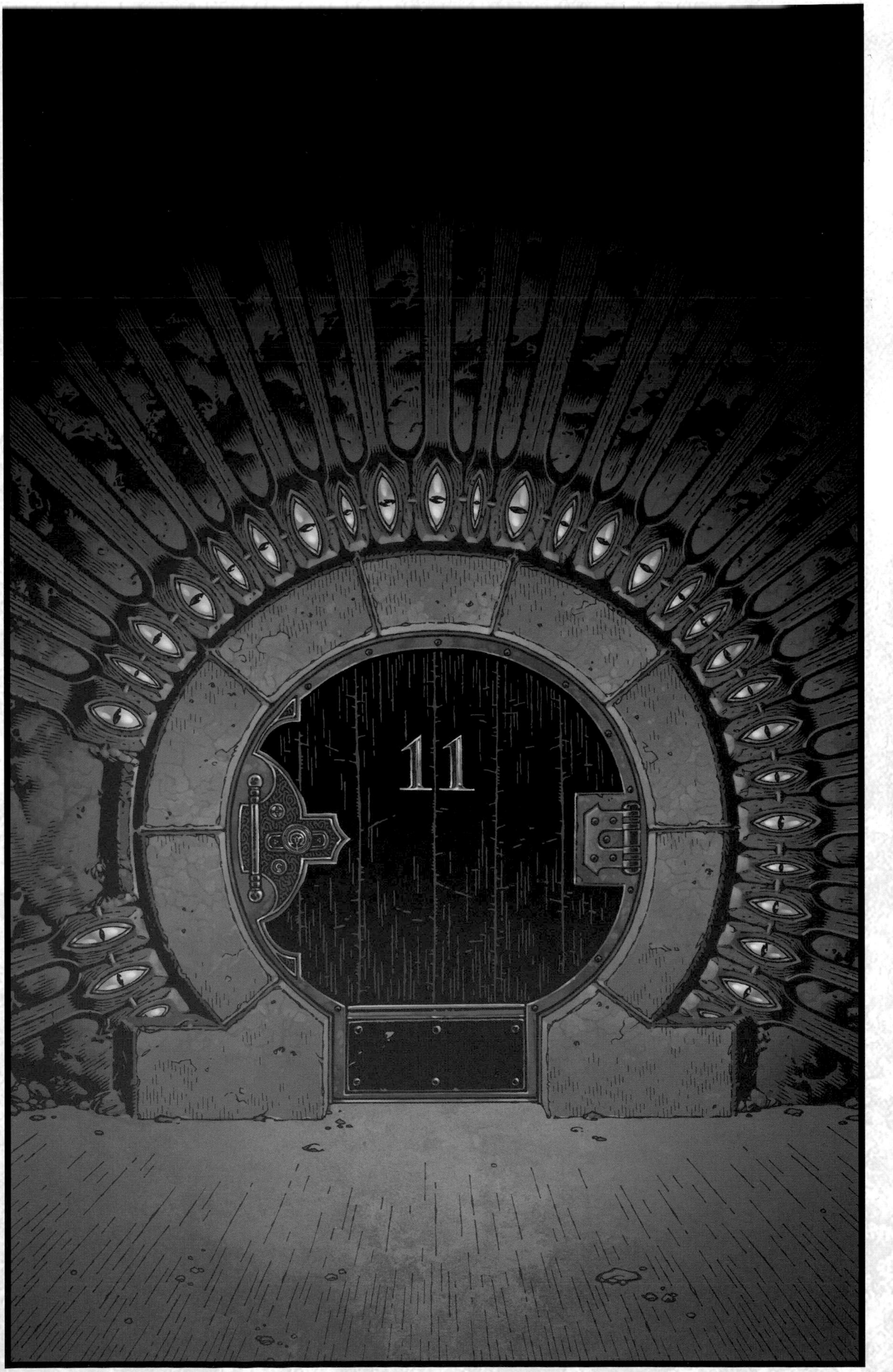
11

- ALPHA & OMEGA -

Chapter Six

ALPHA

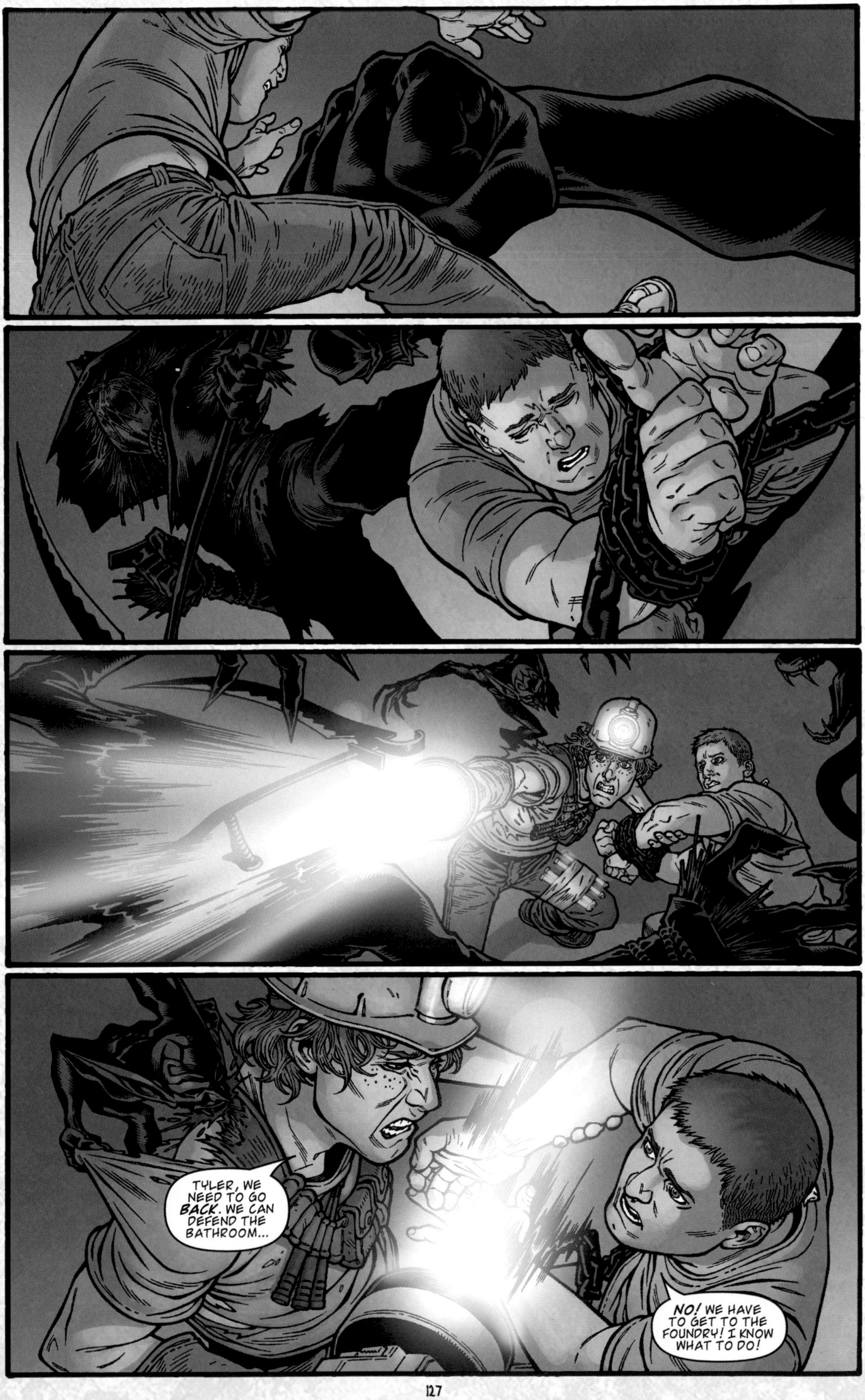
TYLER, WE NEED TO GO BACK. WE CAN DEFEND THE BATHROOM...
NO! WE HAVE TO GET TO THE FOUNDRY! I KNOW WHAT TO DO!

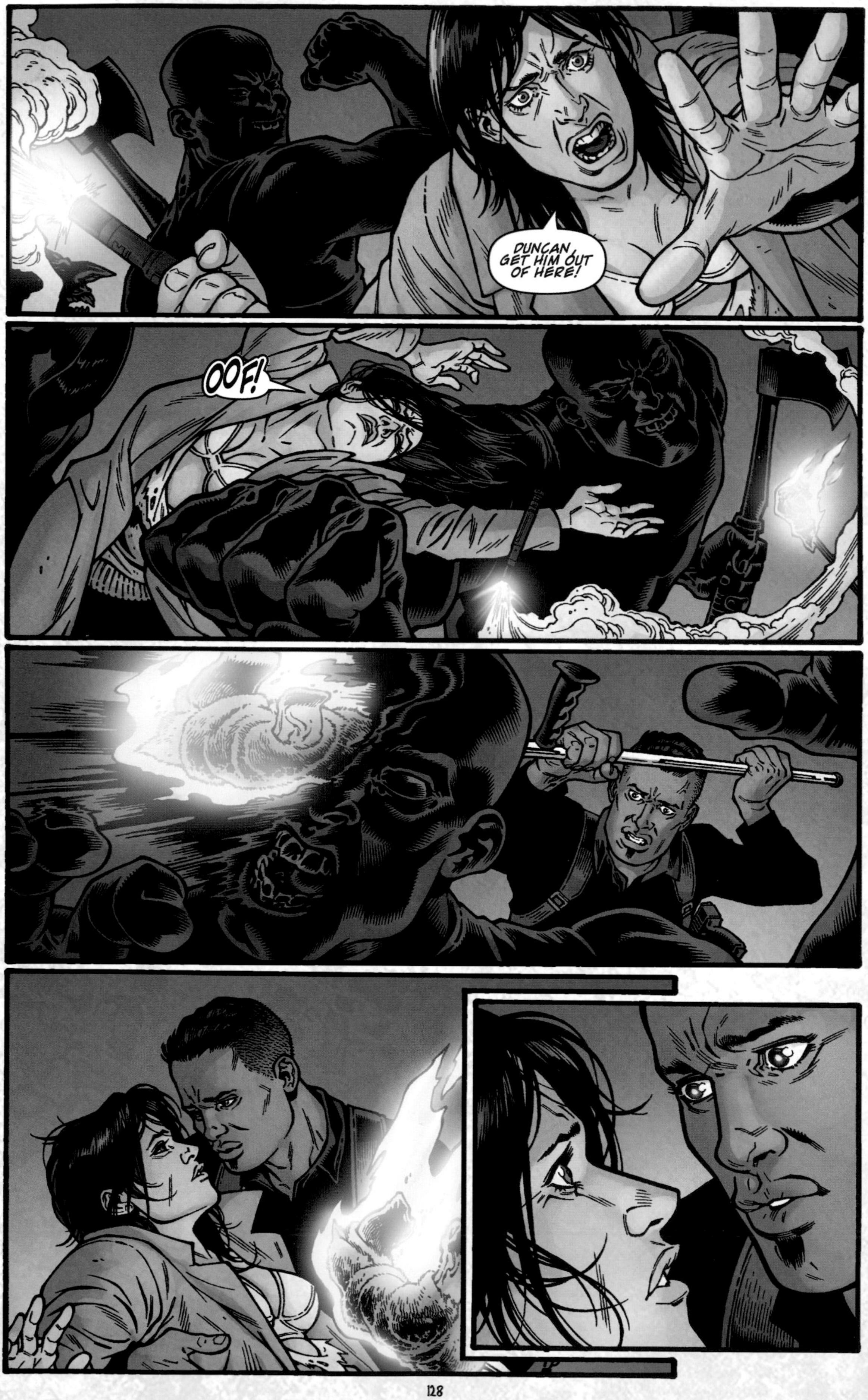
DUNCAN, GET HIM OUT OF HERE!
OOF!

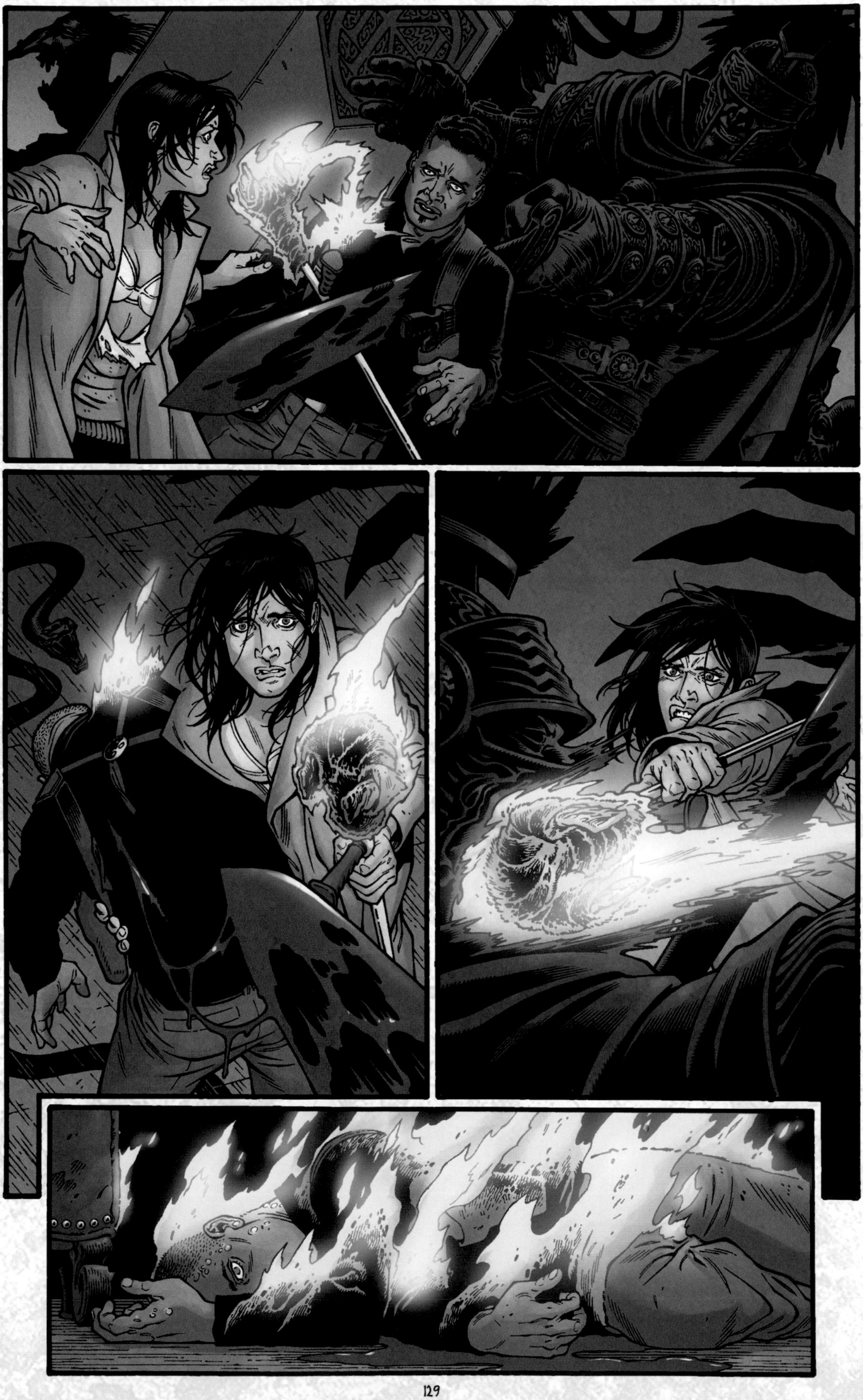

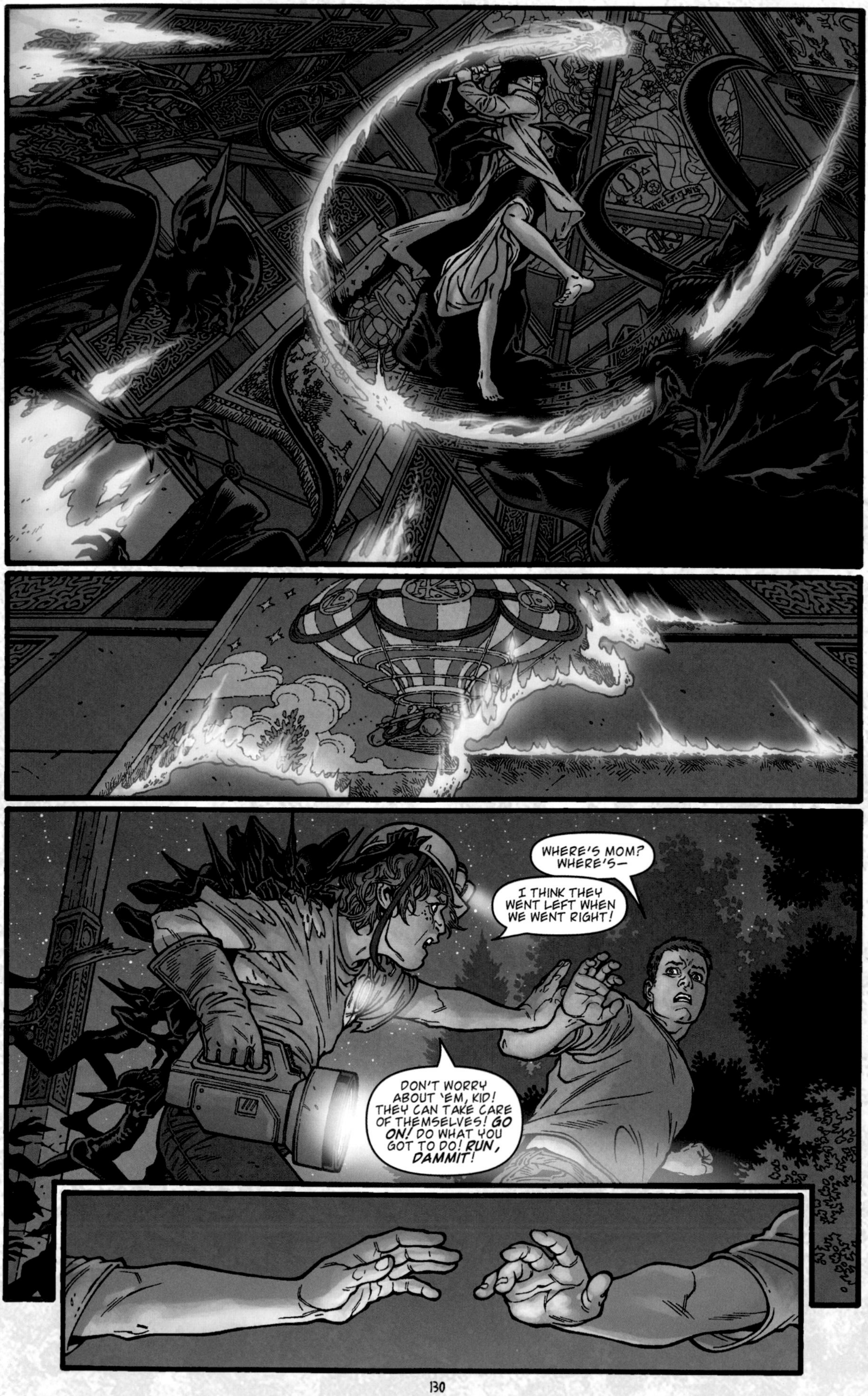
WHERE'S MOM? WHERE'S—
I THINK THEY WENT LEFT WHEN WE WENT RIGHT!
DON'T WORRY ABOUT 'EM, KID! THEY CAN TAKE CARE OF THEMSELVES! GO ON! DO WHAT YOU GOT TO DO! RUN, DAMMIT!

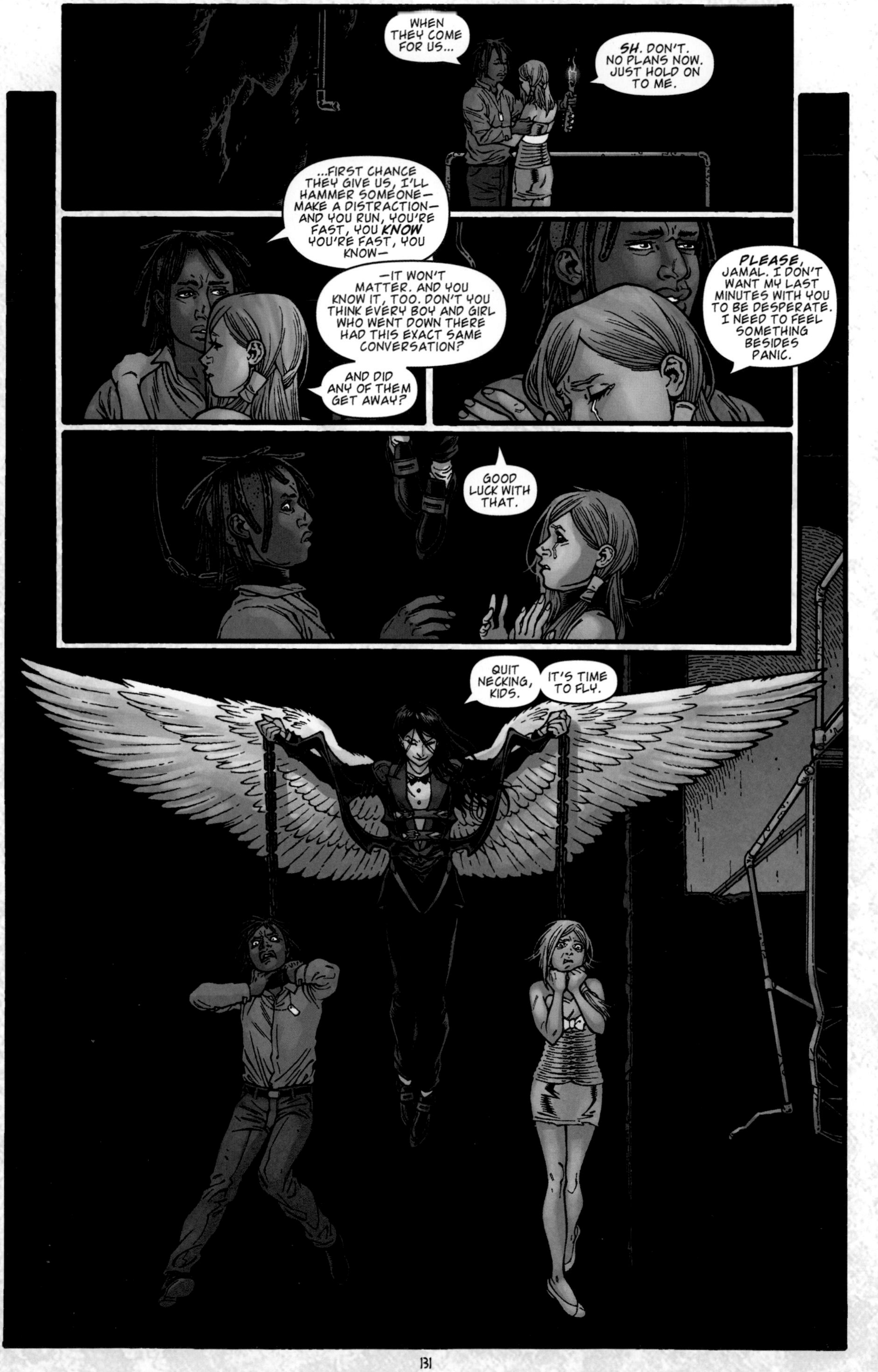

WHEN THEY COME FOR US...
SH. DON'T. NO PLANS NOW. JUST HOLD ON TO ME.
...FIRST CHANCE THEY GIVE US, I'LL HAMMER SOMEONE— MAKE A DISTRACTION— AND YOU RUN, YOU'RE FAST, YOU KNOW YOU'RE FAST, YOU KNOW—
—IT WON'T MATTER. AND YOU KNOW IT, TOO. DON'T YOU THINK EVERY BOY AND GIRL WHO WENT DOWN THERE HAD THIS EXACT SAME CONVERSATION?
AND DID ANY OF THEM GET AWAY?
PLEASE, JAMAL. I DON'T WANT MY LAST MINUTES WITH YOU TO BE DESPERATE. I NEED TO FEEL SOMETHING BESIDES PANIC.
GOOD LUCK WITH THAT.
QUIT NECKING, KIDS.
IT'S TIME TO FLY.

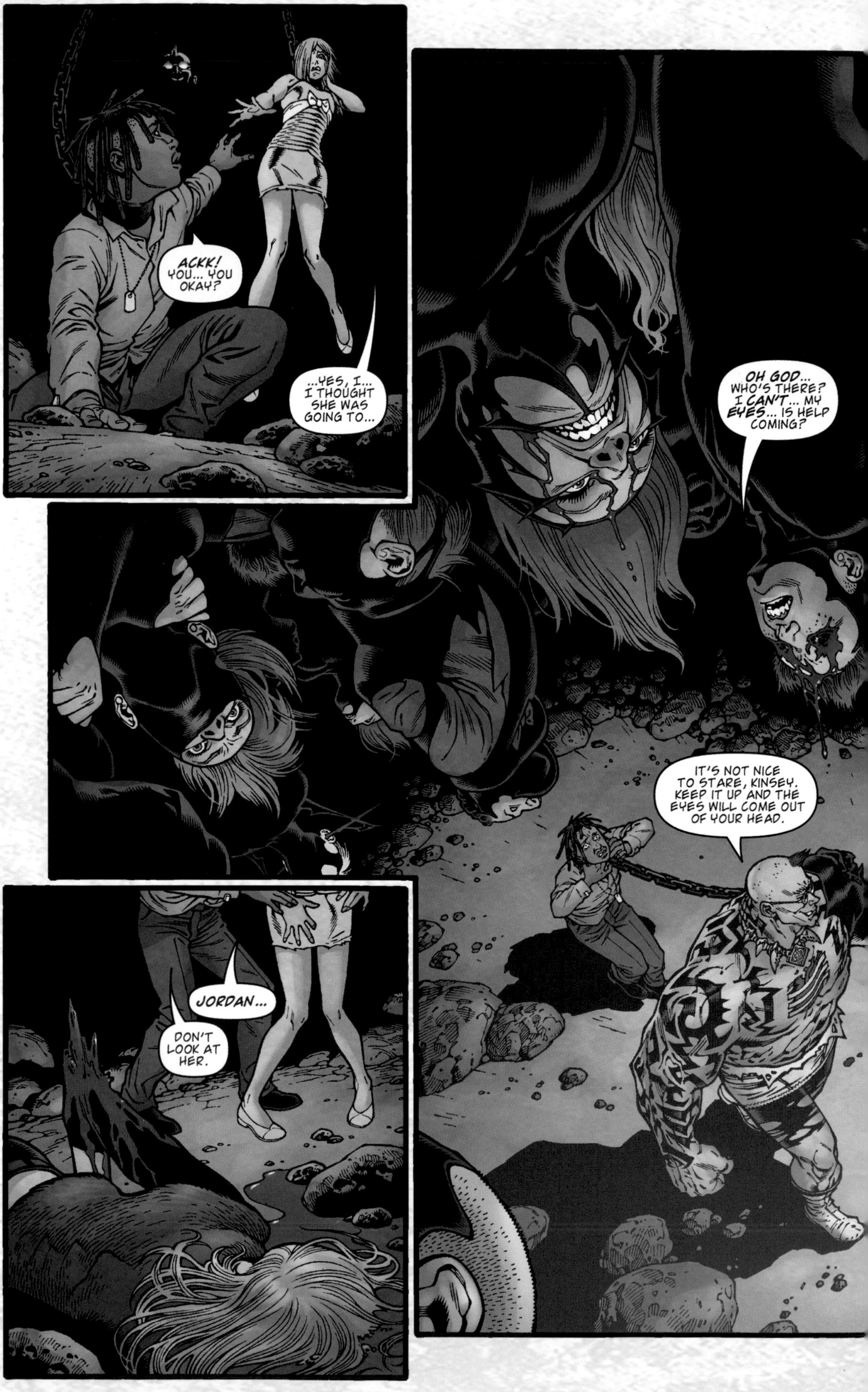
ACKK! YOU... YOU OKAY?
...YES, I... I THOUGHT SHE WAS GOING TO...
OH GOD... WHO'S THERE? I CAN'T... MY EYES... IS HELP COMING?
IT'S NOT NICE TO STARE, KINSEY. KEEP IT UP AND THE EYES WILL COME OUT OF YOUR HEAD.
JORDAN...
DON'T LOOK AT HER.

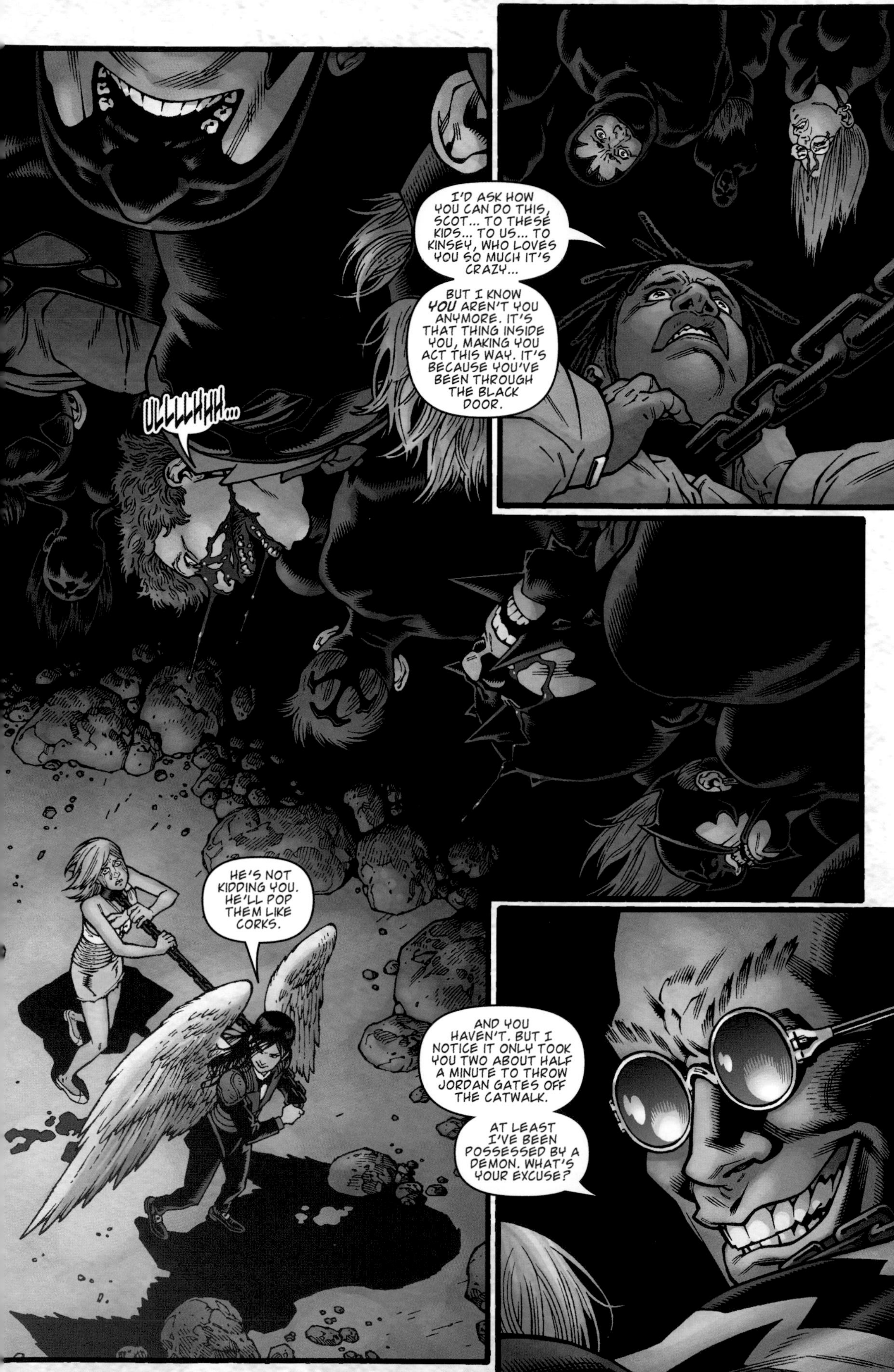
I'D ASK HOW YOU CAN DO THIS, SCOT... TO THESE KIDS... TO US... TO KINSEY, WHO LOVES YOU SO MUCH IT'S CRAZY...
BUT I KNOW *YOU* AREN'T YOU ANYMORE. IT'S THAT THING INSIDE YOU, MAKING YOU ACT THIS WAY. IT'S BECAUSE YOU'VE BEEN THROUGH THE BLACK DOOR.
ULLLLHHH...
HE'S NOT KIDDING YOU. HE'LL POP THEM LIKE CORKS.
AND YOU HAVEN'T. BUT I NOTICE IT ONLY TOOK YOU TWO ABOUT HALF A MINUTE TO THROW JORDAN GATES OFF THE CATWALK.
AT LEAST I'VE BEEN POSSESSED BY A DEMON. WHAT'S YOUR EXCUSE?

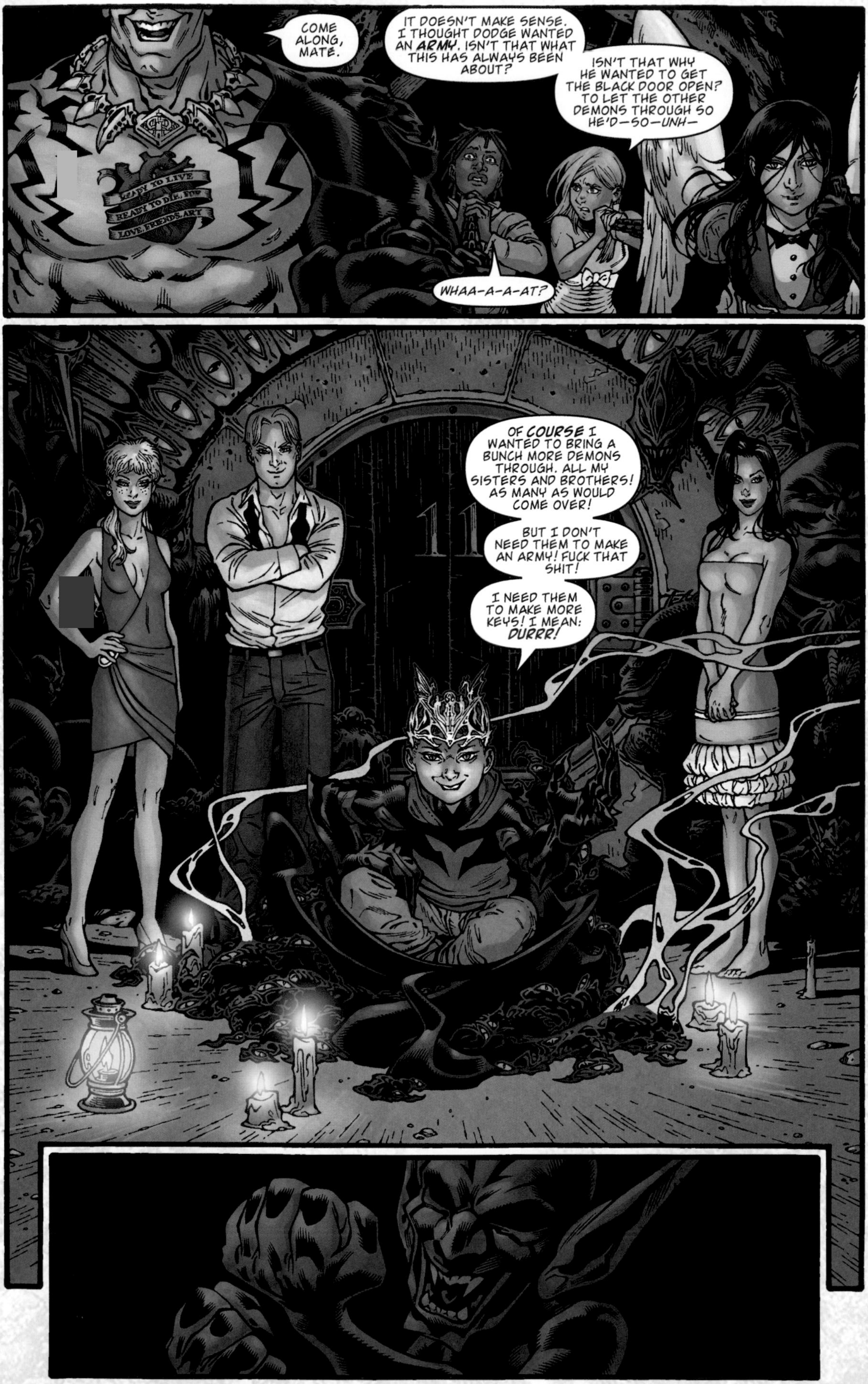
COME ALONG, MATE.
IT DOESN'T MAKE SENSE. I THOUGHT DODGE WANTED AN ARMY. ISN'T THAT WHAT THIS HAS ALWAYS BEEN ABOUT?
ISN'T THAT WHY HE WANTED TO GET THE BLACK DOOR OPEN? TO LET THE OTHER DEMONS THROUGH SO HE'D—SO—UNH—
WHAA-A-A-AT?
OF COURSE I WANTED TO BRING A BUNCH MORE DEMONS THROUGH. ALL MY SISTERS AND BROTHERS! AS MANY AS WOULD COME OVER!
BUT I DON'T NEED THEM TO MAKE AN ARMY! FUCK THAT SHIT!
I NEED THEM TO MAKE MORE KEYS! I MEAN: DURRR!

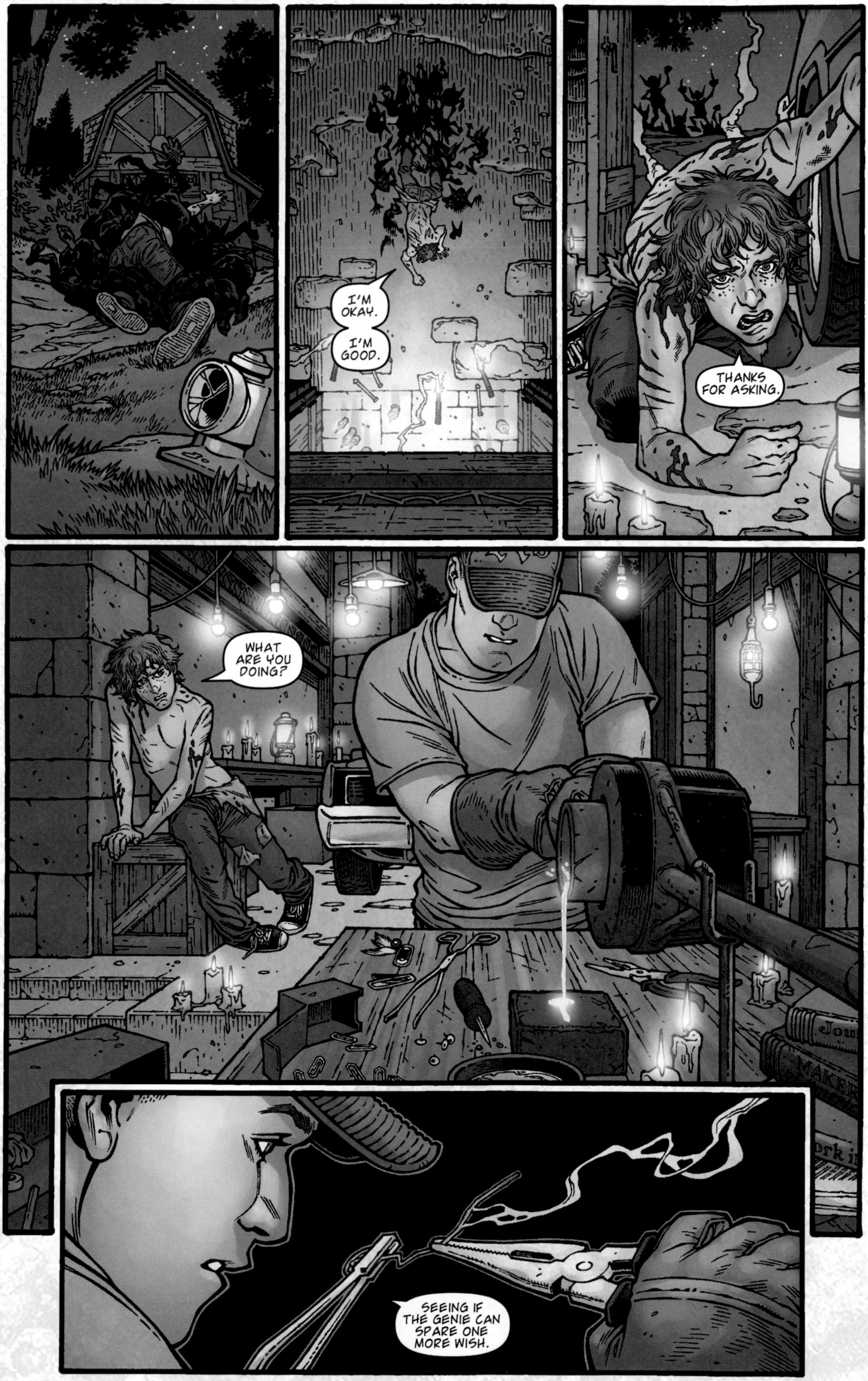
I'M OKAY.
I'M GOOD.
THANKS FOR ASKING.
WHAT ARE YOU DOING?
SEEING IF THE GENIE CAN SPARE ONE MORE WISH.

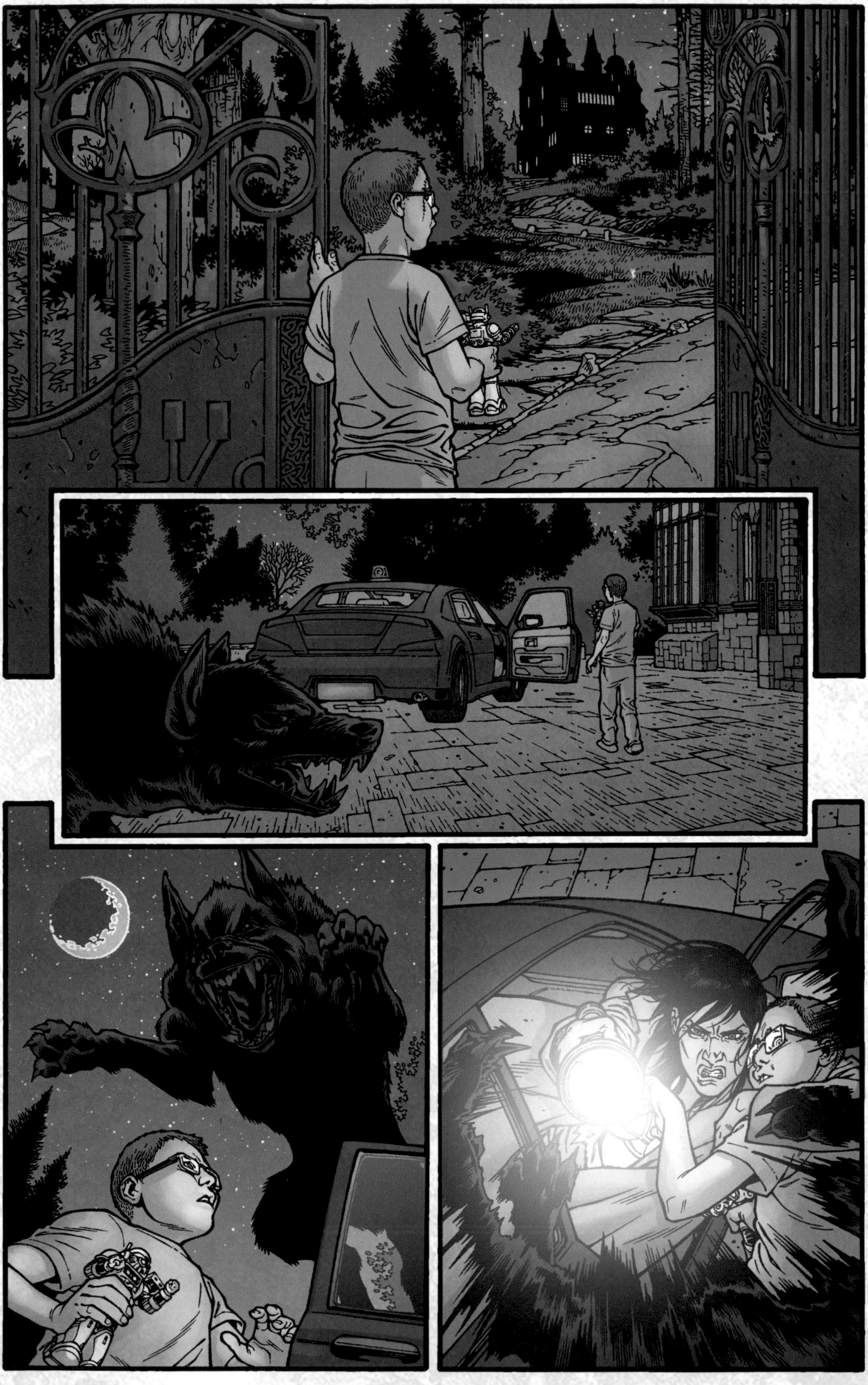

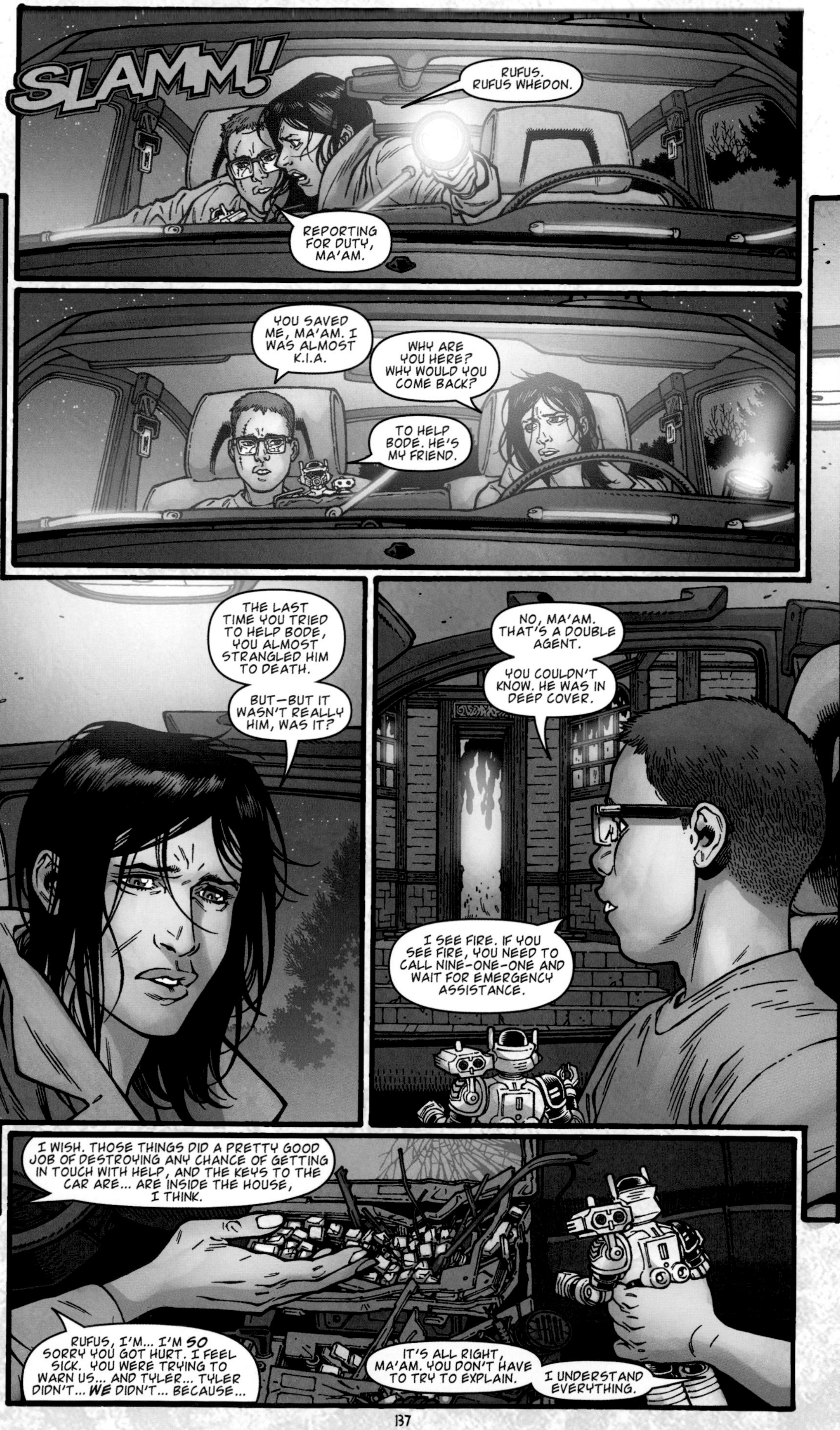
SLAMM!
RUFUS. RUFUS WHEDON.
REPORTING FOR DUTY, MA'AM.
YOU SAVED ME, MA'AM. I WAS ALMOST K.I.A.
WHY ARE YOU HERE? WHY WOULD YOU COME BACK?
TO HELP BODE. HE'S MY FRIEND.
THE LAST TIME YOU TRIED TO HELP BODE, YOU ALMOST STRANGLED HIM TO DEATH.
BUT—BUT IT WASN'T REALLY HIM, WAS IT?
NO, MA'AM. THAT'S A DOUBLE AGENT.
YOU COULDN'T KNOW. HE WAS IN DEEP COVER.
I SEE FIRE. IF YOU SEE FIRE, YOU NEED TO CALL NINE-ONE-ONE AND WAIT FOR EMERGENCY ASSISTANCE.
I WISH. THOSE THINGS DID A PRETTY GOOD JOB OF DESTROYING ANY CHANCE OF GETTING IN TOUCH WITH HELP, AND THE KEYS TO THE CAR ARE... ARE INSIDE THE HOUSE, I THINK.
RUFUS, I'M... I'M SO SORRY YOU GOT HURT. I FEEL SICK. YOU WERE TRYING TO WARN US... AND TYLER... TYLER DIDN'T... WE DIDN'T... BECAUSE...
IT'S ALL RIGHT, MA'AM. YOU DON'T HAVE TO TRY TO EXPLAIN.
I UNDERSTAND EVERYTHING.

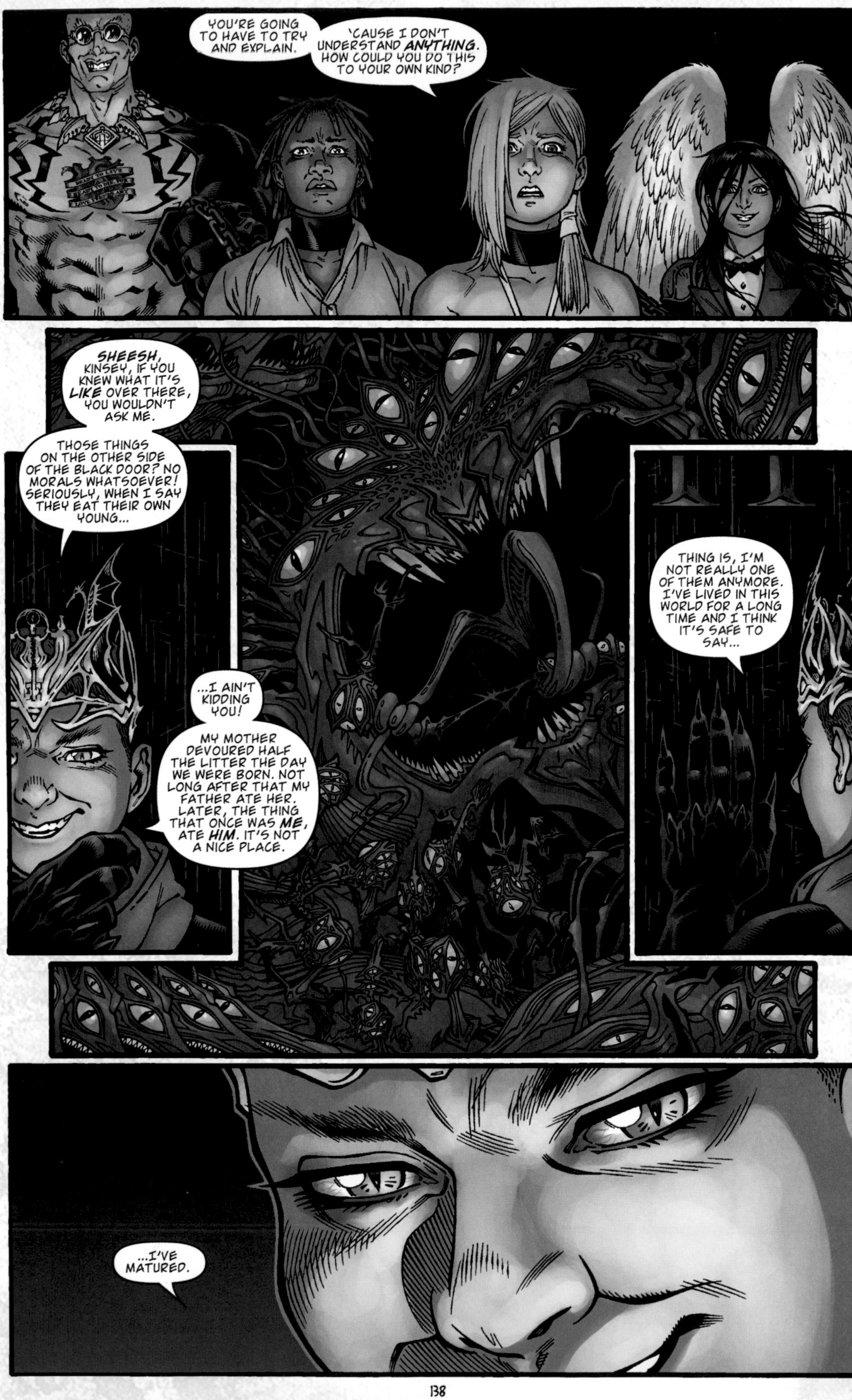

YOU'RE GOING TO HAVE TO TRY AND EXPLAIN.
'CAUSE I DON'T UNDERSTAND ANYTHING. HOW COULD YOU DO THIS TO YOUR OWN KIND?
SHEESH, KINSEY, IF YOU KNEW WHAT IT'S LIKE OVER THERE, YOU WOULDN'T ASK ME.
THOSE THINGS ON THE OTHER SIDE OF THE BLACK DOOR? NO MORALS WHATSOEVER! SERIOUSLY, WHEN I SAY THEY EAT THEIR OWN YOUNG...
...I AIN'T KIDDING YOU!
MY MOTHER DEVOURED HALF THE LITTER THE DAY WE WERE BORN. NOT LONG AFTER THAT MY FATHER ATE HER. LATER, THE THING THAT ONCE WAS ME, ATE HIM. IT'S NOT A NICE PLACE.
THING IS, I'M NOT REALLY ONE OF THEM ANYMORE. I'VE LIVED IN THIS WORLD FOR A LONG TIME AND I THINK IT'S SAFE TO SAY...
...I'VE MATURED.

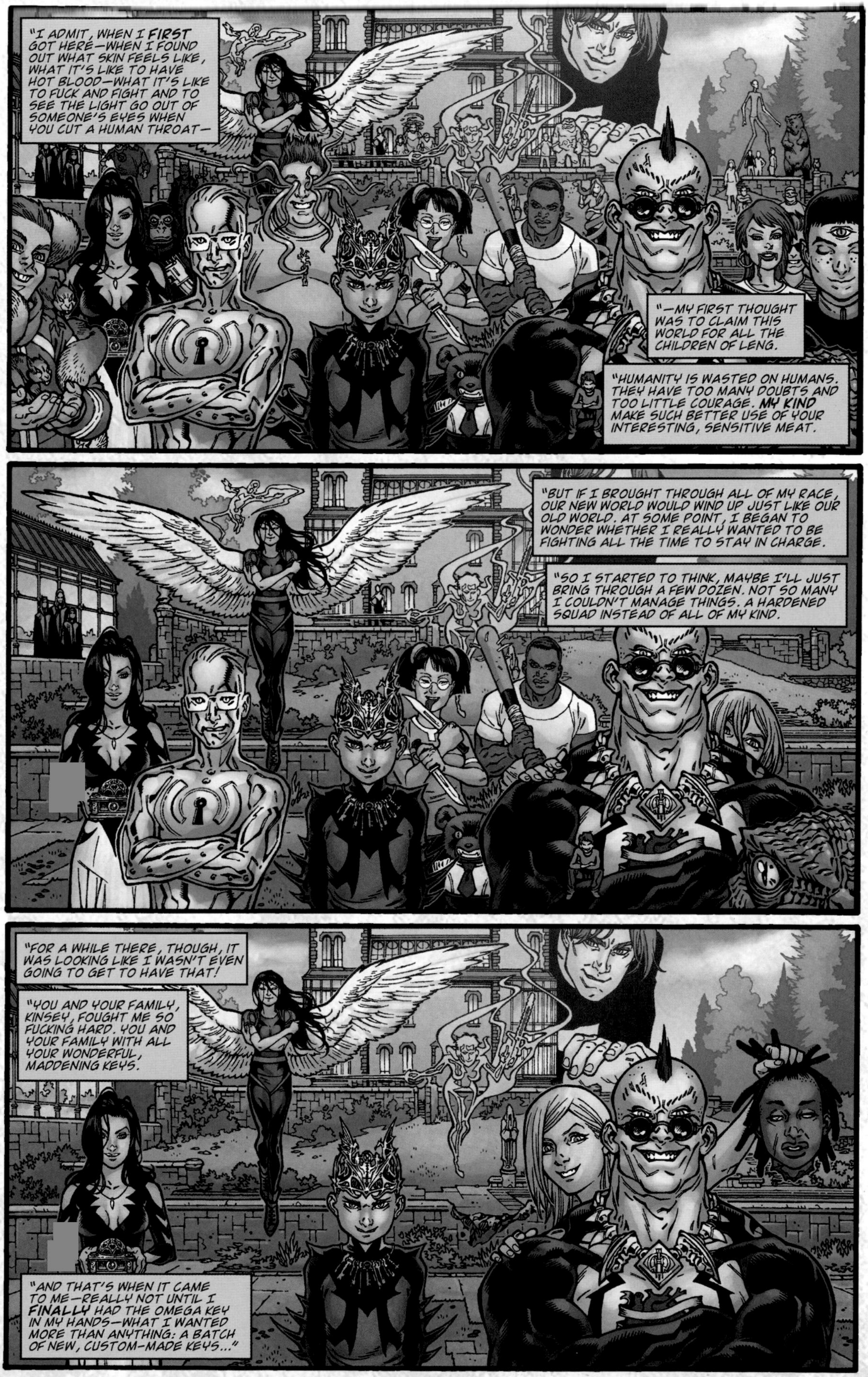
"I ADMIT, WHEN I FIRST GOT HERE—WHEN I FOUND OUT WHAT SKIN FEELS LIKE, WHAT IT'S LIKE TO HAVE HOT BLOOD—WHAT IT'S LIKE TO FUCK AND FIGHT AND TO SEE THE LIGHT GO OUT OF SOMEONE'S EYES WHEN YOU CUT A HUMAN THROAT—
"—MY FIRST THOUGHT WAS TO CLAIM THIS WORLD FOR ALL THE CHILDREN OF LENG.
"HUMANITY IS WASTED ON HUMANS. THEY HAVE TOO MANY DOUBTS AND TOO LITTLE COURAGE. MY KIND MAKE SUCH BETTER USE OF YOUR INTERESTING, SENSITIVE MEAT.
"BUT IF I BROUGHT THROUGH ALL OF MY RACE, OUR NEW WORLD WOULD WIND UP JUST LIKE OUR OLD WORLD. AT SOME POINT, I BEGAN TO WONDER WHETHER I REALLY WANTED TO BE FIGHTING ALL THE TIME TO STAY IN CHARGE.
"SO I STARTED TO THINK, MAYBE I'LL JUST BRING THROUGH A FEW DOZEN. NOT SO MANY I COULDN'T MANAGE THINGS. A HARDENED SQUAD INSTEAD OF ALL OF MY KIND.
"FOR A WHILE THERE, THOUGH, IT WAS LOOKING LIKE I WASN'T EVEN GOING TO GET TO HAVE THAT!
"YOU AND YOUR FAMILY, KINSEY, FOUGHT ME SO FUCKING HARD. YOU AND YOUR FAMILY WITH ALL YOUR WONDERFUL, MADDENING KEYS.
"AND THAT'S WHEN IT CAME TO ME—REALLY NOT UNTIL I FINALLY HAD THE OMEGA KEY IN MY HANDS—WHAT I WANTED MORE THAN ANYTHING: A BATCH OF NEW, CUSTOM-MADE KEYS..."

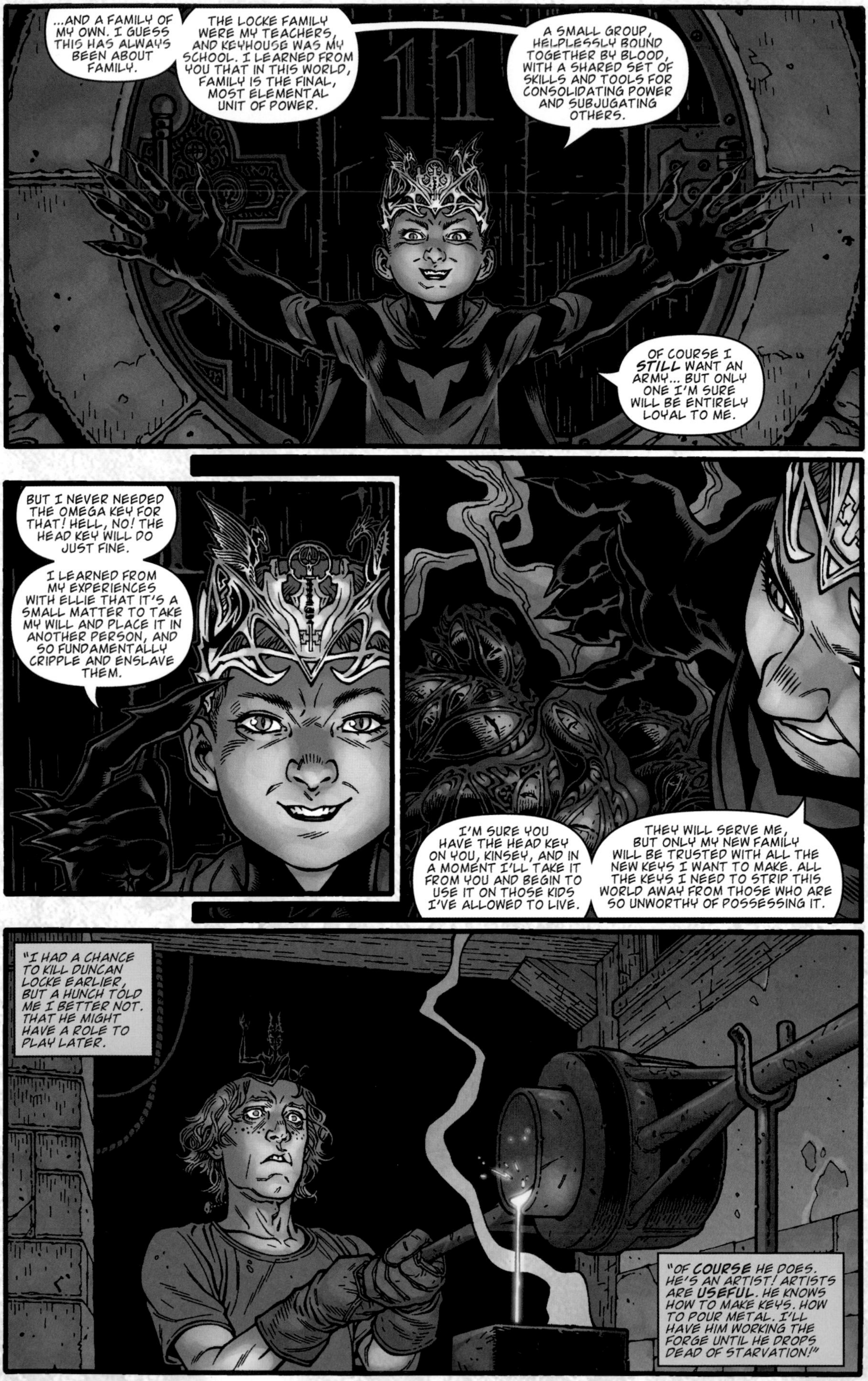
...AND A FAMILY OF MY OWN. I GUESS THIS HAS ALWAYS BEEN ABOUT FAMILY.
THE LOCKE FAMILY WERE MY TEACHERS, AND KEYHOUSE WAS MY SCHOOL. I LEARNED FROM YOU THAT IN THIS WORLD, FAMILY IS THE FINAL, MOST ELEMENTAL UNIT OF POWER.
A SMALL GROUP, HELPLESSLY BOUND TOGETHER BY BLOOD, WITH A SHARED SET OF SKILLS AND TOOLS FOR CONSOLIDATING POWER AND SUBJUGATING OTHERS.
OF COURSE I STILL WANT AN ARMY... BUT ONLY ONE I'M SURE WILL BE ENTIRELY LOYAL TO ME.
BUT I NEVER NEEDED THE OMEGA KEY FOR THAT! HELL, NO! THE HEAD KEY WILL DO JUST FINE.
I LEARNED FROM MY EXPERIENCES WITH ELLIE THAT IT'S A SMALL MATTER TO TAKE MY WILL AND PLACE IT IN ANOTHER PERSON, AND SO FUNDAMENTALLY CRIPPLE AND ENSLAVE THEM.
I'M SURE YOU HAVE THE HEAD KEY ON YOU, KINSEY, AND IN A MOMENT I'LL TAKE IT FROM YOU AND BEGIN TO USE IT ON THOSE KIDS I'VE ALLOWED TO LIVE.
THEY WILL SERVE ME, BUT ONLY MY NEW FAMILY WILL BE TRUSTED WITH ALL THE NEW KEYS I WANT TO MAKE. ALL THE KEYS I NEED TO STRIP THIS WORLD AWAY FROM THOSE WHO ARE SO UNWORTHY OF POSSESSING IT.
"I HAD A CHANCE TO KILL DUNCAN LOCKE EARLIER, BUT A HUNCH TOLD ME I BETTER NOT. THAT HE MIGHT HAVE A ROLE TO PLAY LATER.
"OF COURSE HE DOES. HE'S AN ARTIST! ARTISTS ARE USEFUL. HE KNOWS HOW TO MAKE KEYS. HOW TO POUR METAL. I'LL HAVE HIM WORKING THE FORGE UNTIL HE DROPS DEAD OF STARVATION!"

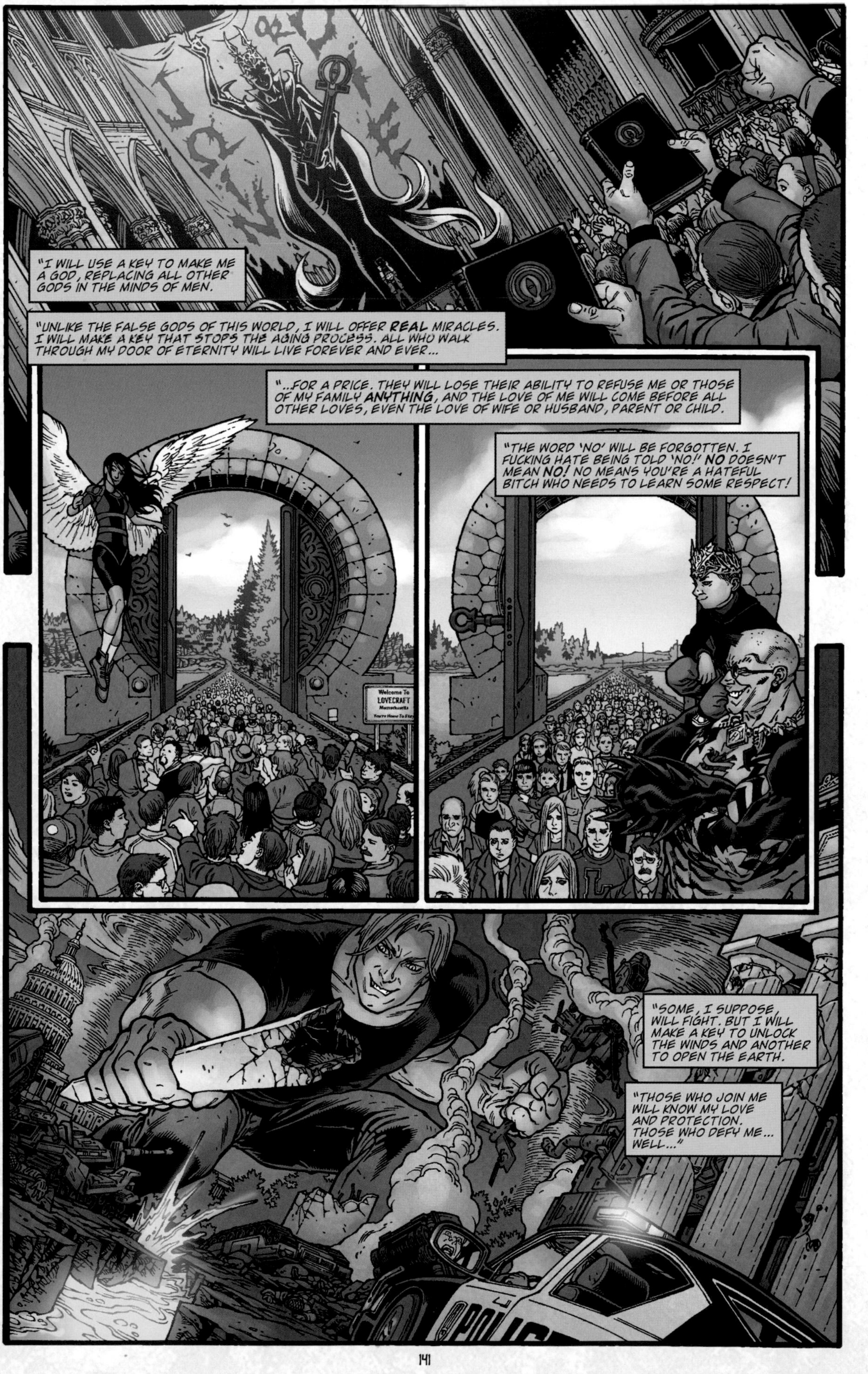
"I WILL USE A KEY TO MAKE ME A GOD, REPLACING ALL OTHER GODS IN THE MINDS OF MEN.
"UNLIKE THE FALSE GODS OF THIS WORLD, I WILL OFFER REAL MIRACLES. I WILL MAKE A KEY THAT STOPS THE AGING PROCESS. ALL WHO WALK THROUGH MY DOOR OF ETERNITY WILL LIVE FOREVER AND EVER...
"...FOR A PRICE. THEY WILL LOSE THEIR ABILITY TO REFUSE ME OR THOSE OF MY FAMILY ANYTHING, AND THE LOVE OF ME WILL COME BEFORE ALL OTHER LOVES, EVEN THE LOVE OF WIFE OR HUSBAND, PARENT OR CHILD.
Welcome To LOVECRAFT Massachusetts You're Home To Stay
"THE WORD 'NO' WILL BE FORGOTTEN. I FUCKING HATE BEING TOLD 'NO!' NO DOESN'T MEAN NO! NO MEANS YOU'RE A HATEFUL BITCH WHO NEEDS TO LEARN SOME RESPECT!
"SOME, I SUPPOSE, WILL FIGHT. BUT I WILL MAKE A KEY TO UNLOCK THE WINDS AND ANOTHER TO OPEN THE EARTH.
"THOSE WHO JOIN ME WILL KNOW MY LOVE AND PROTECTION. THOSE WHO DEFY ME... WELL..."

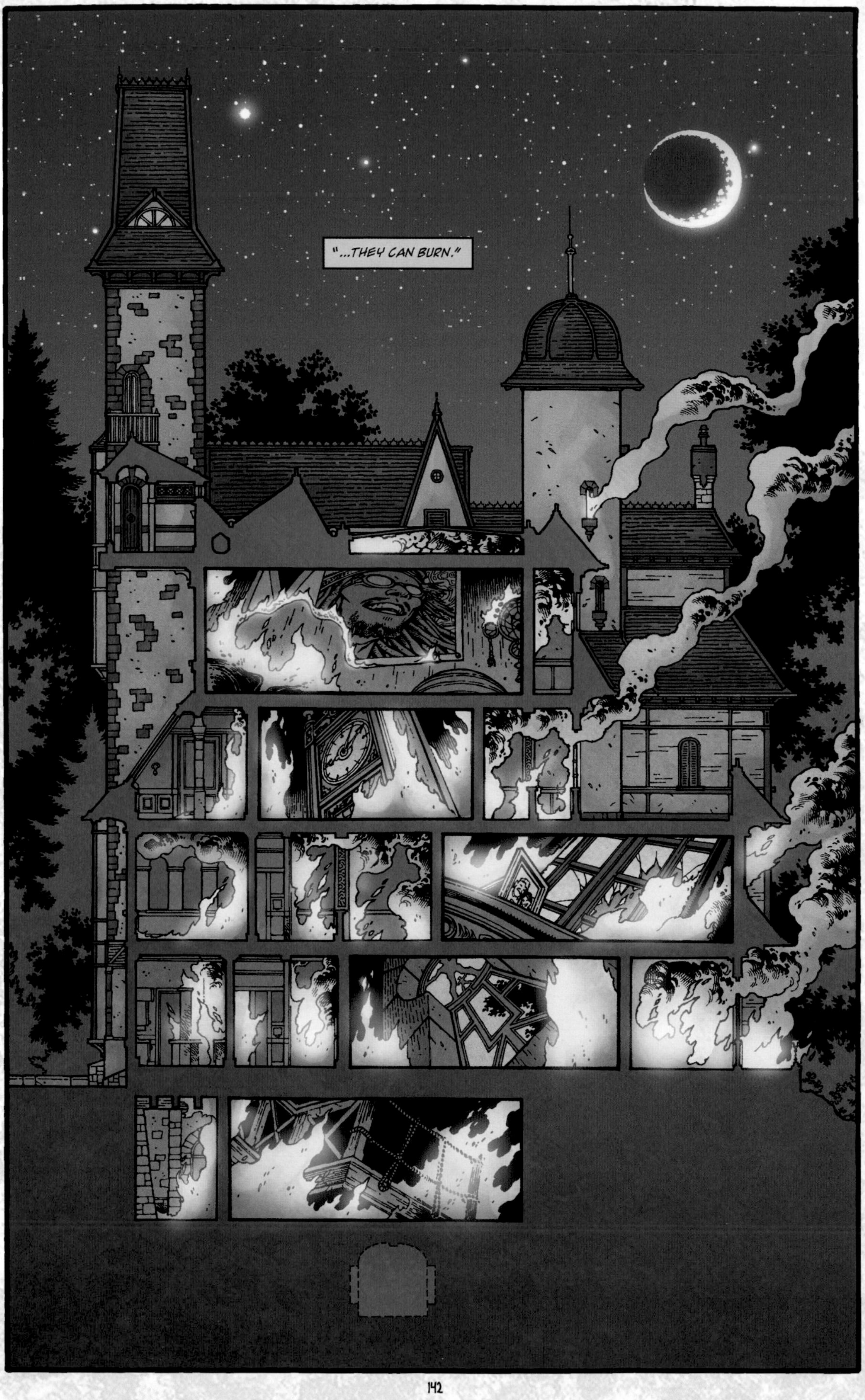
"...THEY CAN BURN."

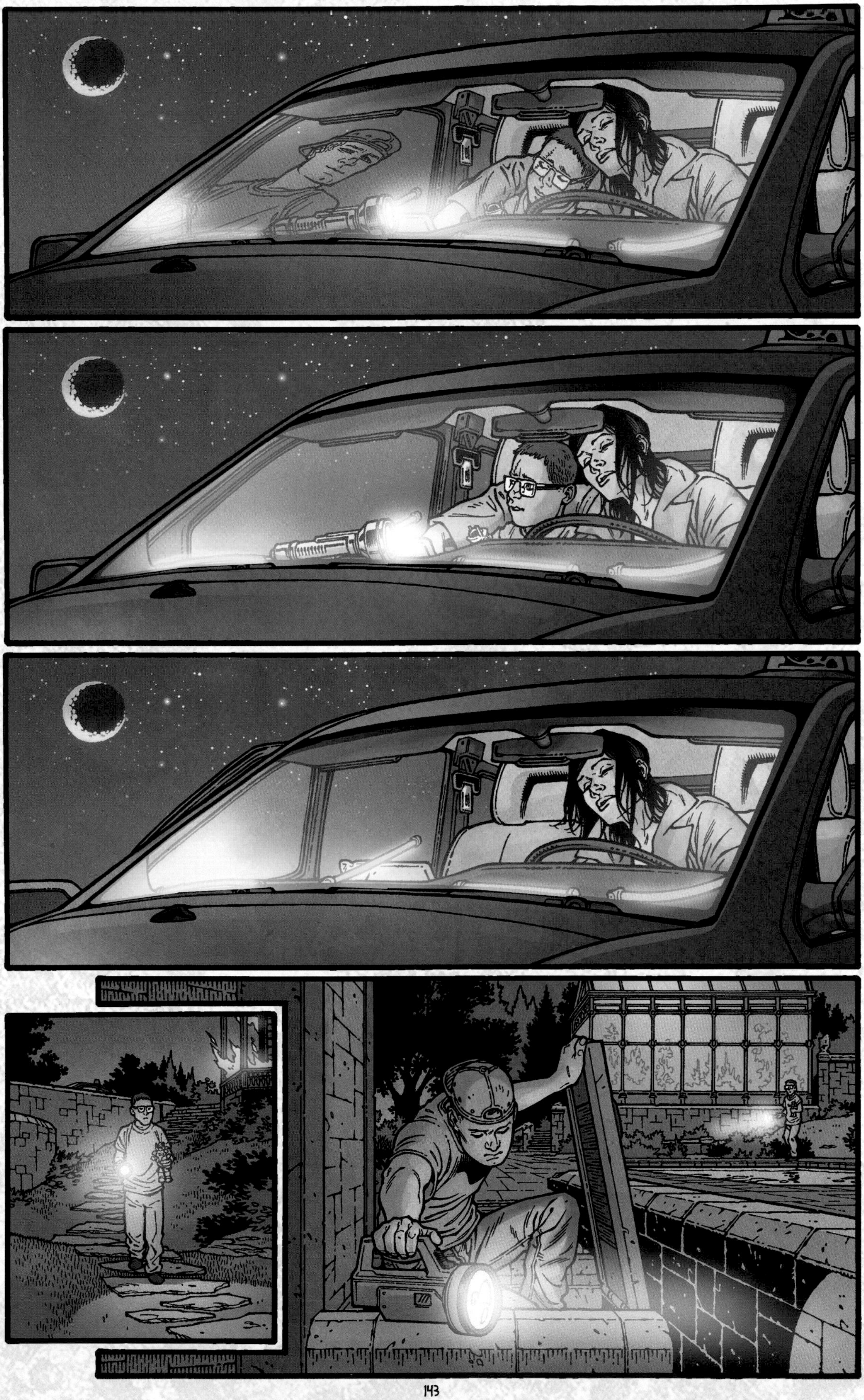

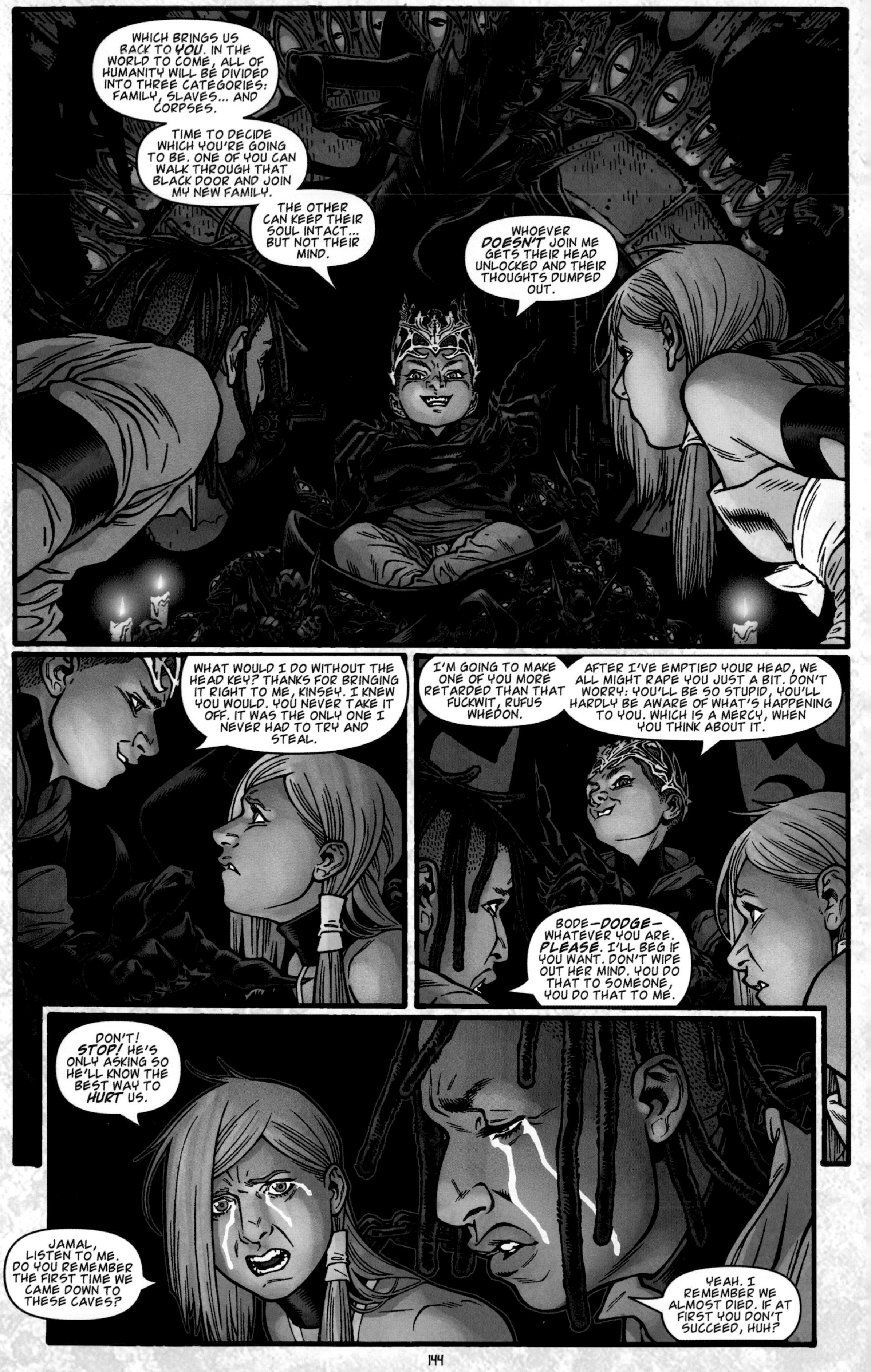
WHICH BRINGS US BACK TO YOU. IN THE WORLD TO COME, ALL OF HUMANITY WILL BE DIVIDED INTO THREE CATEGORIES: FAMILY, SLAVES... AND CORPSES.
TIME TO DECIDE WHICH YOU'RE GOING TO BE. ONE OF YOU CAN WALK THROUGH THAT BLACK DOOR AND JOIN MY NEW FAMILY.
THE OTHER CAN KEEP THEIR SOUL INTACT... BUT NOT THEIR MIND.
WHOEVER DOESN'T JOIN ME GETS THEIR HEAD UNLOCKED AND THEIR THOUGHTS DUMPED OUT.
WHAT WOULD I DO WITHOUT THE HEAD KEY? THANKS FOR BRINGING IT RIGHT TO ME, KINSEY. I KNEW YOU WOULD. YOU NEVER TAKE IT OFF. IT WAS THE ONLY ONE I NEVER HAD TO TRY AND STEAL.
I'M GOING TO MAKE ONE OF YOU MORE RETARDED THAN THAT FUCKWIT, RUFUS WHEDON.
AFTER I'VE EMPTIED YOUR HEAD, WE ALL MIGHT RAPE YOU JUST A BIT. DON'T WORRY: YOU'LL BE SO STUPID, YOU'LL HARDLY BE AWARE OF WHAT'S HAPPENING TO YOU. WHICH IS A MERCY, WHEN YOU THINK ABOUT IT.
BODE—DODGE—WHATEVER YOU ARE. PLEASE. I'LL BEG IF YOU WANT. DON'T WIPE OUT HER MIND. YOU DO THAT TO SOMEONE, YOU DO THAT TO ME.
DON'T! STOP! HE'S ONLY ASKING SO HE'LL KNOW THE BEST WAY TO HURT US.
JAMAL, LISTEN TO ME. DO YOU REMEMBER THE FIRST TIME WE CAME DOWN TO THESE CAVES?
YEAH. I REMEMBER WE ALMOST DIED. IF AT FIRST YOU DON'T SUCCEED, HUH?

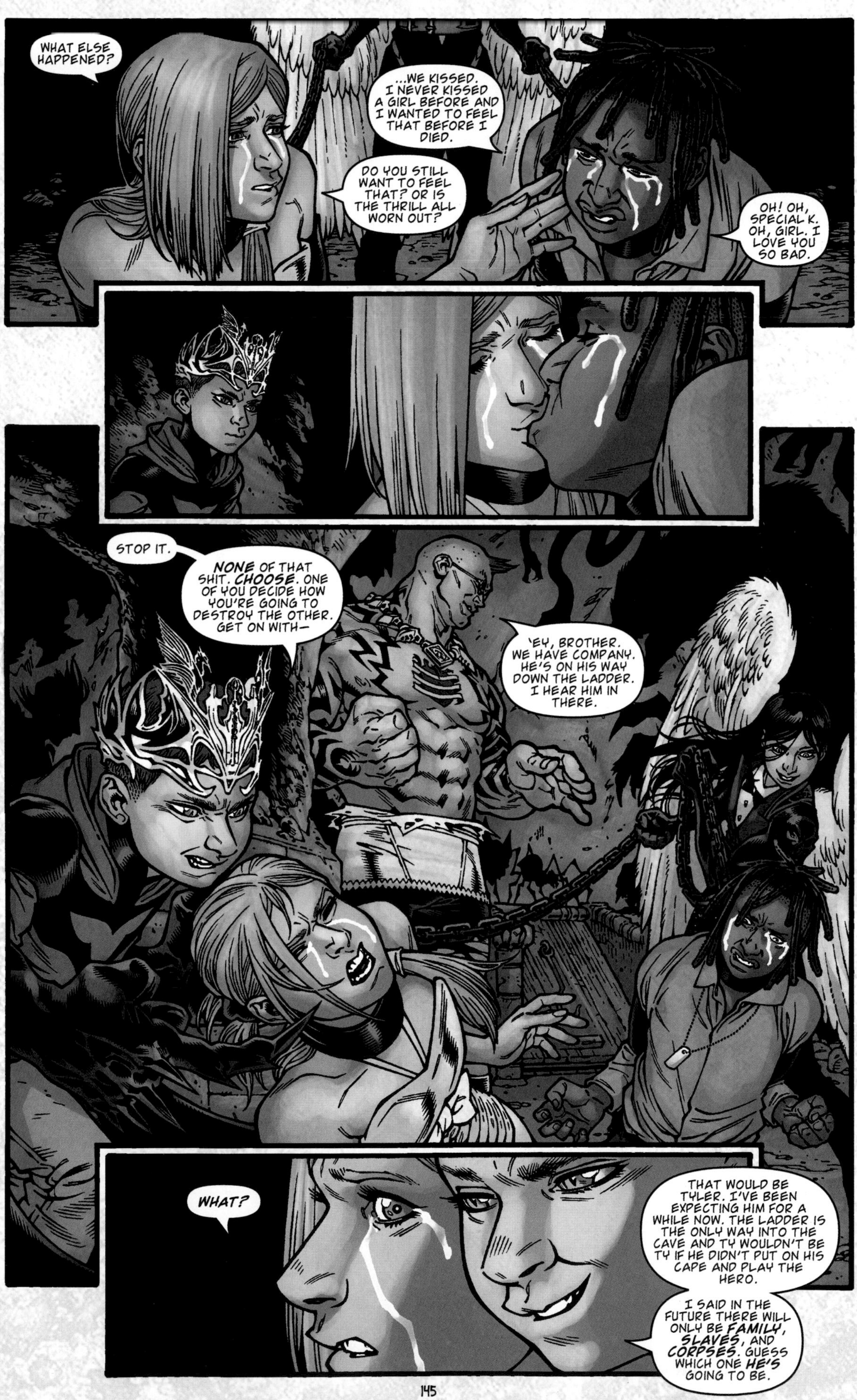
WHAT ELSE HAPPENED?
...WE KISSED. I NEVER KISSED A GIRL BEFORE AND I WANTED TO FEEL THAT BEFORE I DIED.
DO YOU STILL WANT TO FEEL THAT? OR IS THE THRILL ALL WORN OUT?
OH! OH, SPECIAL K. OH, GIRL. I LOVE YOU SO BAD.
STOP IT.
NONE OF THAT SHIT. CHOOSE. ONE OF YOU DECIDE HOW YOU'RE GOING TO DESTROY THE OTHER. GET ON WITH—
'EY, BROTHER. WE HAVE COMPANY. HE'S ON HIS WAY DOWN THE LADDER. I HEAR HIM IN THERE.
WHAT?
THAT WOULD BE TYLER. I'VE BEEN EXPECTING HIM FOR A WHILE NOW. THE LADDER IS THE ONLY WAY INTO THE CAVE AND TY WOULDN'T BE TY IF HE DIDN'T PUT ON HIS CAPE AND PLAY THE HERO.
I SAID IN THE FUTURE THERE WILL ONLY BE FAMILY, SLAVES, AND CORPSES. GUESS WHICH ONE HE'S GOING TO BE.

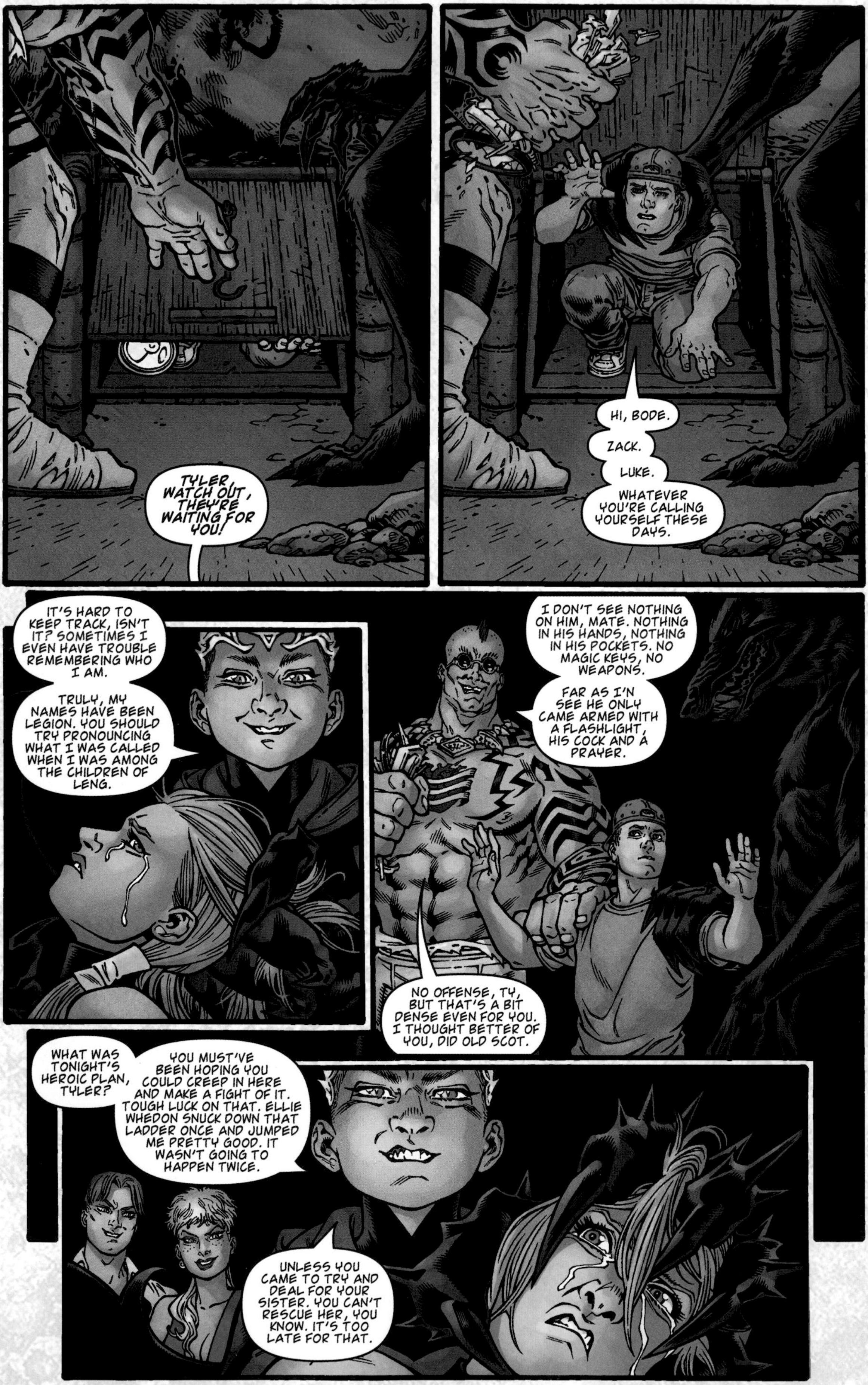
TYLER, WATCH OUT, THEY'RE WAITING FOR YOU!
HI, BODE.
ZACK.
LUKE.
WHATEVER YOU'RE CALLING YOURSELF THESE DAYS.
IT'S HARD TO KEEP TRACK, ISN'T IT? SOMETIMES I EVEN HAVE TROUBLE REMEMBERING WHO I AM.
TRULY, MY NAMES HAVE BEEN LEGION. YOU SHOULD TRY PRONOUNCING WHAT I WAS CALLED WHEN I WAS AMONG THE CHILDREN OF LENG.
I DON'T SEE NOTHING ON HIM, MATE. NOTHING IN HIS HANDS, NOTHING IN HIS POCKETS. NO MAGIC KEYS, NO WEAPONS.
FAR AS I'N SEE HE ONLY CAME ARMED WITH A FLASHLIGHT, HIS COCK AND A PRAYER.
NO OFFENSE, TY, BUT THAT'S A BIT DENSE EVEN FOR YOU. I THOUGHT BETTER OF YOU, DID OLD SCOT.
WHAT WAS TONIGHT'S HEROIC PLAN, TYLER?
YOU MUST'VE BEEN HOPING YOU COULD CREEP IN HERE AND MAKE A FIGHT OF IT. TOUGH LUCK ON THAT. ELLIE WHEDON SNUCK DOWN THAT LADDER ONCE AND JUMPED ME PRETTY GOOD. IT WASN'T GOING TO HAPPEN TWICE.
UNLESS YOU CAME TO TRY AND DEAL FOR YOUR SISTER. YOU CAN'T RESCUE HER, YOU KNOW. IT'S TOO LATE FOR THAT.

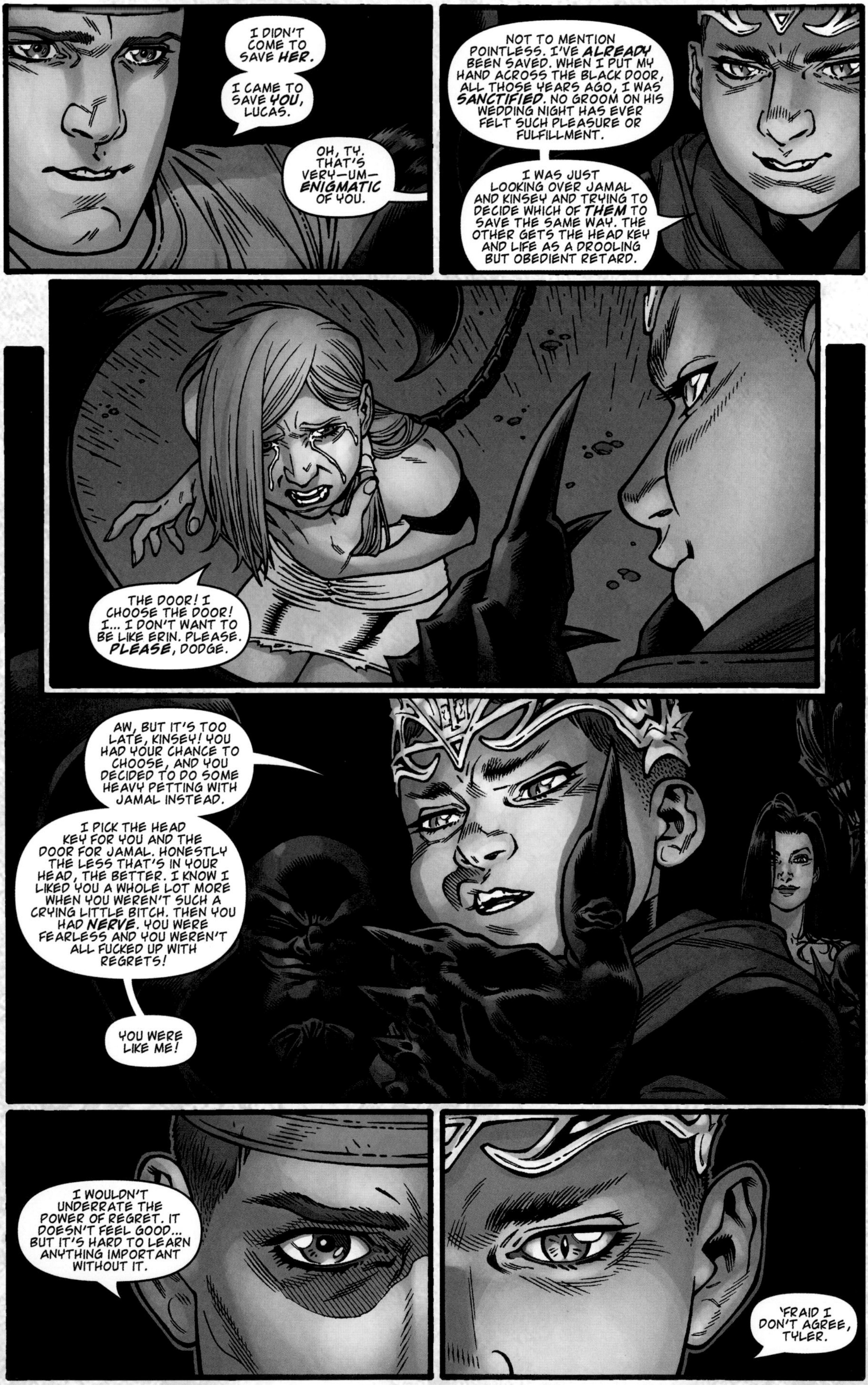
I DIDN'T COME TO SAVE HER.
I CAME TO SAVE YOU, LUCAS.
OH, TY. THAT'S VERY—UM—ENIGMATIC OF YOU.
NOT TO MENTION POINTLESS. I'VE ALREADY BEEN SAVED. WHEN I PUT MY HAND ACROSS THE BLACK DOOR, ALL THOSE YEARS AGO, I WAS SANCTIFIED. NO GROOM ON HIS WEDDING NIGHT HAS EVER FELT SUCH PLEASURE OR FULFILLMENT.
I WAS JUST LOOKING OVER JAMAL AND KINSEY AND TRYING TO DECIDE WHICH OF THEM TO SAVE THE SAME WAY. THE OTHER GETS THE HEAD KEY AND LIFE AS A DROOLING BUT OBEDIENT RETARD.
THE DOOR! I CHOOSE THE DOOR! I... I DON'T WANT TO BE LIKE ERIN. PLEASE. PLEASE, DODGE.
AW, BUT IT'S TOO LATE, KINSEY! YOU HAD YOUR CHANCE TO CHOOSE, AND YOU DECIDED TO DO SOME HEAVY PETTING WITH JAMAL INSTEAD.
I PICK THE HEAD KEY FOR YOU AND THE DOOR FOR JAMAL. HONESTLY THE LESS THAT'S IN YOUR HEAD, THE BETTER. I KNOW I LIKED YOU A WHOLE LOT MORE WHEN YOU WEREN'T SUCH A CRYING LITTLE BITCH. THEN YOU HAD NERVE. YOU WERE FEARLESS AND YOU WEREN'T ALL FUCKED UP WITH REGRETS!
YOU WERE LIKE ME!
I WOULDN'T UNDERRATE THE POWER OF REGRET. IT DOESN'T FEEL GOOD... BUT IT'S HARD TO LEARN ANYTHING IMPORTANT WITHOUT IT.
'FRAID I DON'T AGREE, TYLER.

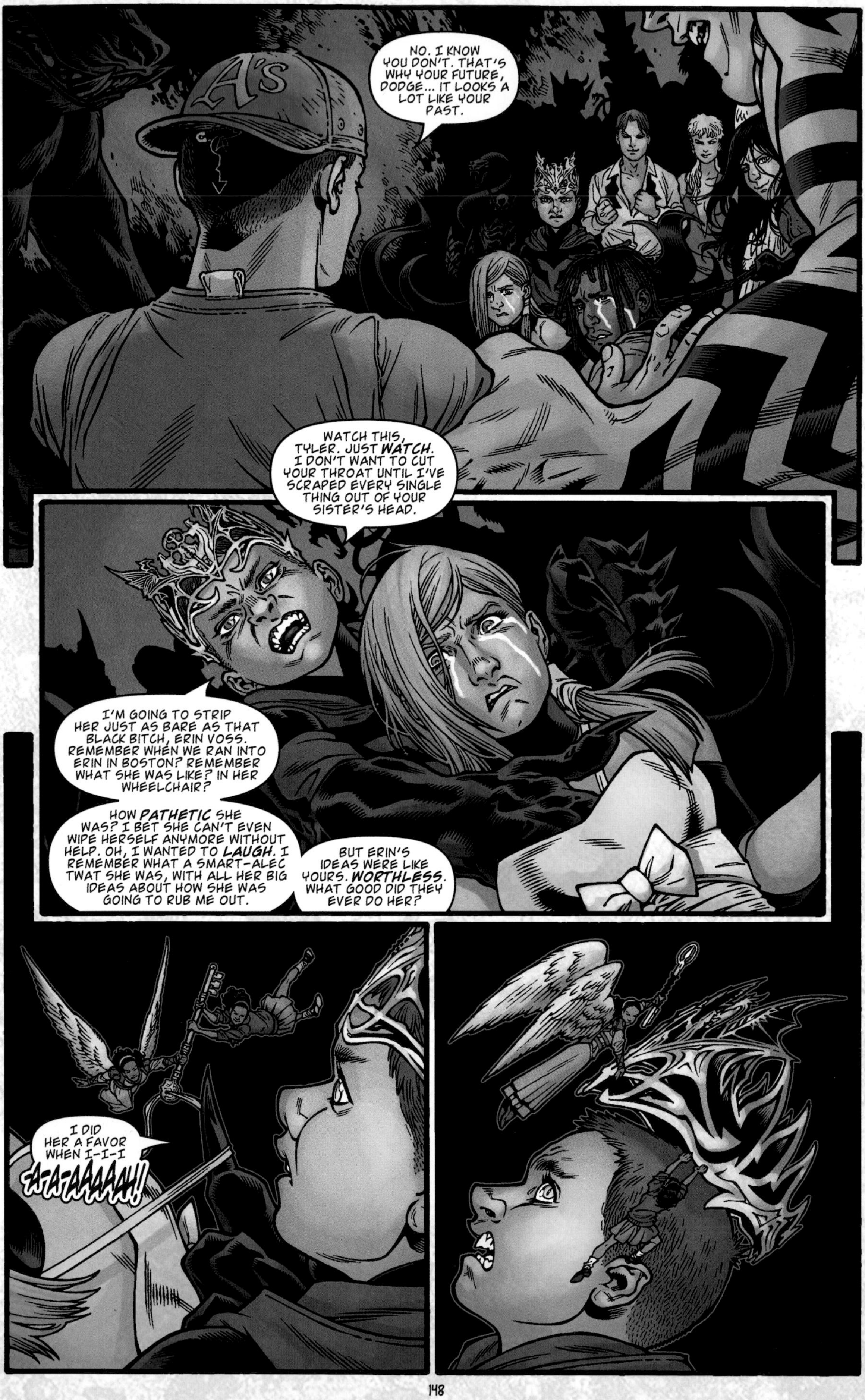

NO. I KNOW YOU DON'T. THAT'S WHY YOUR FUTURE, DODGE... IT LOOKS A LOT LIKE YOUR PAST.
WATCH THIS, TYLER. JUST WATCH. I DON'T WANT TO CUT YOUR THROAT UNTIL I'VE SCRAPED EVERY SINGLE THING OUT OF YOUR SISTER'S HEAD.
I'M GOING TO STRIP HER JUST AS BARE AS THAT BLACK BITCH, ERIN VOSS. REMEMBER WHEN WE RAN INTO ERIN IN BOSTON? REMEMBER WHAT SHE WAS LIKE? IN HER WHEELCHAIR?
HOW PATHETIC SHE WAS? I BET SHE CAN'T EVEN WIPE HERSELF ANYMORE WITHOUT HELP. OH, I WANTED TO LAUGH. I REMEMBER WHAT A SMART-ALEC TWAT SHE WAS, WITH ALL HER BIG IDEAS ABOUT HOW SHE WAS GOING TO RUB ME OUT.
BUT ERIN'S IDEAS WERE LIKE YOURS. WORTHLESS. WHAT GOOD DID THEY EVER DO HER?
I DID HER A FAVOR WHEN I-I-I
A-A-AAAAAH!

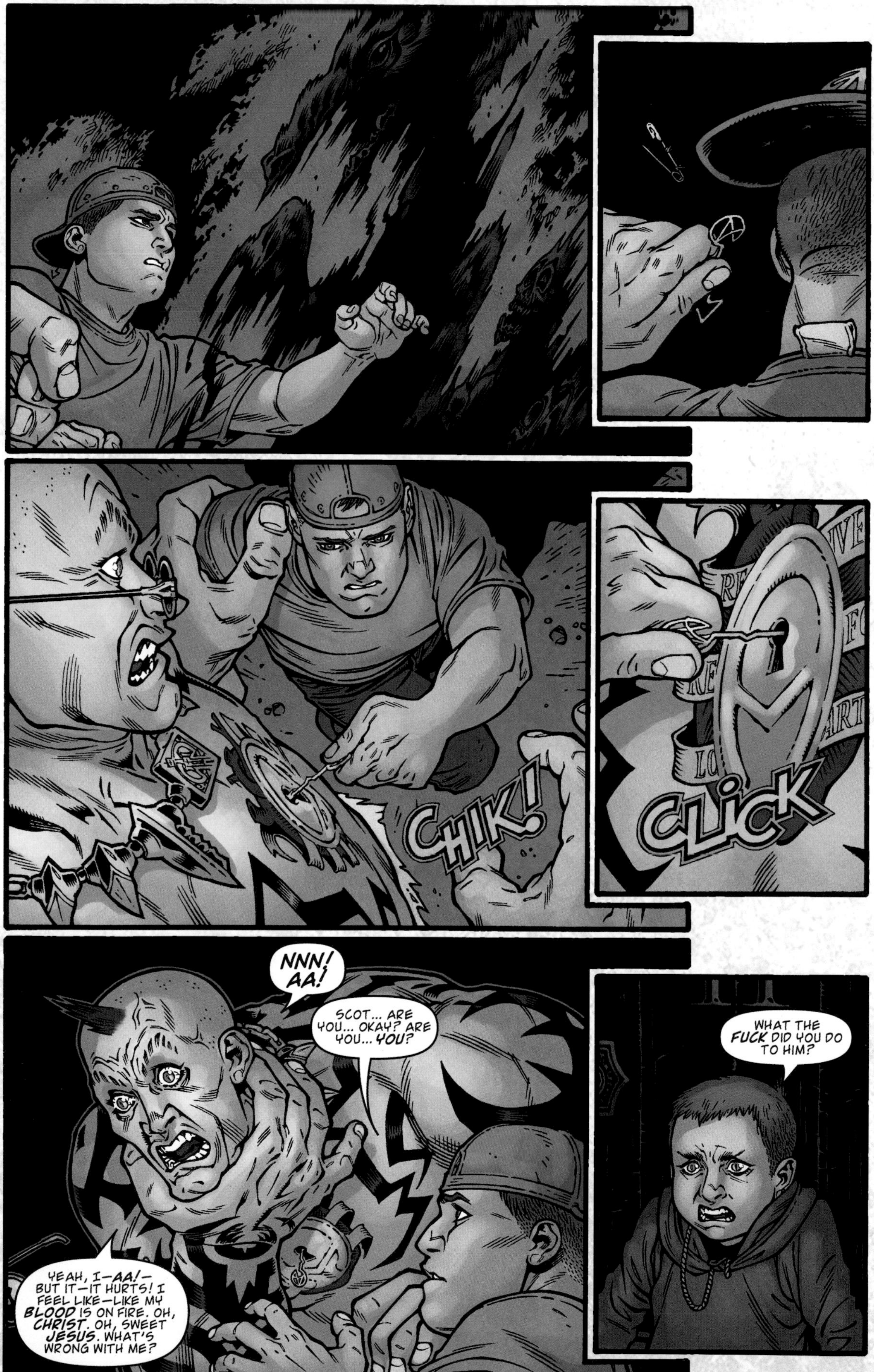
CHIK!
CLICK
NNN! AA!
SCOT... ARE YOU... OKAY? ARE YOU... YOU?
YEAH, I—AA!—BUT IT—IT HURTS! I FEEL LIKE—LIKE MY BLOOD IS ON FIRE. OH, CHRIST. OH, SWEET JESUS. WHAT'S WRONG WITH ME?
WHAT THE FUCK DID YOU DO TO HIM?

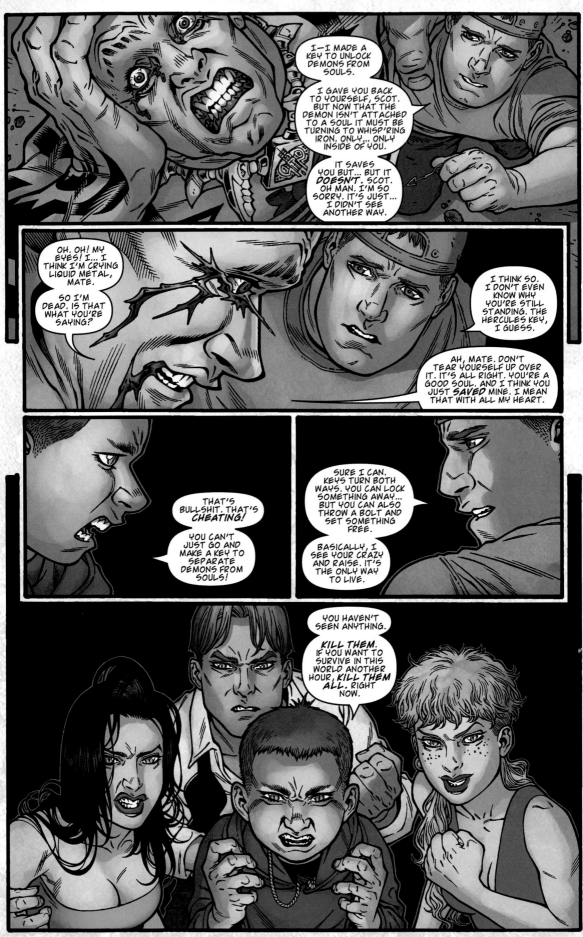

I—I MADE A KEY TO UNLOCK DEMONS FROM SOULS.

I GAVE YOU BACK TO YOURSELF, SCOT. BUT NOW THAT THE DEMON ISN'T ATTACHED TO A SOUL IT MUST BE TURNING TO WHISP'RING IRON, ONLY... ONLY INSIDE OF YOU.

IT SAVES YOU BUT... BUT IT *DOESN'T*, SCOT. OH MAN. I'M SO SORRY. IT'S JUST... I DIDN'T SEE ANOTHER WAY.

OH. OH! MY EYES! I... I THINK I'M CRYING LIQUID METAL, MATE.

SO I'M DEAD. IS THAT WHAT YOU'RE SAYING?

I THINK SO. I DON'T EVEN KNOW WHY YOU'RE STILL STANDING. THE HERCULES KEY, I GUESS.

AH, MATE. DON'T TEAR YOURSELF UP OVER IT. IT'S ALL RIGHT. YOU'RE A GOOD SOUL. AND I THINK YOU JUST *SAVED* MINE. I MEAN THAT WITH ALL MY HEART.

THAT'S BULLSHIT. THAT'S *CHEATING!*

YOU CAN'T JUST GO AND MAKE A KEY TO SEPARATE DEMONS FROM SOULS!

SURE I CAN. KEYS TURN BOTH WAYS. YOU CAN LOCK SOMETHING AWAY... BUT YOU CAN ALSO THROW A BOLT AND SET SOMETHING FREE.

BASICALLY, I SEE YOUR CRAZY AND RAISE. IT'S THE ONLY WAY TO LIVE.

YOU HAVEN'T SEEN ANYTHING.

KILL THEM. IF YOU WANT TO SURVIVE IN THIS WORLD ANOTHER HOUR, *KILL THEM ALL.* RIGHT NOW.

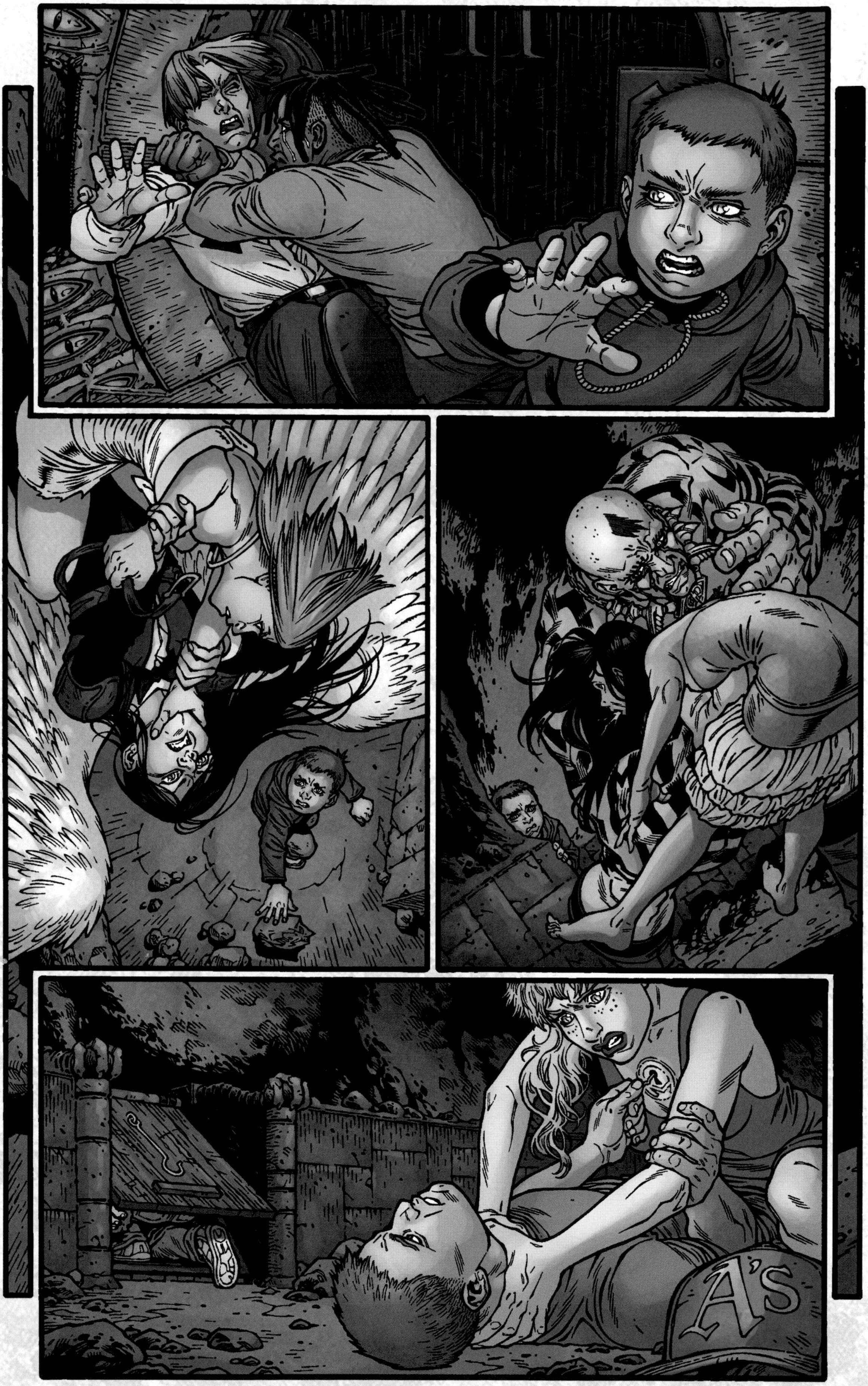

A'S

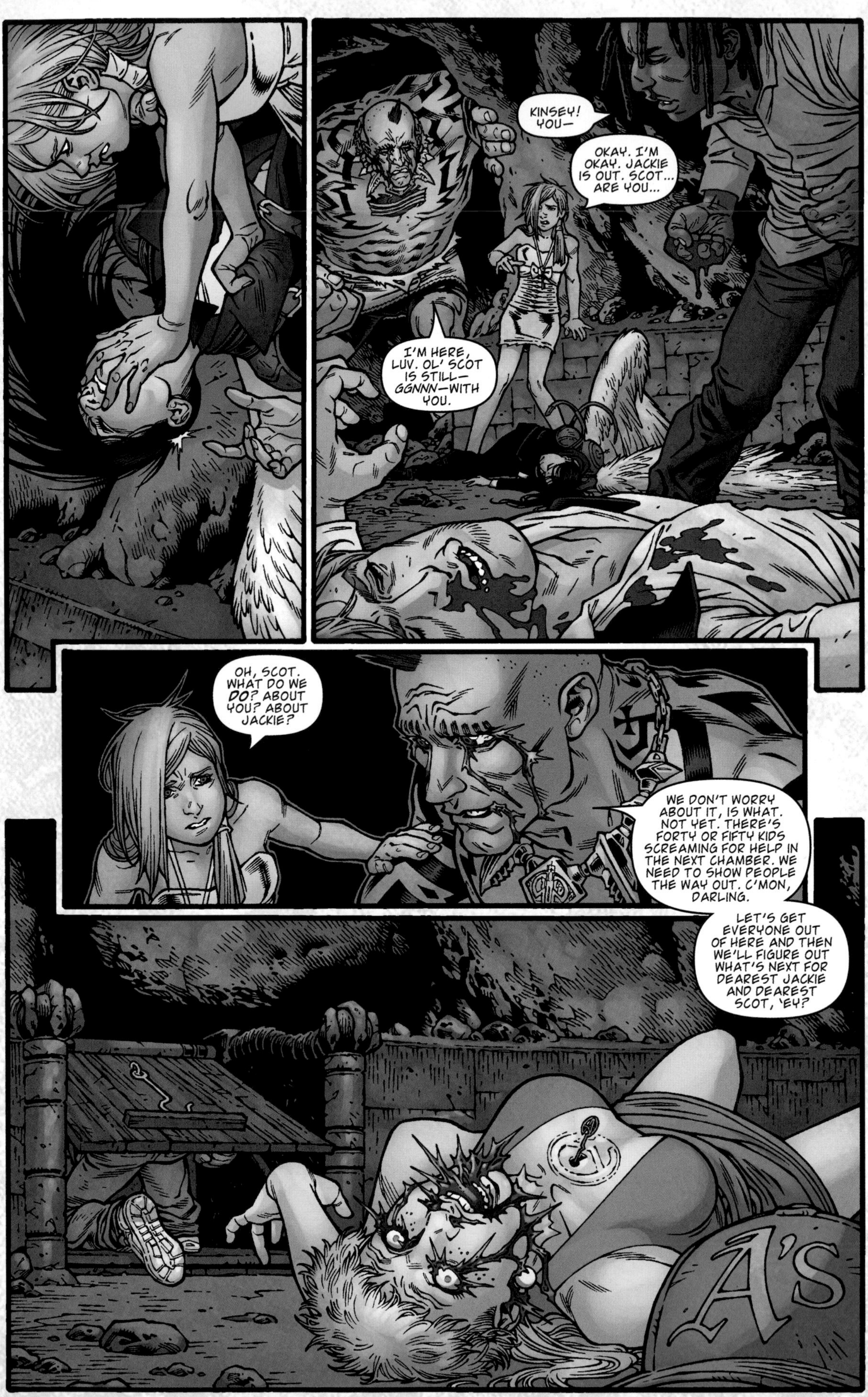
KINSEY! YOU—
OKAY. I'M OKAY. JACKIE IS OUT. SCOT... ARE YOU...
I'M HERE, LUV. OL' SCOT IS STILL— GGNNN—WITH YOU.
OH, SCOT. WHAT DO WE DO? ABOUT YOU? ABOUT JACKIE?
WE DON'T WORRY ABOUT IT, IS WHAT. NOT YET. THERE'S FORTY OR FIFTY KIDS SCREAMING FOR HELP IN THE NEXT CHAMBER. WE NEED TO SHOW PEOPLE THE WAY OUT. C'MON, DARLING.
LET'S GET EVERYONE OUT OF HERE AND THEN WE'LL FIGURE OUT WHAT'S NEXT FOR DEAREST JACKIE AND DEAREST SCOT, 'EY?
A'S

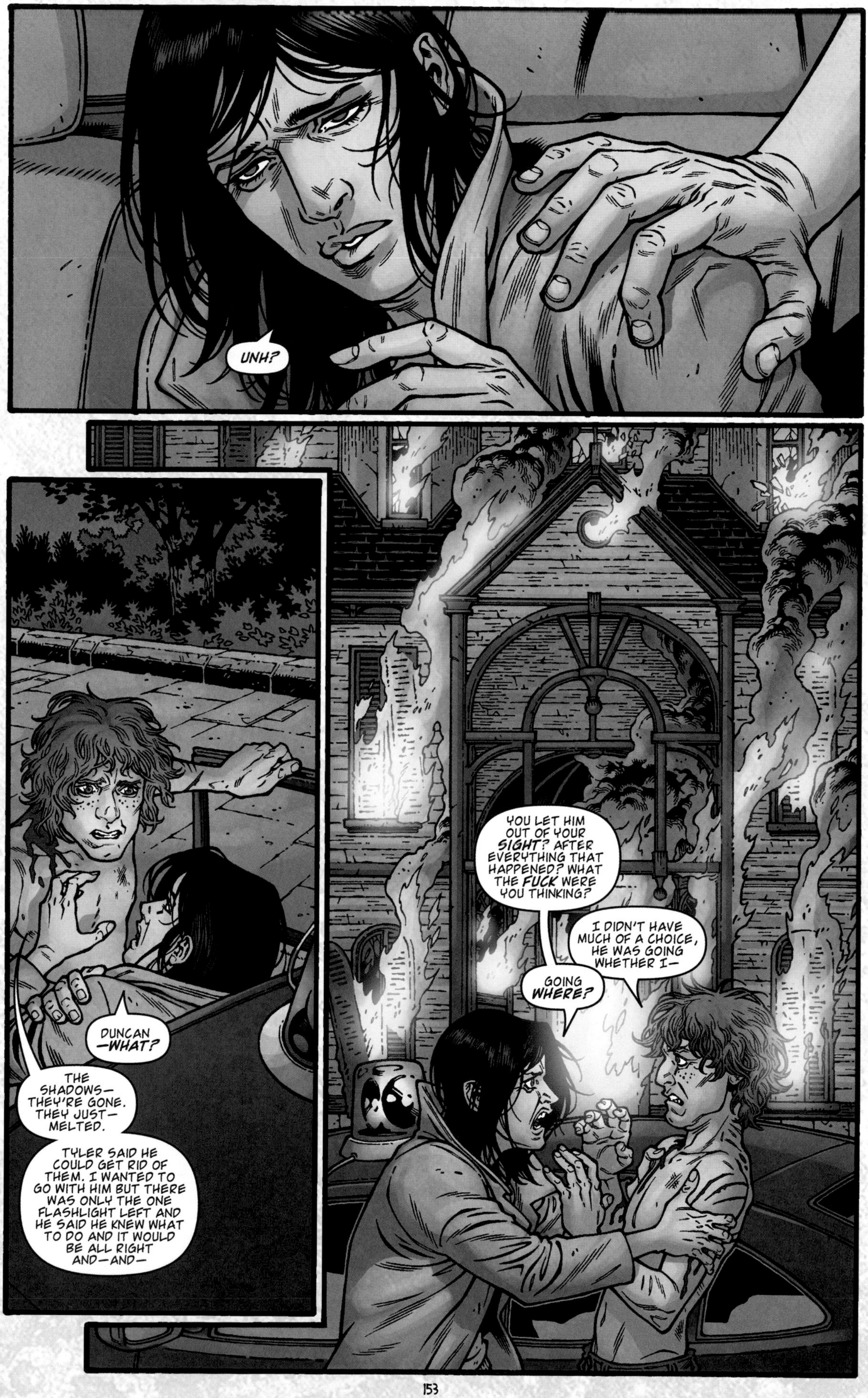
UNH?
DUNCAN —WHAT?
THE SHADOWS— THEY'RE GONE. THEY JUST— MELTED.
TYLER SAID HE COULD GET RID OF THEM. I WANTED TO GO WITH HIM BUT THERE WAS ONLY THE ONE FLASHLIGHT LEFT AND HE SAID HE KNEW WHAT TO DO AND IT WOULD BE ALL RIGHT AND—AND—
YOU LET HIM OUT OF YOUR SIGHT? AFTER EVERYTHING THAT HAPPENED? WHAT THE FUCK WERE YOU THINKING?
I DIDN'T HAVE MUCH OF A CHOICE, HE WAS GOING WHETHER I—
GOING WHERE?

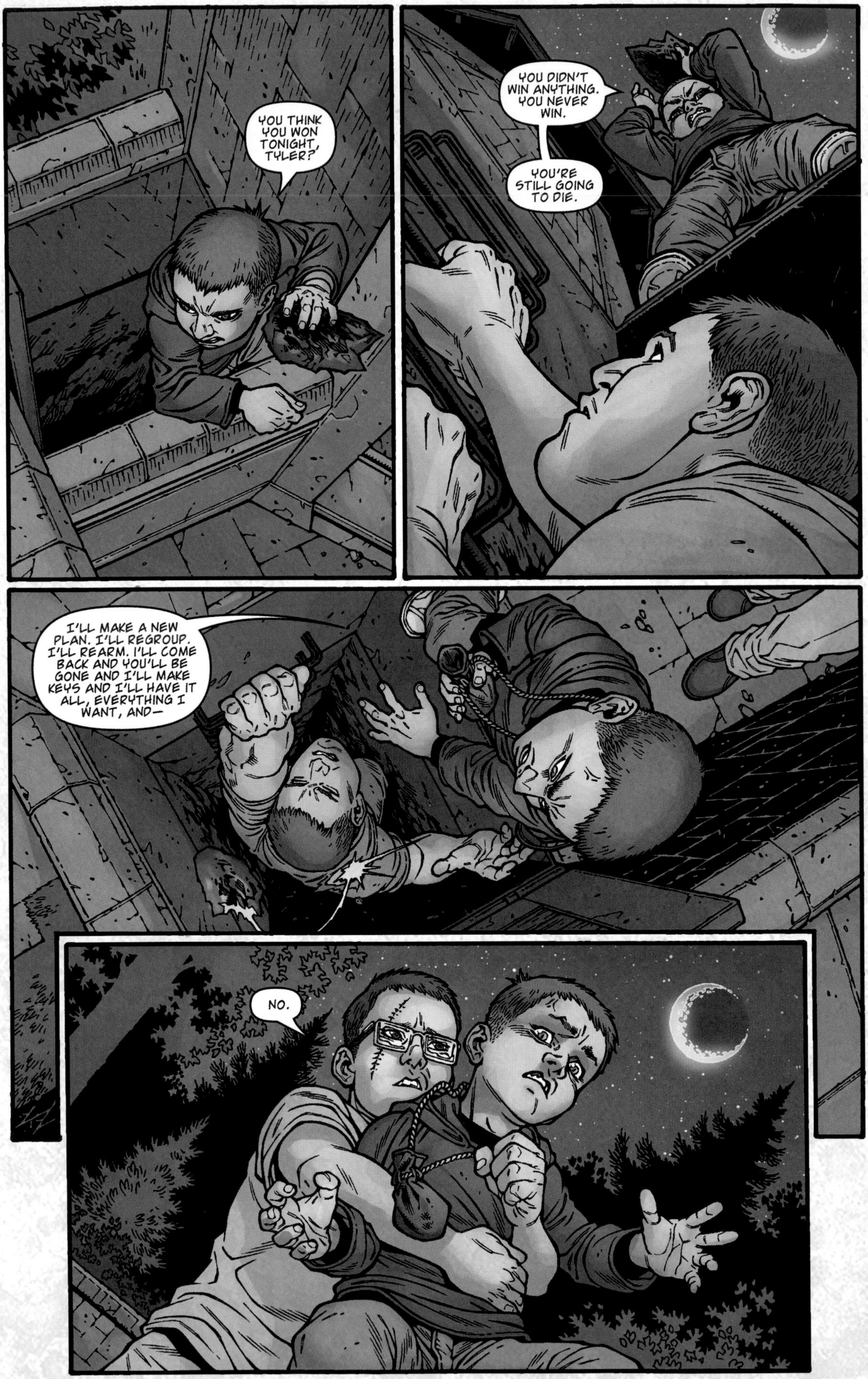
YOU THINK YOU WON TONIGHT, TYLER?
YOU DIDN'T WIN ANYTHING. YOU NEVER WIN.
YOU'RE STILL GOING TO DIE.
I'LL MAKE A NEW PLAN. I'LL REGROUP. I'LL REARM. I'LL COME BACK AND YOU'LL BE GONE AND I'LL MAKE KEYS AND I'LL HAVE IT ALL, EVERYTHING I WANT, AND—
NO.

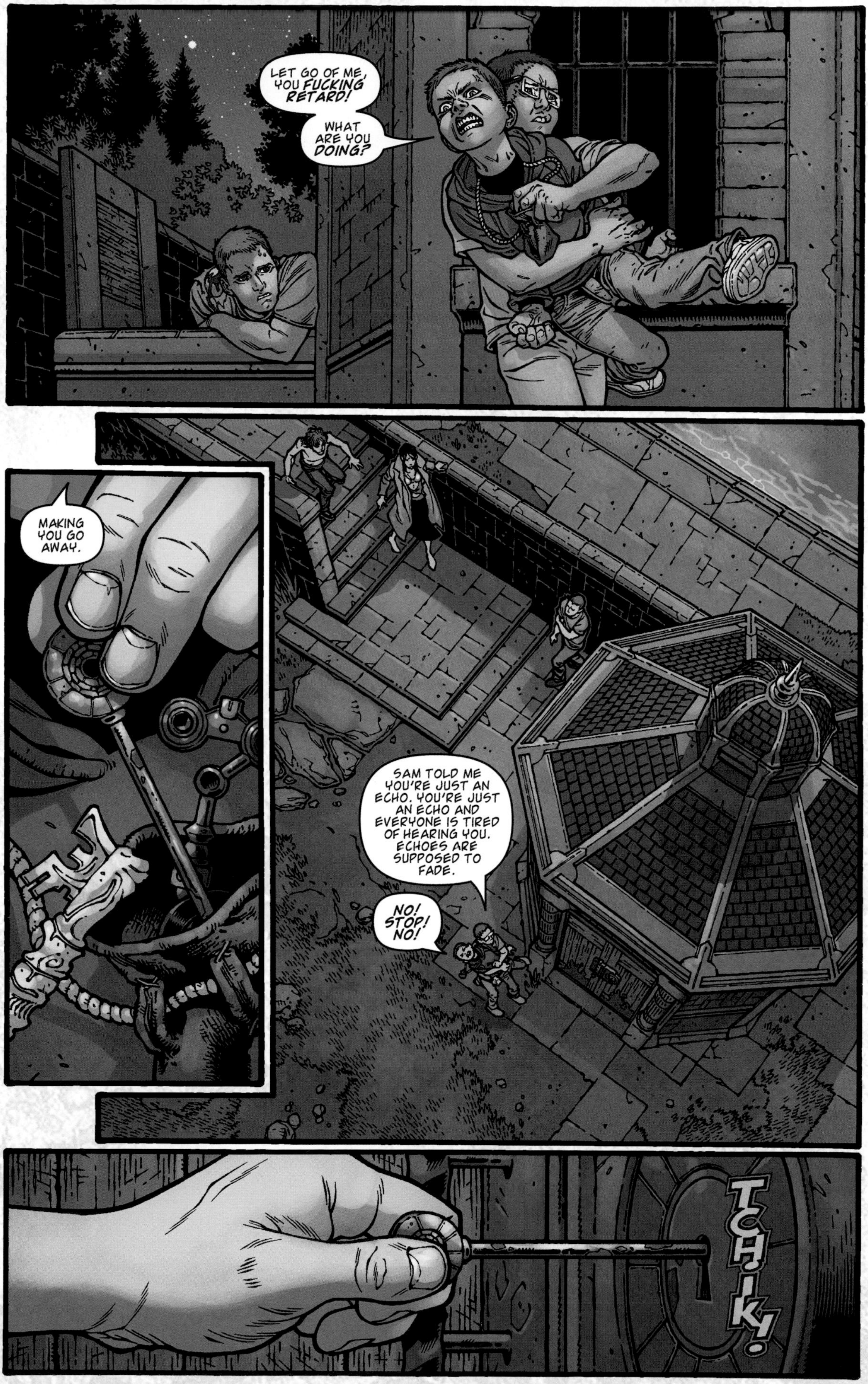
LET GO OF ME, YOU FUCKING RETARD!
WHAT ARE YOU DOING?
MAKING YOU GO AWAY.
SAM TOLD ME YOU'RE JUST AN ECHO. YOU'RE JUST AN ECHO AND EVERYONE IS TIRED OF HEARING YOU. ECHOES ARE SUPPOSED TO FADE.
NO! STOP! NO!
TCHIK!

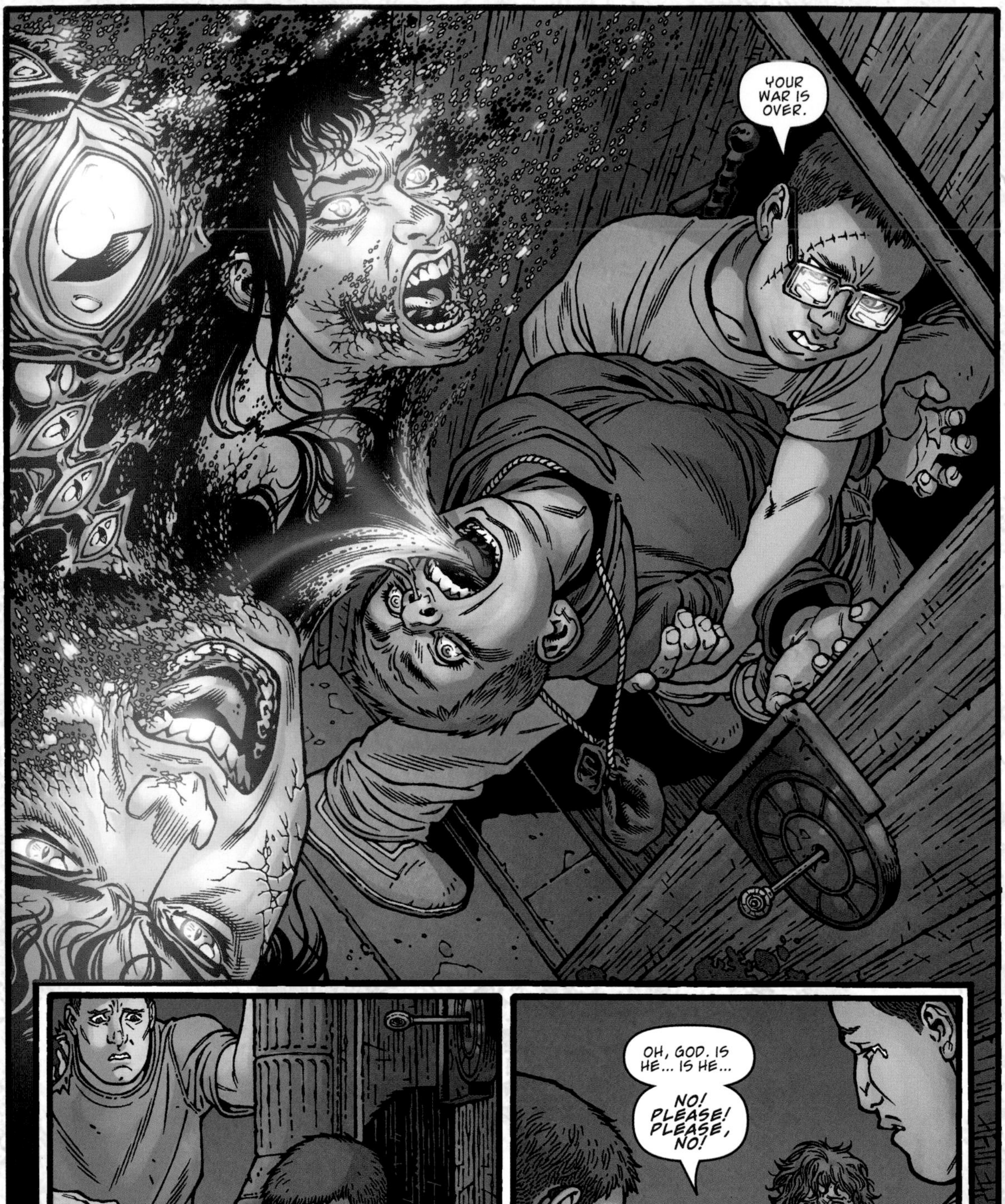
YOUR WAR IS OVER.

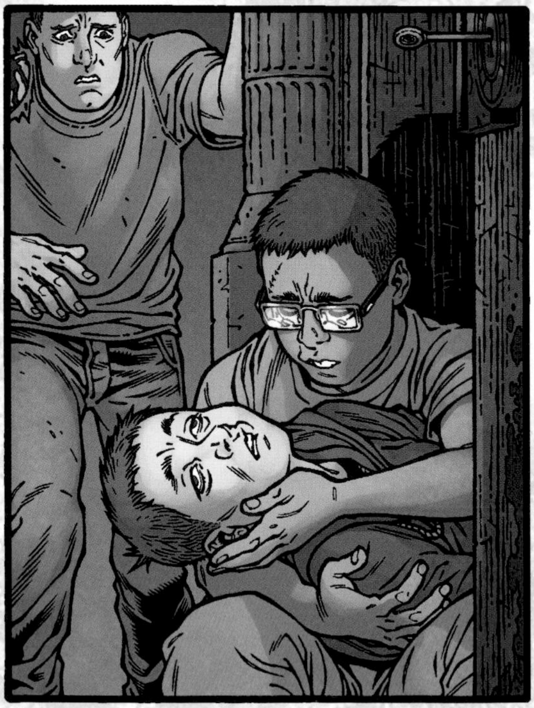

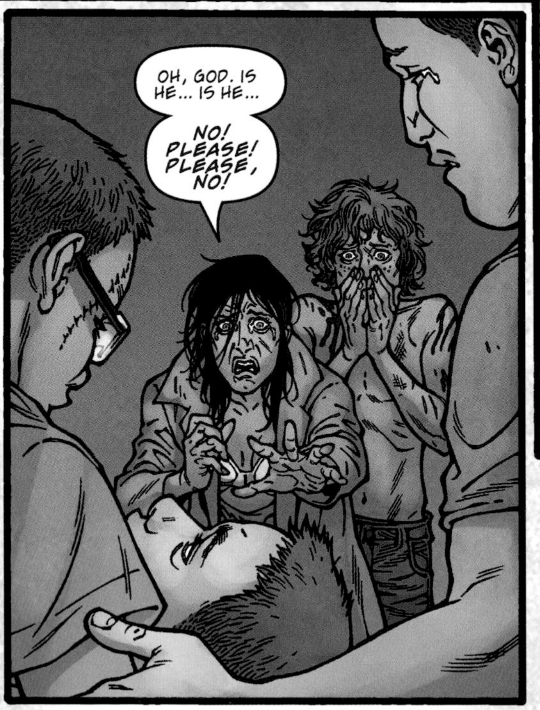
OH, GOD. IS HE... IS HE...
NO! PLEASE! PLEASE, NO!

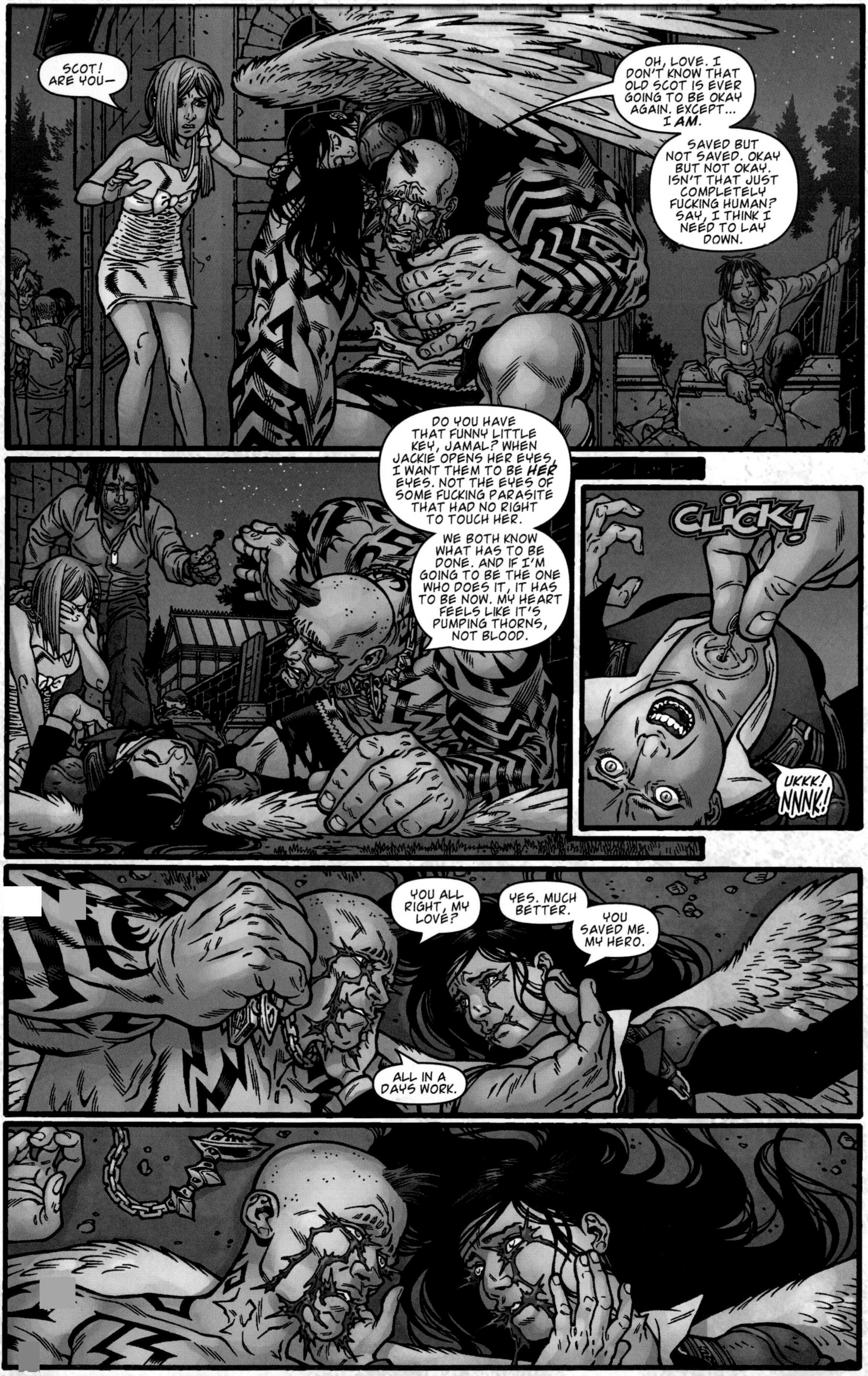
SCOT! ARE YOU—
OH, LOVE. I DON'T KNOW THAT OLD SCOT IS EVER GOING TO BE OKAY AGAIN. EXCEPT... I AM.
SAVED BUT NOT SAVED. OKAY BUT NOT OKAY. ISN'T THAT JUST COMPLETELY FUCKING HUMAN? SAY, I THINK I NEED TO LAY DOWN.
DO YOU HAVE THAT FUNNY LITTLE KEY, JAMAL? WHEN JACKIE OPENS HER EYES, I WANT THEM TO BE HER EYES. NOT THE EYES OF SOME FUCKING PARASITE THAT HAD NO RIGHT TO TOUCH HER.
WE BOTH KNOW WHAT HAS TO BE DONE. AND IF I'M GOING TO BE THE ONE WHO DOES IT, IT HAS TO BE NOW. MY HEART FEELS LIKE IT'S PUMPING THORNS, NOT BLOOD.
CLICK!
UKKK! NNNK!
YOU ALL RIGHT, MY LOVE?
YES. MUCH BETTER.
YOU SAVED ME. MY HERO.
ALL IN A DAYS WORK.

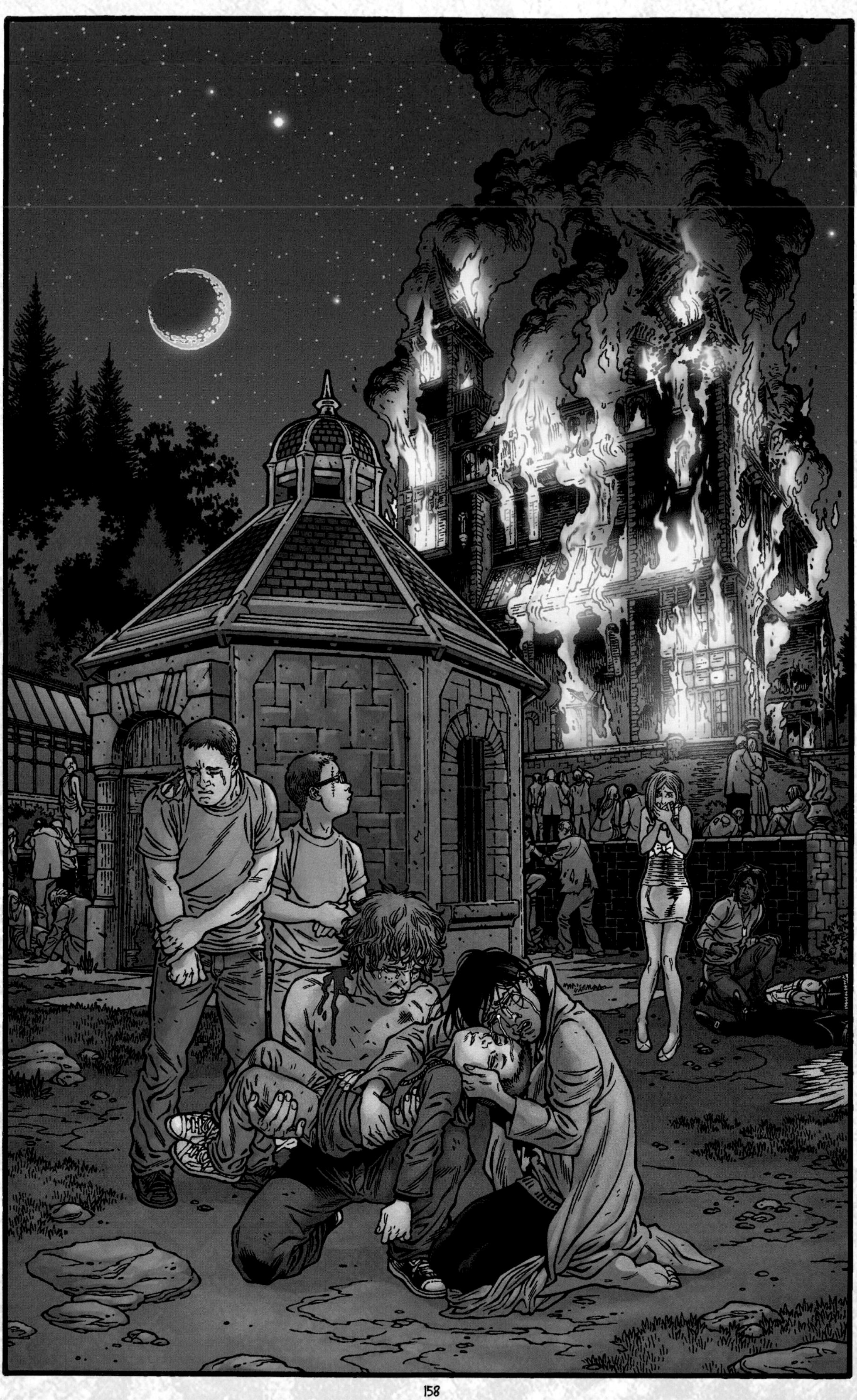

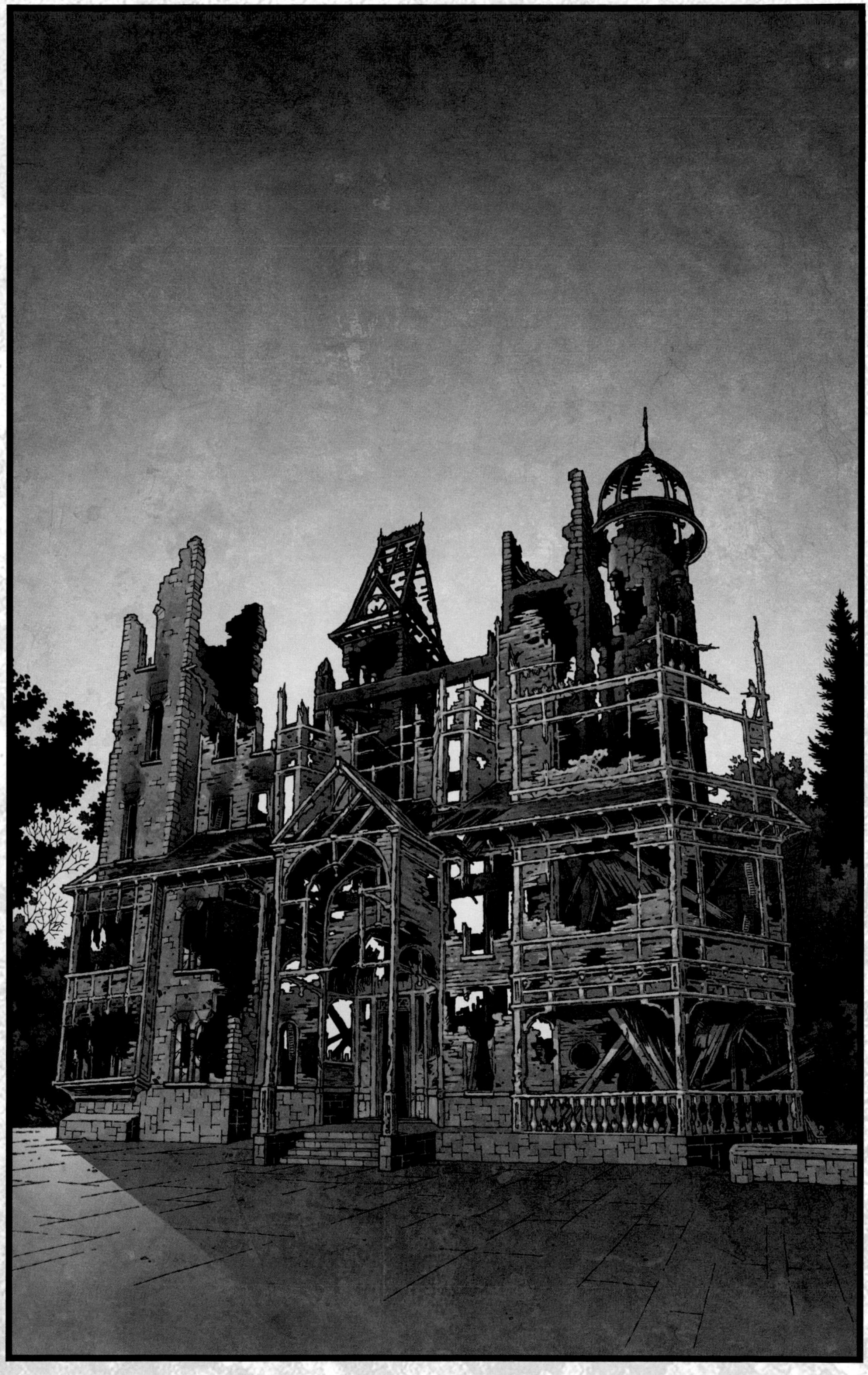

- ALPHA & OMEGA -
Chapter Seven

EPILOGUE: THE LAST DOOR

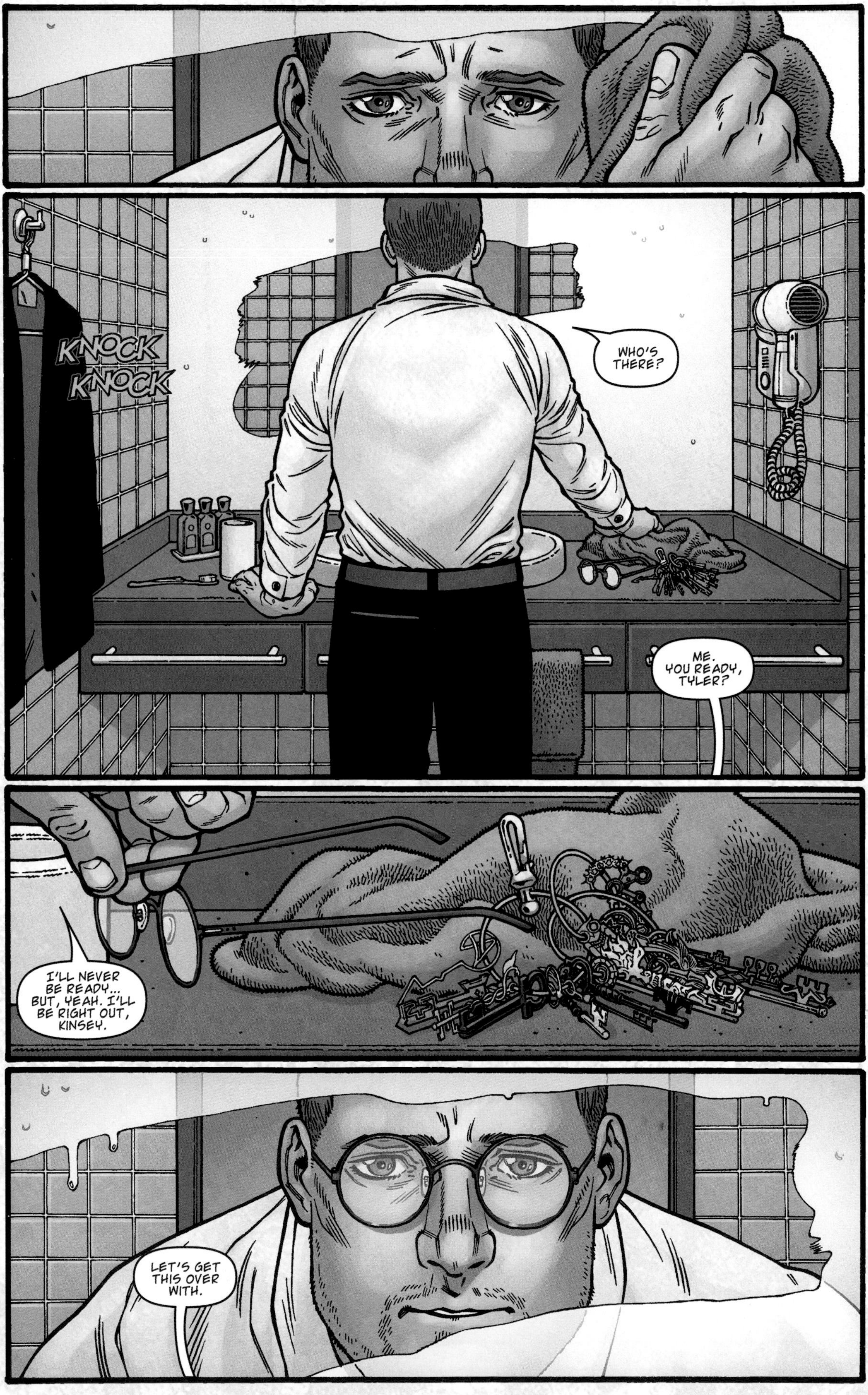
KNOCK
KNOCK
WHO'S THERE?
ME. YOU READY, TYLER?
I'LL NEVER BE READY... BUT, YEAH. I'LL BE RIGHT OUT, KINSEY.
LET'S GET THIS OVER WITH.

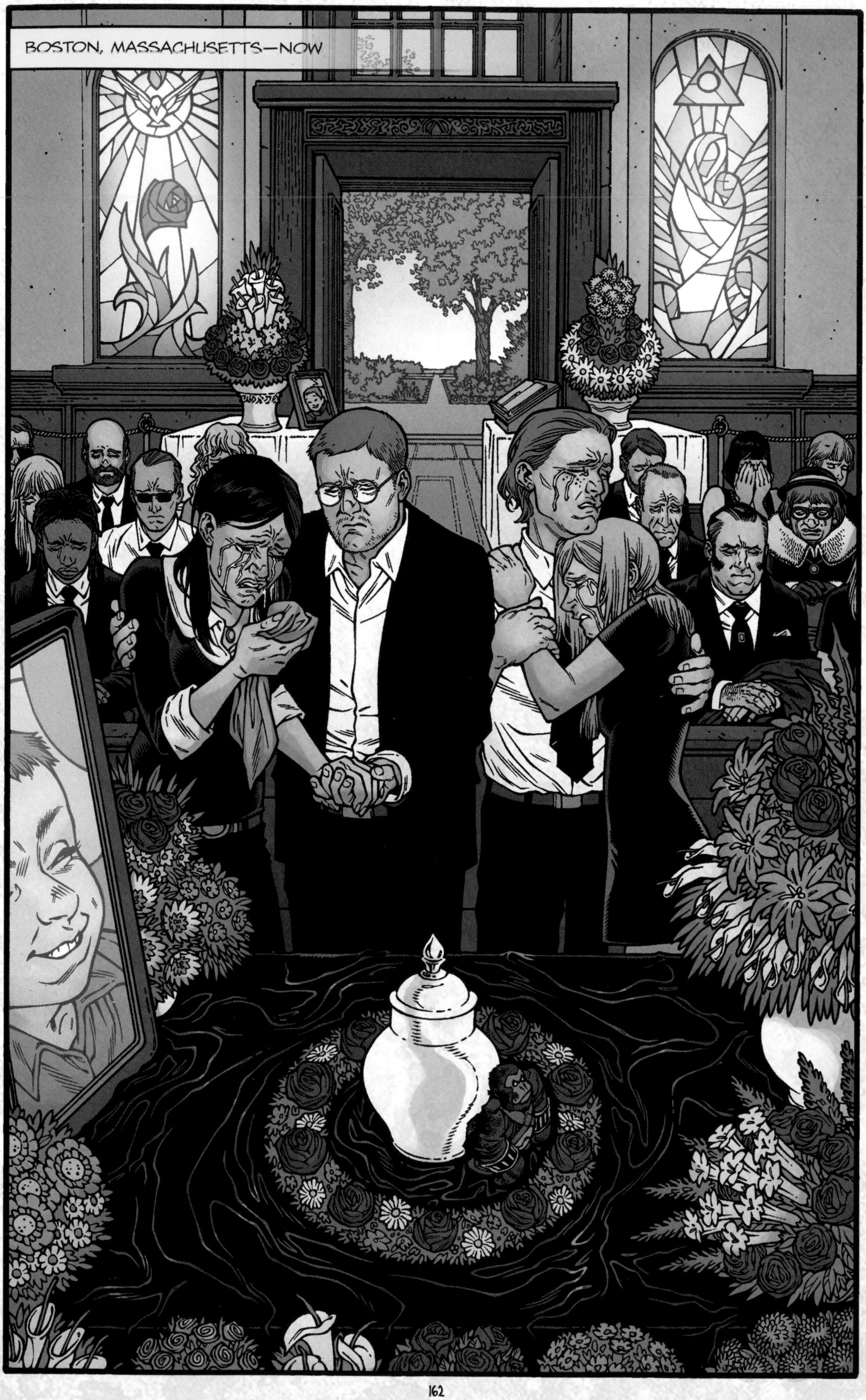
BOSTON, MASSACHUSETTS—NOW

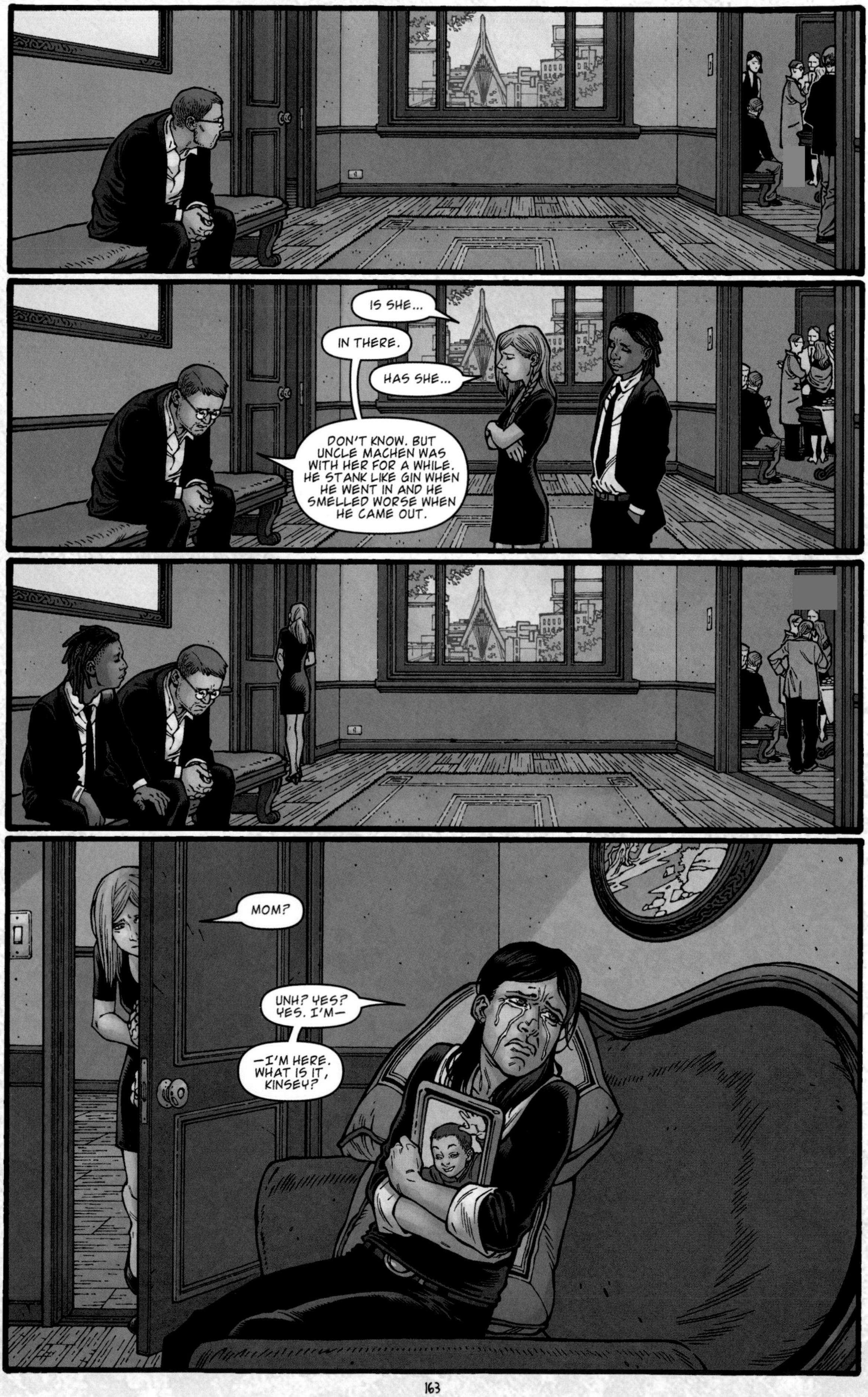
IS SHE...
IN THERE.
HAS SHE...
DON'T KNOW. BUT UNCLE MACHEN WAS WITH HER FOR A WHILE. HE STANK LIKE GIN WHEN HE WENT IN AND HE SMELLED WORSE WHEN HE CAME OUT.
MOM?
UNH? YES? YES. I'M—
—I'M HERE. WHAT IS IT, KINSEY?

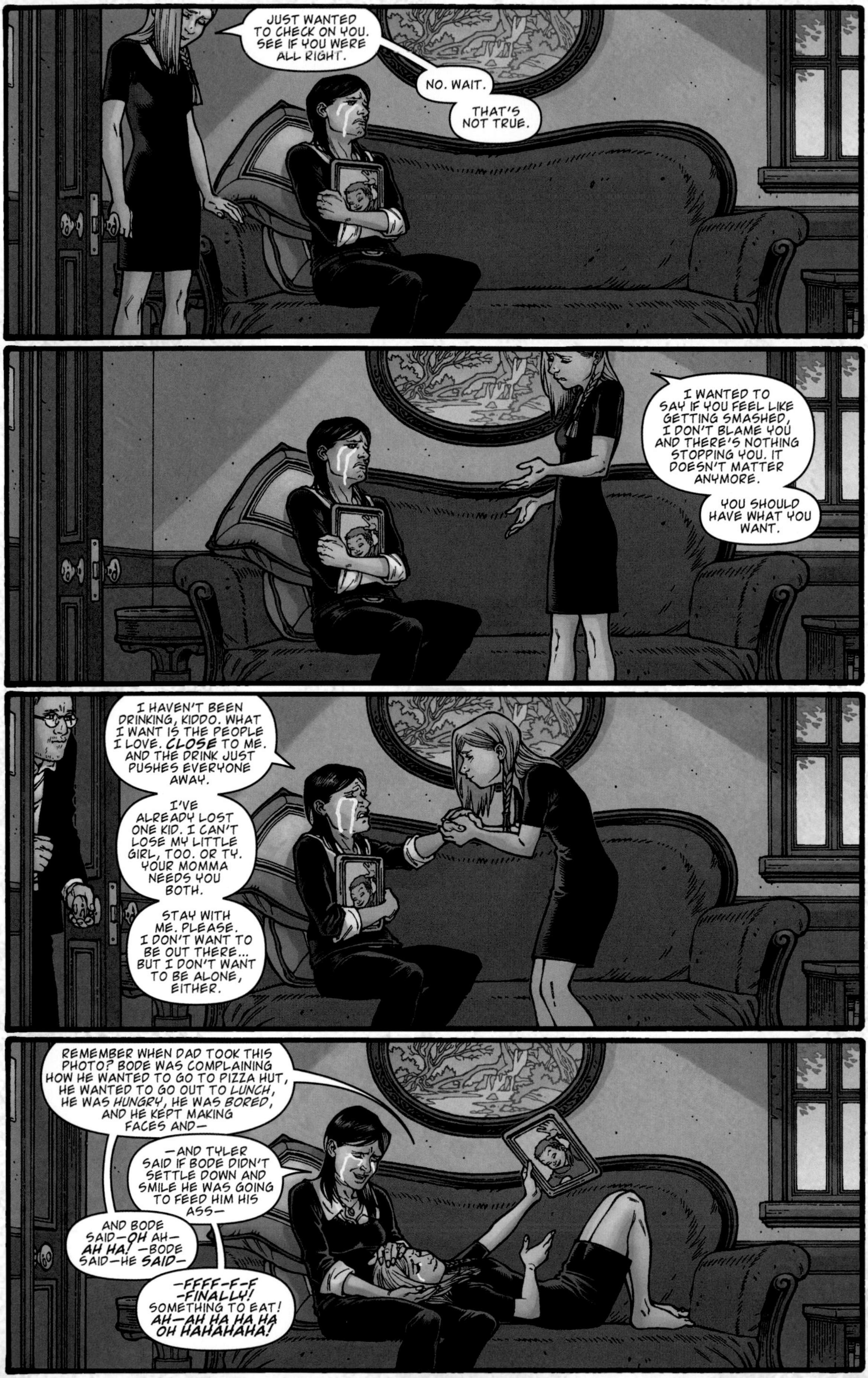
JUST WANTED TO CHECK ON YOU. SEE IF YOU WERE ALL RIGHT.
NO. WAIT.
THAT'S NOT TRUE.
I WANTED TO SAY IF YOU FEEL LIKE GETTING SMASHED, I DON'T BLAME YOU AND THERE'S NOTHING STOPPING YOU. IT DOESN'T MATTER ANYMORE.
YOU SHOULD HAVE WHAT YOU WANT.
I HAVEN'T BEEN DRINKING, KIDDO. WHAT I WANT IS THE PEOPLE I LOVE. CLOSE TO ME. AND THE DRINK JUST PUSHES EVERYONE AWAY.
I'VE ALREADY LOST ONE KID. I CAN'T LOSE MY LITTLE GIRL, TOO. OR TY. YOUR MOMMA NEEDS YOU BOTH.
STAY WITH ME. PLEASE. I DON'T WANT TO BE OUT THERE... BUT I DON'T WANT TO BE ALONE, EITHER.
REMEMBER WHEN DAD TOOK THIS PHOTO? BODE WAS COMPLAINING HOW HE WANTED TO GO TO PIZZA HUT, HE WANTED TO GO OUT TO LUNCH, HE WAS HUNGRY, HE WAS BORED, AND HE KEPT MAKING FACES AND—
—AND TYLER SAID IF BODE DIDN'T SETTLE DOWN AND SMILE HE WAS GOING TO FEED HIM HIS ASS—
AND BODE SAID—OH AH—AH HA! —BODE SAID—HE SAID—
—FFFF-F-F —FINALLY! SOMETHING TO EAT! AH—AH HA HA HA OH HAHAHAHA!

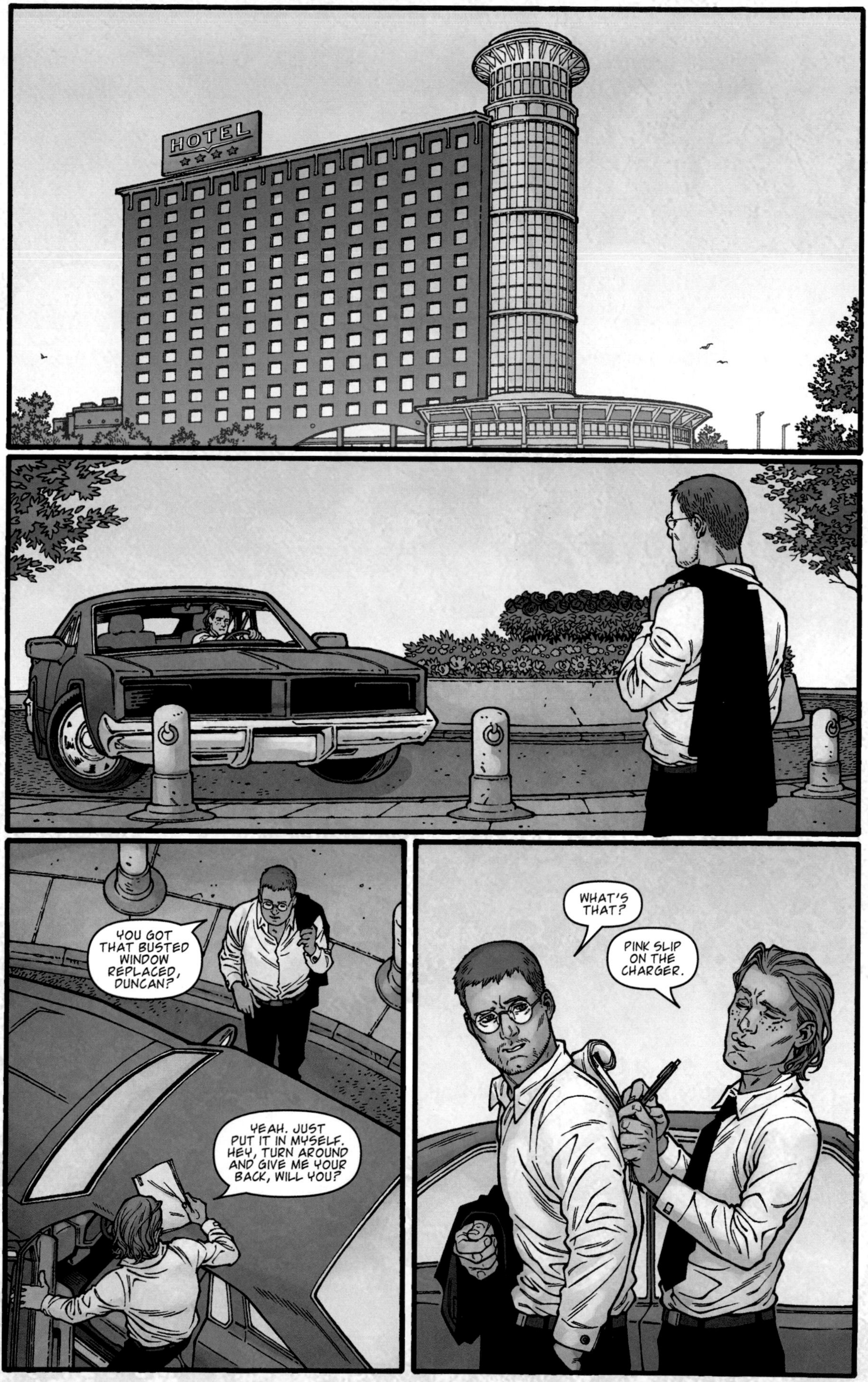
HOTEL
YOU GOT THAT BUSTED WINDOW REPLACED, DUNCAN?
YEAH. JUST PUT IT IN MYSELF. HEY, TURN AROUND AND GIVE ME YOUR BACK, WILL YOU?
WHAT'S THAT?
PINK SLIP ON THE CHARGER.

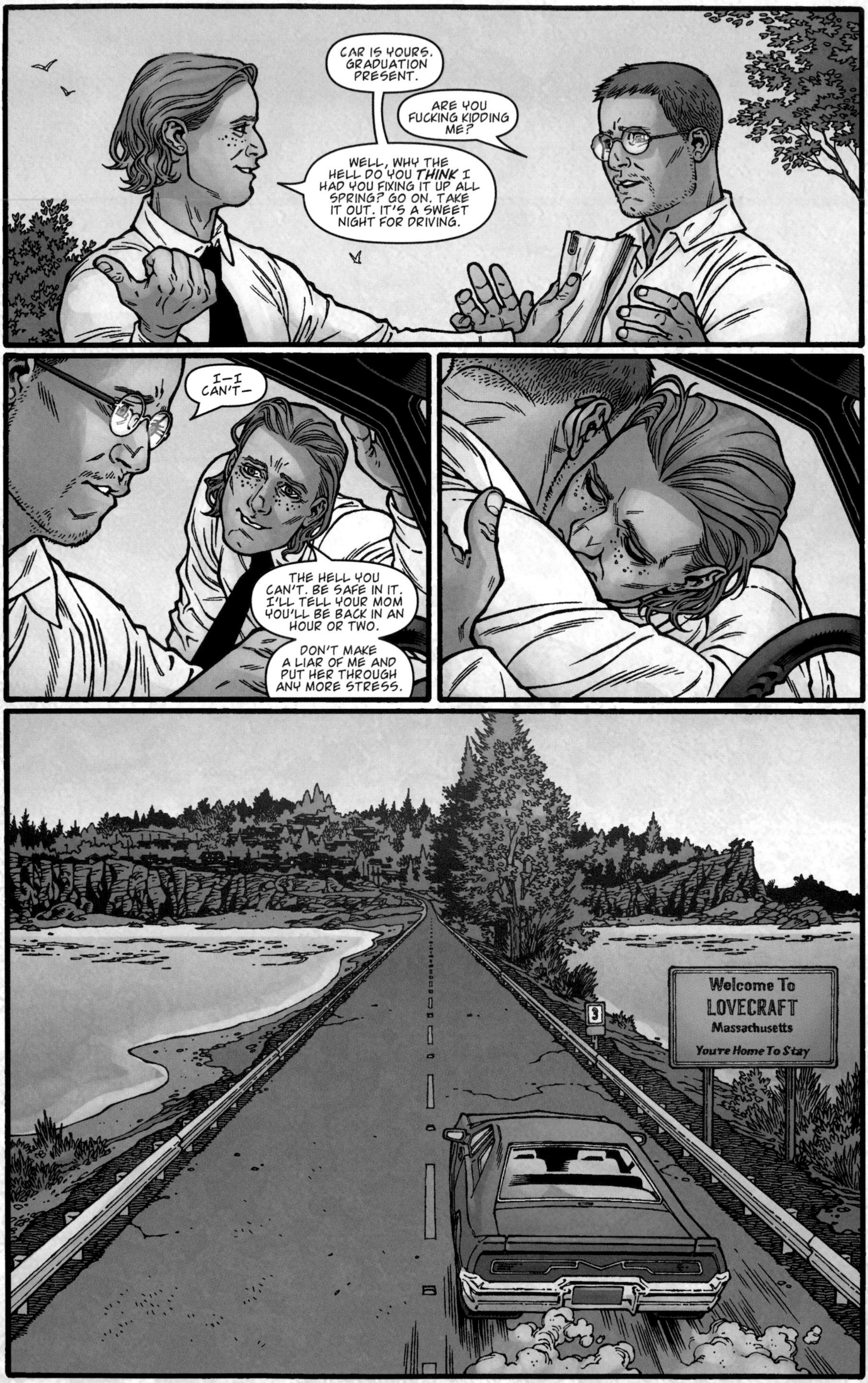
CAR IS YOURS. GRADUATION PRESENT.
ARE YOU FUCKING KIDDING ME?
WELL, WHY THE HELL DO YOU *THINK* I HAD YOU FIXING IT UP ALL SPRING? GO ON. TAKE IT OUT. IT'S A SWEET NIGHT FOR DRIVING.
I—I CAN'T—
THE HELL YOU CAN'T. BE SAFE IN IT. I'LL TELL YOUR MOM YOU'LL BE BACK IN AN HOUR OR TWO.
DON'T MAKE A LIAR OF ME AND PUT HER THROUGH ANY MORE STRESS.
Welcome To
LOVECRAFT
Massachusetts
You're Home To Stay

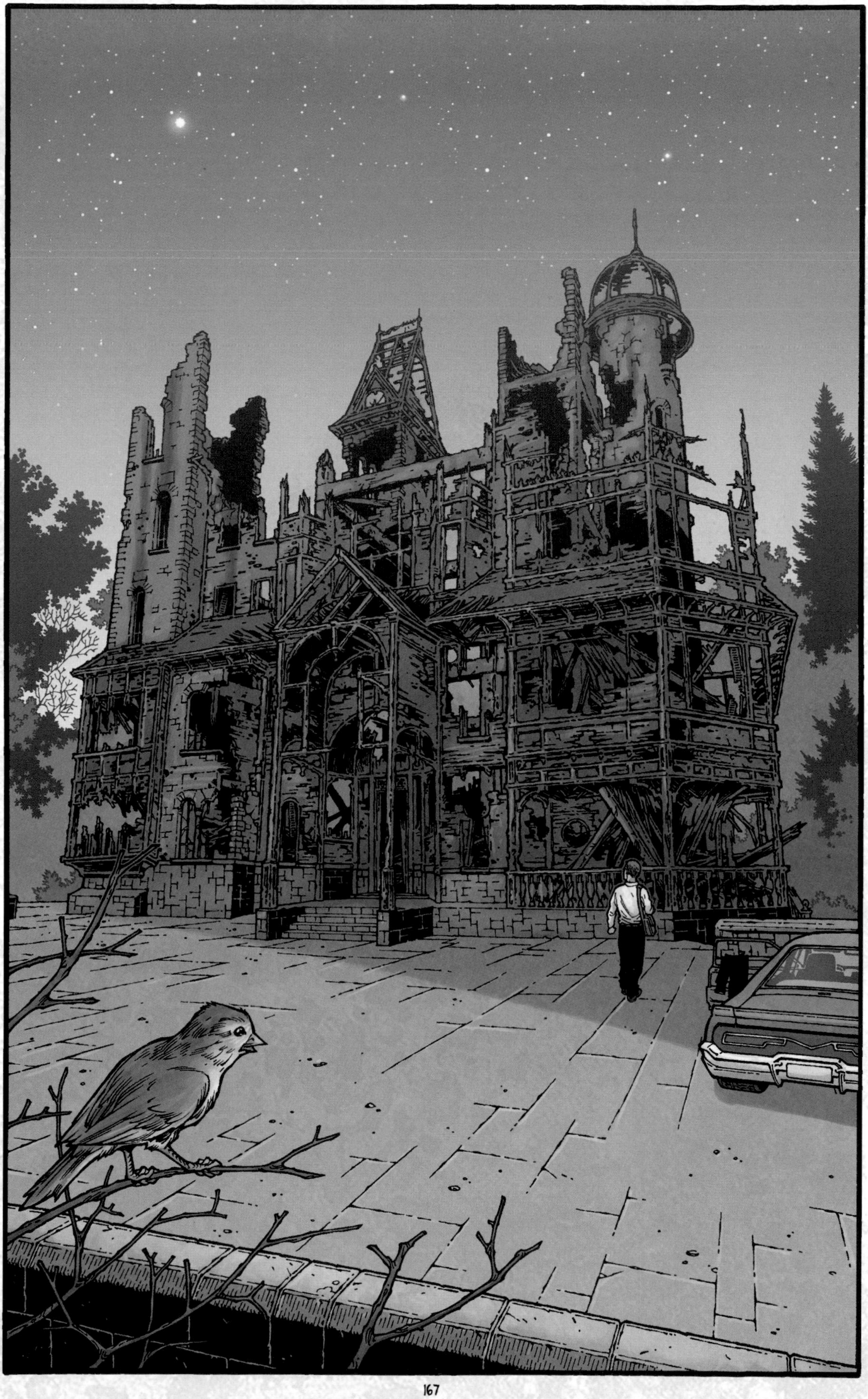

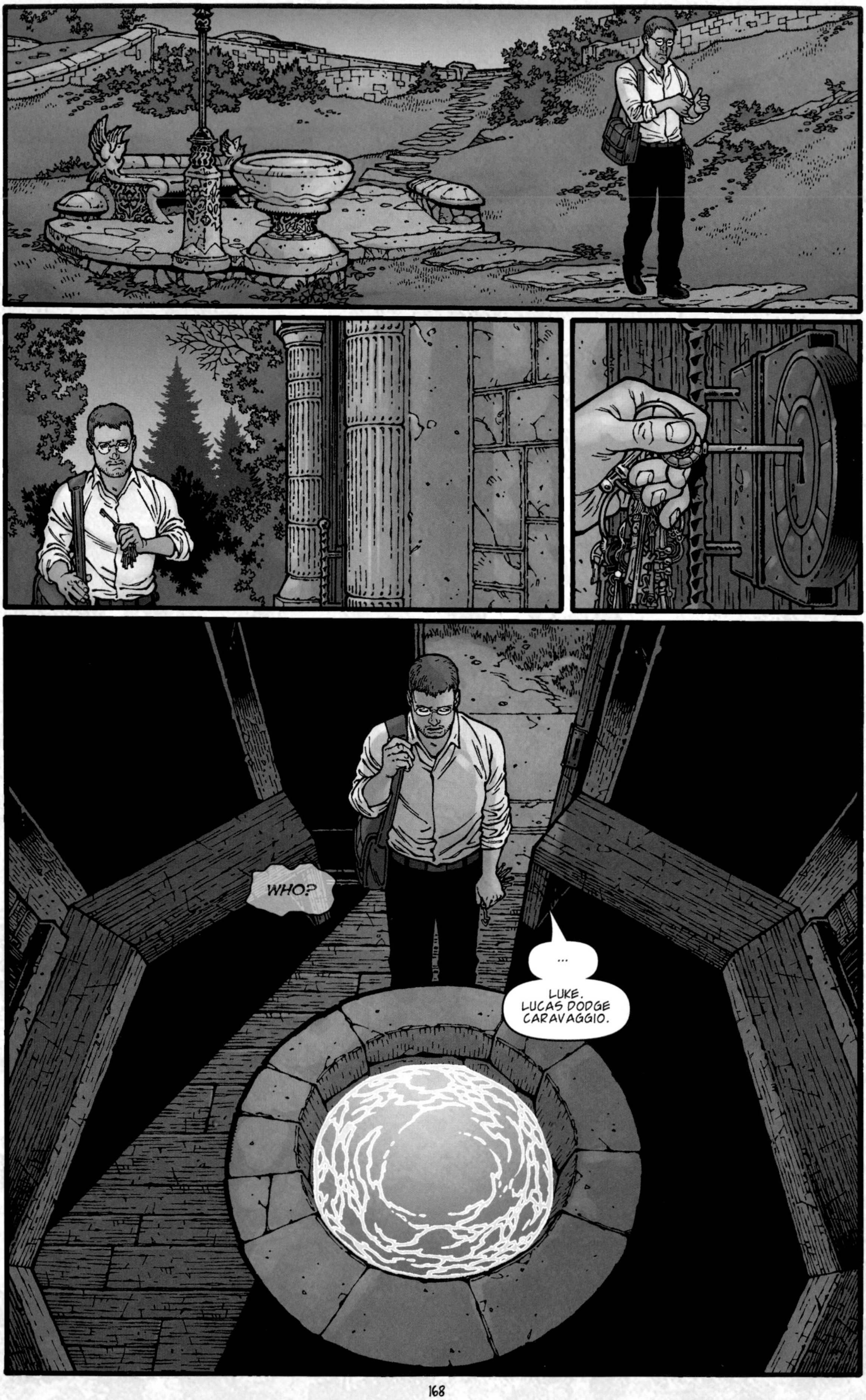
WHO?
...
LUKE.
LUCAS DODGE
CARAVAGGIO.

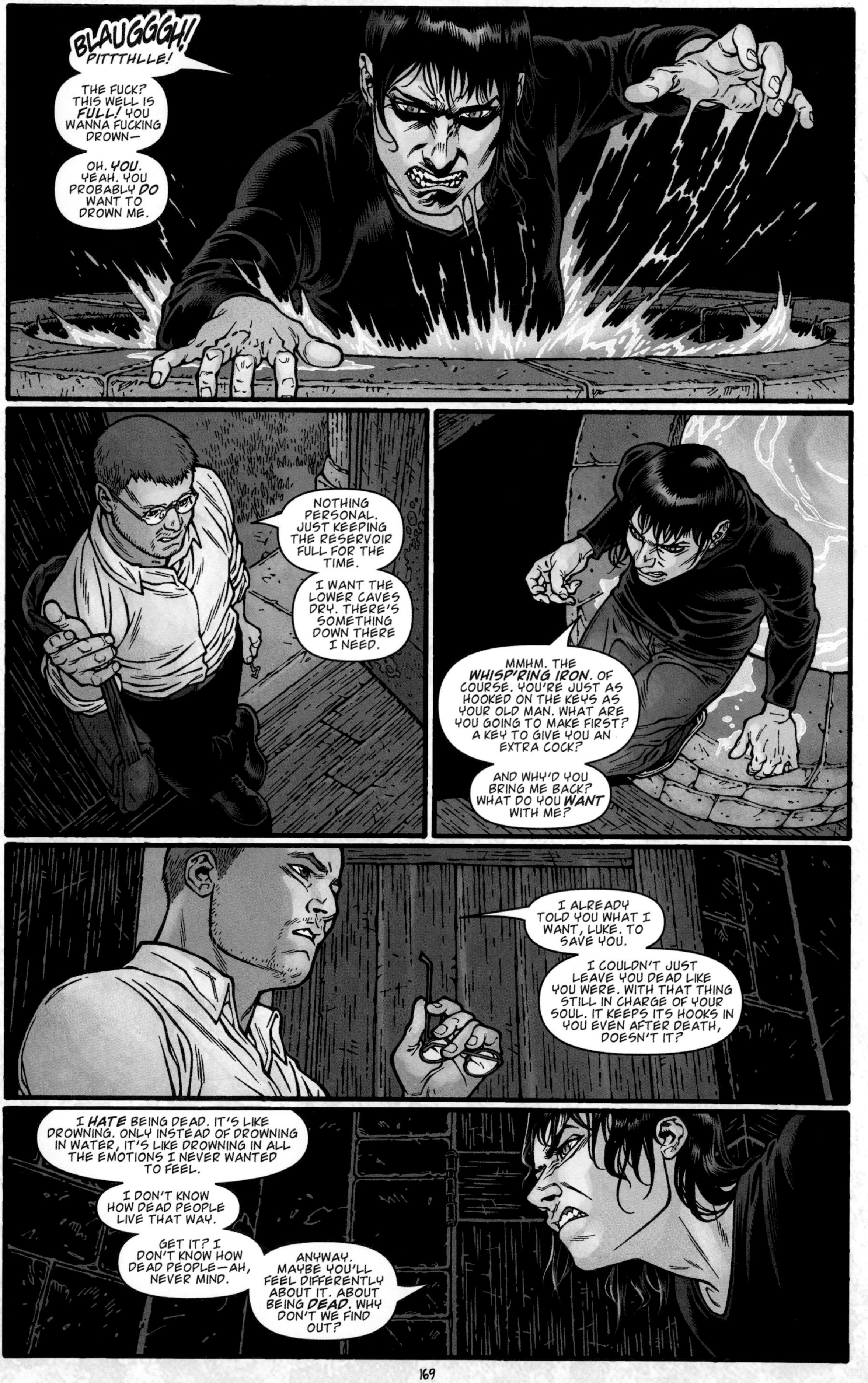

BLAUGGGH! PITTTHLLE!
THE FUCK? THIS WELL IS FULL! YOU WANNA FUCKING DROWN—
OH. YOU. YEAH. YOU PROBABLY DO WANT TO DROWN ME.
NOTHING PERSONAL. JUST KEEPING THE RESERVOIR FULL FOR THE TIME.
I WANT THE LOWER CAVES DRY. THERE'S SOMETHING DOWN THERE I NEED.
MMHM. THE WHISP'RING IRON. OF COURSE. YOU'RE JUST AS HOOKED ON THE KEYS AS YOUR OLD MAN. WHAT ARE YOU GOING TO MAKE FIRST? A KEY TO GIVE YOU AN EXTRA COCK?
AND WHY'D YOU BRING ME BACK? WHAT DO YOU WANT WITH ME?
I ALREADY TOLD YOU WHAT I WANT, LUKE. TO SAVE YOU.
I COULDN'T JUST LEAVE YOU DEAD LIKE YOU WERE. WITH THAT THING STILL IN CHARGE OF YOUR SOUL. IT KEEPS ITS HOOKS IN YOU EVEN AFTER DEATH, DOESN'T IT?
I HATE BEING DEAD. IT'S LIKE DROWNING. ONLY INSTEAD OF DROWNING IN WATER, IT'S LIKE DROWNING IN ALL THE EMOTIONS I NEVER WANTED TO FEEL.
I DON'T KNOW HOW DEAD PEOPLE LIVE THAT WAY.
GET IT? I DON'T KNOW HOW DEAD PEOPLE—AH, NEVER MIND.
ANYWAY. MAYBE YOU'LL FEEL DIFFERENTLY ABOUT IT. ABOUT BEING DEAD. WHY DON'T WE FIND OUT?

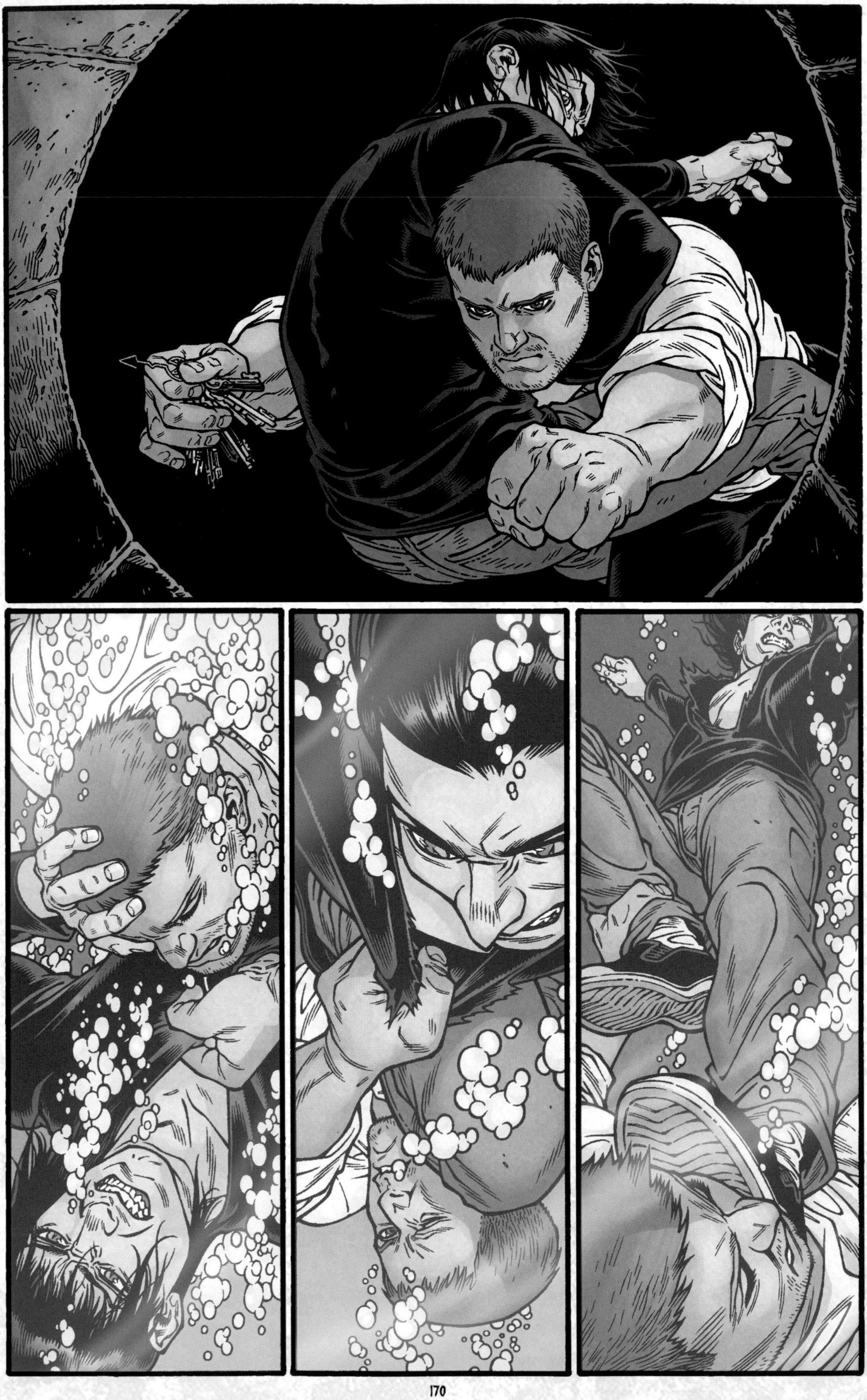

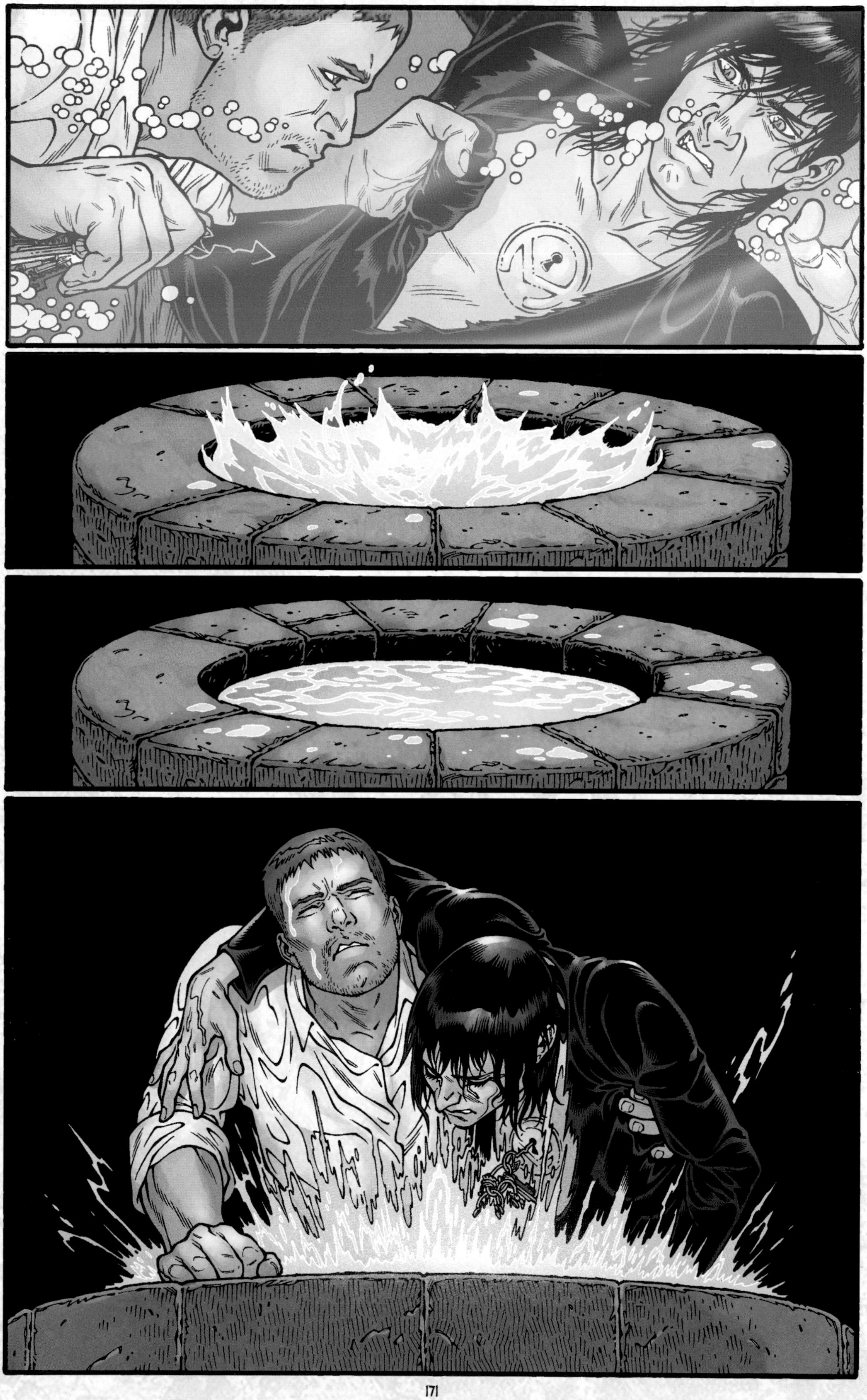

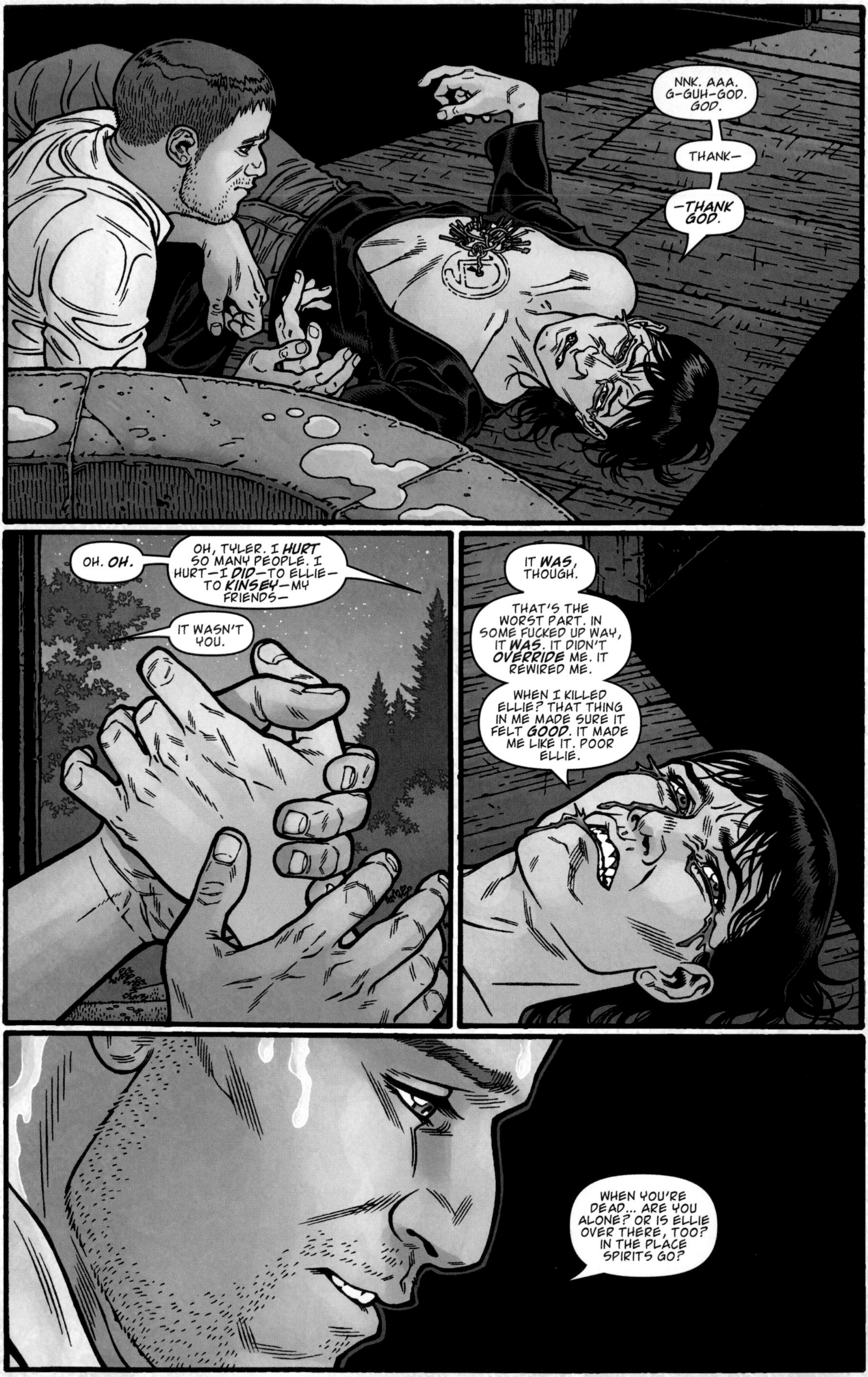
NNK. AAA. G-GUH-GOD. GOD.
THANK—
—THANK GOD.
OH. OH.
OH, TYLER. I HURT SO MANY PEOPLE. I HURT—I DID—TO ELLIE—TO KINSEY—MY FRIENDS—
IT WASN'T YOU.
IT WAS, THOUGH.
THAT'S THE WORST PART. IN SOME FUCKED UP WAY, IT WAS. IT DIDN'T OVERRIDE ME. IT REWIRED ME.
WHEN I KILLED ELLIE? THAT THING IN ME MADE SURE IT FELT GOOD. IT MADE ME LIKE IT. POOR ELLIE.
WHEN YOU'RE DEAD... ARE YOU ALONE? OR IS ELLIE OVER THERE, TOO? IN THE PLACE SPIRITS GO?

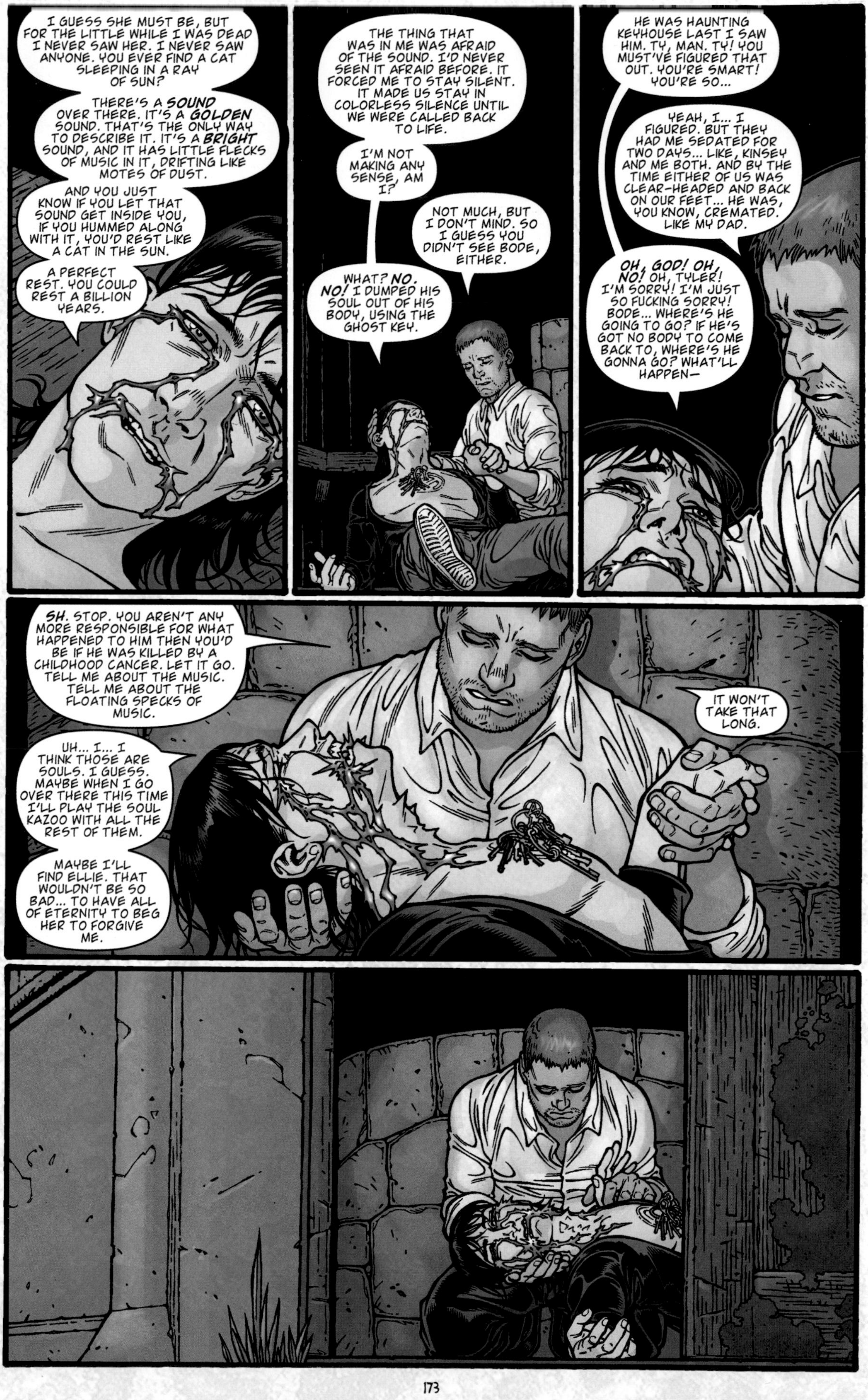
I GUESS SHE MUST BE, BUT FOR THE LITTLE WHILE I WAS DEAD I NEVER SAW HER. I NEVER SAW ANYONE. YOU EVER FIND A CAT SLEEPING IN A RAY OF SUN?
THERE'S A SOUND OVER THERE. IT'S A GOLDEN SOUND. THAT'S THE ONLY WAY TO DESCRIBE IT. IT'S A BRIGHT SOUND, AND IT HAS LITTLE FLECKS OF MUSIC IN IT, DRIFTING LIKE MOTES OF DUST.
AND YOU JUST KNOW IF YOU LET THAT SOUND GET INSIDE YOU, IF YOU HUMMED ALONG WITH IT, YOU'D REST LIKE A CAT IN THE SUN.
A PERFECT REST. YOU COULD REST A BILLION YEARS.
THE THING THAT WAS IN ME WAS AFRAID OF THE SOUND. I'D NEVER SEEN IT AFRAID BEFORE. IT FORCED ME TO STAY SILENT. IT MADE US STAY IN COLORLESS SILENCE UNTIL WE WERE CALLED BACK TO LIFE.
I'M NOT MAKING ANY SENSE, AM I?
NOT MUCH, BUT I DON'T MIND. SO I GUESS YOU DIDN'T SEE BODE, EITHER.
WHAT? NO. NO! I DUMPED HIS SOUL OUT OF HIS BODY, USING THE GHOST KEY.
HE WAS HAUNTING KEYHOUSE LAST I SAW HIM. TY, MAN. TY! YOU MUST'VE FIGURED THAT OUT. YOU'RE SMART! YOU'RE SO...
YEAH, I... I FIGURED. BUT THEY HAD ME SEDATED FOR TWO DAYS... LIKE, KINSEY AND ME BOTH. AND BY THE TIME EITHER OF US WAS CLEAR-HEADED AND BACK ON OUR FEET... HE WAS, YOU KNOW, CREMATED. LIKE MY DAD.
OH, GOD! OH, NO! OH, TYLER! I'M SORRY! I'M JUST SO FUCKING SORRY! BODE... WHERE'S HE GOING TO GO? IF HE'S GOT NO BODY TO COME BACK TO, WHERE'S HE GONNA GO? WHAT'LL HAPPEN—
SH. STOP. YOU AREN'T ANY MORE RESPONSIBLE FOR WHAT HAPPENED TO HIM THEN YOU'D BE IF HE WAS KILLED BY A CHILDHOOD CANCER. LET IT GO. TELL ME ABOUT THE MUSIC. TELL ME ABOUT THE FLOATING SPECKS OF MUSIC.
UH... I... I THINK THOSE ARE SOULS. I GUESS. MAYBE WHEN I GO OVER THERE THIS TIME I'LL PLAY THE SOUL KAZOO WITH ALL THE REST OF THEM.
MAYBE I'LL FIND ELLIE. THAT WOULDN'T BE SO BAD... TO HAVE ALL OF ETERNITY TO BEG HER TO FORGIVE ME.
IT WON'T TAKE THAT LONG.

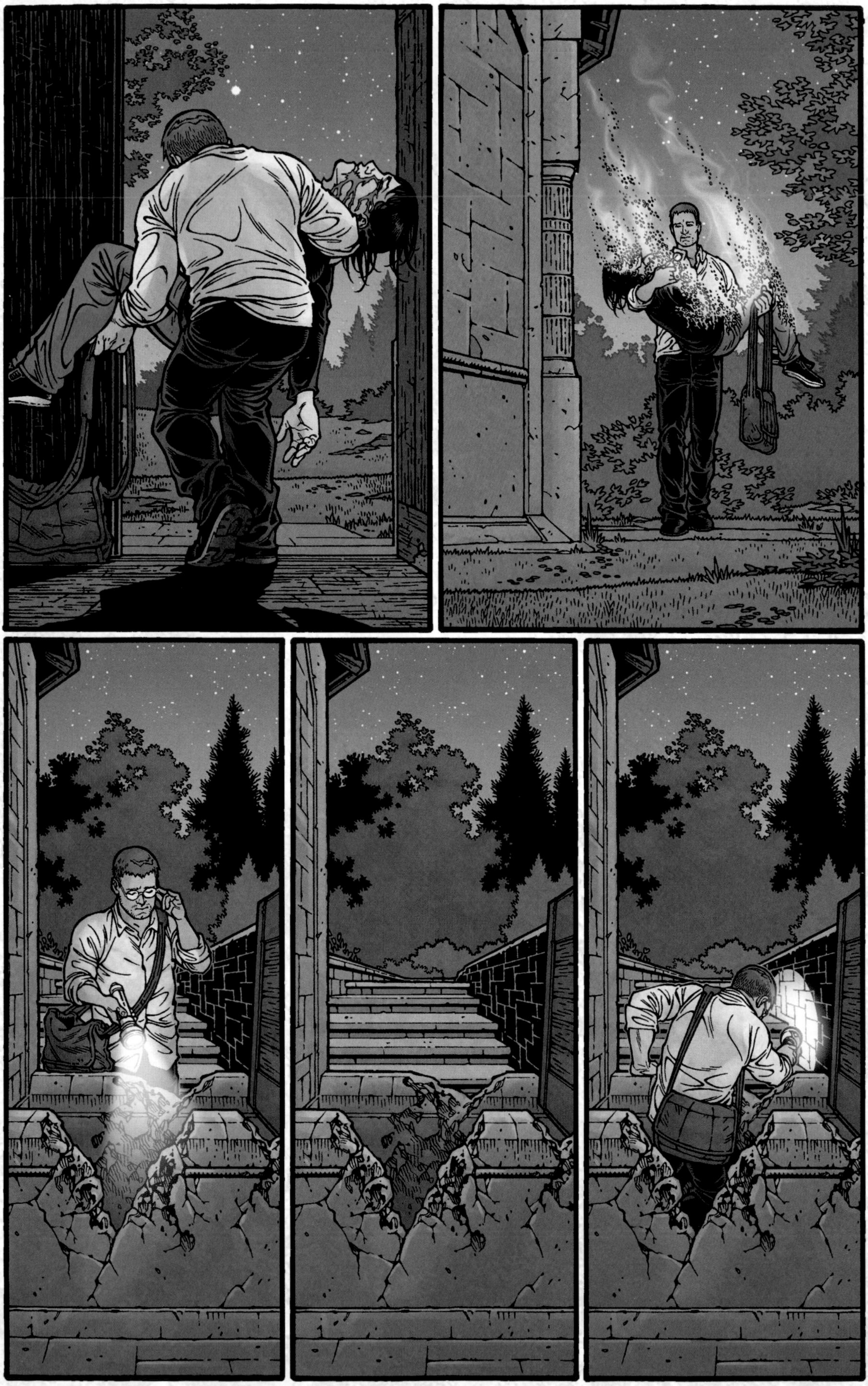

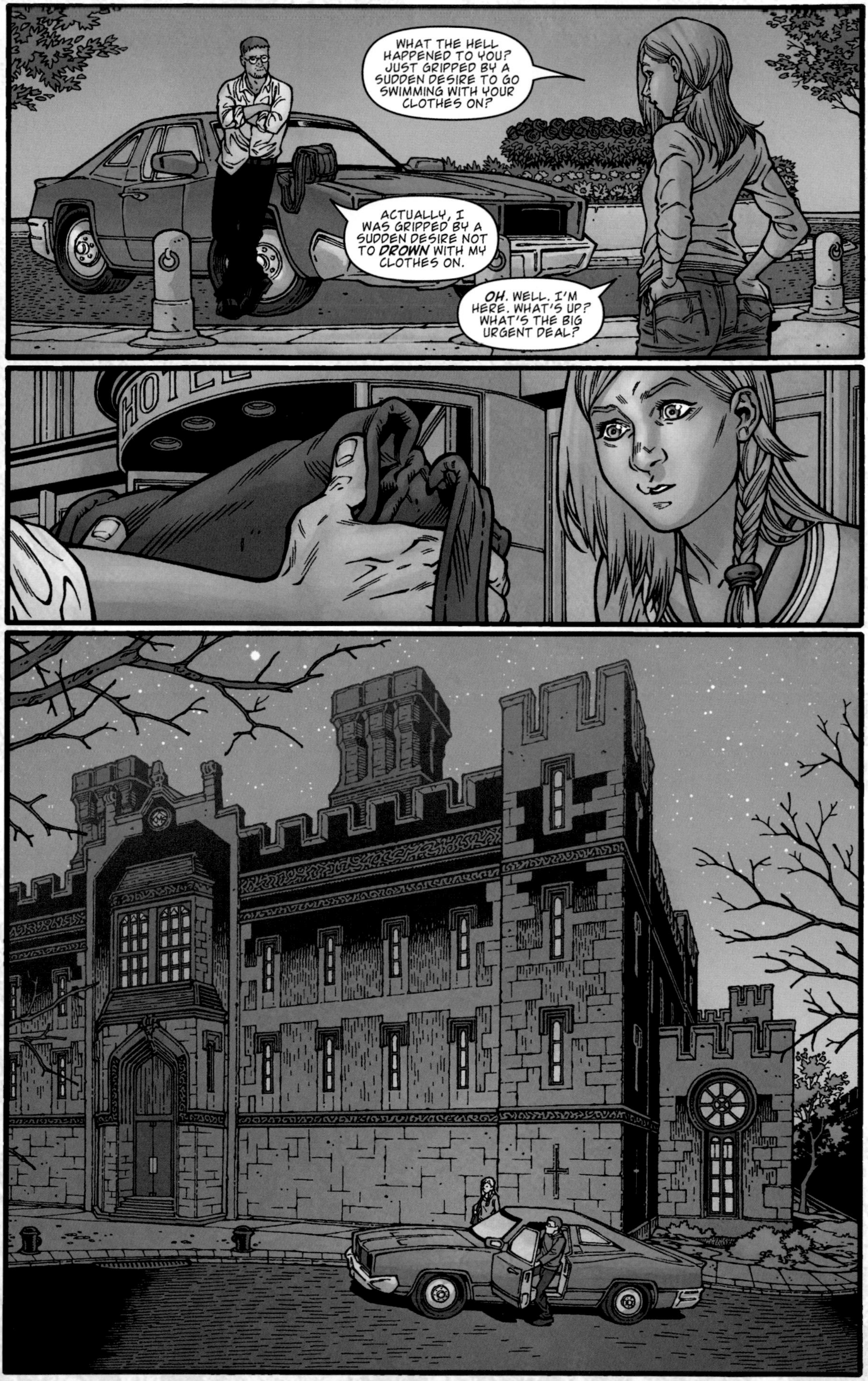
WHAT THE HELL HAPPENED TO YOU? JUST GRIPPED BY A SUDDEN DESIRE TO GO SWIMMING WITH YOUR CLOTHES ON?
ACTUALLY, I WAS GRIPPED BY A SUDDEN DESIRE NOT TO DROWN WITH MY CLOTHES ON.
OH. WELL. I'M HERE. WHAT'S UP? WHAT'S THE BIG URGENT DEAL?
HOTEL

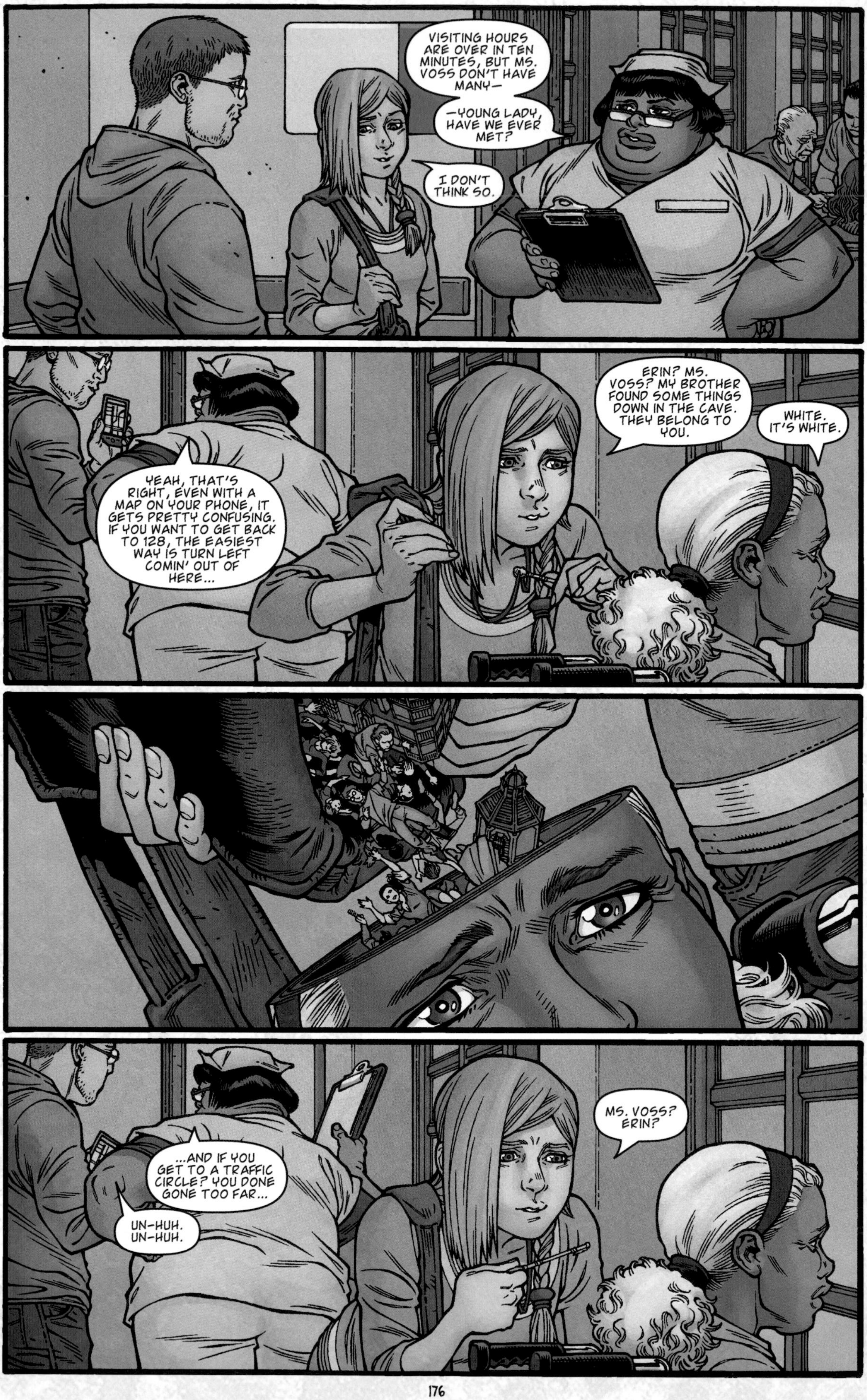
VISITING HOURS ARE OVER IN TEN MINUTES, BUT MS. VOSS DON'T HAVE MANY—
—YOUNG LADY, HAVE WE EVER MET?
I DON'T THINK SO.
YEAH, THAT'S RIGHT, EVEN WITH A MAP ON YOUR PHONE, IT GETS PRETTY CONFUSING. IF YOU WANT TO GET BACK TO 128, THE EASIEST WAY IS TURN LEFT COMIN' OUT OF HERE...
ERIN? MS. VOSS? MY BROTHER FOUND SOME THINGS DOWN IN THE CAVE. THEY BELONG TO YOU.
WHITE. IT'S WHITE.
...AND IF YOU GET TO A TRAFFIC CIRCLE? YOU DONE GONE TOO FAR...
UN-HUH. UN-HUH.
MS. VOSS? ERIN?

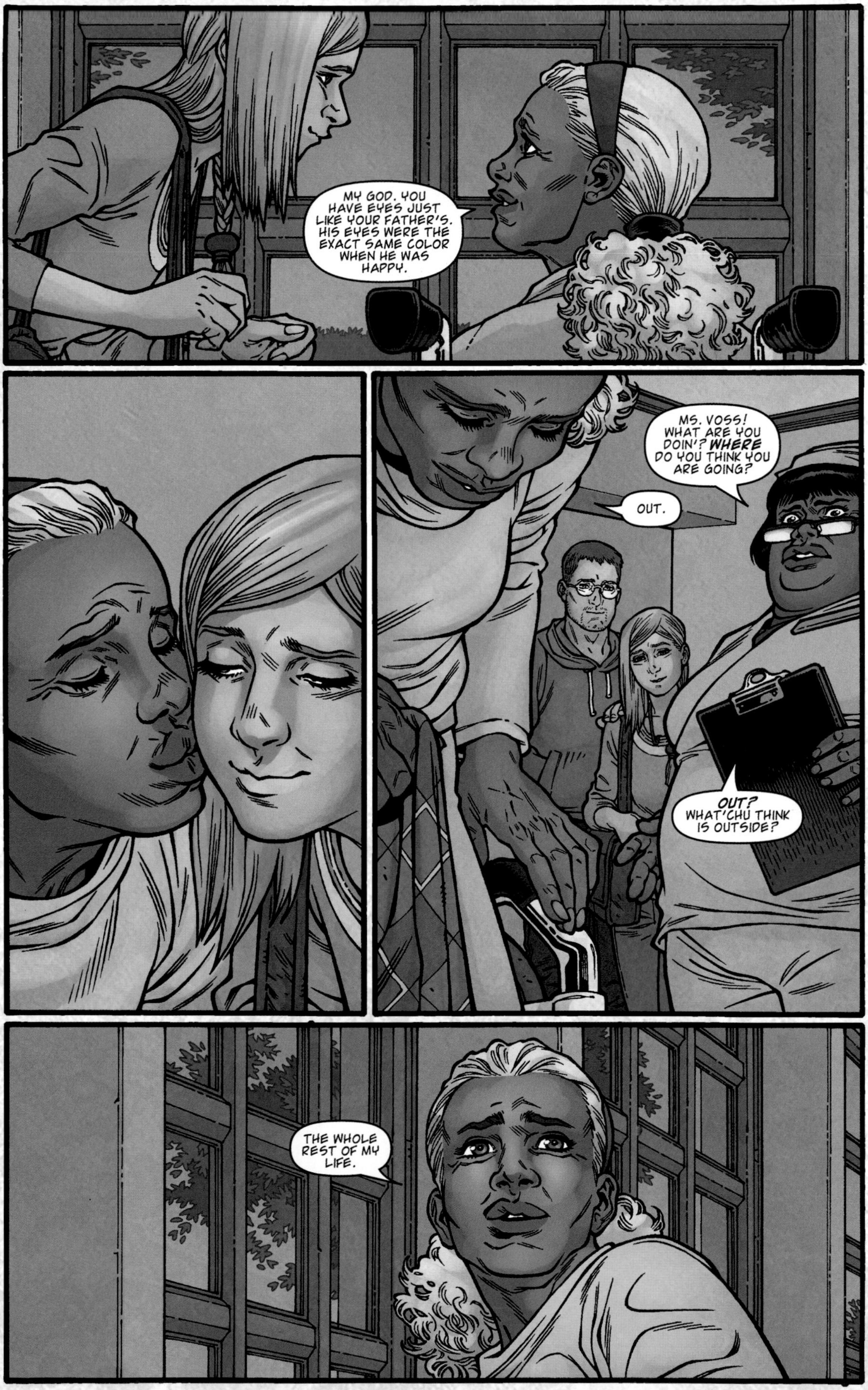
MY GOD. YOU HAVE EYES JUST LIKE YOUR FATHER'S. HIS EYES WERE THE EXACT SAME COLOR WHEN HE WAS HAPPY.
MS. VOSS! WHAT ARE YOU DOIN'? WHERE DO YOU THINK YOU ARE GOING?
OUT.
OUT? WHAT'CHU THINK IS OUTSIDE?
THE WHOLE REST OF MY LIFE.

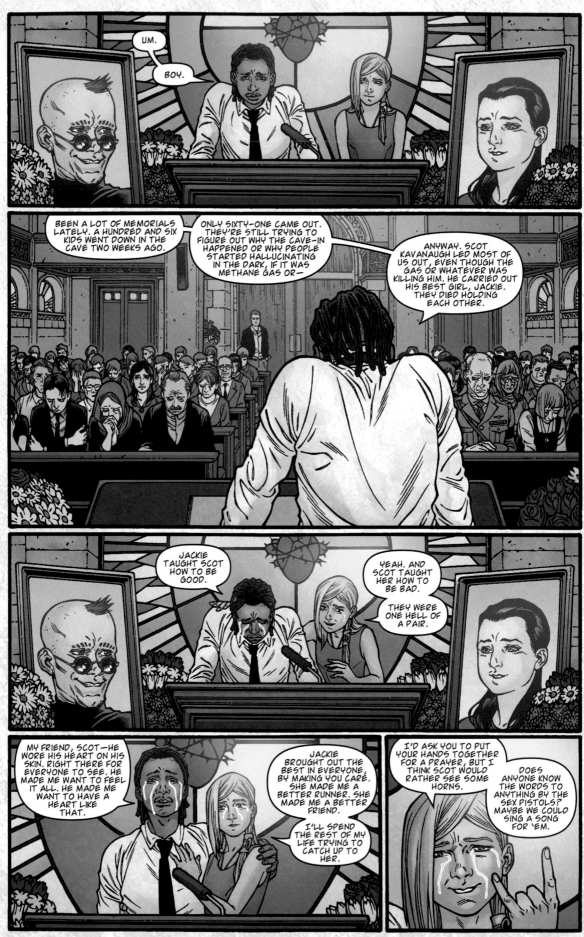

UM.

BOY.

BEEN A LOT OF MEMORIALS LATELY. A HUNDRED AND SIX KIDS WENT DOWN IN THE CAVE TWO WEEKS AGO.

ONLY SIXTY-ONE CAME OUT. THEY'RE STILL TRYING TO FIGURE OUT WHY THE CAVE-IN HAPPENED OR WHY PEOPLE STARTED HALLUCINATING IN THE DARK, IF IT WAS METHANE GAS OR—

ANYWAY. SCOT KAVANAUGH LED MOST OF US OUT, EVEN THOUGH THE GAS OR WHATEVER WAS KILLING HIM. HE CARRIED OUT HIS BEST GIRL, JACKIE. THEY DIED HOLDING EACH OTHER.

JACKIE TAUGHT SCOT HOW TO BE GOOD.

YEAH. AND SCOT TAUGHT HER HOW TO BE BAD.

THEY WERE ONE HELL OF A PAIR.

MY FRIEND, SCOT—HE WORE HIS HEART ON HIS SKIN. RIGHT THERE FOR EVERYONE TO SEE. HE MADE ME WANT TO FEEL IT ALL. HE MADE ME WANT TO HAVE A HEART LIKE THAT.

JACKIE BROUGHT OUT THE BEST IN EVERYONE, BY MAKING YOU CARE. SHE MADE ME A BETTER RUNNER. SHE MADE ME A BETTER FRIEND.

I'LL SPEND THE REST OF MY LIFE TRYING TO CATCH UP TO HER.

I'D ASK YOU TO PUT YOUR HANDS TOGETHER FOR A PRAYER, BUT I THINK SCOT WOULD RATHER SEE SOME HORNS.

DOES ANYONE KNOW THE WORDS TO ANYTHING BY THE SEX PISTOLS? MAYBE WE COULD SING A SONG FOR 'EM.

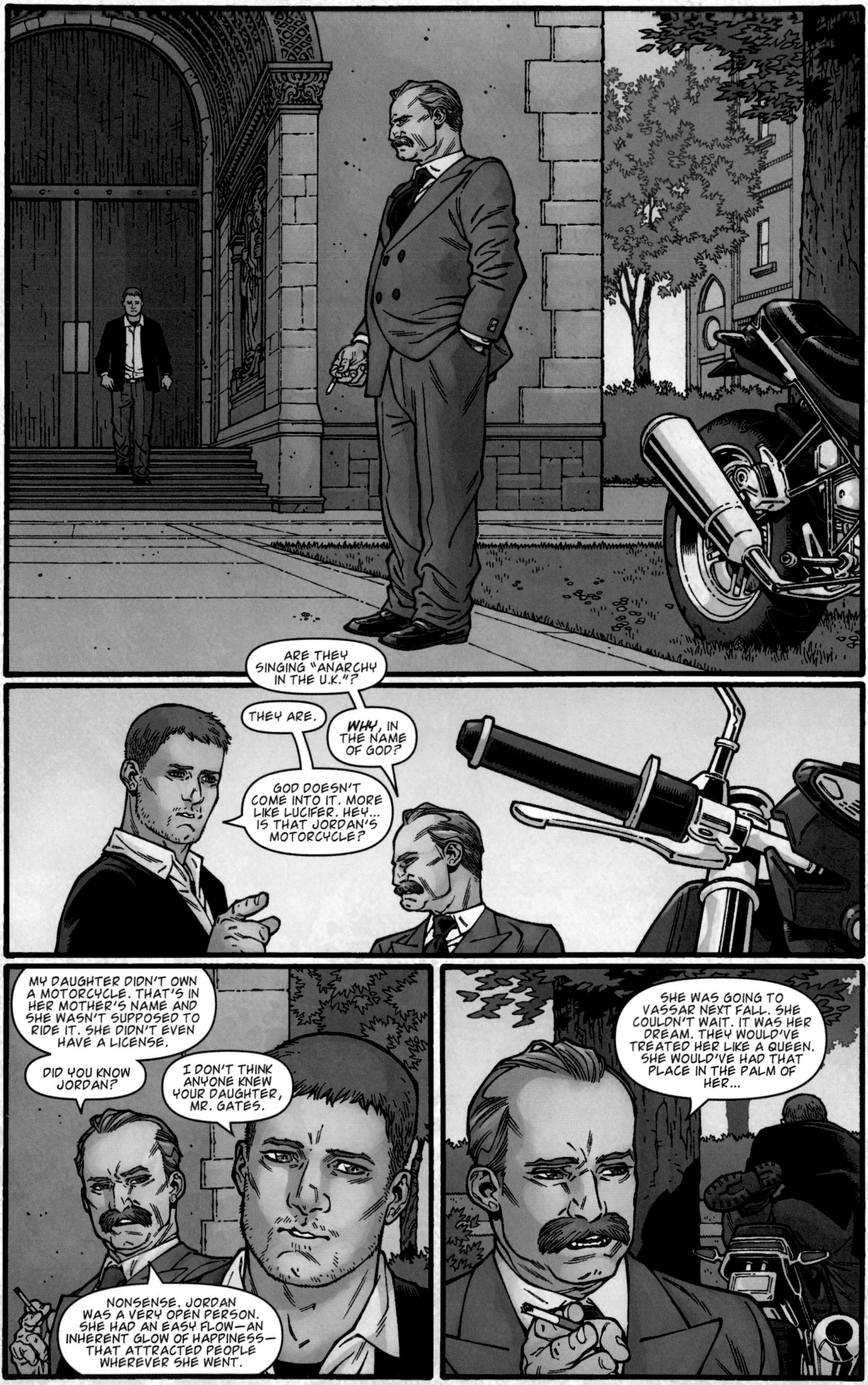

ARE THEY SINGING "ANARCHY IN THE U.K."?
THEY ARE.
WHY, IN THE NAME OF GOD?
GOD DOESN'T COME INTO IT. MORE LIKE LUCIFER. HEY... IS THAT JORDAN'S MOTORCYCLE?
MY DAUGHTER DIDN'T OWN A MOTORCYCLE. THAT'S IN HER MOTHER'S NAME AND SHE WASN'T SUPPOSED TO RIDE IT. SHE DIDN'T EVEN HAVE A LICENSE.
DID YOU KNOW JORDAN?
I DON'T THINK ANYONE KNEW YOUR DAUGHTER, MR. GATES.
NONSENSE. JORDAN WAS A VERY OPEN PERSON. SHE HAD AN EASY FLOW—AN INHERENT GLOW OF HAPPINESS—THAT ATTRACTED PEOPLE WHEREVER SHE WENT.
SHE WAS GOING TO VASSAR NEXT FALL. SHE COULDN'T WAIT. IT WAS HER DREAM. THEY WOULD'VE TREATED HER LIKE A QUEEN. SHE WOULD'VE HAD THAT PLACE IN THE PALM OF HER...

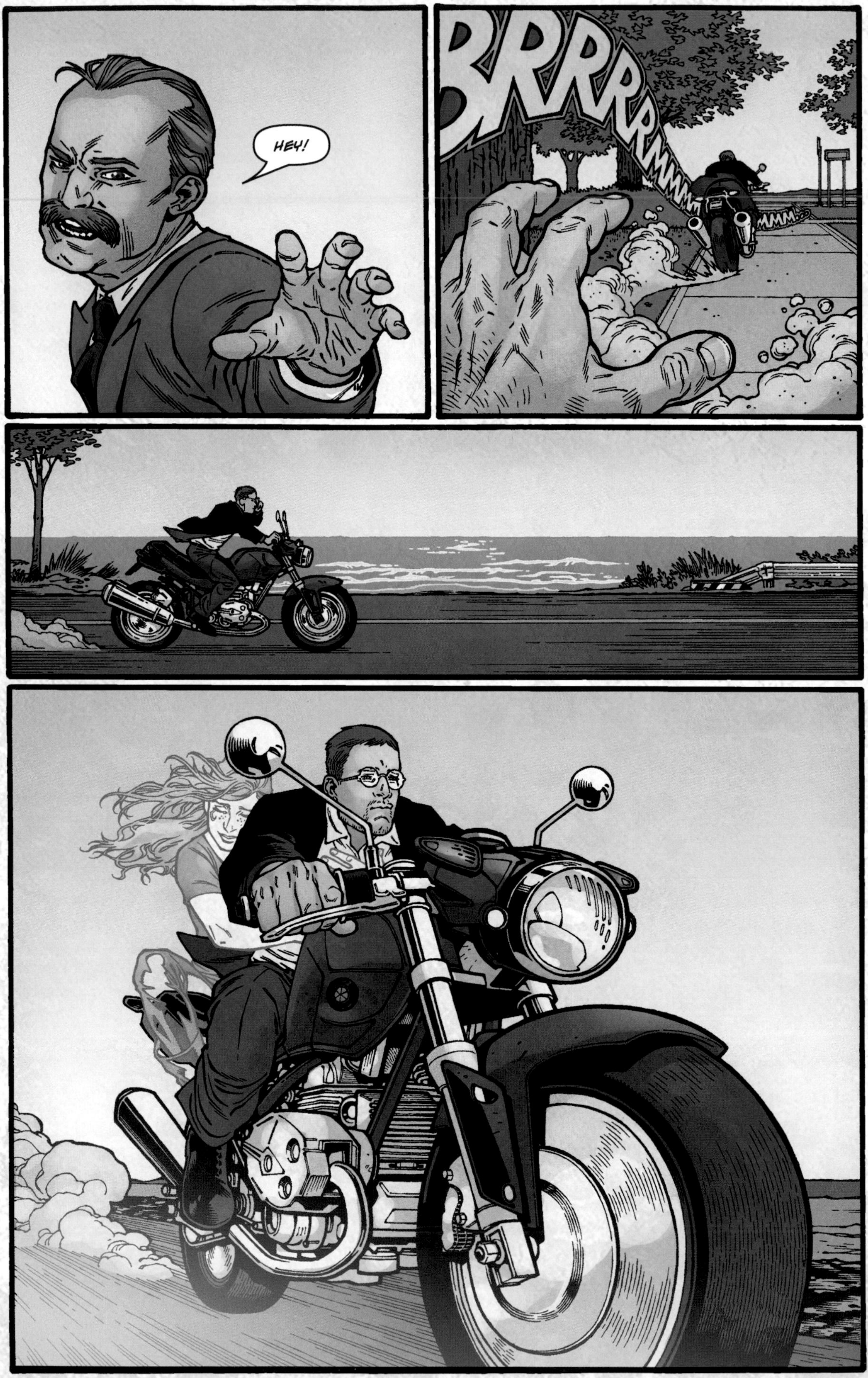
HEY!
BRRRRRMMMMMMMM

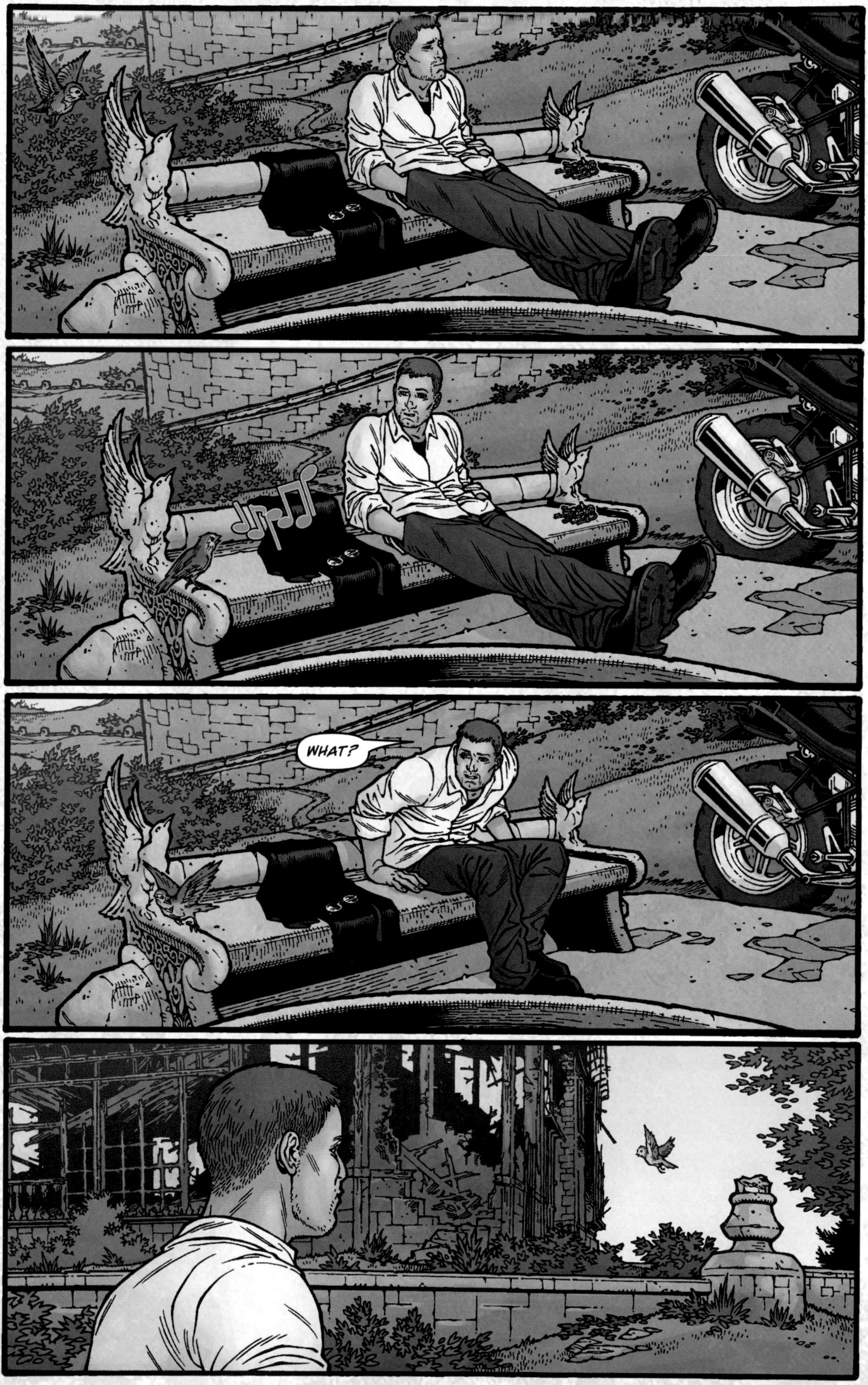
WHAT?

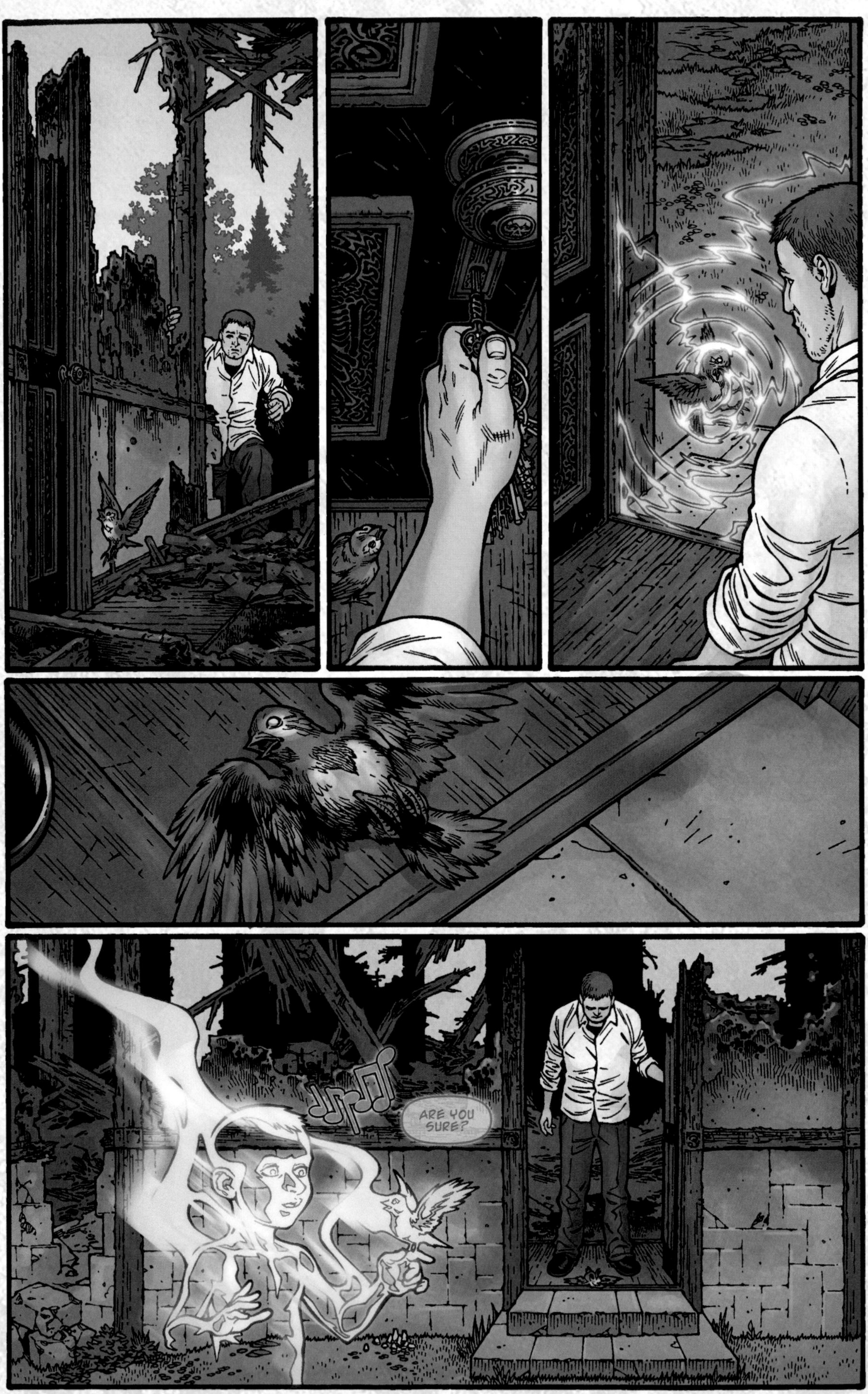
ARE YOU SURE?

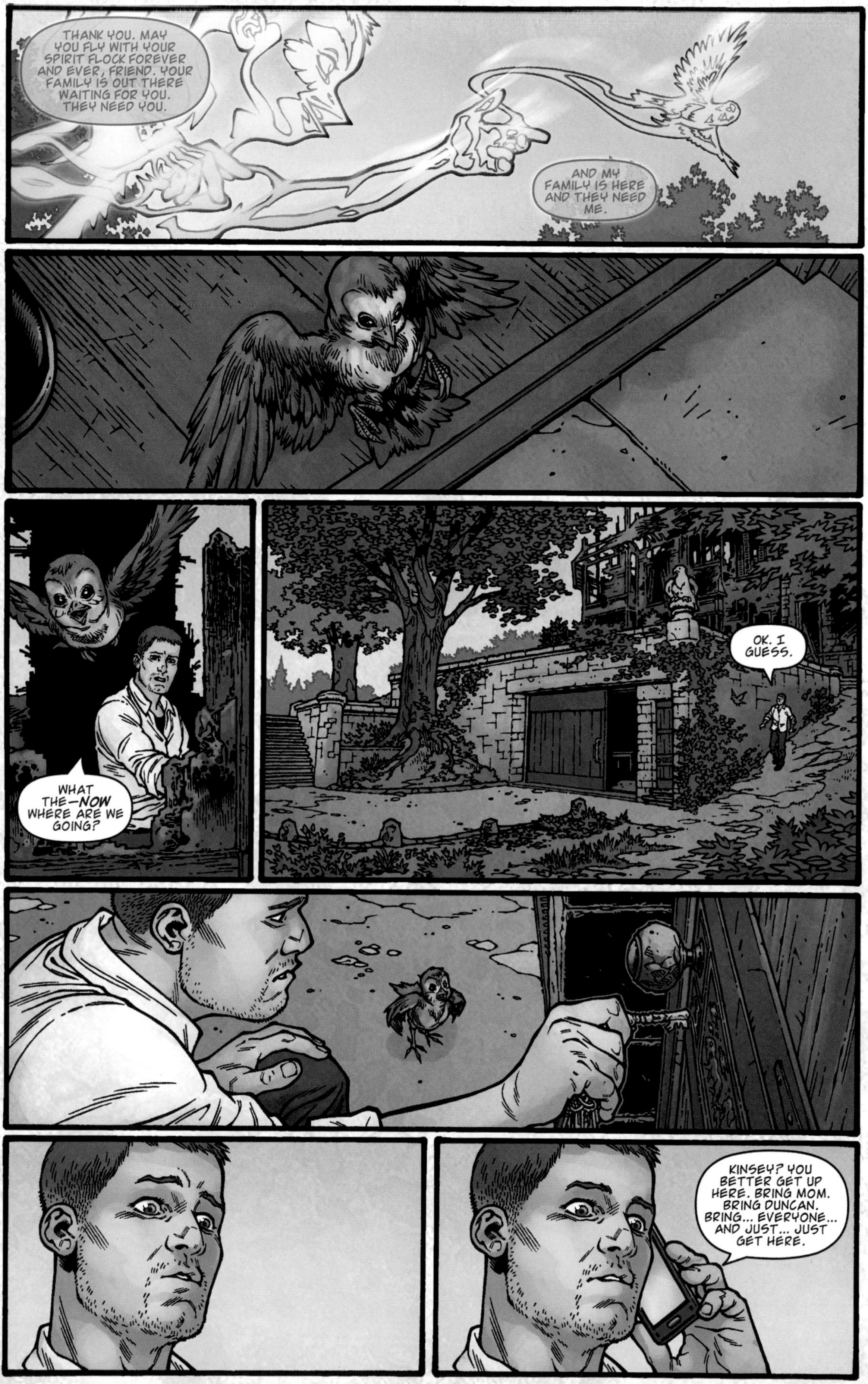
THANK YOU. MAY YOU FLY WITH YOUR SPIRIT FLOCK FOREVER AND EVER, FRIEND. YOUR FAMILY IS OUT THERE WAITING FOR YOU. THEY NEED YOU.
AND MY FAMILY IS HERE AND THEY NEED ME.
WHAT THE—*NOW* WHERE ARE WE GOING?
OK. I GUESS.
KINSEY? YOU BETTER GET UP HERE. BRING MOM. BRING DUNCAN. BRING... EVERYONE... AND JUST... JUST GET HERE.

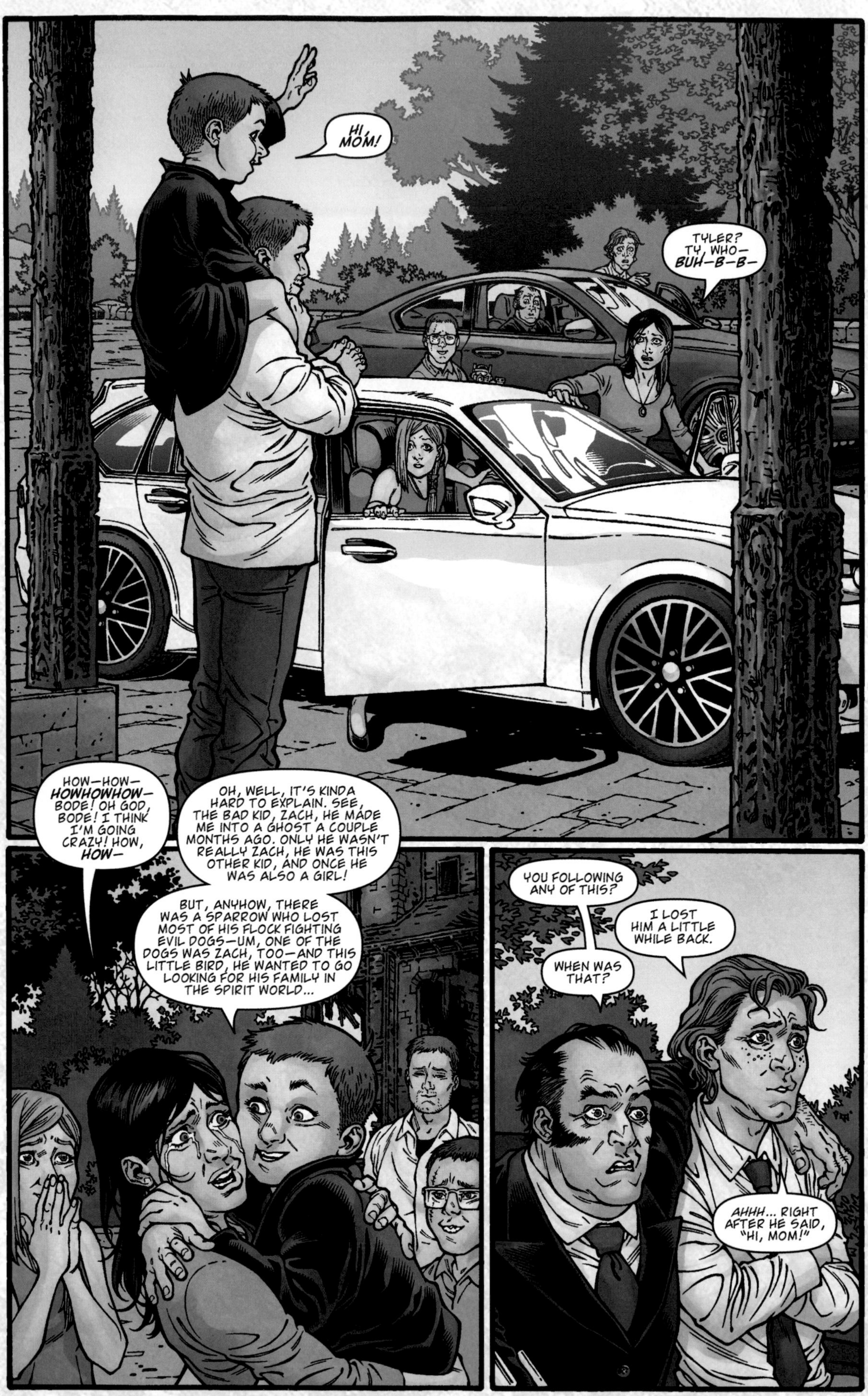
HI, MOM!
TYLER? TY, WHO- BUH-B-B-
HOW-HOW- HOWHOWHOW- BODE! OH GOD, BODE! I THINK I'M GOING CRAZY! HOW, HOW-
OH, WELL, IT'S KINDA HARD TO EXPLAIN. SEE, THE BAD KID, ZACH, HE MADE ME INTO A GHOST A COUPLE MONTHS AGO. ONLY HE WASN'T REALLY ZACH, HE WAS THIS OTHER KID, AND ONCE HE WAS ALSO A GIRL!
BUT, ANYHOW, THERE WAS A SPARROW WHO LOST MOST OF HIS FLOCK FIGHTING EVIL DOGS-UM, ONE OF THE DOGS WAS ZACH, TOO-AND THIS LITTLE BIRD, HE WANTED TO GO LOOKING FOR HIS FAMILY IN THE SPIRIT WORLD...
YOU FOLLOWING ANY OF THIS?
I LOST HIM A LITTLE WHILE BACK.
WHEN WAS THAT?
AHHH... RIGHT AFTER HE SAID, "HI, MOM!"

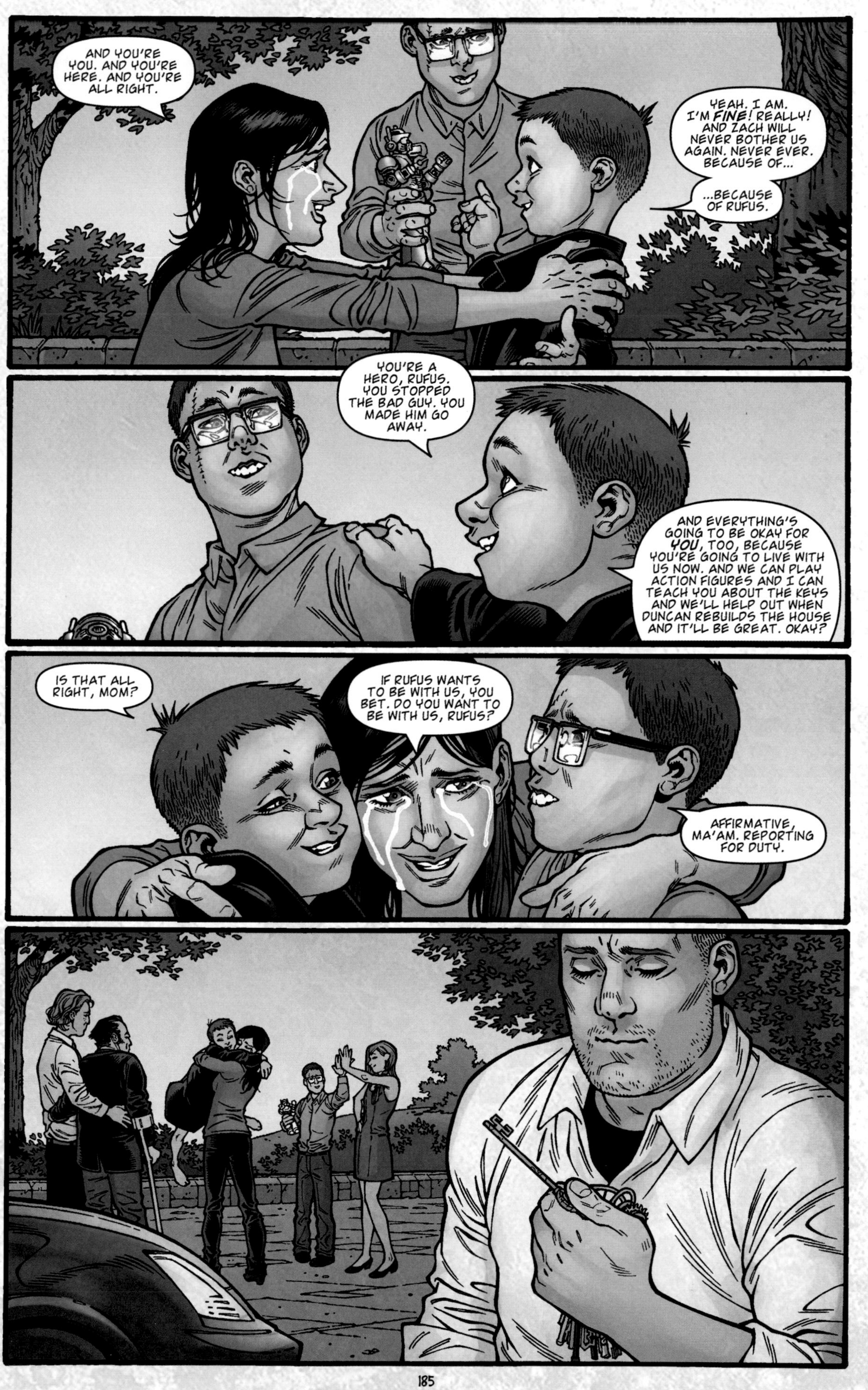
AND YOU'RE YOU. AND YOU'RE HERE. AND YOU'RE ALL RIGHT.
YEAH. I AM. I'M FINE! REALLY! AND ZACH WILL NEVER BOTHER US AGAIN. NEVER EVER. BECAUSE OF...
...BECAUSE OF RUFUS.
YOU'RE A HERO, RUFUS. YOU STOPPED THE BAD GUY. YOU MADE HIM GO AWAY.
AND EVERYTHING'S GOING TO BE OKAY FOR YOU, TOO, BECAUSE YOU'RE GOING TO LIVE WITH US NOW. AND WE CAN PLAY ACTION FIGURES AND I CAN TEACH YOU ABOUT THE KEYS AND WE'LL HELP OUT WHEN DUNCAN REBUILDS THE HOUSE AND IT'LL BE GREAT. OKAY?
IS THAT ALL RIGHT, MOM?
IF RUFUS WANTS TO BE WITH US, YOU BET. DO YOU WANT TO BE WITH US, RUFUS?
AFFIRMATIVE, MA'AM. REPORTING FOR DUTY.

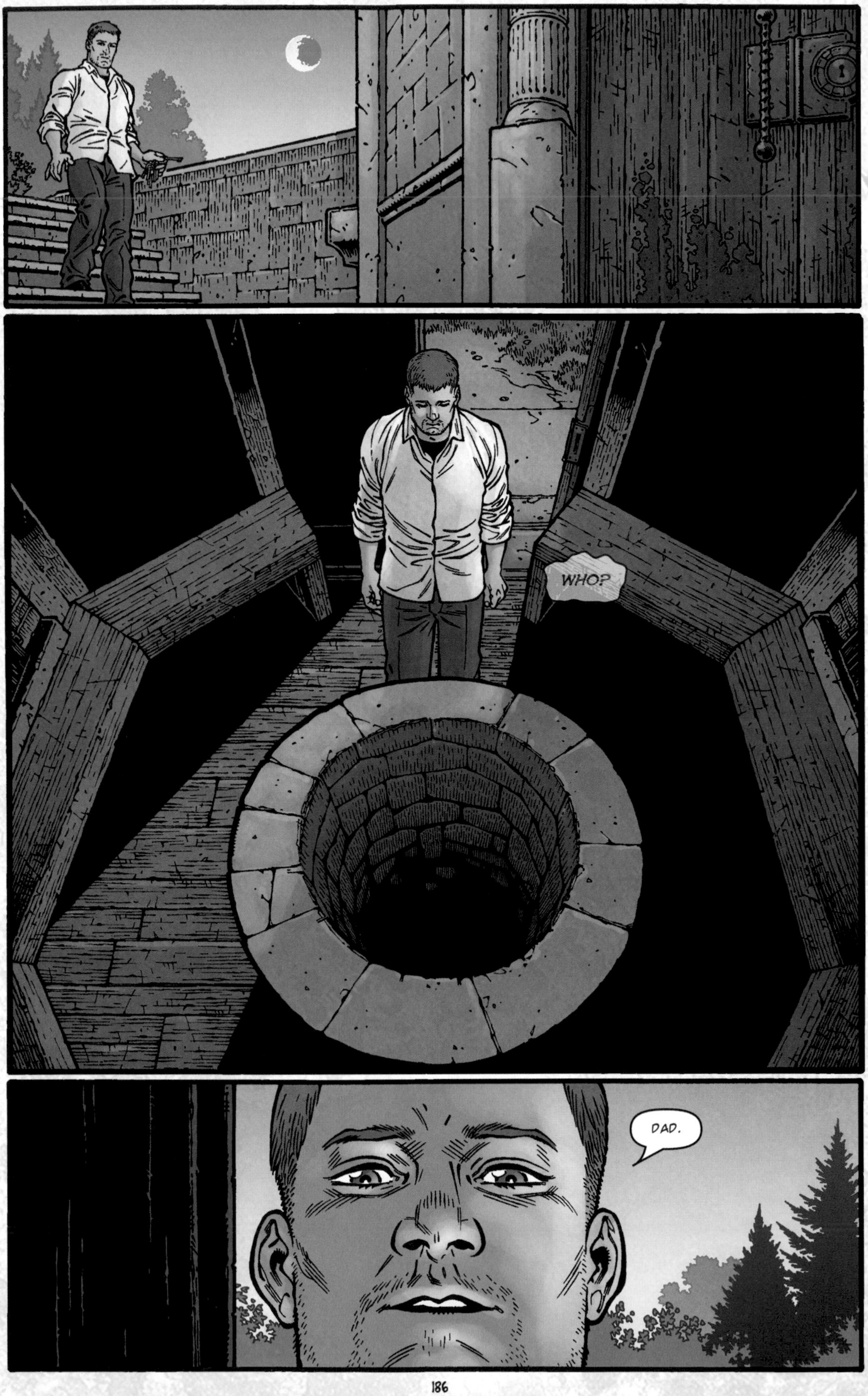
WHO?
DAD.

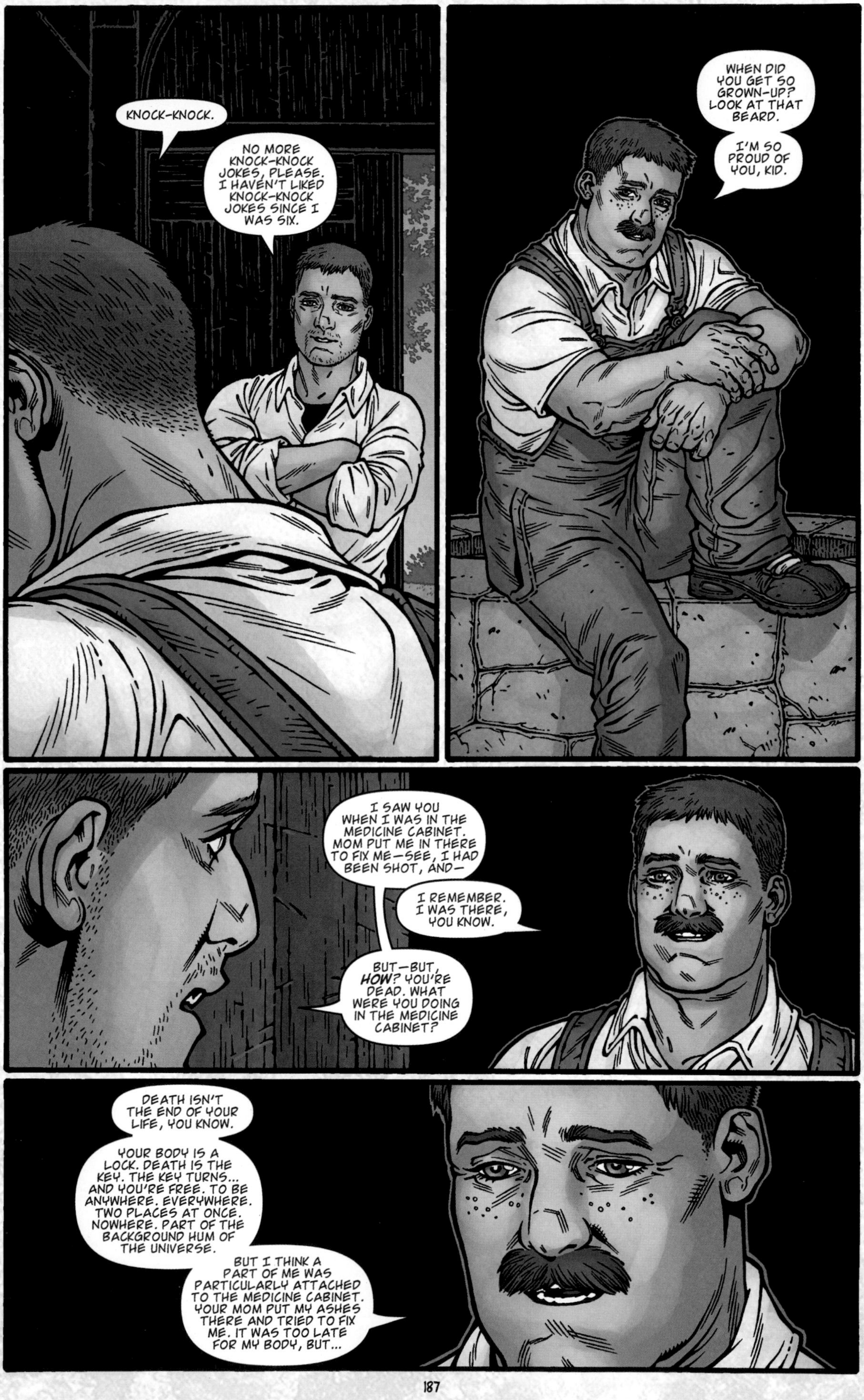
KNOCK-KNOCK.
NO MORE KNOCK-KNOCK JOKES, PLEASE. I HAVEN'T LIKED KNOCK-KNOCK JOKES SINCE I WAS SIX.
WHEN DID YOU GET SO GROWN-UP? LOOK AT THAT BEARD.
I'M SO PROUD OF YOU, KID.
I SAW YOU WHEN I WAS IN THE MEDICINE CABINET. MOM PUT ME IN THERE TO FIX ME—SEE, I HAD BEEN SHOT, AND—
I REMEMBER. I WAS THERE, YOU KNOW.
BUT—BUT, *HOW*? YOU'RE DEAD. WHAT WERE YOU DOING IN THE MEDICINE CABINET?
DEATH ISN'T THE END OF YOUR LIFE, YOU KNOW.
YOUR BODY IS A LOCK. DEATH IS THE KEY. THE KEY TURNS... AND YOU'RE FREE. TO BE ANYWHERE. EVERYWHERE. TWO PLACES AT ONCE. NOWHERE. PART OF THE BACKGROUND HUM OF THE UNIVERSE.
BUT I THINK A PART OF ME WAS PARTICULARLY ATTACHED TO THE MEDICINE CABINET. YOUR MOM PUT MY ASHES THERE AND TRIED TO FIX ME. IT WAS TOO LATE FOR MY BODY, BUT...

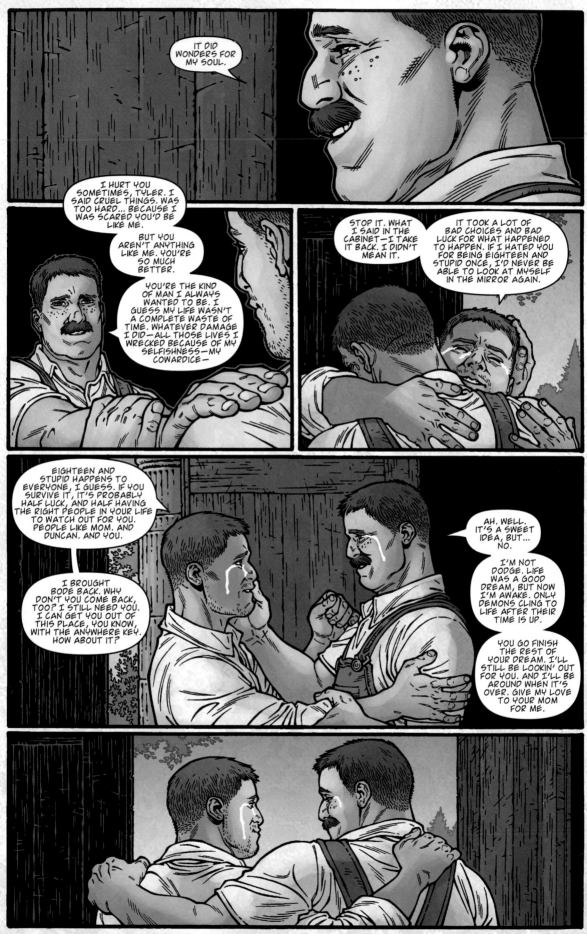

IT DID WONDERS FOR MY SOUL.

I HURT YOU SOMETIMES, TYLER. I SAID CRUEL THINGS. WAS TOO HARD... BECAUSE I WAS SCARED YOU'D BE LIKE ME.

BUT YOU AREN'T ANYTHING LIKE ME. YOU'RE SO MUCH BETTER.

YOU'RE THE KIND OF MAN I ALWAYS WANTED TO BE. I GUESS MY LIFE WASN'T A COMPLETE WASTE OF TIME. WHATEVER DAMAGE I DID—ALL THOSE LIVES I WRECKED BECAUSE OF MY SELFISHNESS—MY COWARDICE—

STOP IT. WHAT I SAID IN THE CABINET—I TAKE IT BACK. I DIDN'T MEAN IT.

IT TOOK A LOT OF BAD CHOICES AND BAD LUCK FOR WHAT HAPPENED TO HAPPEN. IF I HATED YOU FOR BEING EIGHTEEN AND STUPID ONCE, I'D NEVER BE ABLE TO LOOK AT MYSELF IN THE MIRROR AGAIN.

EIGHTEEN AND STUPID HAPPENS TO EVERYONE, I GUESS. IF YOU SURVIVE IT, IT'S PROBABLY HALF LUCK, AND HALF HAVING THE RIGHT PEOPLE IN YOUR LIFE TO WATCH OUT FOR YOU. PEOPLE LIKE MOM. AND DUNCAN. AND YOU.

I BROUGHT BODE BACK. WHY DON'T YOU COME BACK, TOO? I STILL NEED YOU. I CAN GET YOU OUT OF THIS PLACE, YOU KNOW, WITH THE ANYWHERE KEY. HOW ABOUT IT?

AH. WELL. IT'S A SWEET IDEA, BUT... NO.

I'M NOT DODGE. LIFE WAS A GOOD DREAM, BUT NOW I'M AWAKE. ONLY DEMONS CLING TO LIFE AFTER THEIR TIME IS UP.

YOU GO FINISH THE REST OF YOUR DREAM. I'LL STILL BE LOOKIN' OUT FOR YOU. AND I'LL BE AROUND WHEN IT'S OVER. GIVE MY LOVE TO YOUR MOM FOR ME.

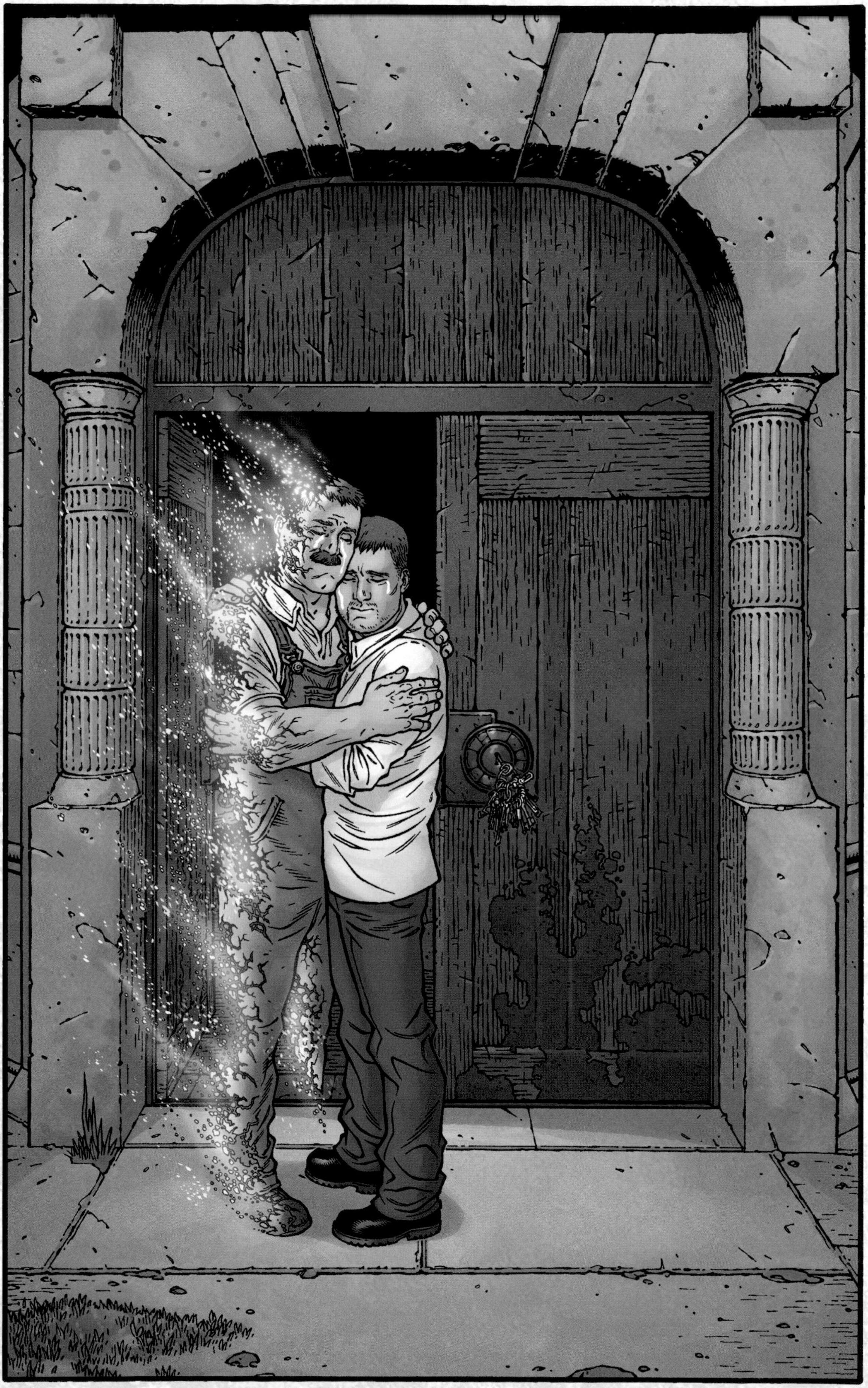

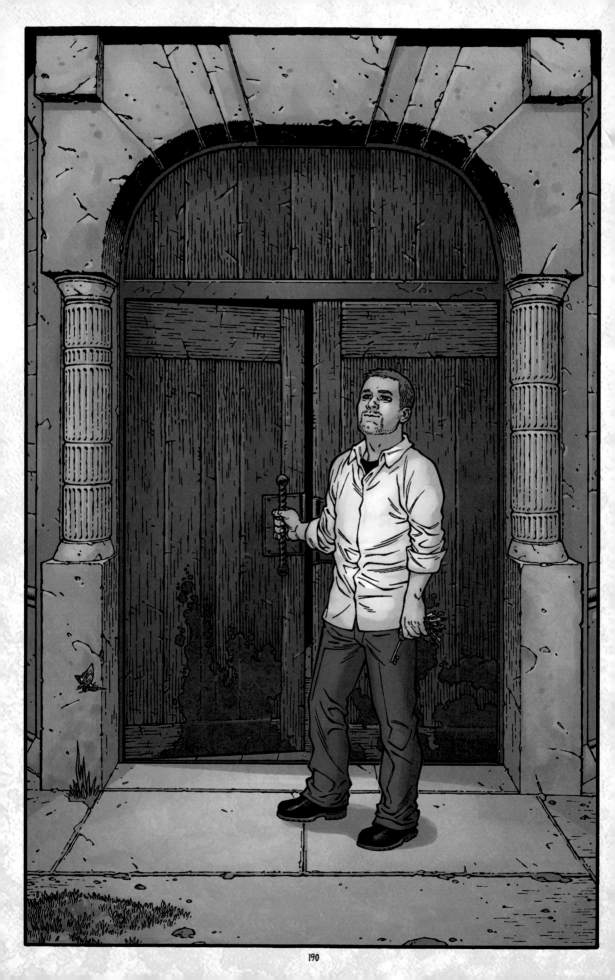

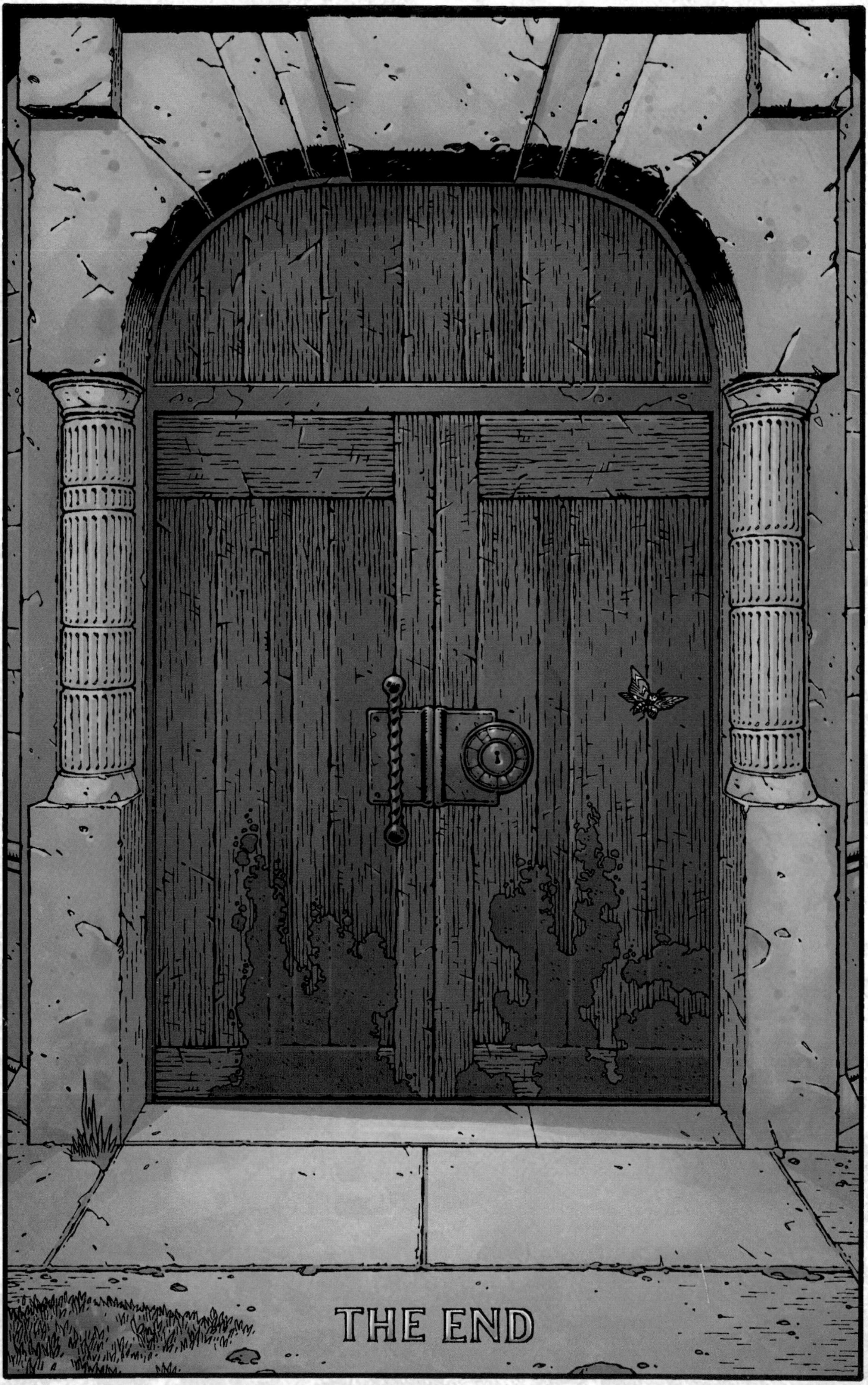
THE END

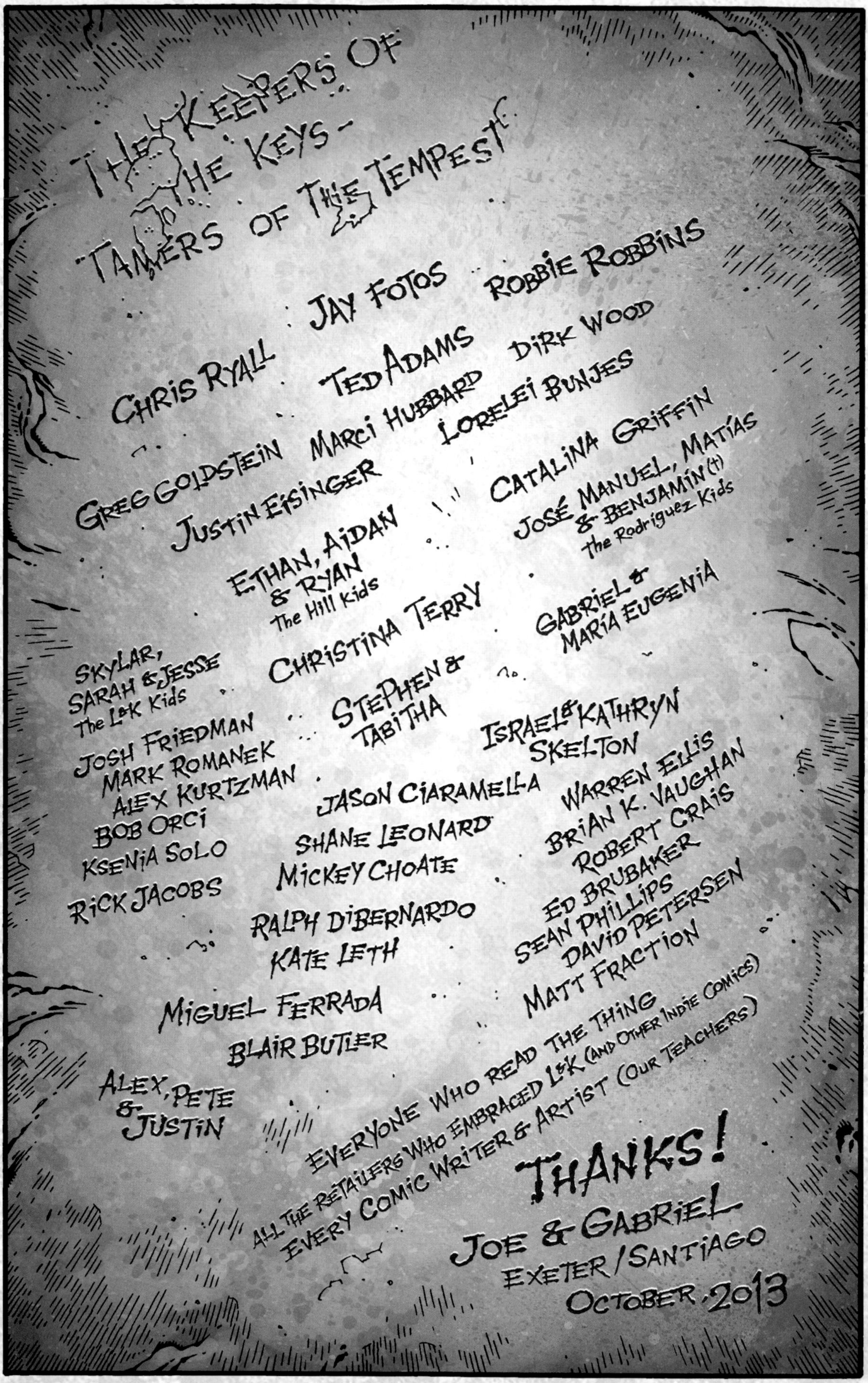
The Keepers of the Keys -
Tamers of the Tempest
Robbie Robbins
Jay Fotos
Chris Ryall
Ted Adams
Dirk Wood
Greg Goldstein
Marci Hubbard
Lorelei Bunjes
Justin Eisinger
Catalina Griffin
José Manuel, Matías & Benjamin (†)
The Rodriguez Kids
Ethan, Aidan & Ryan
The Hill Kids
Christina Terry
Gabriel & María Eugenia
Skylar, Sarah & Jesse
The L&K Kids
Stephen & Tabitha
Israel & Kathryn Skelton
Josh Friedman
Mark Romanek
Alex Kurtzman
Bob Orci
Ksenia Solo
Rick Jacobs
Jason Ciaramella
Shane Leonard
Mickey Choate
Ralph DiBernardo
Kate Leth
Miguel Ferrada
Blair Butler
Warren Ellis
Brian K. Vaughan
Robert Crais
Ed Brubaker
Sean Phillips
David Petersen
Matt Fraction
Alex, Pete & Justin
Everyone who read the thing
All the retailers who embraced L&K (and other indie comics)
Every comic writer & artist (our teachers)
Thanks!
Joe & Gabriel
Exeter / Santiago
October, 2013

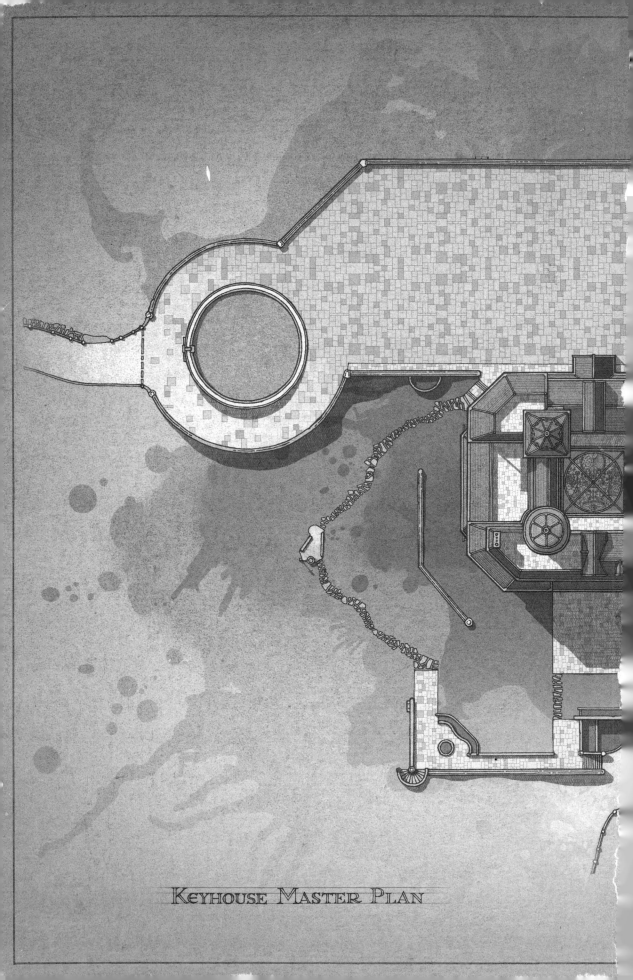

KEYHOUSE MASTER PLAN